W9-AVJ-978

Decade by Decade

Decade by Decade

Peter Haugen

Set Editor: William J. Cannon

BIOLOGY: Decade by Decade

Facts On File, Inc.
An imprint of Infobase Publishing
132 West 31st Street
New York NY 10001

ISBN-10: 0-8160-5530-0
ISBN-13: 978-0-8160-5530-2

Library of Congress Cataloging-in-Publication Data
Haugen, Peter.
Biology : decade by decade / Peter Haugen.
p. cm. — (Twentieth-century science)
Includes bibliographical references and index.
ISBN 0-8160-5530-0 (acid-free paper)
1. Biology—History—20th century—Juvenile literature. I. Title.
QH305.H38 2007
570.9'04—dc22 2006022917

Text design by Dorothy M. Preston and Kerry Casey
Cover design by Dorothy M. Preston and Salvatore Luongo
Illustrations by Bobbi McCutcheon
Photo research by Elizabeth H. Oakes

Printed in the United States of America

VB KT 10 9 8 7 6 5 4 3 2 1

This book is printed on acid-free paper.

For Marcus E. Haugen and Lucas A. Haugen,
and in memory of Dick Swanson

Contents

Preface

The 20th century witnessed an explosive growth in science and technology—more scientists are alive today than have lived during the entire course of earlier human history. New inventions including spaceships, computer chips, lasers, and recombinant deoxyribonucleic acid (DNA) have opened pathways to new fields such as space science, biotechnology, and nanotechnology. Modern seismographs and submarines have given earth and ocean scientists insights into the planet's deepest and darkest secrets. Decades of weather science, aided by satellite observations and computer modeling, now produce long-term, global forecasts with high probabilities (not certainties) of being correct. At the start of the century, science and technology had little impact on the daily lives of most people. This had changed radically by the year 2000.

The purpose of Twentieth-Century Science, a new seven-volume book set, is to provide students, teachers, and the general public with an accessible and highly readable source for understanding how science developed, decade by decade, during the century and hints about where it will go during the early decades of the 21st century. Just as an educated and well-informed person should have exposure to great literature, art, and music and an appreciation for history, business, and economics, so too should that person appreciate how science works and how it has become so much a part of our daily lives.

Students are usually taught science from the perspective of what is currently known. In one sense, this is quite understandable—there is a great deal of information to master. However, very often a student (or teacher) may ask questions such as "How did they know that?" or "Why didn't they know that?" This is where some historical perspective makes for fascinating reading. It gives a feeling for the dynamic aspect of science. Some of what students are taught today will change in 20 years. It also provides a sense of humility as one sees how brilliantly scientists coped earlier with less funding, cruder tools, and less sophisticated theories.

Science is distinguished from other equally worthy and challenging human endeavors by its means of investigation—the scientific method—typically described as

a) observations
b) hypothesis

c) experimentation with controls

d) results, and

e) conclusions concerning whether or not the results and data from the experiments invalidate or support the hypothesis.

In practice, the scientific process is not quite so "linear." Many related experiments may also be explored to test the hypothesis. Once a body of scientific evidence has been collected and checked, the scientist submits a paper reporting the new work to a peer-reviewed journal. An impartial editor will send the work to at least two reviewers ("referees") who are experts in that particular field, and they will recommend to the editor whether the paper should be accepted, modified, or rejected. Since expert reviewers are sometimes the author's competitors, high ethical standards and confidentiality must be the rule during the review process.

If a hypothesis cannot be tested and potentially disproved by experiment or mathematical equations it is not scientific. While, in principle, one experiment can invalidate a hypothesis, no number of validating experiments can absolutely prove a hypothesis to be "the truth." However, if repeated testing, using varied and challenging experiments by diverse scientists, continues to validate a hypothesis, it starts to assume the status of a widely accepted theory. The best friend a theory can have is an outstanding scientist who doubts it and subjects it to rigorous and honest testing. If it survives these challenges and makes a convert of the skeptical scientist, then the theory is strengthened significantly. Such testing also weeds out hypotheses and theories that are weak. Continued validation of an important theory may give it the stature of a law, even though it is still called a theory. Some theories when developed can revolutionize a field's entire framework—these are considered "paradigms" (pronounced "paradimes"). Atomic theory is a paradigm. Advanced about 200 years ago, it is fundamental to understanding the nature of matter. Other such paradigms include evolution; the "big bang" theory; the modern theory of plate tectonics, which explains the origin of mountains, volcanoes, and earthquakes; quantum theory; and relativity.

Science is a collective enterprise with the need for free exchange of information and cooperation. While it is true that scientists have strong competitive urges, the latter half of the 20th century witnessed science's becoming increasingly interdisciplinary. Ever more complex problems, with increasing uncertainty, were tackled and yet often eluded precise solution.

During the 20th century, science found cures for tuberculosis and polio, and yet fears of the "dark side" of science (e.g., atomic weapons) began to mount. Skepticism over the benefits of science and its applications started to emerge in the latter part of the 20th century even as its daily and positive impact upon our lives increased. Many scientists were sensitive to these issues as well. After atomic bombs devastated Hiroshima and Nagasaki, some distinguished physicists moved into the life sciences and others started a magazine, now nearly 60 years old, *The Bulletin of the Atomic Scientists*, dedicated to eliminating the nuclear threat and promoting peace. In 1975, shortly after molecular biologists developed recombinant deoxyribonucleic acid (DNA), they held a conference at Asilomar, California, and imposed voluntary limits on certain experiments. They encouraged adoption of regulations in this revolutionary new field. We are in an era when there are repeated and forceful attempts to blur the boundaries between religious faith and science. One argument is that fairness demands equal time for all "theories" (scientific or not). In all times, but especially in these times, scientists must strive to communicate to the public what science is and how it works, what is good science, what is bad science, and what is not science. Only then can we educate future generations of informed citizens and inspire the scientists of the future.

The seven volumes of Twentieth-Century Science deal with the following core areas of science: biology, chemistry, Earth science, marine science, physics, space and astronomy, and weather and climate. Each volume contains a glossary. Each chapter within each volume contains the following elements:

- background and perspective for the science it develops, decade by decade, as well as insights about many of the major scientists contributing during each decade
- black-and-white line drawings and photographs
- a chronological "time line" of notable events during each decade
- brief biographical sketches of pioneering individuals, including discussion of their impacts on science and the society at large
- a list of accessible sources for Additional Reading

While all of the scientists profiled are distinguished, we do *not* mean to imply that they are necessarily "the greatest scientists of the decade." They have been chosen to represent the science of the decade because of their outstanding accomplishments. Some of these scientists were born to wealthy and distinguished families, while others were born to middle- and working-class families or into poor families. In a century marked by two world wars, the cold war, countless other wars large and small, and unimaginable genocide, many scientists were forced to flee their countries of birth. Fortunately, the century has also witnessed greater access to the scientific and engineering professions for women and people of color, and ideally all barriers will disappear during the 21st century.

The authors of this set hope that readers appreciate the development of the sciences during the last century and the advancements occurring rapidly now in the 21st century. The history teaches new explorers of the world the benefits of making careful observations, of pursuing paths and ideas that others have neglected or have not ventured to tread, and of always questioning the world around them. Curiosity is one of our most fundamental human instincts. Science, whether done as a career or as a hobby, is after all, an intensely human endeavor.

Acknowledgments

My thanks to molecular biologist Karen K. Bernd of Davidson College, Davidson, N.C., and to science historian Eric D. Kupferberg of Harvard University for sharing their knowledge. Many people graciously helped to track down information. At the University of Wisconsin–Madison, thanks to Karen Dunn of Steenbock Memorial Library, Micaela Sullivan-Fowler of the History of the Health Services Library, Lisa Wettleson of the Biology Library, and women's studies librarian Phyllis Holman Weisbard. At Cornell University, thanks to Jeff Diver and Jim Morris-Knower, both of Mann Library, and to Katherine Regan of the Division of Rare and Manuscript Collections of University Archives. Thanks to George Schlukbier of the Library of Congress, Keith W. Anderson of the U.S. Geological Survey, and entomologist/chemical ecologist Murray S. Blum of the University of Georgia for his support and encouragement.

Thanks also to Frank K. Darmstadt, executive editor of science and mathematics, for overseeing and coordinating all the books in this set (an enormous job). Special thanks to Amy L. Conver for copyediting this book. Warm thanks to line illustrator Bobbi McCutcheon for her skill and for cheerfully putting up with a sometimes-befuddled author and to Elizabeth Oakes for researching and obtaining the photos. Thanks most of all to Deborah Blum, who helped in innumerable ways.

Introduction

Civilization marks time by centuries, although the passage from one 100-year period into the next seldom means very much. Momentous changes in the way people live and think—in areas ranging from politics to religion to science—are as likely to happen 30 or 50 years into a century as at the very beginning or the very end. For example, the American Revolution, a world-changing event—began in the 1770s. The Nuclear Age started, literally with a bang, in 1945.

Biology: Decade by Decade is about an extremely important century in the history of biology, and its writing was made easier by at least a few coincidences of timing, in which important breakthroughs happened, or came to light, just as the 19th century was ending and the 20th beginning. In the period around 1900, a handful of European biologists discovered groundbreaking research that reshaped the way they and their peers thought about *genetic* heredity and biological evolution. That research into patterns of inherited physical traits, conducted by an Austrian monk named Gregor Mendel (1822–84), had been ignored decades earlier when Mendel published it. But in 1900 and 1901, Mendel's amateur work—modestly undertaken in a monastery garden plot—meshed with professional biologists' growing eagerness to discover the physical mechanism by which living things replicate themselves.

Gregor Mendel's painstaking experiments provided a foundation for 20th-century genetic research. (MendelWeb)

When he identified rules that apply to that mechanism—patterns by which individual traits appear to be passed on independently of one another—Mendel gave his successors a fresh perspective on the theory of the evolution of species, which English naturalist Charles Darwin (1809–82) had put forward in 1859. By 1900, Darwin's theory had gained wide acceptance, although even enthusiastic Darwinians sometimes expressed reservations regarding specifics. Darwin's ideas about natural selection, for example, sparked discussions that lasted into and through the 20th century.

Overall, the theory of evolution had raised more questions than it answered, but they were fascinating, stimulating questions. Chief among those questions was this: How do species reproduce? This is not a facetious inquiry. Scientists knew about sexual reproduction, of course, just as growers of crops and livestock had understood basic techniques of breeding, including aspects of selective breeding and cross-breeding, for a long time. What biologists wanted to know was what it is, exactly, that makes a new animal or plant come to life. What triggers the new to grow into the image of the old? How does nature perform this alchemy?

Centuries begin in years ending in 01 (because there was no year 0), so it was almost precisely at the beginning of the 20th century, in 1901, that one young American biologist, Walter Stanborough Sutton (1877–1916), provided a vital clue to this scientific mystery of life. Sutton found strong microscopic evidence that *chromosomes*, tiny paired structures within the *nucleus* of the living cell, carry the even smaller microscopic units of inheritance. Mendel had called these theoretical units "factors." Within a few years of Sutton's observation the units would be called genes. *Biology: Decade by Decade* recounts the rise of Mendel's and Sutton's field of study, genetics, which came of age and gave rise to newer, more specific, subdisciplines in the 20th century.

That story is perhaps the most exciting tale that the history of biology in the 20th century presents. Beginning with Sutton and his contemporaries, it builds to the dramatic point in 1953 when James Watson (1928–) and Francis Crick (1916–2004) worked out the structure of the DNA molecule. Then it races to a climax with the *biotechnology* revolution of the 1970s through the 1990s. That story is not, however, the only one to be told here. There are many other plot lines that unfolded within biology over those 100 years, most of them intertwined. Before mentioning a few of these, it may be prudent to consider the field of biology at large. When did it arise, and what are its boundaries?

Biological inquiry, like astronomy and mathematics, traces to antiquity. Ancient people observed the world around them and tried to understand how things worked. Forerunners of modern biologists wondered if plants and animals had a predetermined purpose. Did a superior being put other living things here to give people something to eat? If so, why were some plants inedible? Why were some animals, locusts for example, a plague rather than a blessing? Were other living things like people? Did they have spirits? Other living things performed functions much like human beings. They ate, grew, and mated. They gave birth. They eliminated waste.

The Greek philosopher Aristotle (387–322 B.C.E.) studied virtually everything he could observe. He wrote in exquisite detail about many plants and animals and speculated about their respective places in the universe.

In the early 19th century—almost 23 centuries after Aristotle—the common terms for people who studied the workings of nature, especially living things, remained "natural philosopher" and *naturalist.* They observed and cataloged the world's diverse varieties of plants and animals. They gave these species names and separated them into categories based on similarities and differences. Pioneered in the 18th century by Sweden's Carl von Linné (1707–78; often cited by the Latin version of his name, Carolus Linnaeus), this is an area of science that today goes under the heading *taxonomy*, a subdiscipline of biology.

Louis Pasteur first demonstrated the role of microorganisms in disease and fermentation. (M. Ladrey in *L'Illustration*)

As the 19th century progressed, biological study probed deeper and wider, foreshadowing a multifaceted future. In France, Louis Pasteur (1822–95) unlocked the secrets of fermentation in the 1850s, establishing the role of *microorganisms* in that process. He followed by showing that all living things are produced by other living things, disproving the popular ancient notion that lesser life-forms, such as worms, sprang from inanimate matter such as dust, mud, and horsehair. Not long after, Swiss chemist Johann Friedrich Miescher (1844–95) isolated DNA (*deoxyribonucleic acid*) from the nuclei of white blood cells, although the full significance of the substance would not be made clear for almost a century.

While studying white blood cells, Johann Friedrich Miescher isolated DNA, which he called "nuclein." (Friedrich Miescher Institute)

Around this time, Mendel did his work, painstakingly keeping records of traits passed on from generation to generation of garden peas. These experiments would lead toward an understanding of what Miescher had found and what it meant. As mentioned above, other scientists overlooked Mendel's patterns of heredity until decades later. By contrast, Darwin won considerable attention in his own time and sparked fierce debate with his book *On the Origin of Species*, unveiling the theory of evolution.

DNA pioneer Miescher's 19th-century laboratory, with its vaulted ceiling, in Tübingen, Germany (Friedrich Miescher Institute and University of Tübingen Library)

Charles Darwin's innovative way of thinking about nature cast a brilliant new light on the work of earlier naturalists. (Harvard University)

Darwin—who began as an old-style naturalist, or taxonomist, and developed an innovative way of thinking about nature—became the most important biologist of the 19th century. His insights cast a brilliant new light on the work of earlier thinkers such as Linné. Linné's system was the basis for the categorizations biologists still use, with like species grouped together into a *genus;* similar genera (the plural of genus) joined into families, families into orders, and so on. Darwin's theory transformed such organization from a static chart of life into something fluid and exciting. The relationships between similar species became a story of adaptation and the struggle to survive. It illustrated how plants and animals responded to changes in where they lived, to what they found to eat, to what tried to eat them, and to any other challenges they had to overcome. Animating life science, Darwin's work inspired generations of researchers who followed him—some to build on what he had found, others to expose flaws in his ideas.

As the 19th century flowed into the 20th, biology branched into new specialties, growing into a dizzying array of disciplines and subdisciplines and sub-subdisciplines, many of them dependent on one another. Some biologists studied moss while others examined the tree on which it grows. Still others studied the dog that sniffs the tree, the flea in the dog's fur, or the *bacterium* inside the flea's digestive system. A *virus* that attacks the bacterium inside the flea merited study, as did the *molecules* within the bacterium's cellular nucleus, and even the chemical processes within those molecules.

Biology treats parts of living things—the structure of the flea's mouth—and relationships between living things—how the tree and the moss; the dog and the flea; or the flea, the bacteria, and the virus affect one another. Biologists also pick apart the ways living things interact with the broader environments in which they live—oceans, deserts, forests, and so on. Fields as seemingly different from each other as medicine and forestry fall under the vast umbrella of biology, along with mycology (the study of *fungi*), virology (viruses), and neurobiology (the nervous systems of animals and people).

Biological sciences can be lumped together under general labels such as botany (the study of plants)

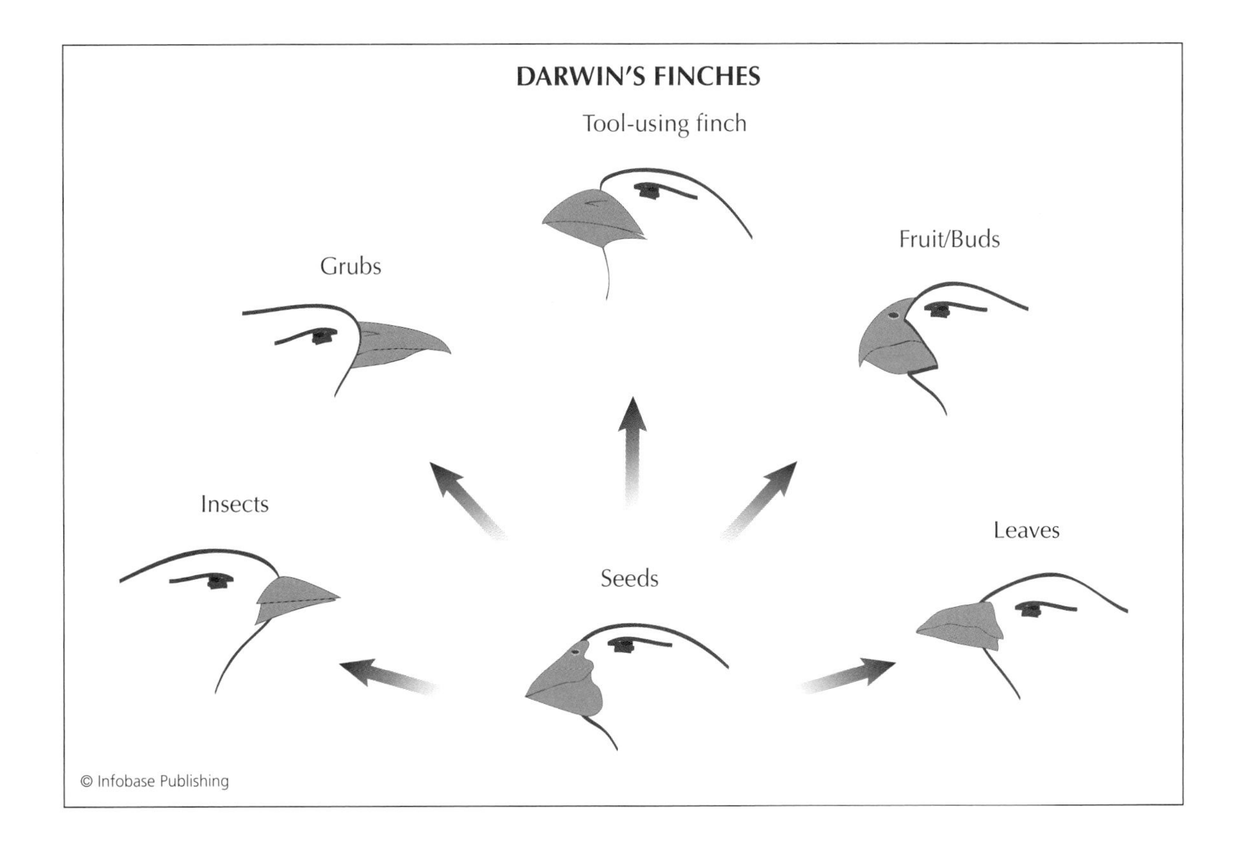

In the Galápagos Islands, Charles Darwin observed 14 species of finches whose beaks, adapted to different feeding habits, illustrated for him how descendants of a single species can evolve to fit divergent niches in nature.

and zoology (the study of animals) or sorted into innumerable specialties. Within zoology, there are ichthyology (fish), entomology (insects), herpetology (reptiles and amphibians), and protozoology (microscopic animals called *protozoa*). There are too many other "'ologies" to list them all, but the branches of biology also include

- Morphology—studying the shape and structure of plants and animals
- Physiology—learning about functions of cells, tissues, organs, and organ systems
- Ecology—how living things interact with their environment, including other organisms
- Embryology—how the embryo (an example being the human fetus) forms in animals and plants
- Genetics—how plants and animals pass down traits as they reproduce and how they change over generations

As with zoology, these also have subcategories. Within morphology, for example, you can study anatomy, histology, and cytology.

- Anatomy means the study of how living things are built at the level seen by the naked eye. It includes how bones and muscles fit together.
- Histology looks closer, at microscopic structures within living things.
- Cytology takes it down to the cellular level and, focusing ever tighter, gives way to molecular biology, looking at the matter that makes up cells.

Solving a problem within one biological specialty almost always involves understanding something about other, related specialties. All biologists need to know some chemistry, and many specialize in the chemistry of life. Ecologists are biologists who must understand a broad range of subjects, including meteorology (the weather) and geology. Geology is even more important to paleontologists, who study the petrified remains of ancient life-forms. Because life is a complicated web with innumerable crisscrossing strands, so is biology.

In treating the story of 20th-century biology, this book cannot adequately address even a tiny fraction of the entire, diverse narrative. It will, however, trace major avenues. The practice of medicine, for example, saw great advances in the 19th century, especially after Pasteur showed that microorganisms cause disease and then became the first to develop vaccines against rabies and anthrax. Such breakthroughs pointed toward the medical "miracles" (for so they seemed) of the 20th century. Discoveries, techniques, and treatments that sprang from biological research saved countless lives that would otherwise have been lost to disease and injury.

In another area where biologists directly affected people's everyday lives, agricultural practices ranging from plant breeding and animal husbandry to advances in veterinary medicine revolutionized the way farmers (and, increasingly, large agribusinesses) grew food. There again, 19th-century breakthroughs had paved the way toward astonishing progress. For example, the self-taught botanist Luther Burbank (1849–1926) bred hundreds of new plant varieties. Despite a lack of orthodox scientific method, Burbank's success and widespread popularity caught the imagination of better-educated plant geneticists who were eager to marry his enigmatic (and, it proved, nearly inimitable) techniques to the lessons gained from Mendel's research.

Both of the above stories—medicine and scientifically enhanced agriculture—melded, especially late in the 20th century, into what might be called the DNA narrative, the one in which geneticists probed, unlocked, and learned to manipulate the molecular and submolecular secrets of life.

Also in the 20th century, naturalists and biological researchers led the way to a profound new awareness of the way plants, animals, and the Earth itself rely upon each other and affect each other, for better

Naturalist John Muir, with beard, showing President Theodore Roosevelt the beauty of the Sierra Nevada. Muir expressed intuitively what 20th-century research would later show about the interconnectedness of all living things. (Library of Congress)

and too often (in the case of human beings' impact on their surroundings) for worse. Naturalist John Muir (1838–1914), founding father of the century's conservation movement, described such an awakening in his 1911 book *My First Summer in the Sierra.* "When we try to pick out anything by itself," he wrote, "we find it hitched to everything else in the universe."

In many ways, ecological science and the rise of environmental awareness may be seen as another aspect of the DNA story. As biologists probed deeper and deeper into the innermost workings of life, they came to a far better understanding of what every living thing has in common, of the shared biochemical and evolutionary history of all that is alive. At the same time, scientists studying plants and animals in nature found resounding echoes of this most basic, microscopic, truth on a vast, *macroscopic* stage. They discovered layer upon layer upon layer of interdependencies between seemingly unrelated species and the world those species populate.

From the 1960s forward, ecologists and environmentalists sounded widespread alarms over the damage that human technology was causing, and potentially could cause, to natural systems. Such activism led to laws protecting the natural environment in many industrialized countries, including the United States. Those laws in turn brought resistance and backlash from business and agricultural interests that found such restrictions too costly.

By century's end, many industries employed for commercial gain the very techniques—genetic engineering, cloning, biotechnology—that had resulted from the DNA story, techniques developed by geneticists, molecular biologists, and biochemists. Agribusiness and the medical-pharmaceutical field were among the most prominent of these industries. Many considered these commercial uses of biotechnology a mixed blessing or even a curse. In some cases, the heirs of Sutton, Watson, and Crick found themselves at odds with heirs of Muir. For environmentalists and others wary of unchecked change, genetically altered organisms raised the most troubling ecological questions yet, such as: What potential havoc might a biologically engineered life-form, loosed upon the environment, wreak? Is such an organism significantly different from a hybrid that was achieved by traditional selective breeding? What limits, both scientific and ethical, will apply to cloning technology?

Questions of that sort do not respect the arbitrary boundary between centuries. They continue to be asked in the 21st century and will accompany biological innovation well into the future.

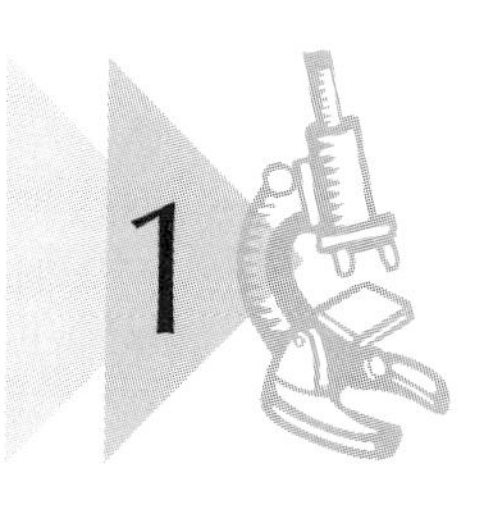

1 1901–1910: Breakthroughs in Genetics Set Century's Scientific Tone

An Age of Potential

To people in the United States and Europe, the beginning of the 20th century seemed filled with astonishing possibilities. Human life and knowledge had seen radical changes through the century before. Steam power, the telegraph, and the rise of mechanized factories had transformed the way people traveled, communicated, and worked. Newer inventions—the telephone, the electric light, the horseless carriage, the moving picture show—promised a future beyond the imaginations of most. Inventors on both sides of the Atlantic raced to devise a practical winged flying machine.

This spirit of innovation, of possibility, affected biological inquiry as well. Researchers linked diseases to microscopic causes; they devised new cures and therapies. Another field of biological study seemed, at the time, less practical and perhaps audacious. It was the quest to understand how life replicated itself. Was it possible to uncloak this ancient mystery—the very mechanics of biological reproduction? The idea struck some as outrageous. They thought of reproduction as a function of the supernatural, at the hands of a divine creator. Solving that mystery, they thought, was not just impossible, it was improper. Such misgivings live on in today's debates over biotechnology and its uses.

Biologists thought it both possible and desirable to tackle the problem. They were eager to learn life's secrets. Armed with the data that pea-breeding amateur Gregor Mendel had collected, inspired by the insights of Charles Darwin, they pushed on. In 1900, European scientists working independently of one another—Hugo de Vries (1848–1935) of the Netherlands, Erich Tschermak von Seysenegg (1871–1962) of Austria, and Karl Erich Correns (1864–1933) of Germany—discovered Mendel's long-ignored paper "Experiments with Plant Hybrids."

In the winter of 1865, Mendel had read the paper to an audience of scientists and naturalists (both professionals and his fellow amateurs) in Brünn, Moravia (now Brno, Czechoslovakia), at meetings of the Brünn

Society for Study of the Natural Sciences. Mendel—portly, shy, and not used to public speaking—had read the paper in two installments, the first on February 8 and the second on March 8. Both readings took about an hour. On neither occasion did anyone in the room ask a question. The next year, the detailed paper, 44 pages long, appeared in published form in *Proceedings of the Brünn Society for Study of Natural Sciences*—a book-length annual publication including all the papers read at the society's meetings over a year. Mendel ordered 40 copies of *Proceedings* and sent at least a dozen of them out to biologists around Europe, among them Charles Darwin. After Darwin's death in 1882, his copy still sat on one of his shelves, the pages uncut. (Books, in those days, were issued with pages connected both within the spine, or binding, and on the other side, where they had to be carefully cut the first time someone opened a book.)

Other copies apparently lay unread, as well, and those people that did read Mendel's paper seemed to see it as a guide to breeding hybrid peas rather than as a discovery of laws of genetic inheritance. Although "Experiments with Plant Hybrids" was sometimes cited by biologists over the following decades, there is no evidence that anyone during that

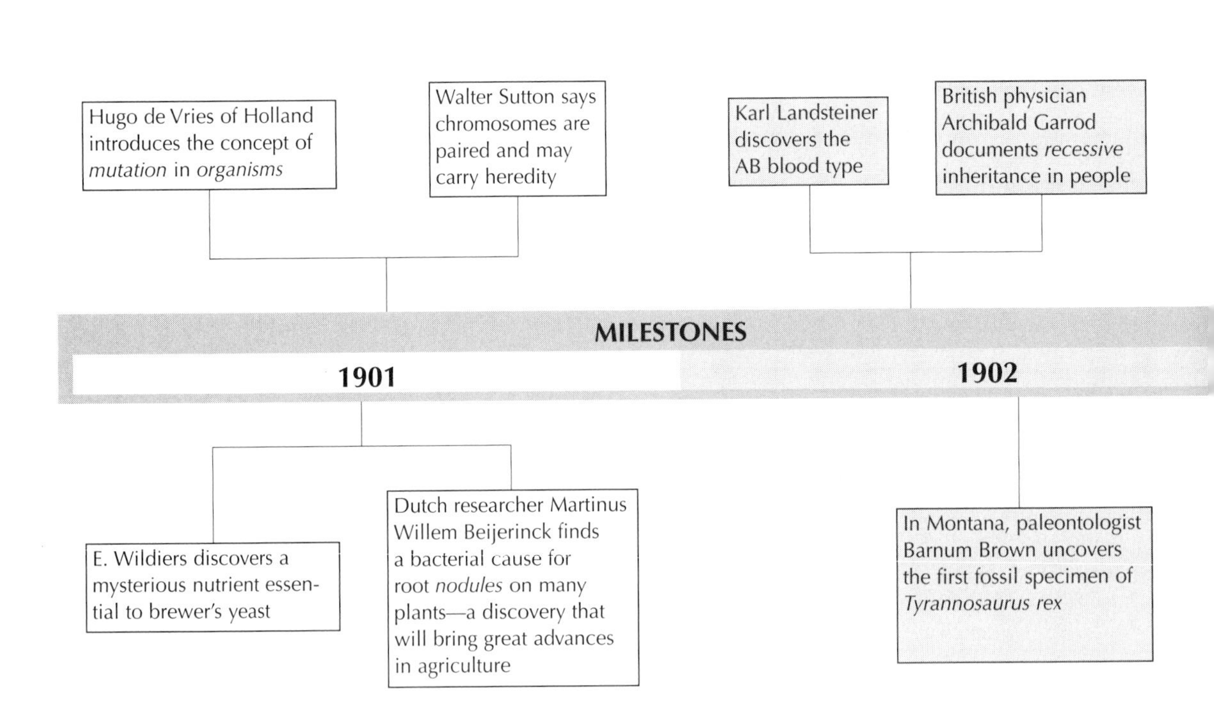

time grasped the importance of what the monk had discovered about the way pea plants passed on characteristics such as height and color.

By the late 1890s, one of those neglected copies had somehow found its way into the library of Dutch botanist Martinus Willem Beijerinck (1851–1931). Mendel's findings struck Beijerinck as similar to those of his contemporary, Hugo de Vries, another Dutch botanist. Beijerinck sent the publication to de Vries, who carefully cited Mendel in a 1900 paper of his own. At the same time, early 1900, both Tschermak von Seysenegg and Correns also ran across Mendel's paper and cited it. That seems a tremendous coincidence, but it becomes understandable in light of the fact that these men were researching patterns of genetic inheritance—just becoming a hot topic in European and American botany and zoology. They were conducting their own experiments, and in the course of those studies, they sought any previous work that might be related.

The sudden flurry of Mendel citations caught the attention of outspoken English zoologist William Bateson (1861–1926), who saw in it confirmation of his own ideas. In May 1900, Bateson, of St. John's College, Cambridge, delivered a lecture to the Royal Horticultural Society in London in which he trumpeted Mendel's findings. According to the pub-

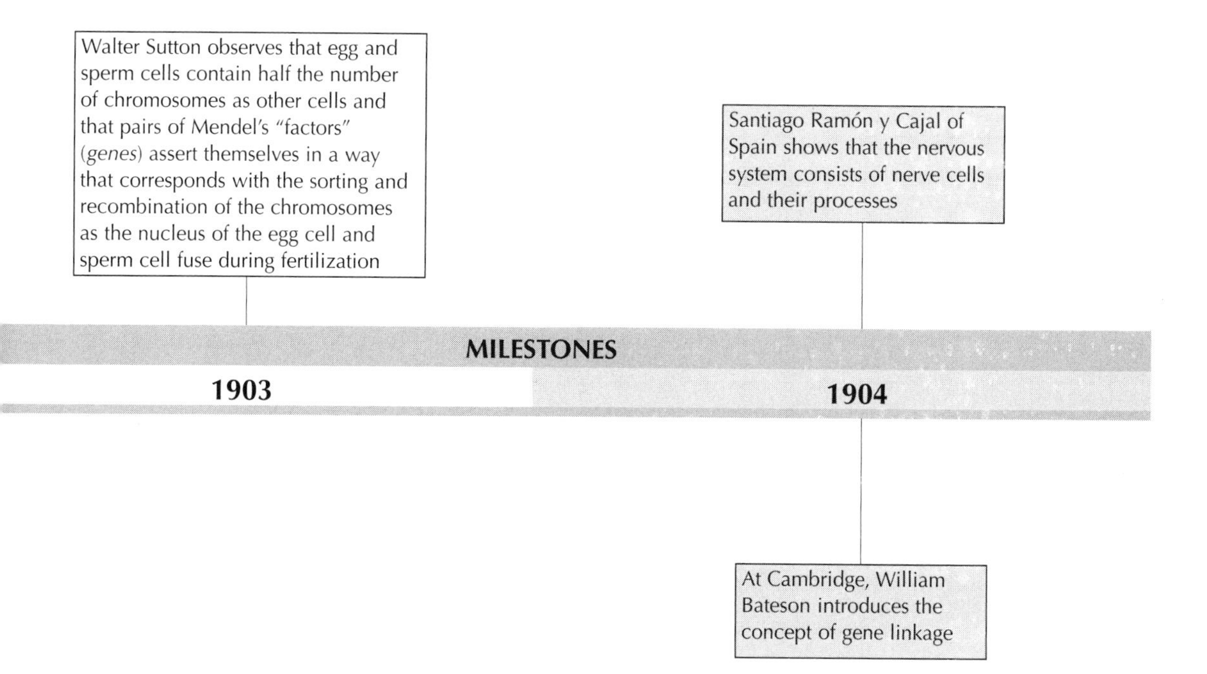

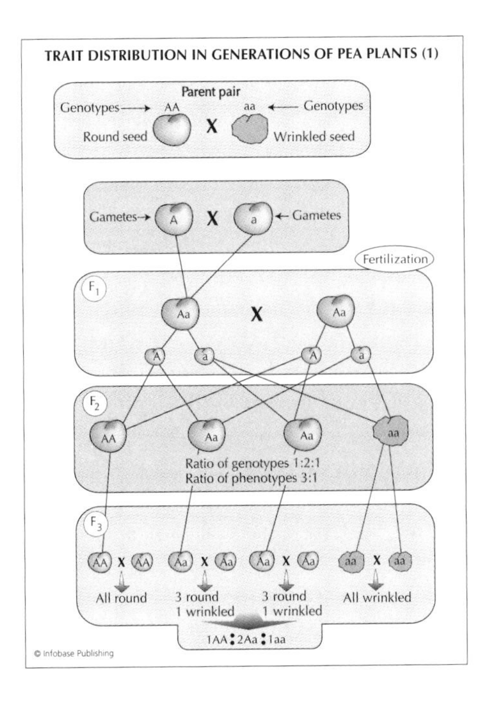

Mendel crossed a strain that produced all smooth, round seeds with one that produced all wrinkled seeds. Offspring were all smooth, yet when that generation self-pollinated, the result was a second generation (f2) of three plants with smooth peas to every one with wrinkled peas. When that generation self-pollinated, the 3:1 ratio held in the next, or f3 generation.

lished version of that speech, he said, "An exact determination of the laws of heredity will probably work more change in man's outlook on the world, and in his power over nature, than any other advance in natural knowledge that can be foreseen. There is no doubt whatever that these laws can be determined."

Mendel's work, confirmed through new research by these four—de Vries, Tschermak von Seysenegg, Correns, and finally Bateson—demonstrated statistical basics of how traits pass from generation to generation, especially in the way one trait (the color of a plant's flower) can be passed along independently

MILESTONES

1905

Nettie Maria Stevens of Bryn Mawr College publishes a study showing that chromosomes determine gender in *Tenebrio molitor* beetles

1906

In Brussels, Belgium, Jules Bordet and Octave Gengou grow the bacterium *Bordetella pertussis* and establish the likelihood that it causes whooping cough

British biochemist Sir Frederick Gowland Hopkins shows that foods contain what he calls "accessory factors" in addition to proteins, carbohydrates, fats, minerals, and water. They appear essential to growth and health

The Bronx Zoological Park in New York displays Ota Benga, a captured African Forest Person, or "Pygmy" from what would later be the Democratic Republic of the Congo

1907

After extensive experimentation with sea urchin eggs, Theodor Boveri reports that individual chromosomes carry individual traits

from another (the length of the stem) and also how some traits (such as red flowers) prove dominant and others (white flowers) recessive. Soon other scientists would also be pursuing parallel lines of experimentation.

Yet there was a difference between charting the statistical patterns of inheritance and understanding the mechanics behind those patterns. Biologists did not even know why a pig gave birth to a baby pig instead of a kitten. They did not understand why chicks, instead of ducklings, emerged from chicken eggs. They knew for sure that each species reproduced in kind, of course, but they did not

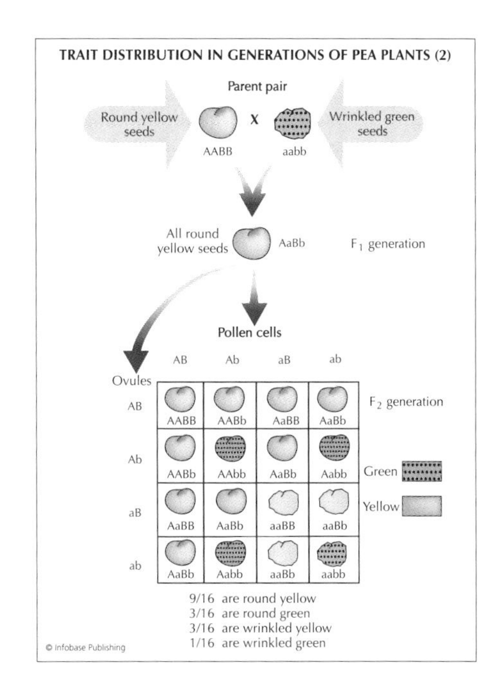

Mendel found that genetic traits do not blend but are inherited independent of one another.

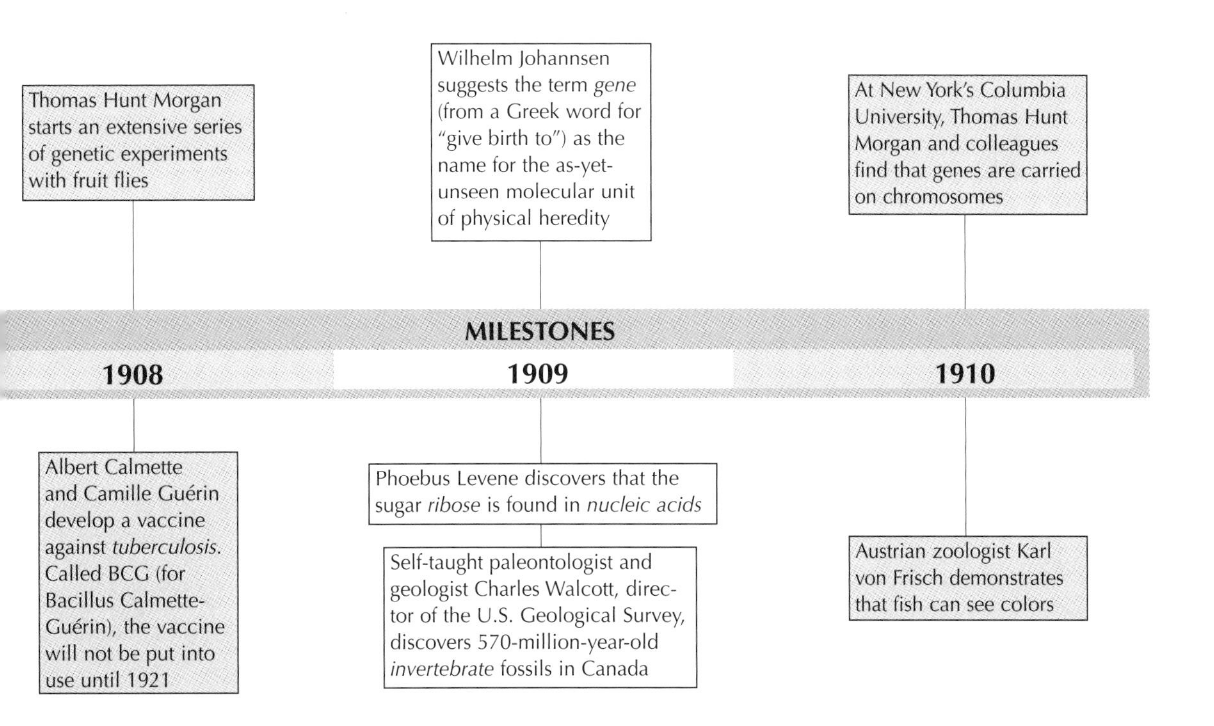

know what it was within egg and sperm that caused new pigs and chicks to turn out like their parents.

That compelling mystery drove scientists ranging from the widely respected William Bateson to Kansas undergraduate Walter Sutton, who found an important clue—one that would set the tone for the decade ahead—in the wheat fields of his family's farm.

The Grasshopper and the Cytologist

If Walter Sutton had not grown up on a farm, and if Sutton had not been such a dutiful brother, biological science might have had to wait for a key observation that helped illuminate the burgeoning field of genetic research. As it was, his observation that chromosomes play a central role in determining physical heredity came almost as soon as the century began.

An undergraduate at the University of Kansas in Lawrence, the personable young Sutton went home to Russell County, Kansas, in the summer of 1897 to help out two of his brothers who had taken over the family farm from their father. Harvesting wheat with a horse-drawn machine called a *header* was familiar work to Sutton, who at age 10 had come west with his family from Utica, New York. This particular summer, though, the curious biology major looked at one detail of the harvest with newly educated eyes. Along with the heads of wheat, the header collected hundreds, if not thousands, of grasshoppers—pests that had to be picked out of the crop. As Sutton picked, he paid particular attention to one type of hopper, the extremely large species called the plains lubber grasshopper, *Brachystola magna*. An enthusiastic and gifted student, he had spent the previous academic year assisting in the laboratory of his histology professor, Clarence E. McClung (1847–1946). McClung and Sutton had been investigating the way grasshoppers produce sperm cells, but McClung had chosen as his research subjects "long-horned" grasshoppers from the insect family *Tettigoniidae*, which includes katydids. By applying his laboratory training to his work in the field (literally), Sutton discovered a much better subject, *B. magna*, in the related family *Acrididae*. The most obvious difference between Tettigoniidae and Acrididae is that the first has long, threadlike antennae (thus the common name long-horned), and the second has shorter, thicker antennae. That, however, was not the difference that caught Sutton's attention.

On the farm, Sutton dissected several plains lubber grasshoppers and examined their sex organs, as he had learned to do in McClung's tiny office-laboratory. He found that the insects' germ cells (the male's sperm as well as the female's egg) were very large, making the sperm especially easy to study. He sent a sample to McClung, who asked Sutton to collect as many lubber grasshoppers as he could.

Within a very few years, *B. magna* was a favorite research subject for cytologists around the world. Yet that was not the extent of Sutton's contribution. When he returned to Lawrence in the fall, he used this grasshopper species to observe that chromosomes, mysterious rodlike structures within the cell, retained their individual characteristics within forming germ cells. This was surprising because most biologists of the time assumed that chromosomes were essentially all the same. McClung, meanwhile, caught the first documented glimpse of an X chromosome in a lubber germ cell.

Sutton continued his explorations at New York's Columbia University, which in 1901 awarded the prodigious Kansan a graduate fellowship to study under Edmund B. Wilson (1856–1939), a leading cytologist. There he worked on the article "On the Morphology of the Chromosome Group in *Brachystola Magna*," published in 1902 in *Biological Bulletin*. The paper detailed the way chromosomes retain individuality. He followed in 1903 with "The Chromosomes in Heredity," also published in *Biological Bulletin*. In that article, Sutton unveiled a breakthrough finding based on his observations of *meiosis*, or reduction cell division. This is the kind of cell division that takes place during sexual reproduction. Sutton saw that after each chromosome paired with another chromosome physically similar to it, the chromosomes separated and one member of each pair went to a different cell. If one was from the mother and the other from the father (an assumption at that point), this behavior fit with Mendel's findings. Sutton's paper suggested that chromosomes contain the mechanism for Mendelian inheritance.

Sutton was not the first to have looked closely at chromosomes. Twenty years before in Belgium, Edouard van Beneden (1846–1910) had studied the organization of the structures in the fertilized eggs of worms and other organisms. His results led German zoologist Wilhelm Roux (1850–1924) to say in the 1880s that these structures (soon to be called chromosomes) contained the stuff of heredity. Some prominent biologists—Columbia's Wilson among them—agreed, but the theory had failed to catch on.

Why did Sutton's report find greater acceptance? At least in part, it was because of lucky timing. Mendel's experiments were just becoming known among biologists in 1901, thanks to the scientists who had embraced the monk's work as supporting their own research. The widely respected Bateson was especially influential and particularly enthusiastic about spreading Mendel's ideas. In 1900, Bateson sponsored and supervised an English translation of Mendel's paper "Experiments with Plant Hybrids." The next year he expanded its ideas into the book *Mendel's Principles of Heredity*. Bateson came from England to New York around this time to spread Mendelian ideas, making a powerful impression on young Sutton.

The Columbia graduate student had already observed that egg and sperm cells contain only half the number of chromosomes as other cells in the same organism. Then he realized that the sorting and recombination of the chromosomes during fertilization, as the nucleus of the egg cell and sperm cell fuse, matched the distribution of traits as Mendel had recorded them. In other words, whatever it is that makes physical heredity work, apparently it happens in the chromosomes.

Working independently, German cell researcher Theodor Boveri (1862–1915), who also had studied under Columbia's Wilson, made observations that supported Sutton's, strengthening the Kansan's case. As Wilson later recalled, Sutton believed he had discovered "why the yellow dog is yellow." He had not quite made that discovery, but the young scientist had put generations of geneticists on the right track.

Walter Sutton, Renaissance Researcher

According to one stereotype, scientists are obsessively single-minded about their research, working long days and forgoing vacations for years on end in pursuit of a single intriguing answer. Some scientists actually live that way, but not all. Although a hard worker, Walter S. Sutton—who found the link between chromosomes and genes—did not fit the stereotype.

Unlike many biologists, Sutton chose his field rather late. Growing up on a farm near Russell, Kansas, he showed a particular facility for repairing farm machinery. In 1896, he went off to the University of Kansas in Lawrence as an engineering major.

The next summer, Sutton's parents and his four brothers fell ill with typhoid fever. Of the family, only Walter remained well, so it was his job to nurse the rest. This was a life-changing experience, especially the death of Walter's 17-year-old brother, John. (John's letter of acceptance to the U.S. Naval Academy arrived on the day of his funeral.)

Walter went back to Lawrence that fall and switched his major to biology, the preparation for becoming a medical doctor. That was where he met his first research mentor, Clarence McClung, and began the research that made Sutton famous in the history of cellular biology.

Young Sutton pursued interests outside of the laboratory, some having nothing to do with science. He and McClung enjoyed the new game of basketball (invented in 1891). And when the sport's inventor, James Naismith (1861–1939), formed the first KU varsity basketball team in 1899, Walter Sutton and his brother William were both on the team. (Naismith was also versed in a field of biology. He was a medical doctor and served simultaneously as coach, athletic director, university chaplain—he had a degree in divinity as well—and campus physician.)

Sutton did not continue as a geneticist. He chose instead a many-faceted career in which he never abandoned his earlier passion for engineering or his determination to heal. All his life, he designed machines and tools. For McClung's lab, he invented a paraffin-melting system. After his stellar work as a graduate student at New York's Columbia University, Sutton returned to Kansas, where he worked in the state's oil fields. There he designed and won patents for devices that improved the efficiency of oil drilling and pumping.

Sutton then returned to medical school and became an accomplished Kansas surgeon. Serving as a U.S. Army medical officer in France during World War I, he invented a number of tools for removing bullets and shrapnel from battlefield wounds. Sutton survived the war, only to die the next year in Kansas City, Kansas, after an operation to remove his inflamed appendix.

Beyond Mendel: Some Genes Go Together

As much as Bateson championed Mendel's work, he also noticed important exceptions to the monk's finding that one factor (a gene) controlled one inherited trait and that each factor worked independently.

Around 1902, Reginald Crundall Punnett (1875–1967), a young zoology researcher at Cambridge University, wrote to Bateson to express his interest in genetic studies. Bateson invited Punnett to join him in research with pea plants, and then poultry. Their inquiries went beyond Mendel. The studies confirmed that certain features were consistently inherited together—an idea that seemed to contradict Mendel's findings. The phenomenon came to be known as gene linkage, later understood as the result of genes lying close to one another on the same chromosome. The studies also indicated that some traits—purple flowers in a sweet pea plant, *Lathyrus odoratus*, for example—seemed caused by a set of genes acting in concert. The concept of gene linkage would lead to gene maps that actually described the order of linked genes.

Bateson was one of the important geneticists of the time who did not agree with Walter Sutton's idea that chromosomes contained the mechanism for genetic inheritance—not until much later. Bateson would finally change his mind, citing research conducted by another leading geneticist who at first doubted the chromosome's role. That was Thomas Hunt Morgan (1866–1945), a native of Lexington, Kentucky, who had earned his Ph.D. in marine biology from Johns Hopkins University, in Baltimore.

Morgan came from a prominent Kentucky family. His father had served as a U.S. diplomat. His uncle, Brigadier General John Hunt Morgan, was known as "the thunderbolt of the Confederacy" during the Civil War. Although those circumstances have little to do with Morgan's scientific career, they were part of him. They shaped him. They rooted him in a culture, a time, and a place. He spoke with a Kentucky accent all of his life. Many writers of scientific history commit the error of failing to depict researchers as people—individuals with family histories, personal lives, and eccentricities. It is not surprising such accounts invariably fail to engage the reader. Where possible, given space, this book will attempt to allow the reader a glimpse of the human side of science and scientists.

The boy Morgan found himself excited by nature's wonders from an early age. He spent many young hours outdoors, observing and collecting samples—rocks, shells, insects, birds' eggs. He went on to study natural history at Kentucky State University, where he was valedictorian of the class of 1886. That may not have been a great honor, considering that he was one of only three graduates that year, but Morgan clearly was destined for a career in research.

Morgan taught biology and continued his studies, now specializing in embryology, at Bryn Mawr College, in Pennsylvania, before arriving at

Columbia in 1904 as a zoology professor. (Sutton had just finished his graduate work in New York and, in an unlikely career choice, had gone west to work in the oil fields of his home state.) Widely recognized by his uncombed hair, wild beard, and disheveled clothes, the easy-going and friendly Morgan quickly developed a reputation for carelessness about many things—but not about his attitude toward science. In that, he was uncompromising, arguing that a researcher should maintain skepticism toward every hypothesis, particularly his own.

Morgan believed science should go beyond the kinds of observations that Sutton and Bovari (and for that matter, Darwin himself) had made. No matter how careful the observations, he doubted them unless they could be confirmed by painstaking experiment.

Unwilling to accept Mendel's newly revived conclusions without his own investigation, Morgan tried breeding all-brown wild mice with white-bellied house mice, but he could not produce results that matched either Mendel's or those that Bateson and Punnett had recently achieved in Britain using poultry. Morgan worked with many other animals, including the tiny, aphid-like grape phylloxera, *Daktulosphaira vitifoliae*, a serious pest in vineyards.

In 1908, on the advice of Harvard University researcher William Castle (1867–1962), Morgan assigned a graduate student to breed the common fruit fly, *Drosophila melanogaster*. The student was trying to see if fruit flies deprived of light for scores of generations would become congenitally blind. If that happened, it would confirm an idea about evolution that had been advanced much earlier by the French nobleman Jean-Baptiste-Pierre-Antoine de Monet, chevalier de Larmarck (1744–1829). Lamarck, who coined the term *biology*, thought that an acquired trait could be inherited. He thought that giraffes, for example, had devel-

Rapid reproduction and clear genetic variation made D. melanogaster *ideal for genetic research.*

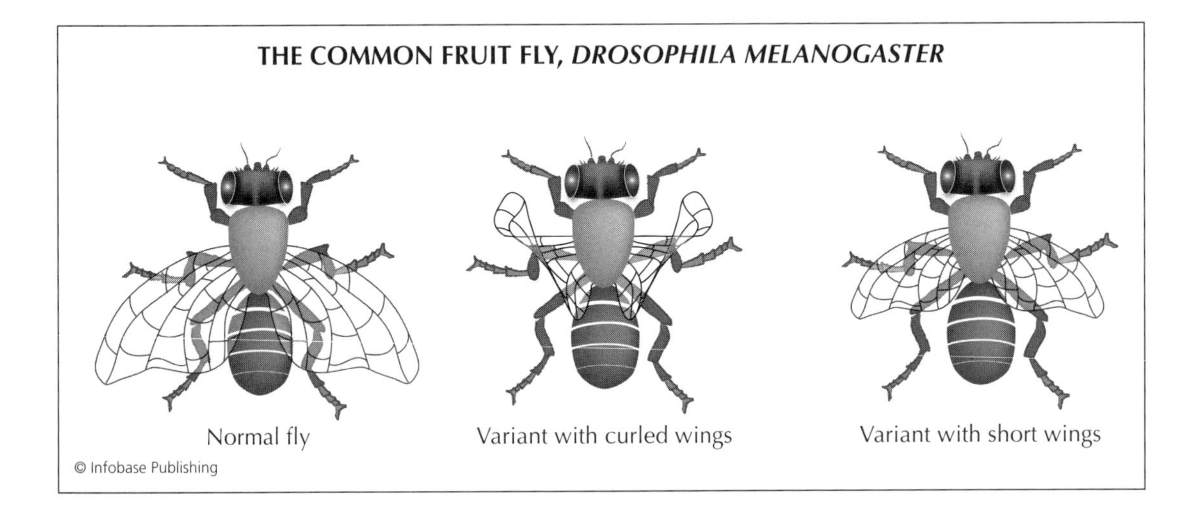

Thomas Hunt Morgan surrounded by the hundreds of milk bottles that housed his experimental subjects (A. F. Huettner/Caltech Archives)

oped their long necks through generations of stretching for leaves. The parent's neck, elongated through use, was passed on to the calf, which in turn spent a lifetime stretching its neck and passed the resulting elongation on to the next generation.

Morgan's student found no evidence that generations of fruit flies raised in darkness produced blind or eyeless offspring. Yet the experiment produced a more important discovery. It demonstrated to Morgan that *D. melanogaster* was a nearly perfect laboratory animal for genetic experiments. The tiny insects (also called vinegar flies or banana flies) breed at four days old and produce a new generation in just over a week. They lay hundreds of eggs at a time, a rich source of data, and display clear genetic variation in traits that include wing size, wing shape, bristle shape, and eye color.

Each fruit fly is about .12 inch (3 mm) long, not much bigger than a pinhead, and although that makes the creature difficult to see clearly without magnification, it meant that Morgan and his team could breed thousands upon thousands, feeding them with a little mashed banana and housing them in rows of milk bottles along the wall of Morgan's small laboratory at Columbia University. By 1910, Morgan's lab would become famous (or notorious for its mess and odor) as "the Fly Room." This untidy, rudely furnished laboratory, measuring 23 feet (7.01 m) wide and 27 feet (8.23 m) long, was where Morgan and associates embarked upon decades of experiments into the patterns by which genetic traits are passed from generation to generation of *D. melanogaster*. Columbia's Fly Room was where Morgan would establish in the next decade (and in the next chapter of this book) that despite his own initial misgivings, and those of William Bateson, the mechanism for genetic inheritance is indeed carried by chromosomes.

Linking Sex to the "X"

Morgan's breakthrough, described in the following chapter, would involve the mysterious X chromosome, the structure first observed in grasshoppers by Clarence McClung in Kansas. But it was while Morgan remained unconvinced of the importance of chromosomes that one of his former Bryn Mawr students, Nettie Maria Stevens (1861–1912), first established that the chromosome was the likely determinate of gender in insects. Hers was some of the earliest work to suggest that genetic material, rather than the embryonic environment, determined whether an organism would be female or male. This provided her peers, including Morgan, with a solid connection between a heritable trait and a particular chromosome.

Originally from Vermont, Nettie Stevens was that rare woman of her time who not only attended college (State Normal School in Westfield, Massachusetts) but also went on to graduate studies. "Normal" schools of the era, precursors of state colleges and universities, specialized in training teachers. Their mission was to establish norms of elementary and secondary education. Most women who attended these colleges planned careers in the classroom. Stevens did teach school, but she decided in her thirties to pursue another career path, as a biological researcher. After earning a master's degree at Stanford University in California in 1900, she returned east to begin working on a Ph.D. at Bryn Mawr. Her research in taxonomy and morphology focused on a *phylum* of single-celled animals, the protozoan Ciliophora. The work took her to Italy and Germany before she earned her doctorate in 1903. The next year, she collaborated with Morgan in a study of cell regeneration. Although five years younger, he was a mentor to Stevens. (The subject of cell regeneration fascinated Morgan throughout his long career.)

The Genesis of "Gene"

How did the basic unit of physical heredity come to be called a "gene"? It happened well before any biologist knew that a gene would prove to be a specific sequence of *nucleotides* found on a chromosome.

Many histories of science credit Danish botanist Wilhelm Ludvig Johannsen (1857–1927) with first using the term *gene* to mean the unit of inheritance that Gregor Mendel had called a factor. Johannsen did not have to reach very far for the term, however. He was among the first scientists to support his Dutch peer Hugo de Vries's theory that unprecedented traits arise through abrupt *mutations.* (This contradicted Charles Darwin's theory that new varieties and species of plants and animals arose as the result of long, gradual changes.) From his correspondence with de Vries, Johannsen was well aware of his colleague's use of the term *pangene,* or *pangen,* which in German means something akin to "all-begetting." De Vries used *pangene* to mean the basic unit of heredity as early as 1889.

Gene appears to have been a simple shortening of pangene. Regardless of who first used it, the term is related to ancient Greek words such as *genea,* meaning family heritage, and *genos,* meaning racial heritage. The Bible's book about the beginning of the world bears the title Genesis, which also is a common noun in English referring to something's beginning. By 1859, Darwin was already using the term *genetic* to mean biological heritage, and in 1905, William Bateson suggested that the emerging field of study concerned with biological heredity be called genetics. *Gene* was part of the English language by 1911.

In 1905, Stevens turned her attention to chromosomes. Using the yellow mealworm beetle, *Tenebrio molitor*, a serious pest in grain elevators, as her subject, she announced that the chromosomes known as X and Y determined the beetle's sex. This observation, also reported around the same time by Edmund Wilson at Columbia, and later confirmed by Morgan and company in their work on *D. melanogaster*, pointed toward a new era in genetic research.

Stevens, on faculty at Bryn Mawr, continued to contribute to the field, exploring the chromosome makeup of various insects until her death at age 51.

Chemistry Counts

While some scientists studied the frequency with which traits showed up in successive generations and others looked closely at the structures within a cell, yet another line of research began to sort out the chemicals that comprise living matter. That is where Phoebus Levene (1869–1940) made his contributions.

Although his Jewish parents named him Fishel when he was born in Sagor, Russia, they renamed him two years later when they moved the family to St. Petersburg. With the more Russian-sounding moniker Feodor, the boy enjoyed a rich education in the city. Although Jews suffered cruel discrimination in czarist Russia, Levene's father, a custom shirtmaker, did well in St. Petersburg and sent young Feodor (nicknamed "Fedya") to schools where he learned to read classical literature in Greek and Latin. The boy became fluent in German and French, picked up a smattering of Italian and English, and scored so high on the entrance exams that he won admission to the St. Petersburg Royal Medical Academy. This was a considerable feat because few Jews were allowed to study at the academy.

Before he could finish his course of study, anti-Semitism became so violent in Russia that the Levene family, Fedya included, decided to immigrate to New York. Thinking he was choosing the English equivalent of Feodor, the young man somehow hit upon Phoebus (pronounced Fee-bus) as his new name, instead of the more correct Theodore. (He might have gone down in the history of science as "Ted.") He later took Theodore as a middle name.

After briefly practicing medicine, Levene studied chemistry at Columbia University and then devoted the bulk of his career to experiments studying the chemistry of life at the Rockefeller Institute for Medical Research. That is where, in 1909, he isolated ribose, a five-carbon sugar, from the *ribonucleic acid* (RNA) molecule—a big step in unraveling the chemical building blocks of life. RNA would later in the century be found to be the stuff that transfers encoded genetic messages from DNA to a cell's protein-manufacturing mechanism.

The Case of the Black Diaper

Although they struggled with the details, many biologists of the early century already understood that heredity's rules must flow from processes within the molecules of the living cell—chemical processes. A few of those scientists reasoned that if genes were chemical in their actions, perhaps the broader chemical functions, and chemical malfunctions, of an organism could also be understood as genetic traits. If so, such traits might be passed along by rules similar to those that predicted flower color in pea plants or wing shape in fruit flies.

One scientist in particular embraced such reasoning and applied it not to laboratory plants and animals but directly to people—patients at London's St. Bartholomew's and Sick Children's hospitals. In 1896, Dr. Archibald E. Garrod (1857–1936) became interested in the rare disorder *alkaptonuria*, or black diaper disease. The problem causes some people's urine to turn dark when exposed to air. Garrod, noting that the condition seemed to run in families, combined what he knew of the new science of biochemistry with the emerging discipline of genetics in considering a cause.

At the time, alkaptonuria was thought to be a bacterial infection. Garrod found instead that patients with alkaptonuria actually lacked an *enzyme* that helps the chemical *alkapton*, or *homogentisic acid*, break down into *acetoacetic acid* in the body's urinary tract. What matters about that is this: The urine emerges into the air full of unbroken-down alkapton, which turns black when exposed to oxygen. Thus, the startling color of baby's wet diapers.

Careful data-keeping allowed Garrod to declare in 1902 that the condition was *congenital*—a rare recessive trait. It fit the pattern of inheritance described by Mendel in his experiments with peas. Ahead of his time, Garrod came up with the phrase "inborn errors of metabolism." (Another such recessive trait is albinism, a lack of pigment in skin, eyes, and hair.) Although Garrod collaborated and consulted with Bateson and with respected biochemist Frederick Gowland Hopkins (1861–1947), this work attracted little attention at the time. It would be decades before the field of chemical genetics would find its place within medicine and biological research. When it did, Garrod was hailed as its founder.

The First Chemotherapeutic Agent

By the year 1900, Paul Ehrlich (1854–1915) of Berlin, Germany, was well established as a pioneer of biochemistry and immunology, having devoted decades to the study of cell chemistry and the body's natural defenses against diseases such as diphtheria. The cigar-puffing scientist had already done the work on immunity that would win him a share of the 1908 Nobel Prize in physiology or medicine. Originally from Silesia, a region that was then under Prussian rule but now part of Poland, Ehrlich was the son of a prominent Jewish-German industrialist. Although trained to become a physician, he had no formal education in applied biochemistry or bacteriology. Those disciplines were not yet part of standard medical studies when he was at the University of Leipzig. Yet they were the fields in which he excelled as a researcher.

Immunologist Paul Ehrlich developed the first chemotherapeutic drug, a treatment for syphilis. (Smith Collection, Rare Book & Manuscript Library, University of Pennsylvania)

In the new century's first decade, he turned his attention to the stubborn disease agent *Treponema pallidums*, the spirochete (one of group of corkscrew-shaped, burrowing bacteria) that causes the sexually transmitted disease syphilis.

With his Japanese colleague Sahachiro Hata (1872–1938), Ehrlich pursued a theory that chemicals with a special attraction for certain cells can be used to attack specific diseases. After trying many formulas of arsenic mixed with other ingredients, they arrived upon what they called preparation 606. It was not a cure, but it proved so effective in treating syphilis that

Élie Metchnikoff's Despair and Triumph

The Russian biochemist Élie Metchnikoff (1845–1916), winner of a 1908 Nobel Prize, attempted suicide twice before he arrived at his most important discovery—a natural process called *phagocytosis,* which is important in immunology.

Troubled by weak eyesight and a lifelong heart condition, Metchnikoff fell into a deep despondency in 1873. This severest kind of depression came over him after his first wife, Ludmilla, died of tuberculosis. She had been ill when they married five years earlier—so weak that she had to be carried to the church on a chair for their wedding—but Metchnikoff was unprepared for the loss. It hit him so hard that he took a massive dose of opium in an attempt to join her in death.

Metchnikoff survived and married again, but after his second wife, Olga, fell ill with typhoid fever, he again fell into despair and exposed himself to what he hoped was a fatal disease by injecting bacteria into his bloodstream. Again he lived, although he suffered terribly from the fever he had given himself.

Metchnikoff, whose original name in Russia had been Ilya Ilich Mechnikov, was always interested in nature and science. As a little boy in Kharkhoff, he lectured his younger brothers and their friends on points of botany and geology. The son of a landowner, he enjoyed a diverse university education that took him to Germany and Italy. In 1867, he came back to Russia and taught zoology at the University of Odessa and then the University of St. Petersburg.

As Metchnikoff was recovering from his self-inflicted illness, St. Petersburg became dangerously chaotic. This was in the wild time after a terrorist bomb killed Czar Alexander II in 1881. The next year, Metchnikoff resigned his position and fled back to Italy.

In the city of Messina, he continued his research into embryology. That is where he discovered phagocytosis. It is a phenomenon in which cells wrap themselves around other matter, sealing it off and consuming it. Metchnikoff arrived at his breakthrough after observing unusual cells in the larvae of starfish. He thought these cells, which could move around in the organism, might function as a natural defense. To test his idea, he placed tiny thorns from a tangerine tree into the larvae. The next morning, the thorns were surrounded by the mobile cells. This struck him as similar to the way some white blood cells behave, seemingly in response to infection. He thought that these white blood cells, *leucocytes,* were a type of phagocyte (bacteria-eating cell) that might surround and digest bacteria that get into the body.

This fundamental discovery in immunology earned Metchnikoff a share of the 1908 Nobel Prize in physiology or medicine (Ehrlich was cowinner). Although it took some time for the idea of phagocytes and cellular immunity to catch on, Metchnikoff knew he had made a great success of something. It changed him from a gloomy, pessimistic sort to a much more optimistic man. His troubles were not over, however. Appointed to a public health office back in Russia, he struggled against local resistance to modern vaccine treatment and eventually fled his native country again. He spent the rest of his life studying immunity at the Pasteur Institute in Paris, where he became known by the French version of his name, Élie Metchnikoff. There he developed a reputation for eccentricity. He let his hair and beard grow long and tangled. He wore overshoes no matter the weather. He often accidentally sat on his hat.

Metchnikoff grew depressed again in 1914 over the outbreak of World War I. His lifelong heart trouble, no doubt compounded by his black mood, finally killed him two years later.

Ehrlich nicknamed it his "magic bullet." Under the trade name Salvarsan, this substance became the first drug used for *chemotherapy*.

Nutrition Becomes a Science

The most obvious link between chemistry and biology lies in the commonplace reality that living things consume fuel, processing it by chemical means. Until the 20th century, however, scientists had but a very rudimentary idea of how nutrition might work. Physicians could only guess at the subtler biochemical aspects. They knew nothing of vitamins.

Earlier clues had suggested the importance to health of minor substances in food, but the substances eluded detection. In 1747, a British Navy surgeon, James Lind (1716–84), had shown that he could cure scurvy—then a common disease among sailors—by feeding oranges and lemon juice to those afflicted. The active ingredient in the fruit—later named vitamin C—remained a mystery.

The very concept that animals burn food to produce energy and heat may be common sense, but science embraced it only after Antoine-Laurent Lavoisier (1743–94) discovered the process of combustion—that oxygen is consumed and carbon dioxide given off—in a fireplace and likewise in respiration. Lavoisier, credited as the founder of biochemistry, might have gone on to greater discoveries, but unfortunately, he was beheaded, for no other reason than his noble rank, during the darkest time of the French Revolution. In "Elegy to Lagrange," an article included in the 1812 book *Mémoires de l'Institut*, Jean-Baptiste-Joseph Delambre (1736–1813) quoted the mathematician Joseph-Louis Lagrange (1736–1813) mourning Lavoisier: "It took them only an instant to cut off that head, but it is unlikely that a hundred years will suffice to reproduce a similar one."

As it turned out, more than a century passed between Lavoisier's death and a more sophisticated approach to nutrition study. An obscure medical student, known to history only as E. Wildiers (d. 1906) became one of the first to write about nutritionally essential chemicals that occur in tiny amounts in food. Studying under Manille Ide (1866–ca. 1945) at the Laboratory of Biological Chemistry in Louvain, Belgium, Wildiers and fellow students discovered in 1901 a substance that occurs in minute amounts but that they found indispensable to the growth and fermentation of brewer's yeast. (Yeasts, single-cell fungi that live in colonies, are like every other living thing in that their nutritional needs must be met for them to survive and thrive.) Wildiers called the substance "bios," from the Greek "to live." Although the Belgian team never managed to identify its chemical composition, bios may have been *pantothenic acid*, a part of the B-vitamin complex that is important to yeast and many other forms of life.

A few years earlier in Indonesia, the Dutch biologist Christiaan Eijkman (1858–1930) had noted, but failed to understand, that malnutri-

Scientist of the Decade: William Bateson (1861–1926)

In a widely told, though perhaps somewhat fanciful story, pioneering geneticist William Bateson first read Gregor Mendel's 1865 paper "Experiments in Plant Hybridization" while traveling by train from Cambridge to London on May 8, 1900. Bateson was on his way to deliver a lecture that, according to this story, he quickly rewrote so that he could publicly hail Mendel's findings and proclaim the underlying principles as revolutionary to the study of heredity.

In reality, Bateson's conversion to the Mendelian model of inherited traits may not have come over him quite so dramatically—perhaps taking a matter of days or even a few weeks. However quickly he took up this cause, Bateson was uniquely well prepared to understand and embrace Mendel's work as a new foundation for the biological field—which it indeed turned out to be.

Born in 1861 in Whitby, Yorkshire (northeast England), William had been the second of six children born to Anna Aikin and William Henry Bateson, who was master of St. John's College at Cambridge University. The elder William Bateson was known as an independent-minded reformist, and his children took after him. They loved to read, think, and argue.

In young William's case, however, that did not necessary translate into a love of school. At Rugby (birthplace of a particularly rough-and-tumble brand of football), he was only a so-so student, inclined to follow his own interests instead of the official curriculum. From early on, those interests included the controversial new theories of Charles Darwin. Bateson had wanted to be a naturalist. Fearing he was not good enough, he once thought he would have to resign himself to what he considered a far lesser career, as a physician.

When he arrived to study at Cambridge, Bateson was fortunate to fall under the tutelage of Scottish embryologist Francis Maitland Balfour (1851–82), one of the top researchers of the time. As a postgraduate student, Bateson traveled widely to observe nature, collect samples, and confer with other scientists. Within a few years after graduation, he had won considerable attention and a research position at St. John's by rewriting a chapter of evolutionary science. Bateson's research, much of it conducted during postgraduate studies in the United States, established a previously unsuspected genetic link between an obscure group of invertebrate marine creatures called acorn worms, which are various species of the genus *Balanoglossus,* and vertebrates. His research, which continues to hold up well in the 21st century, established worms of this sort as likely ancestors of every beast with a backbone, including human beings.

A formidable-looking Victorian gentleman with a receding hairline, large mustache, and basset-hound eyes, Bateson was 40 when he discovered Mendel. A widely respected zoologist, he was also a principal combatant in a continuing scientific debate over how species give rise to new species. Darwin's theory of evolution had by 1900 become widely accepted among scientists. His view of natural selection, however, remained controversial. Darwin himself, having died in 1882, was no longer able to participate in the discussion, but many among his scientific heirs clung to Darwin's notion that natural selection worked through slow, gradual changes as variants within a species proved advantageous to survival, causing those variants to be more widely inherited.

Bateson disagreed. From the 1880s, his observations in the fields of morphology and embryology had shown him many cases in which there was a sharp break in characteristics between one animal and its offspring, such as an extra toe or limbs. He expanded his data through extensive surveys of horticulturists and stock breeders. Soon Bateson came to argue that genetic changes took place in fits and starts—sudden variations—although he could not explain a mechanism for this.

In his massive 1894 book *Materials for the Study of Variation,* Bateson cataloged more than 800 variations in animal form and challenged the idea of gradual natural selection by stating that species in transition seemed tellingly absent.

Bateson's theory of *discontinuity* in evolution resounded through the 20th century, especially as it was taken up by prominent paleontologists such as Harvard University's Stephen Jay Gould (1941–2002).

Seeking a hard scientific underpinning for his theories, Bateson bred poultry and flowers. By 1899, the year before he encountered Mendel, Bateson had realized that physical inheritance worked by some principle other than the simple blending of characteristics from each parent.

Mendel wrote of hereditary elements, or factors, that were like particles. He noted that they took two forms, *dominant* and *recessive.* Bateson was excited to realize that his own research at Cambridge fit the outline of Mendel's results. In his 1902 book *Mendel's Principals of Heredity,* Bateson coined new scientific terms to describe Mendelian ideas—the ideas that would fire an explosion in genetic research. Bateson's new language of genetics, now standard textbook terminology, included *allele, heterozygous,* and *homozygous.*

Working with Reginald Punnett, Bateson charted the inheritance of traits through generations of sweet peas, *Lathyrus odoratus.* Although related to Mendel's experimental subjects, garden peas (Mendel used *Pisum sativum* and a few other varieties), sweet peas are grown not for food but for their fragrant, attractive flowers. The biologists found that when a plant inherited purple flowers it almost always also inherited elongated pollen grains. They further found that plants with red flowers were virtually always endowed with round pollen grains. This surprised them because it did not fit with Mendel's finding that characteristics are inherited independently of each other. Thus, Bateson introduced the concept of gene linkage, later found to be caused by genes that are close to each other on the chromosome and so likely to be inherited together. Linkage was a crucial concept, leading to the first gene maps and, ultimately, to greatly increased understanding of how inheritance works. Bateson and Punnet's experiments also demonstrated that certain physical traits result from a combination of two or more genes.

Bateson has been a somewhat controversial figure for more than a century. Some historians of science refer to him as the singular founder of modern genetics. Others count him alongside Thomas Hunt Morgan as a cofounder. (Mendel, of course, is credited as the primary forerunner of the field.) Bateson's stature, however, among succeeding generations has suffered from his resistance, until quite late in his career, to the correct idea that chromosomes carry Mendel's units of inheritance.

Whether he founded the field or not, Bateson certainly named it. In a 1905 letter to geologist Adam Sedgwick, Bateson commented that there was not yet a word that meant the study of inheritance and variation. He wrote, "such a word is badly wanted and if it were desirable to coin one, Genetics might do." The word *genetic* was not new as an adverb or as an adjective (as explained in the sidebar "The Genesis of Genes" on page 13). By Bateson's conceit, however, *genetics* quickly became a noun and the name of a new academic chair at Cambridge. In 1908, Bateson was the first scientist awarded that position, Chair of Genetics.

As for Bateson's notorious slowness to embrace chromosome theory, according to 21st-century biologist Patrick Bateson (not a descendant but a cousin two generations removed), it may have been rooted in an unwillingness to embrace a theory so unformed. Some of the early speculation about the role of chromosomes treated the *intracellular* structures as if they themselves—rather than genes carried within them—were the units of inheritance. This would have aroused a deep suspicion in a scientist such as Bateson, whose research had found more complex patterns of inheritance than adequately could be explained if chromosomes were genes. At any rate, once Bateson had seen how conclusively Thomas Hunt Morgan's experiments (inspired, in part, by Bateson's work) had linked the distribution of traits in fruit flies to the pairings of chromosomes, he agreed that the gene must be therein contained.

(continues)

(continued)

Regardless of his shortcomings, and whether or not it is appropriate to call him founder of genetics, Bateson was undoubtedly a pivotal figure. He was at the center of genetics, and even of biology at large, in the first decade of the 20th century. It was not only his groundbreaking research that made him so, it was also the way he saw the importance of others' creative research—not just Mendel's, but work being done by contemporaries such as de Vries, Tschermak von Seysenegg, Correns, and Garrod.

Bateson was quick to recognize the importance of his Continental contemporaries' confirmation of Mendel's results. He quickly grasped the genetic implications of Garrod's research into black diaper disease. Not least, Bateson stood at the center because of his advocacy, interpretation, and expansion of Mendel's ideas—spurring the innovative thinking of American pioneers Walter Sutton and Morgan, among many other scientists. He was the most influential biologist from 1901 to 1910.

Bateson worked in the field he had named for the rest of his life. Until his death in 1926, he served as director of London's John Innes Horticultural Institution, which he had transformed into a center for genetic research.

tion caused the debilitating nerve disease beriberi, a common complaint in the region. At his laboratory in Jakarta, Eijkman observed chickens that were fed with leftover white rice from the Dutch army officers' mess. (Jakarta, then called Batavia, was the capital of what was the Dutch East Indies). The birds became listless and developed other symptoms similar to those of people with beriberi. When the army cook decided that leftover officers' rice was too good for the birds and started sending them unpolished, brown rice instead, the chickens recovered.

Eijkman knew there was something about their diet that affected the chickens' health. He may not have known, however, that a link between nutrition and beriberi had already been accepted by the Japanese military, which had dramatically reduced the incidence of the disease by adding a little meat, wheat, and extra vegetables to its men's diet of mostly white rice and bits of fish. What Eijkman failed to see was that the sickness resulted from something missing. He thought instead that the white rice contained a harmful bacterium. It took his successor, Gerrit Grijns (1865–1944) to realize in 1901 that the unpolished rice contained a nutrient in its outer layer, or bran, that the white rice, with the bran layer polished away, did not contain. The absence of that substance, later found to be vitamin B_1, or thiamine, caused disease in birds and in people.

Grijns's observation meshed with what Britain's Frederick Hopkins saw in his laboratory rats. Hopkins, affectionately known to his friends as "Hoppy," was the same biochemist that was helping Garrod with the black diaper disease mystery. Meanwhile, in Hopkins's own laboratory, he noted that rodents failed to grow on a diet of artificial milk but that when he added a little cow's milk to the formula, they grew quickly. Hopkins realized that protein, fat, and carbohydrate are not enough to sustain life, not even with mineral salts added. What was missing?

In 1901, Hopkins isolated the amino acid tryptophan from the protein in cow's milk. (Although it is not a vitamin, tryptophan enables the human body to produce niacin, or vitamin B_3, essential for growth.) In 1906, Hopkins advanced the theory that animals need "accessory substances" in their food in order to sustain growth and life. Hopkins's accessory substances would soon be known as vitamins.

Further Reading

Allen, Garland E. *Thomas Hunt Morgan: The Man and His Science.* Princeton, N.J.: Princeton University Press, 1978. A biography of American genetics pioneer.

Bateson, Patrick. "William Bateson: A Biologist Ahead of His Time." *Journal of Genetics* 81, no. 2 (August 2002): 49–59. Available online. URL: http://www.ias.ac.injgenet/Vol81No2/JG532.PDF. Accessed April 1, 2006. Historical essay posits William Bateson's importance as a founding figure of genetics.

Bateson, William. *Materials for the Study of Variation with Especial Regard to Discontinuity in the Origin of Species.* London: Macmillan, 1894. Landmark volume in which British genetics pioneer put forth his theory of discontinuity.

———. *Mendel's Principles of Heredity.* London: H. K. Lewis, 1902. William Bateson introduces English-speaking world to Mendel's findings.

BBC Online. "Historic Figures: William Bateson." Available online. URL: http://www.bbc.co.uk/history/historic_figures/bateson_william.shtml. Accessed July 29, 2004. Biographical information about early geneticist.

———. "James Lind." Available online. URL: http://www.bbc.co.uk/history/historic_figures/lind_james.shtml. Accessed July 29, 2004. Biography of physician hailed as the father of nautical medicine, nutrition pioneer.

Bern, Alexander G. *Archibald Garrod and the Individuality of Man.* New York: Oxford University Press, 1993. Biography of the founder of chemical genetics.

Biozentrum, University of Würzberg. "Theodore Boveri." Available online. URL: http://www.biozentrum.uni-wuerzburg.de/thepersontheodor.html. Accessed April 1, 2006. Profile of German cytologist who made early observations about nature of chromosomes.

Bolton, Sarah K. *Famous Men of Science.* New York: Thomas Y. Crowell, 1946. Biographies of scientists through history, including Darwin and Pasteur.

Cold Spring Harbor Laboratory: DNA from the Beginning. "Nettie Maria Stevens." Available online. URL: http://www.dnaftb.org/dnaftb/concept_9/con9bio.html. Accessed July 29, 2004.

———. "Reginald Crundall Punnett." Available online. URL: http://www.dnaftb.org/dnaftb/concept_5/con5bio.html. Accessed July 29, 2004. Biography of cytologist who made important observation about chromosomes.

Corsi, Pietro. *The Age of Lamarck*. Berkeley: University of California Press, 1989. Explanation of Lamarckianism and its legacy in genetic theory.

Gould, Stephen J. *Ever since Darwin*. New York: W. W. Norton, 1977. Paleontologist's thoughtful and entertaining essays about natural history and evolution.

Henig, Robin Marantz. *The Monk in the Garden: The Lost and Found Genius of Gregor Mendel, the Father of Genetics*. Boston/New York: Houghton Mifflin, 2000. Biography examines life and legacy of first genetics researcher.

Kothare, S. N., and Sanjay A. Pai. *An Introduction to the History of Medicine*. Chap. 7, "Nutrition and Disease." Available online. URL: http://www.histmedindia.org. Accessed July 29, 2004. Account of early inquiries into nutritional needs and discovery of vitamins.

Lephalophodon. University of California, Santa Barbara. Available online. URL: http://www.nceas.ucsb.edu/~alroy/lefa/Bateson.html. Accessed July 29, 2004. An appreciation of William Bateson's contributions to field of genetics.

Linné, Carl von. *Systema Vegetabilium* (English). Lichfield, England: Leigh and Sotheby, 1783. An example of the great Swedish taxonomist's precedent-setting system of classification.

Margulis, Lynn, and Karlene V. Schwartz. *Five Kingdoms: An Illustrated Guide to the Phyla of Life on Earth*. New York: W. H. Freeman, 1997. Shows a modern approach to taxonomy, greatly changed by the progress of science but still rooted in Linné's system.

Mendel, Gregor. "Experiments in Plant Hybridization" (1865). Available online. URL: http://www.mendelweb.org/Mendel.html. Accessed April 1, 2006. Mendel's paper translated into English.

Metchnikoff, Olga. *Life of Élie Metchnikoff*. North Stratford, N.H.: Ayer Co. Publishers, 1972. Biography of microbiologist who discovered phagocytosis.

Muir, John. *My First Summer in the Sierra*. New York: Penguin Books, 1987. Pioneering naturalist's first-person account includes insights into workings of natural systems.

Ogilvie, M. B., and C. J. Choquette. "Nettie Maria Stevens (1861–1912): Her Life and Contributions to Cytogenetics." *Proceedings of the American Philosophical Society* 125, no. 4 (August 21, 1981): 293–311. Biographical article evaluates work of pioneering cytogeneticist.

Sutton, Walter S. "The Chromosomes in Heredity." *Biological Bulletin* 4 (1903): 231–251. Seminal paper on chromosome theory.

Wilhelm Johannsen Centre for Functional Genome Research. "About Wilhelm Johannsen." Available online. URL: http://www.wjc.ku.dk/Wilhelm. Accessed April 1, 2006. Biographical material on Danish geneticist, contemporary of Bateson who helped shape the field of study.

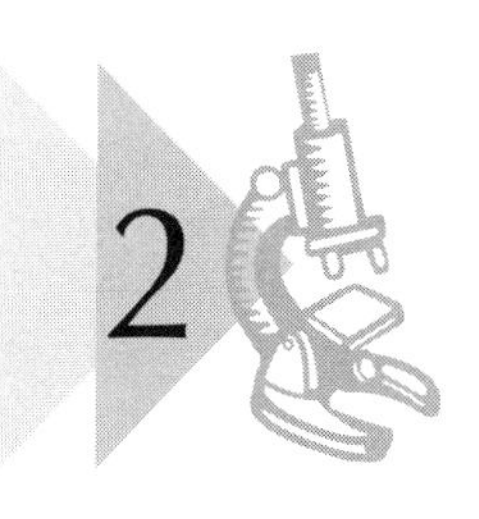

2 1911–1920: Research Perseveres in Time of War

Conflict Mocks Human Enlightenment

For people who believe that the world is bettered by civilization, science, education, and the advances they bring, war can be a humbling business—especially when it involves the so-called advanced countries at the forefront of learning and research.

The second decade of the 20th century was a time of great international tension that erupted into a widespread war—even more widespread and demoralizing than any the world had seen before it. Germany and its allies, the Austro-Hungarian and Ottoman empires, fought a group of countries that included France, Russia, Britain, and eventually the United States.

War colored every aspect of the decade, including biological endeavor. Military physicians such as Walter Sutton of the United States, who had been a genetic researcher, struggled to repair horrific battle wounds and to counter the devastating effects of chemical weapons. Some scientists—supposedly enlightened researchers such as Nobel Prize–winning Fritz Haber (1868–1934)—notched up the cruelty of war by working on and promoting the use of such weapons. Haber helped add chlorine gas, phosgene, and the horrible blistering agent known for its pungent smell as mustard gas (*dyichlorethyl sulfide*) to his native Germany's military arsenal. Away from the front lines, science suffered.

Fritz Haber, 1918 Nobel laureate in chemistry, promoted Germany's use of chemical weapons in World War I. (Smith Collection, Rare Book & Manuscript Library, University of Pennsylvania)

Many researchers diverted their work from pure science to the war effort. Thus, William Lawrence Bragg (1890–1971) and William Henry Bragg (1862–1942)—physicists whose work paved the way for later biological studies—concerned themselves with submarine detection, and biochemist Chaim Weizmann (1874–1952) worked on processes for manufacturing explosives. From 1915 to 1919, the Nobel Assembly at the Karolinska Institutet in Sweden—the body charged with choosing Nobel Prize awardees in the area of physiology or medicine—found no work worthy of the prize. Yet laboratory work and field work continued.

The decade of the Great War, as it was called, brought advances in areas of applied biology such as immunology, bacteriology, food science, and crop breeding—especially in the United States, an ocean away from the battle lines. The Mendelian ideas being spread by British geneticist William Bateson, discussed in chapter 1, found their way into the research stations of the U.S. Department of Agriculture (USDA). Meanwhile, other biologists, such as the USDA's Alice Catherine Evans (1881–1975), pursued diseases to their sources. One devastating disease—a worldwide plague of influenza—left doctors and immunologists frustrated and humbled.

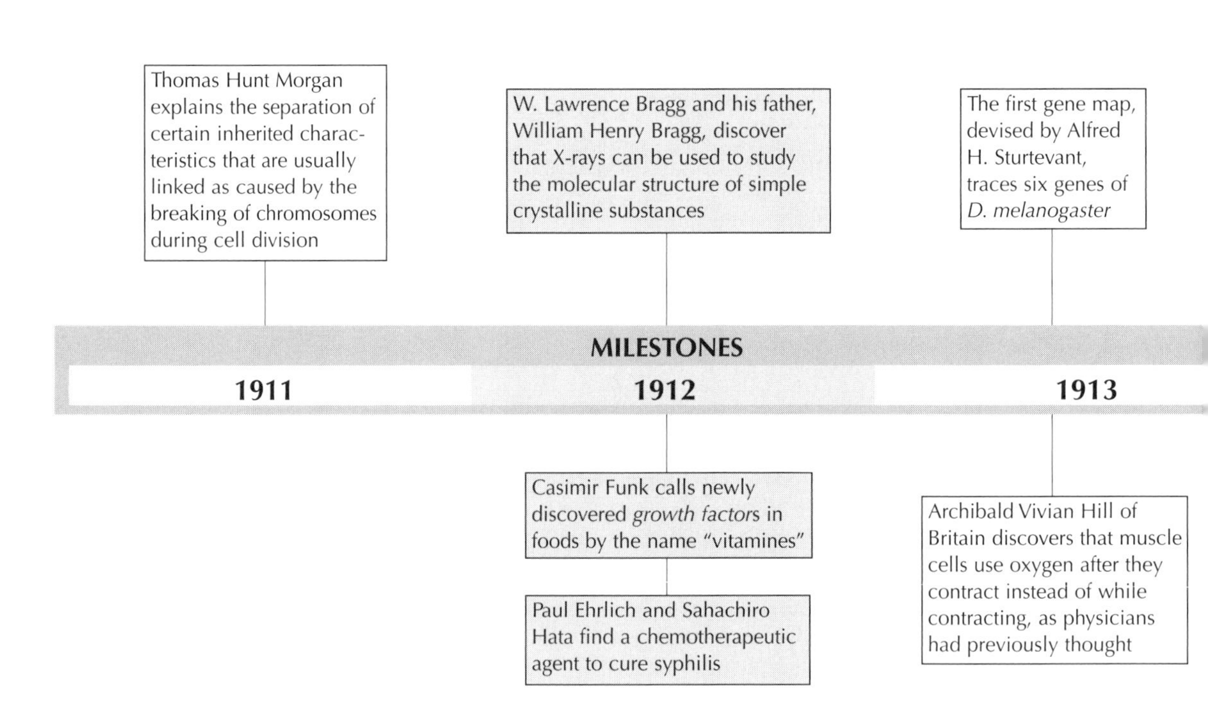

Bananas hang amid the clutter in Thomas Hunt Morgan's crowded laboratory at Columbia University. (Caltech Archives)

MILESTONES

1914

In England, Henry Hallett Dale, a physiologist, isolates the chemical acetylcholine and theorizes that it is involved in sending nerve impulses

U.S. biologist Edward Calvin Kendall identifies thyroxin, secreted by the thyroid gland

1915

English bacteriologist Frederick W. Twort describes bacteriophages, the relatively large viruses that attack and destroy bacteria

Thomas Hunt Morgan, Calvin Bridges, Alfred H. Sturtevant, and Hermann Joseph Muller publish the influential book *The Mechanism of Mendelian Heredity*

Chaim Weizmann uses a *microbe, Clostridium acetobutylicum,* to produce acetone and butyl alcohol, essential to the British munitions program during World War I

1916

Princeton professor George Harrison Shull, a pioneering corn breeder, publishes the first issue of the scientific journal *Genetics*

As in the century's first decade, the most exciting quest in biology seemed to lie within the living cell itself—at the most fundamental layers of life. A few biologists still resisted the idea that chromosomes carried the information for genetic heredity, but in the Fly Room, which was the informal name for Thomas Hunt Morgan's laboratory at Columbia University, a team of geneticists moved beyond proving the vital function of the chromosome. Amid the smell of fermenting mashed banana (food for their experimental subjects), Morgan's group plunged forward to the business of figuring out where certain trait-linked genes occurred on the chromosomes of fruit flies.

Scientists approached a basic and very ancient question: What is it that makes living matter differ from physical matter? This inquiry belonged as much to physics and chemistry as to biology.

Glimpsing a Geography of Genes

Early in 1910, Thomas Hunt Morgan was in his second year of hands-on heredity experiments on the fruit fly species *Drosophila melanogaster*. Thus far, he had balked at adopting the idea that a chromosome could

MILESTONES

1917

Sewall Wright of the U.S. Department of Agriculture shows that production of the pigment determining coat color in mammals requires biochemical steps, taking place in a certain order, and suggests that each step is mediated by a different, specific enzyme

D'Arcy Wentworth Thompson of Scotland publishes *On Growth and Form,* showing the importance of different growth rates in the development of different animal forms from a basic design that they have in common

Félix d'Hérelle publishes his findings regarding bacteria that attack viruses, which he has identified independently from Twort. He coins the word *bacteriophage*

1918

Herbert M. Evans chairman of the anatomy department at the University of California, Berkeley, determines (incorrectly, it will turn out) that human cells contain 48 chromosomes

Bacteriologist Alice Catherine Evans of the U.S. Department of Agriculture links undulant fever, or Malta fever, in people to a bacterial disease of cows that spreads via milk. She advocates pasteurization to prevent the potentially fatal illness

A worldwide *epidemic* of influenza kills 25 million people, far more than died as a result of World War I

carry specific hereditary traits. Very soon, however, he would become well-known among fellow biologists for showing dramatically that chromosomes *do* contain the stuff of heredity.

Morgan's position, when he started the Fly Room experiments at Columbia University, had been that even though Mendel's theories corresponded with the way chromosomes paired in germ cells and even though the theories could predict the distribution of physical traits in breeding experiments, the proponents of Mendel's ideas had yet failed to describe how heredity worked. In this, Morgan sided with William Bateson, the British researcher who had recently helped found and name this new branch of biological inquiry, genetics.

Soon, however, breeding experiments would convince Morgan and Bateson of the crucial role of the chromosome. A key to this conversion was the Columbia team's observation of a mutant male *D. melanogaster* with white eyes instead of the usual red eyes. Morgan wanted to see if this unusual trait would be passed along to the fly's offspring—and especially if the trait would be inherited in a way that corresponded with Mendel's hereditary factors. So Morgan crossed the white-eyed male fly with a normal female, one with red eyes. According to what Morgan later wrote,

Theobald Smith describes the microbe *Vibrio fetus,* responsible for fetal membrane disease in cattle

MILESTONES

1919

1920

The Ecological Society of America publishes the first issue of the quarterly journal *Ecology*

the resulting generation all had red eyes. (Accounts at the time noted 1,237 red-eyed flies and three—all of them male—with white eyes.) The point was that the gene for red eyes was overwhelmingly dominant over the white.

Then, just as Mendel had done with his pea plants, Morgan crossed two flies from that second generation with each other. Out of 4,252 flies in this next generation, 782 had white eyes. But here came a surprise that could not be overlooked: All 782 white-eyed flies were male—nearly half the males in the entire generation. This puzzled Morgan. Why were there no white-eyed female flies?

The Fly Room crew—including Morgan's student assistants Alfred H. Sturtevant (1891–1970), Calvin B. Bridges (1889–1938), and Hermann J. Muller (1890–1967)—was on the verge of a major discovery. Perhaps it is best, however, to approach what they learned by first reviewing a bit of what has, since Morgan's time, become a basic understanding of chromosomes.

Chromosomes determine gender in organisms that have sexual differentiation. Specifically, it is the X chromosome that determines the sex of the fruit fly larva (or the human baby). In these and many other species (although not all), an individual with two X chromosomes is female. An individual with only one X chromosome—joined to a shorter Y chromosome—is male. If, during fertilization, the egg (always X) hooks up with an X sperm, the resulting *zygote* (fertilized egg) is XX—that is, female. If, on the other hand, the egg joins with a Y sperm, the zygote is an XY and will develop into a male.

In *D. melanogaster*, the gene for white eyes occurs on the X chromosome. Genes on the X chromosome that determine a trait are called sex-linked. In Morgan's experiment, the recessive white-eye trait expressed itself only when there was not a dominant red-eye trait opposite it—that is, virtually exclusively in XY, or male individuals. Morgan's results fit Mendel's observations about dominant and recessive genes but also hit upon the fact that the gene for white eyes was unlike any other previously noted Mendelian recessive trait. It was a sex-linked trait, expressed overwhelmingly in males although carried upon a particular stretch of the X chromosome of the mother. The Fly Room experiments confirmed Nettie Stevens's earlier observations that the X chromosome determines gender and further showed that genes not only were contained within chromosomes but that they also occurred in specific places on specific chromosomes.

Morgan's team members developed the *D. melanogaster* work into an overall theory of heredity. They began with location. They argued that the location of genes along chromosomes caused the phenomenon in which certain traits are often inherited together, rather than always independently, as Mendel had observed in his pea plants. This work built on Bateson's discovery of linked traits (discussed in chapter 1). The Fly

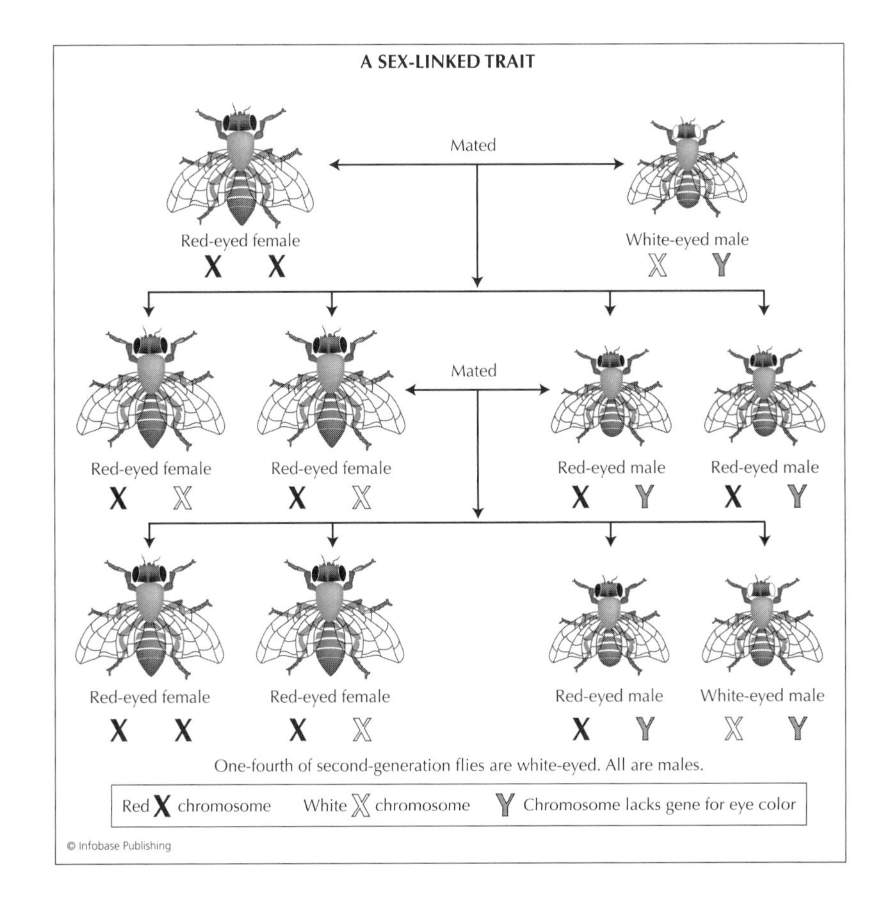

The distribution of the white-eye mutation in Drosophila *confirmed the idea that the responsible gene was carried on the X chromosome.*

Room scientists thought that these simple linked traits—which are not the same as sex-linked traits—were the result of genes that were physically next to or near each other on the chromosome. When the genes recombine during reproduction, similar to when a player "cuts" a deck of cards while shuffling, those genes close to each other are much less likely to separate from each other than those farther apart on the length of the chromosome.

The Cartography of the Chromosome

Sturtevant, a young midwesterner who had yet to earn his bachelor's degree, first realized that the predictable distribution of traits in generations of fruit flies made it possible to draw a map of the species' chromosomes. The tiny distance of a few millionths of an inch between genes and the order in which they occurred on the chromosome showed in the way traits such as eye color, abdomen color, and wing size and shape were passed on independently or in combination from generation to generation.

Alfred Sturtevant, the first gene mapper, would later follow mentor Thomas Hunt Morgan from Columbia University to Caltech, where he remained on the faculty until his death in 1970. (Reed Sturtevant, sturtevant.com)

"I suddenly realized that the variations in the strength of linkage, already attributed by Morgan to differences in the spatial separation of the genes, offered the possibility of determining sequences in the linear dimensions of a chromosome," Sturtevant wrote decades later in a published memoir about Morgan and the Fly Room work. "I went home and spent most of the night (to the neglect of my undergraduate homework) in producing the first chromosome map."

Genetic Numbers Game

Until Morgan's breakthrough, it had not occurred to biologists—even those that championed the genetic importance of chromosomes—just how those tiny, rod-shaped bodies might carry the stuff of heredity. There were not enough chromosomes to account for all the information that must somehow be passed along. One trait per chromosome certainly was not a conceivable way for the formula to work. If the number of chromosomes meant anything, then why did that number vary so widely from species to species?

The name chromosome refers to color (the Greek *chroma*), because when dye is applied to a microscope slide, chromosomes take on the dye's color and stand out from the rest of the cell's nucleus. Yet even that did not make the tiny structures easy for Morgan and his contemporaries to see. The only time they could make out what they were looking for, using the best microscopes of the time, was during cell division, or *mitosis,* when the thin, tangled strands, or *chromatids,* coil and thicken into the familiar chromosome rod.

Chromosomes seemed bafflingly inconsistent from species to species. *D. melanogaster* has eight chromosomes (four pairs, although Morgan for quite a while thought it was five), while a goldfish has 104. Dogs have 78 and so do chickens. Horses have 64. Human beings have 46, although nobody was sure of that until 1956, when Swedish botanist Albert Levan (1905–98) and American geneticist Joe Hin Tijo (d. 2001) announced the correct number.

For almost four decades before that, most researchers thought humans carried 48—24 pairs—based on a 1918 announcement by anatomist Herbert M. Evans (1882–1971). In 1921, zoologist Theophilus Shickel Painter (1889–1969) also attempted to count the number of human chromosomes by examining a slice of human testicle under a microscope. He counted the same number as had Evans.

Evans, of the University of California, Berkeley, and Painter, of the University of Texas, were not bad scientists. Evans was a highly successful and well-regarded researcher and educator. Painter (discussed in chapter 4) made important discoveries in his research with *Drosophila* cells. In their shared miscalculation, they simply made a mistake. People err in biological research, as in every other discipline. Sometimes it takes many years to correct an error.

The group learned to map gene positions—something they could not even begin to see through their microscope lenses—with increasing precision. They spread the word through Morgan's 1913 book *Sex and Heredity* and in their jointly written 1915 book The *Mechanism of Mendelian Heredity*. These laid the foundation for succeeding generations of genetic research.

Bragg, Bragg, and the Birth of Crystallography

Herbert Evans's mistake (as discussed in the sidebar "Genetic Numbers Game" on page 30) resulted from the difficulty of analyzing something as small as chromosomes, tucked as they are within the nucleus of a *eukaryotic* cell. Biologists of his generation lacked a tool for seeing such structures clearly. Their successors would gain the ability to investigate structures far smaller than the chromosome—the crystalline molecular structures within which the chromosome carries the coding for genetic heredity. In the second decade of the century, two innovative physicists were developing a technique that would later enable photographs of such tiny bits of living matter.

No single researcher or group of researchers can investigate a very broad range of phenomena in detail, so scientists have, over decades and centuries, segregated their lines of inquiry into hundreds, if not thousands, of specialties. As they probed a scientific category more deeply, many researchers inevitably narrowed their focus. The best specialists, however, are those open to ideas that cross the boundaries between specialized areas of inquiry—even seemingly basic lines such as those drawn between physics and chemistry and biology. Living matter is, after all, matter. Cells are made of chemicals also found in inanimate solids, liquids, and gases. Living matter obeys physical and chemical laws that apply to inanimate matter. A 1912 breakthrough by William Henry Bragg and his son William Lawrence Bragg (who went by his middle name) has meant so much to later generations of biologists because it allowed them to see and better understand the microscopic structure of crystals. Crystals are an important component of life on the molecular level.

William Bragg and Lawrence Bragg were well prepared for crossing the boundaries between intellectual fields. Both set out to become mathematicians. Both switched to physics, a discipline in which they shared the Nobel Prize in 1915.

The senior Bragg was born and educated in England but had spent much of his teaching and research career in Australia, where he won a professorship in 1885. His restless mind liked to jump from problem to problem, field to field. He made the transition from mathematics to physics largely based on his capacity for self-study. In his early forties, he began experimenting with ionizing radiation, which is high-energy radiation that causes the formation of ions as it passes through matter. (An ion is an atom with a negative or positive charge as the result of having lost

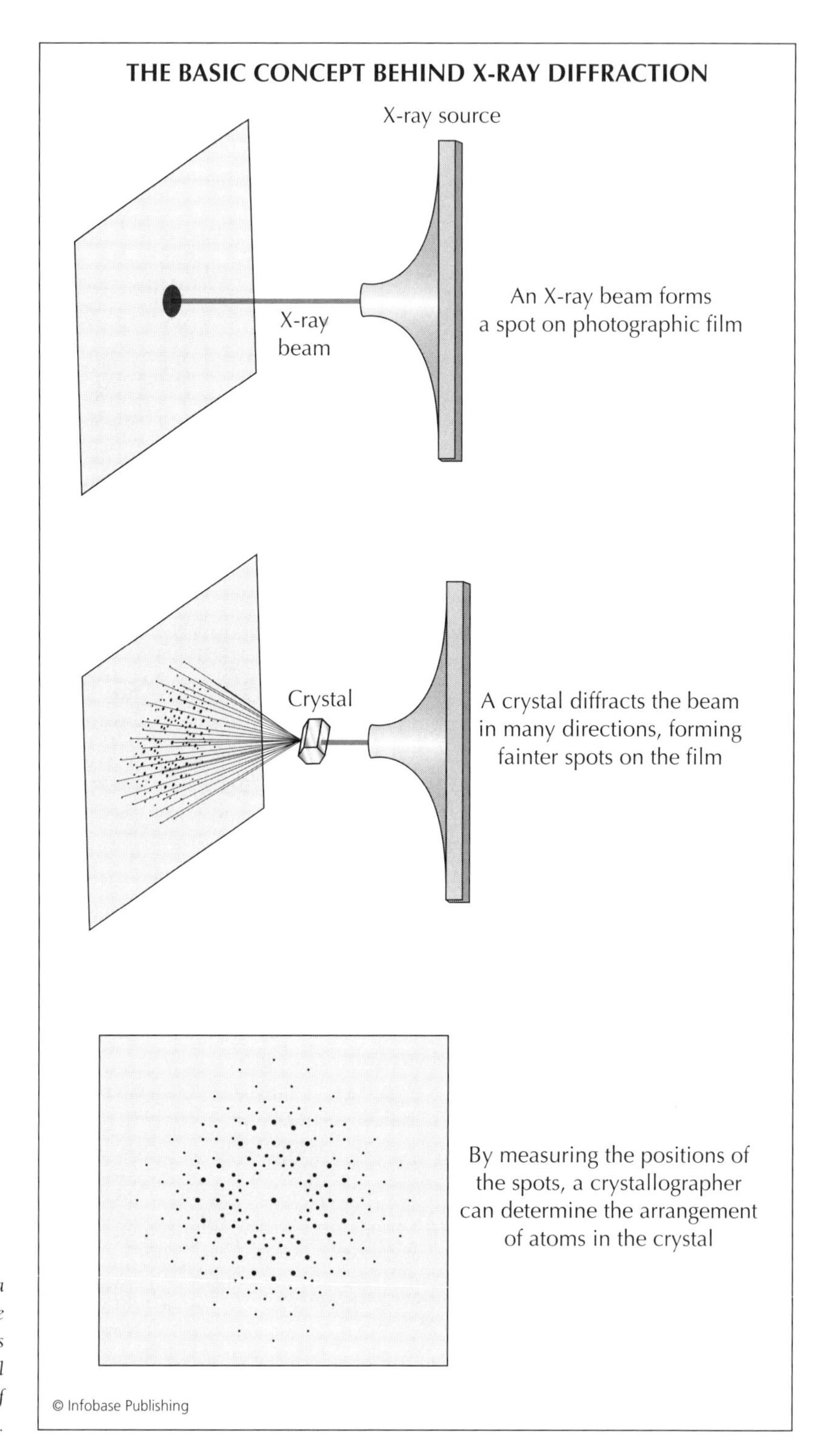

Bragg and Bragg devised a method to explore the structure of crystals using X-rays. This would prove an important tool in probing the molecules of living things.

Chaim Weizmann: Scientist and Statesman

Biochemist Chaim Weizmann, like the Braggs, used his scientific expertise to aid in Britain's war effort. Also like the Braggs, he would not be confined by the boundaries of his scientific discipline. Weizmann, however, is remembered as much for his work outside of science as for the innovative way he harnessed a biological by-product to aid the weapons industry.

The son of a lumber merchant in Motol, Russia, Weizmann from his youth showed both a gift for science and dedication to the dream of a Jewish homeland. Because of limits on the number of Jews allowed into Russia's universities, Weizmann studied in Germany and Switzerland, earning his Ph.D. in 1900. While a lecturer at Geneva University, his organic chemistry experiments led to patents for several dyes and scents. In 1904, Weizmann accepted a post at the University of Manchester and moved with his wife, Vera, a physician, to England.

In World War I, his research in biochemistry proved exactly what Britain needed. Weizmann had been seeking a biochemical solution to a growing rubber shortage. The popularity of bicycles and motorcars had created a great demand for pneumatic tires. The rubber tree industry had struggled to fill the need. To develop a polymer substitute—a synthetic rubber—on a practical industrial scale, Weizmann needed a great deal of dioctyl phthalate, a liquid that can be mixed with a chemical resin such as polyvinyl chloride to give the resulting material flexibility.

Weizmann determined that dioctyl phthalate can be derived from butyl alcohol, an organic compound given off by some microorganisms during fermentation. After many trials, he found that the bacterium *Clostridium acetobutylicum,* when fed any of a wide range of inexpensive starch sources, gave off a significant amount of butyl alcohol.

Weizmann's discovery aided Britain in the war because besides synthetic rubber, another

(continues)

or gained one or more electrons. "Ion" can also mean a group of such charged electrons.) This is the kind of radiation used in modern radiation treatment of cancer. X-rays also are ionized radiation.

William Bragg's early work on this topic brought him such favorable attention that he won a position back in England, at the University of Leeds. Sailing from Australia, he traveled with his eldest son, Lawrence, a university student who had been studying math. Accepted to Cambridge, Lawrence also changed his focus to physics.

Early in 1912, Max von Laue (1879–1960) of Germany discovered that X-rays could be diffracted by crystals. That is, if a ray was aimed at the crystal, the ray's direction and intensity changed. This caught the interest of both Braggs. The father thought the phenomenon could be used to learn more about the nature of X-rays. The son, by then a graduate student, was interested in what the diffracted rays could tell physicists about the structure of crystals.

Using special equipment designed by William, the father-son team directed X-rays at common salt (sodium chloride), a simple inorganic crystal. Measuring the diffracted beams and interpreting their patterns

(continued)

important industrial substance, acetone, could be derived from butyl alcohol. Also called dimethyl ketone, acetone is a solvent crucial to the manufacture of cordite, a smokeless explosive. Appointed director of the British Admiralty Laboratories in 1916, Weizmann developed a multistage process by which a great deal of acetone, and thus cordite, could be made using *C. acetobutylicum*.

The Admiralty took over a London distillery and set Weizmann to work developing his fermentation process on a large scale. The process faltered, however, because the biochemist needed a reliable source of food starch that he could feed to the bacteria. Britain, under blockade by the Germans, had run low on wheat and other grains. For a while, Weizmann tried distilling acetone from horse chestnuts. Eventually, Britain moved the Weizmann process to distilleries in Canada and India. In 1917, the United States set up a plant to make acetone with the Weizmann process, using midwestern corn as the carbohydrate source.

Weizmann's biochemical process won him recognition from Parliament and gave him access to the highest echelons of British government. Still a Zionist, he seized the opportunity to lobby for the 1917 Balfour Declaration, expressing the empire's support for "the establishment in Palestine of a national home for the Jewish people."

In 1934, Weizmann became founding director of the Daniel Seiff Research Institute (now Israel's Weizmann Institute). As a British subject in Palestine, he worked toward the creation of Israel. In talks with President Harry Truman, he secured U.S. recognition and a $100 million loan for the newly declared state in 1948. The next year, the scientist was elected Israel's first president.

was an incredibly difficult, labor-intensive series of calculations, a process in which Lawrence took the lead. (Such calculations did not become easier until computerization arrived much later in the century.) He was able to work out a surprising fact about the compound. Its molecules were not paired atoms (one sodium to one chloride) bonded by ionization, as expected. Instead, the compound consisted of a geometrically rigid lattice—a structure of flat surfaces and angles—built of regularly spaced sodium and chloride ions.

This was the birth of a new science, X-ray crystallography. It won the Braggs their Nobel Prize and paved the way for a generation of specialists who would use the technique to analyze a range of crystalline substances. When biologists finally figured out the structure of the DNA molecule itself, they would include biologists trained in physics and relying heavily on crystallography.

Because of World War I, the Braggs turned their attention to more immediate problems of practical physics. Britain mobilized in 1914, and both father and son served His Majesty's military, concentrating on submarine detection.

Putting Gene Theory to Work

North American corn became a convenient raw material for making World War I cordite (as discussed in the sidebar "Chaim Weizmann: Scientist and Statesman" on page 33) because the crop had become abundant in the United States. Beginning in the 1870s, the U.S. Department of Agriculture (USDA) encouraged corn growing to ease what was perceived as a surplus of wheat. With USDA-funded biologists devoted to improving the corn crop, the government effort succeeded, and corn, by the early 20th century, had outstripped wheat and other field crops in volume.

The corn of the time was already the result of many centuries of selective breeding. Prehistoric growers in Mexico and Central America had learned that seeds from the best plant produced the best crop. Agriculturists of the early 20th century clearly understood plant husbandry, so they saw little novelty in the revelation that Mendel had altered pea plants through crossing varieties. Yet the idea of statistical rules by which the results of hybridization could be reliably predicted piqued farmers' interest. Such rules promised a rapid improvement in seed stock, meaning higher crop yields and more money.

When British geneticist William Bateson came to New York in the late summer of 1902, to speak to the International Conference on Plant Breeding and Hybridization, he had been greeted by commercial breeders as well as biologists such as Walter Sutton. On the whole, the breeders tended to be the more enthusiastic about his message. These businesspeople focused on the practical application of Bateson's message. So did another significant part of Bateson's audience, agricultural biologists. The latter were both experimental scientists and practical breeders.

Employed by the USDA and by state colleges, botanists had already made great strides toward establishing plant breeding as a science, even though much of the discipline remained in the realm of art. The best-known plant breeder of the early 20th century was Luther Burbank, developer of the Burbank potato, the Satsuma plum, the Shasta daisy, and hundreds of other commercially viable species variants. Although he found inspiration in the writings of Charles Darwin, Burbank was no scientist. He did not keep detailed notes and did not follow established scientific methods. His prolific results, however, were so impressive that better-educated botanists and geneticists such as Holland's Hugo de Vries (one of the codiscoverers of Mendel's work) traveled to Santa Rosa, California, to try to understand how Burbank did what he did. In that effort, de Vries failed. So did leading geneticist George Harrison Shull (1874–1954), who spent fruitless months over a period of years following the idiosyncratic Burbank through his Santa Rosa gardens, fields and greenhouses.

Although he failed to capture Burbank's magic, Shull emerged in the second decade of the 20th century as a revolutionary—and thoroughly scientific—crop breeder in his own right. Shull, the son of a farmer, built on the work of Mendel, Bateson, and de Vries as he applied genetic theory to American Indian corn, often referred to in technical contexts by the more precise name, maize. At the Carnegie Station for Experimental Evolution, Cold Spring Harbor, New York, Shull isolated genetic traits in commercially grown corn. He focused, for example, on the number of rows of kernels on an ear, crossing varieties over and over and charting the results. Shull joined the faculty of Princeton University, where he continued his corn hybrid experiments through the second decade of the 20th century. In 1915, he founded the journal *Genetics*. In its early issues, the publication featured papers by researchers such as Calvin Bridges of Columbia University, one of Thomas Hunt Morgan's "Fly Boys."

Shull's work intersected with similar research that Edward Murray East (1879–1938), an agricultural chemist turned geneticist, was conducting. When the two scientists realized what they had in common, they collaborated. East had begun his career at the University of Illinois, where he had analyzed the protein and fat content of corn being grown as animal feed. This led him to experiments in which, like Shull, he isolated "pure" or homozygous strains of self-pollinated corn and then genetically crossed the strains so that he could chart the resulting traits. (Each corn plant possesses both the male *stamen* and female *pistil*. The stamen flower is the corn tassel. The pistil, which receives the fertilizing pollen from the stamen, is in the spike that matures into the plant's kernel-bearing ear.) East continued his work at the Connecticut Experimental Station and then at Harvard University, where in 1914 he welcomed a gifted young Kansan, Donald Forsha Jones (1890–1963), as a graduate student.

Jones had gone from Kansas State College of Agriculture and Applied Science (now Kansas State University), where he earned his bachelor of science degree in 1911, to work for the USDA at the Arizona Agricultural Experiment Station in Tucson. He then successfully applied to Harvard's graduate program. At Harvard, Jones began working with East, building on the teacher's work and that of Shull. In 1917, Jones successfully combined two hybrid corn varieties—each the result of crossing two of East's pure, self-pollinated strains. The resultant double cross was notably more vigorous and hardier than either its homozygous grandparents or its single-cross hybrid parents. This new hybrid produced more abundant, uniform kernels. Hybrid seeds, marketed commercially, would within a few years greatly increase crop yields—allowing farmers to grow far more corn on far fewer acres. Breeders and geneticists hailed Jones's hybrid (credited to Shull and East as well) as a practical triumph of Mendelian genetic theory. In 1919, East and Jones published *Inbreeding and Outbreeding*, a book that firmly established Mendelian principles as the basis of developing hybrid crops.

Safe as Milk

Farmers readily adopted hybrid corn when it became commercially available in the 1920s, but other food producers did not always welcome biological researchers' findings. The dairy industry proved especially resistant in 1918 when USDA bacteriologist Alice C. Evans (1881–1975) called for milk to be pasteurized before it was sold.

Pasteurization, a heat treatment to kill *pathogenic* microorganisms in beverages and some foods, dates back to the 1860s, when Louis Pasteur of France showed that the fermentation within wine and beer could be stopped by heating the beverages to 135°F (57°C) for a few minutes. By halting fermentation, the process preserved the drinks and prolonged their shelf life. Yet by the second decade of the 20th century, Pasteur's method had not been widely or uniformly applied to milk. Evans changed that when she traced a disease in cows to a disease in people and showed that it was spread through raw milk.

Alice Evans, like geneticist Nettie Stevens, began her career as a schoolteacher before becoming a biological researcher. After attending Susquehanna Collegiate Institute in Towanda, Pennsylvania, as a teenager, Evans taught in a rural elementary school for four years. Then she entered a nature course designed for schoolteachers at Cornell University. The exposure to higher education convinced her that instead of returning to her former profession, she should stay at Cornell to pursue biological science. With the help of a scholarship, she earned a bachelor's degree in bacteriology in 1909 and proceeded to the University of Wisconsin, where she was awarded a master of science degree, also in bacteriology, in 1910.

Her professors urged her to continue working toward a Ph.D., but Evans chose to forgo a doctorate and accept a position as a USDA bacteriologist, at first based in Madison, Wisconsin. The first woman to hold such an appointment, her status with the USDA's Bureau of Animal

Alice Evans became the first woman president of the Society of American Bacteriologists. (National Library of Medicine, National Institutes of Health)

Husbandry, Dairy Division, was elevated from "temporary" to "permanent" in 1913, upon her transfer to Washington, D.C. At George Washington University, Evans began working on the *bovine* disease known at the time as Bang's disease, after Danish veterinarian Bernhard L. F. Bang (1848–1932), who had described the disorder in 1897. The illness was also called Bang's abortion, because it often caused pregnant cows to lose their fetal calves.

Evans perceived a connection between Bang's disease and Malta fever, a debilitating and sometimes fatal illness in people that British military doctor Sir David Bruce (1855–1931) had in the 1880s traced to what he thought at first was a bacterium from the genus *Micrococcus*. The microbe turned out to belong to a previously unidentified genus that was later (in 1930) named after Bruce, as *Brucella*. Bruce and his wife, Mary, his research partner, traced the human sickness—also known as Mediterranean fever, among other names—to goats' milk. By 1915, biologists in the United States had traced a similar disease, called undulant fever, to cows' milk. Like Malta fever, undulant fever brought fever, painful joints, night sweats, and prolonged fatigue, but dairymen and physicians alike believed that when it was contracted through milk, poor sanitation was to blame. They argued that if the milk was handled properly, with improved sanitary practices, the disease could be eliminated from cow's milk altogether.

Alice Evans disagreed. Through her laboratory work in Washington and then at the University of Chicago, she showed that a species of *Brucella* bacterium that made people sick also sickened the cow. It was the source of Bang's disease. By conclusively linking the human and bovine diseases (and also linking them to the disease spread by goats' milk that the Bruces had identified), Evans showed that the bacterium was in the milk of infected, undiagnosed cattle. She argued that it spread to people regardless of how carefully the milk was handled during and after milking. Citing the danger of raw milk, Evans in 1917 read her paper "The Large Numbers of Bacteria Abortus Var. Lipolyticus Which May Be Found in Milk" to the American Society of Bacteriologists, proposing that the dairy industry begin routinely pasteurizing its products. Published in March of that year in the *Journal of Bacteriology*, the paper cited the relationship between Bang's disease and the illness in humans. Fellow biologists, physicians, and dairy farmers alike, however, were not convinced. Many dismissed Evans's work, including a 1918 follow-up paper titled "Further Studies on Bacterium Abortus and Related Bacteria," published in the *Journal of Infectious Diseases*, as inconclusive.

Theobald Smith (1859–1934), the dean of U.S. pathologists and powerfully influential, was particularly slow to accept Evans's results. The director of the department of animal pathology of the Rockefeller Institute in New York, and a renowned expert on the subject of bovine diseases, he resisted her findings. It had been a tenet of bacteriology orthodoxy since the turn of the century that diseases of cattle could not be spread to people through milk. Smith said that Bang's disease was not caused by the same bacterium as the one that spread Malta fever from goats to people and that Evans's call for pasteurization was unwarranted. Invited in the 1920s to chair a National Research Council Committee on Infectious Abortion, Smith declined, saying in a telegram that his own studies of the so-called Malta fever were not ready and that he would be in opposition to another committee member, meaning Evans.

Putting the "Amin" in Vitamins

In another branch of food science—nutrition—researchers in the century's second decade achieved significant progress in tracing and identifying those "accessory factors" that England's Frederick Hopkins had in 1906 found essential for life and growth. Casimir Funk (1884–1967), a Polish chemist working in England, was the first to put a specific name to such a substance.

Funk achieved this breakthrough in 1912. Examining the outer layer of brown (unpolished) rice, he discovered that this layer—called the bran—contains a water-soluble compound made of nitrogen bound to three hydrogen atoms (NH_3). He classified this compound among a class of organic, ammonia-derived substances called amines. This amine, Funk proposed, was what was lacking in a diet of white (or polished) rice. For this reason, people or animals who subsisted on a diet of white rice alone eventually fell ill with beriberi—a result of malnutrition. Symptoms include inflammation of the digestive system, nerves, and heart—sometimes resulting in heart failure.

Since the amine was necessary for life, Funk called it vitamine, for "vital amine." The word was spelled with a final "e."

The name caught on, not just for the amine that Funk had discovered—known today as vitamin B_1, or thiamine—but for all accessory factors, as they were discovered. The problem with the name that Funk had selected, however, was that as vitamines were later isolated and their chemical structures fully elucidated, many proved not to be amines. Rather than find a new term, biochemists dropped the final "e" to create the word *vitamin*.

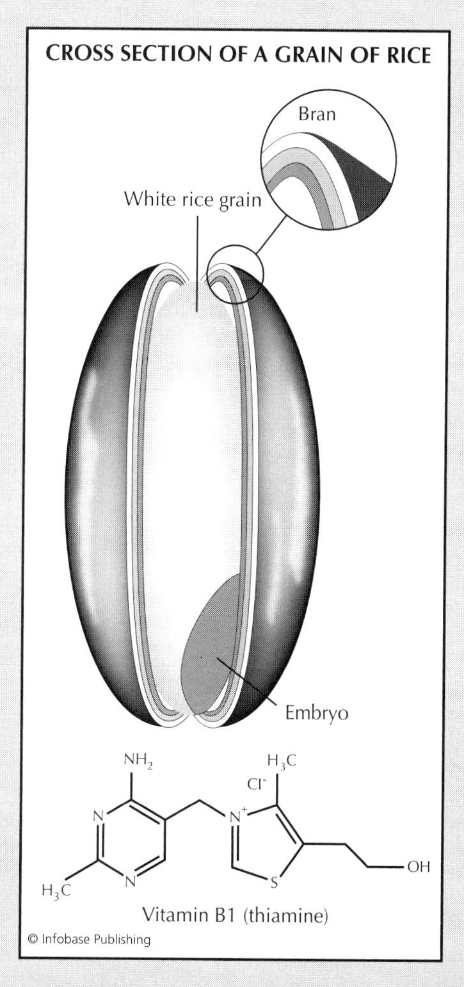

Casimir Funk found that whole-grain rice contains thiamine, lost when the bran layer is polished away.

After a 1925 speech to the American Society of Tropical Medicine, meeting in Washington, D.C., Evans opened the floor to discussion. As reported by biographer Virginia Law Burns, drawing from Evans's memoirs, many of the researchers and physicians in the audience that day spoke in support of Evans's call for pasteurization. Then the meeting's master of ceremonies, William H. Welch (1850–1934), stood up to conclude the discussion. The dean of the School of Hygiene and Public Health at Johns Hopkins Medical School, Welch stated flatly, "I cannot believe that cows' milk might be the source of human infection."

Evans stuck by her arguments. Slowly, as other bacteriologists confirmed her results, she won converts. Based on her work, scientists acknowledged four species of *Brucella* that can spread from animals to humans. They are *Brucella abortus*, which Evans found in cattle; *B. melitensis*, traced to goats and sheep; *B. suis* in pigs; and *B. canis* in dogs. In the 1920s, European dairy producers began responding to this evidence by routinely pasteurizing their product. Finally, in the 1930s, the United States made pasteurization of milk mandatory.

Evans suffered for her cause, and not just because other scientists at first rejected her results. In the course of her research, she accidentally infected herself with *B. melitensis* and contracted undulate fever, or brucellosis, as the human version of the disease came to be called. She endured years of fever and weakness. In 1922, she was hospitalized with the fever for 10 weeks. In 1929, a recurrence of brucellosis put Evans, by then the first woman president of the Society of American Bacteriologists (now the American Society for Microbiology), in the hospital again. For decades after her discovery won acceptance, she was respected as a world authority on *B. abortus*, brucellosis, and other diseases.

The Bacteria Eaters

In late 19th-century India, bacteriologist Ernest Hankin had noticed that Hindu worshippers who drank the water of the sacred Ganges River did not contract cholera. This struck Hankin as curious, since the polluted river certainly contained the cholera bacteria, but as he investigated, he found that the water also contained an antibacterial agent. It was something tiny enough to pass through a chemist's porcelain filter, a filter so fine as to strain out the bacteria themselves.

It was not until 1915, however, that another English bacteriologist, Frederick Twort (1887–1950), isolated the bacteria-fighting microbe and described it as a type of virus. (Dutch biologist Martinus W. Beijerinck [1851–1931] had first identified viruses in 1898). Limited by a war-reduced science budget, Twort did not follow up on his discovery.

Canadian microbiologist Félix d'Hérelle (1873–1949) had first observed the bacteria-killing phenomenon a few years earlier in Mexico, where he was trying to invent a way of using microbes to control crop-destroying locusts. He recognized it again in the summer of 1915, working at the

Pasteur Institute in Paris where he grew cultures of a bacterium that attacked the digestive systems of insects. In his cultures of this bacterium, odd clear spots, free of bacteria, would appear with no apparent cause.

HOW A BACTERIOPHAGE ATTACKS BACTERIUM

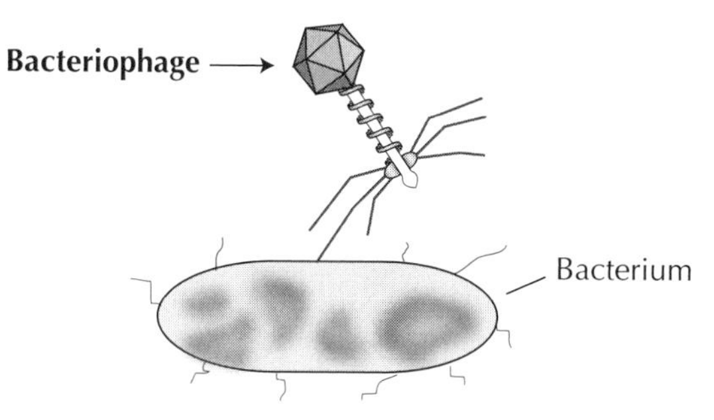

Bacteriophage lies dormant until a leg fiber makes contact with a host bacterium

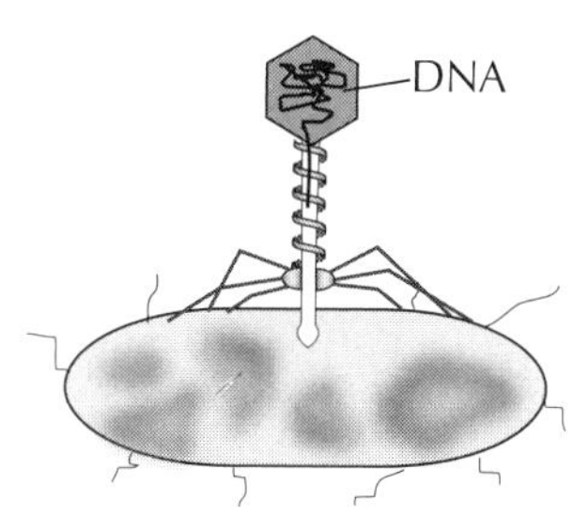

Bacteriophage attaches and penetrates the bacterium

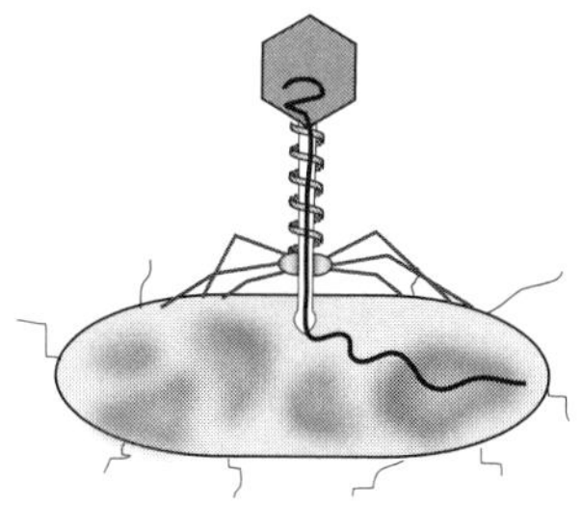

Bacteriophage injects DNA into the bacterium then produces masses of new viruses

Although Félix d'Hérelle envisioned the bacteriophage as consuming bacteria, it actually takes over a bacterium's reproductive mechanism.

Asked to investigate an outbreak of bloody dysentery in a French cavalry unit stationed on the city's outskirts, d'Hérelle took samples of hospitalized soldiers' liquid feces. Using porcelain filters like the one that Hankin had used in India, the microbiologist strained out all solids, down to and including the bacteria. Then he prepared samples in which he reintroduced the dysentery-causing bacterium. The samples quickly became cloudy with bacteria cultures, but then those familiar clear patches began to appear in d'Hérelle's petri dishes. Something—at first he called it "an invisible microbe"—was killing the bacteria.

That microbe, he discovered, was a virus. In 1916, the Canadian named it bacteriophage, which means "eats bacteria."

D'Hérelle saw in his discovery the potential for bacteriophage therapy against bacterial infections. He traveled to Indonesia, where his studies of bacteria-borne diseases in people and animals led him to a technique for isolating bacteriophages that attacked specific microbial colonies. Later, as a health officer for the League of Nations, based in Egypt, he achieved some success using bacteriophage therapy to treat contagious diseases that sometimes spread through the Middle East as large numbers of Muslims traveled on their pilgrimage to Mecca. D'Hérelle's work, promising relief from a wide range of ailments, caught the imagination of immunologists and physicians worldwide.

D'Hérelle brought the study of the bacteriophage to Yale University, where he taught the first classes in protobiology (as the field was then called). He continued to keep a home in Paris where, with his son, he set up a company to develop and market specific bacteriophages—soon nicknamed "phages"—for medical use. Soviet medical officials were especially receptive to the promise of phage therapy, and the government of the USSR invited d'Hérelle to help establish laboratories dedicated to the line of inquiry. In Tbilisi, Georgia, he cofounded and helped direct the Eliava Institute of Bacteriophage, Microbiology, and Virology, where numerous field studies confirmed the medical usefulness of phages.

Phage therapy in the West, meanwhile, stumbled. Many physicians tried using antibacterial phages through the 1920s to fight diseases, and many achieved limited successes. Pharmaceutical companies ventured into the manufacture of phage-based medicine, but these preparations proved less than reliable. Few pharmacists or physicians understood how narrowly specific phages attacked specific bacteria, a subject that d'Hérelle's research continued to probe. Worse, the drug companies did not understand how to prepare, preserve, or store the viruses. D'Hérelle once examined 20 different commercial preparations and found that not one of them contained live phages.

A 1931 study, commissioned by the American Medical Association, found that phage therapy had not proved effective except against bacteria-caused cysts and local *staphylococcus* infections. The study questioned whether phages were in fact live viruses or an inert substance, such as an enzyme. After that, the use of phage therapy dropped off in the West, especially after German pathologist Gerhard Domagk announced in 1932 that a group of chemicals called sulfonamides possessed "bacteriostatic" properties, that is, they inhibit bacteria growth. Sulfa drugs became a standard therapy against infection until the large-scale manufacture of antibiotics, starting with penicillin, in the 1940s.

By the end of the 20th century, many disease-causing bacteria, including some responsible for forms of gonorrhea and tuberculosis, had evolved into strains resistant to antibiotics. Some researchers began looking once again toward phage therapy as an alternative way to fight bacteria. Entrepreneurial bacteriologists founded companies such as Phage Therapeutics, Inc., of Washington, D.C. (in 1997) and Intralytics Inc. of Baltimore (1998) to develop new bacteriophage-based medicines and therapies.

Phages may not have borne out d'Hérelle's hopes for them, but they have played a crucial role in laboratory research. Because of their simple structure and genetic makeup, and also because they can be grown easily in the lab, they proved useful for studying life at the molecular level. Nobel Prize winner Max Delbrück (1906–81), a physicist who studied microbiology, referred to the phage, the simplest genetic system known, as the hydrogen atom of biology.

Carl Merril, chief of biochemical genetics lab at the National Institutes of Medical Health, summarized the importance of phages to researchers in a 2000 interview with *Smithsonian* magazine: "If you look at the early Nobel Prizes in molecular biology, half of the awards went to researchers using phages."

A Humbling Plague

Viruses are better known as disease agents than as disease fighters. It was a virus that during World War I caused one of the most deadly epidemics in human history.

On the morning of March 11, 1918, U.S. Army Private Albert Gitchell, a mess cook at Camp Funston, Kansas, reported to sick call. He had a sore throat and his limbs ached. The next day, 40 soldiers arrived at the army infirmary of nearby Fort Riley with the same complaints. A week later there were more than 500.

Most recovered quickly, but 46 of them died before the fast-moving illness, apparently a severe strain of influenza, appeared to have run its course at the fort. What the army doctors could not know was that this was only the beginning of a pandemic—that is, an epidemic that would sweep the world.

That same spring, the army's 89th Division shipped out of Kansas, headed for Europe. Soon after they arrived in France, the flu began spreading through the trenches of the Western Front. At first, most

Scientist of the Decade: Thomas Hunt Morgan (1866–1945)

When a Nobel Prize was awarded for the first time to a geneticist in 1933, the recipient was one whose work—especially that work done in the years between 1911 and 1920—had shaped the emerging field of study. Discoveries that came out of Thomas Hunt Morgan's laboratory at Columbia University, the Fly Room, did more to illuminate the role of chromosomes and the function of genes than any other before the molecular structure of DNA was finally understood in the 1950s.

Columbia's Fly Room was rightly famous for the work being done there, but it was also famous because of the colorful personality of the man his students called "The Boss."

He was the son of Charlton Hunt Morgan (1839–1912), who as a young U.S. diplomat in Italy fought on the side of revolutionary nationalist leader Giuseppe Garibaldi. Then Charlton Morgan returned home to Kentucky and joined the Confederate Cavalry regiment led by his elder brother, the legendary raider John Hunt Morgan (1825–64).

Thomas Hunt Morgan with Dutch biologist Hugo de Vries, one of the scientists who had rediscovered and confirmed Gregor Mendel's work at the turn of the 20th century. (Caltech Archives)

Charlton Morgan's son was no soldier, but he attacked scientific questions with uncompromising zeal. As a zoology student, Thomas Hunt Morgan had decided that there was no substitute for experimentation and proofs. Mere observation was inadequate; conjecture inadmissible. In his 1907 book *Experimental Zoology,* Morgan wrote: "The essence of the experimental method consists in requiring that every suggestion (or hypothesis) be put to the test of experiment before it is admitted to a scientific status. . . . The investigator must . . . cultivate also a skeptical state of mind toward all hypotheses—especially his own—and be ready to abandon them the moment the evidence points the other way."

Yet Morgan was anything but rigid in bearing or habits. At a glance, the tall, bearded biologist fit the stereotype of an absent-minded professor. He was known to use a string to hold up his trousers. He once asked a colleague to paste a piece of white paper over a hole in his shirt before he gave a speech. During a stay with the Morgan family in New York, geneticist William Bateson wrote to his wife about his host's tattered coat and shoes. Morgan once sailed for Europe with luggage that consisted of a comb, razor, bar of soap, and an extra pair of socks.

His informality carried over to his work. Students, including undergraduates, were free to disagree or even argue with their leader, although he usually prevailed. Tove Mohr, a biologist and the wife of Morgan's first European assistant—postdoctoral student Otto Mohr of Norway—was struck by the contrast between authoritarian European professors and the easy-going geneticist. His research crew worked in concert, with each new result discussed freely, regardless of whether it was Morgan's or that of undergraduate assistant Alfred Sturtevant. Sturtevant was actually employed in the lab as a bottle washer, but after he spotted a crucial mutation—a white-eyed male—through the thick glass of one of the milk bottles used to house the subjects, Morgan immediately made the young man a researcher.

Morgan's collegial style encouraged independent research by his staff, many of whom—including the Nobel Prize–winning Hermann Muller—went on to distinguished research careers of their own.

As a researcher, Morgan was at once meticulous (with data) and unspeakably sloppy (with everything else). While the other researchers on his team threw discarded fruit flies into a jar of oil that they called "the morgue," Morgan simply smashed his flies against the white porcelain plate he used for counting them. He would leave the accumulating mess until someone else—often the wife of one of his students—felt compelled to wash the plate. His mail, usually unopened, lay in a massive pile that cluttered his lab table until somebody threw it away.

Although a distant cousin of industrialist J. Pierpont Morgan (1857–1913), the professor had grown up in genteel poverty, a circumstance that may have underlaid his eccentricities about money. He hated to spend his university's funds. At Columbia, he only reluctantly allowed his researchers to replace their handheld magnifiers with simple microscopes. Among the reasons he loved fruit flies as research subjects is that he could feed an entire laboratory of them for 10 cents a day. Later, when he established a new biology division at the California Institute of Technology, Morgan had only one telephone installed on each floor of the building for all the faculty and staff to share.

On the other hand, Morgan was generous with experimental results and his lab subjects—often shipping fruit flies to other universities and laboratories without asking for compensation. He was also gracious in sharing his private money. Although he never took credit, it was widely known that the mysterious anonymous fellowships that sometimes helped young Columbia graduate students finish their degrees were actually gifts from The Boss.

At Woods Hole Marine Laboratory in Massachusetts, where he spent many summers of research, Morgan socialized with peers and students alike, swimming and joining in games. He enjoyed the company of children; he and wife Lilian had four of their own. Tove Mohr observed that when Morgan was at play with children, he *was* a child.

The congenial personality was paired with a restless intellect. Throughout his career—including the Fly Room years—Morgan ran multiple outside experiments. According to biographers Ian Shine and Sylvia Wrobel, the scientist joked that his experiments fell into three categories: ". . . fool experiments, damn fool experiments and those that are still worse."

Morgan thought of himself not as a geneticist but as an embryologist. Many of his experiments focused on the question of tissue differentiation in embryos. From early in his career, he had been fascinated with one basic question: If a zygote divides into two identical cells, and those cells divide into four identical cells, then eight, sixteen and so on—all just alike (all what later generations of embryologists would term *embryonic stem cells*)—then what causes these stem cells to eventually and inevitably differentiate into bone cells, blood cells, nerve cells, and so on? It was a profound question, one that would not be answered during Morgan's lifetime.

victims recovered quickly. Doctors called it "the three-day flu." (The men called it "the Spanish flu," although there was no evidence it had come from Spain.)

The illness seemed just another hardship of war until later in the summer, when it evolved into something much more serious. The death rate grew alarmingly, to one-third of those stricken. Symptoms broke out on both sides of the front lines and then beyond the troops. Before the year was out, 400,000 German civilians would be dead of the disease. Back in the United States, the flu took at least 450,000 lives in 1918.

Everything about this illness alarmed and frustrated the doctors and immunologists who tried to treat it, but one aspect in particular struck them as most frightening. Unlike other influenzas, unlike illnesses in general, it targeted people in the prime of their lives—not the chronically ill, not the elderly, not babies. Most of those who got it, and by far most who died of it, were between 20 and 40 years of age and, until they caught the flu, healthy.

Hitting seaport cities first, the virus penetrated Britain. Then it was in Spain (where it was called "the French flu"), then Italy, then around the Mediterranean, and eastward through Asia.

More than 25 million people died worldwide, an estimated 12,550,000 of those in India alone. Some estimates put the death toll as high as 35 million. The flu killed nearly three times the estimated 9 million who died in the war. The United States's death toll from influenza reached 550,000. Subsequent outbreaks of the disease killed hundreds more through the 1920s, but each return of the disease was a little less virulent than its predecessor. Succeeding generations of immunologists looked to the 1918 crisis as a reason to learn all they could about viral diseases.

Further Reading

Allen, Garland E. *Thomas Hunt Morgan: The Man and His Science.* Princeton, N.J.: Princeton University Press, 1978. Biography of influential, eccentric, Nobel Prize winner.

Burns, Virginia Law. *Gentle Hunter: A Biography of Alice C. Evans, Bacteriologist.* Bath, Mich.: Enterprise Press, 1993. Biography of bacteriologist who linked raw milk to disease.

Chemical Achievers, The Chemical Heritage Foundation. "William Henry Bragg and William Lawrence Bragg." Available online. URL: http://www.chemheritage.org/EducationalServices/chemach/ppb/whlb.html. Accessed August 16, 2004. Biography of father-son team of physicists responsible for X-ray crystallography.

Collier, Richard. *The Plague of the Spanish Lady: The Influenza Pandemic of 1918–1919.* New York: Athenaeum, 1974. Story of devastating pandemic during World War I.

Cravens, Hamilton. *The Triumph of Evolution: The Heredity-Environment Controversy, 1900–1941.* Baltimore: Johns Hopkins University Press, 1988. Author discusses and documents debate over nature v. nurture in the early 20th century.

East, Edward M., and Donald F. Jones. *Inbreeding and Outbreeding.* Philadelphia: Lippincott, 1919. Landmark book on crop genetics.

Evans, Alice C. "Further Studies on Bacterium Abortus and Related Bacteria. II. A Comparison of Bacterium Abortus with Bacterium Bronchisepticus and with the Organism Which Causes Malta Fever." *Journal of Infectious Diseases* 22 (1918): 580–593. Bacteriologist offers more evidence in her case for pasteurizing milk.

———. "The Large Numbers of Bacteria Abortus Var. Lipolyticus Which May Be Found in Milk." *Journal of Bacteriology* 2, no. 2. (March 1917): 185–186. Bacteriologist describes link between bacterial disease agent and raw milk.

Harrow, Benjamin. *Casimir Funk: Pioneer in Vitamins and Hormones.* New York: Dodd, Mead, 1955. Biography of biochemist who discovered thiamin.

Koerner, Brendan I. "Phages: Bacteria-Killing Viruses May Fight for Humankind Again." *Sightings.* Available online. URL: http://www.rense.com/health/phages.htm. Accessed August 16, 2004. Article looks at return of phage therapy in age of antibiotic-resistant microbes.

Kruif, Paul Henry de. *Microbe Hunters.* New York: Harcourt, Brace, 1926. History of bacteriology, early virology, and immunology.

Lewis, Edward B. "About A. H. Sturtevant." National Academy Press. Available online. URL: http://www.nap.edu/readingroom/books/biomems/asturtevant.pdf. Accessed August 16, 2004. Background on geneticist who started as one of T. H. Morgan's laboratory assistants.

Morgan, Thomas Hunt. *Experimental Zoölogy.* New York: Macmillan, 1907. Morgan's early work lays out principles of his uncompromising approach to research.

———, Calvin Bridges, Alfred H. Sturtevant, and Hermann Joseph Muller. *The Mechanism of Mendelian Heredity.* New York: Johnson Reprint Corp., 1972. Morgan and his team of researchers lay out their findings regarding genetic heredity patterns in fruit flies.

Rose, Norman. *Chaim Weizmann: A Biography.* New York: Penguin, 1986. Biography of innovative biochemist who was also a Zionist diplomat and politician.

Shine, Ian, and Sylvia Wrobel. *Thomas Hunt Morgan: Pioneer of Genetics.* Lexington, Ken.: University Press of Kentucky, 1976. Biography of Nobel Prize–winning geneticist.

Smith, C. Wayne. *Crop Production: Evolution, History, and Technology.* Hoboken, N.J.: Wiley, 1995. History examines application of genetic theory to 20th-century agriculture.

Snustadt, Peter D., and Michael J. Simmons. *Principles of Genetics.* Hoboken, N.J.: Wiley, 2002. Text is a helpful primer in how chromosomes and genes function.

Sturtevant, Alfred H. "Thomas Hunt Morgan." *National Academy of Sciences Biographical Memoir* 33 (1959): 283–325. Geneticist Sturtevant recalls his scientific mentor.

Thompson, D'Arcy Wentworth. *On Growth and Form.* New York: Macmillan, 1948. Veteran naturalist looks at embryology and cell differentiation as it was understood in Morgan's time.

Wakefield, Julie. "The Return of the Phage." *Smithsonian* magazine, October 2000. Available online. URL: http://www.smithsonianmag.com/issues/2000/october/phenom_oct00.php. Accessed October 10, 2006. Article looks at return of phage therapy in age of antibiotic-resistant microbes.

1921–1930: Biology in the Public Arena

The Push and Pull of "Normalcy"

After World War I, many people in the United States and Europe felt that civilization had been to the brink of destruction and pulled back just in time. The 1920s was a decade of rebuilding and reveling—a time when the surging U.S. economy, in particular, fueled an air of invincibility. It was not just business that was stimulated; the decade also saw manic activity and great achievement in arts, entertainment, sports, and not least in scientific research.

Not everyone welcomed change. Warren G. Harding won the U.S. presidency in 1920 with his postwar call for a "return to normalcy." Traditionalists decried innovations—women's suffrage, jazz music, and the theory of evolution—as immoral and degenerate. Many put the widely taught theory of evolution first among these modern abominations. Some ranked it as evil blasphemy—an affront to God.

The idea that species gave rise to new species through evolution was so widely accepted among academics that it had become a foundation of the life sciences. Charles Darwin's theory was standard textbook fare. In the 1920s, however, came a concerted effort to ban the teaching of evolution in U.S. schools. When pro-evolutionists in Tennessee deliberately challenged such a ban, they brought about the famous legal case remembered as the Scopes Monkey Trial.

Meanwhile, at the university level, geneticists and microbiologists—for whom the evolutionary process was a given—accelerated their quest to find out just how the chemistry of life passes information from an organism to its offspring. Some of the work within this decade, such as Hermann J. Muller's observations on the structure of chromosomes, predicted discoveries to come—as if Muller and others could see into the future.

Just as 1920s sports produced such phenomena as baseball slugger Babe Ruth and heavyweight boxing champion Jack Dempsey, just as 1920s literature produced Ernest Hemingway and F. Scott Fitzgerald, so did megastars emerge in 1920s research. Among them was dashing dinosaur hunter Roy Chapman Andrews (1884–1960), who popularized the quest to understand prehistoric life. Though nominally a zoologist, Andrews was more explorer than scientist, yet the paleontologists traveling with him—especially the self-effacing Walter Granger (1872–1941)—greatly expanded what was known about prehistoric mammals and dinosaurs.

This also was the decade that Linus Pauling (1901–94), a chemist and physicist, arrived as a researcher. At the California Institute of Technology from 1922, young Pauling began sorting out the physical laws that determine how atoms are arranged inside molecules. His research provided groundwork for those scientists, including Pauling himself, who would race in future decades to figure out the structure of the DNA molecule.

In the case of another scientific star, Great Britain's Alexander Fleming (1881–1955), his breakthrough discovery—penicillin—came in the 1920s but would bear fruit only later. Its bacteria-fighting properties would be virtually ignored until other researchers turned it into a medical revolution.

Shadows hovered over the economic and cultural euphoria of the 1920s. U.S. farmers were having a rough time, an early sign of the Great Depression to come. Postwar economic uncertainty bred social discontent in Germany, leading to extremism in politics.

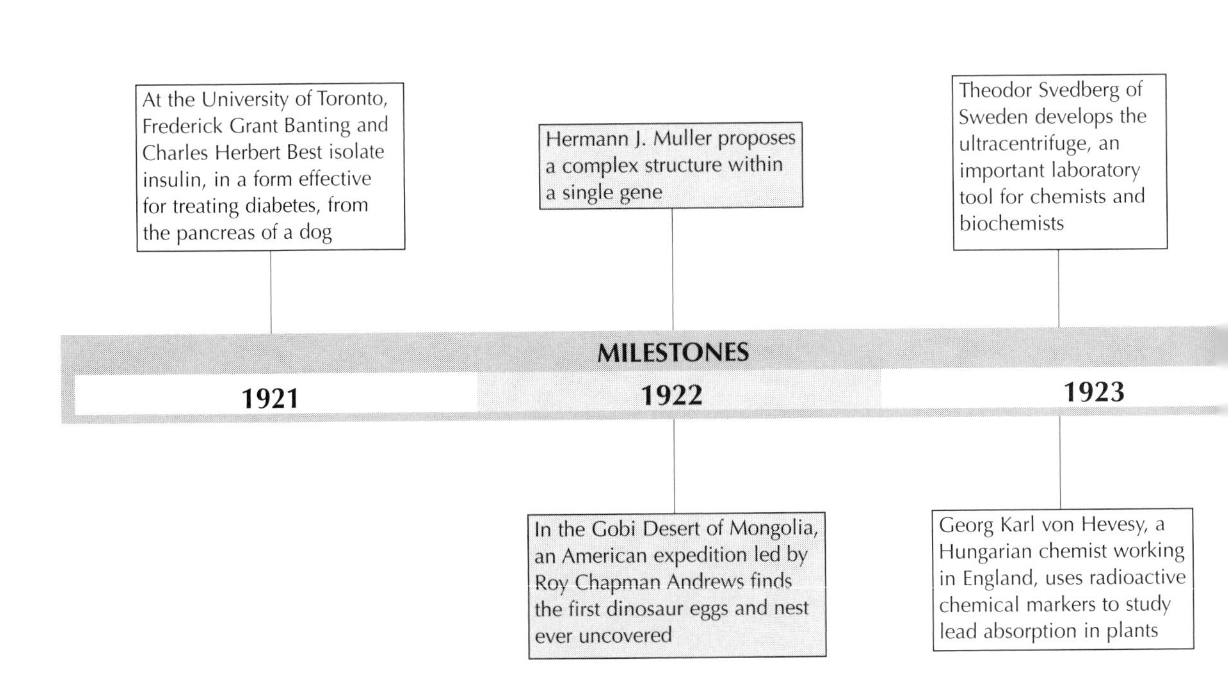

German political extremists were among those who seized onto a misconceived social theory—unfortunately linked to Darwinism and genetic science—and later put it to horrible use. This theory, eugenics, argued that in human beings, genetic inferiority was prevalent among certain social classes and ethnic groups. Most dangerous, it argued for social-biological engineering to root out undesirable traits. The idea had advocates in other countries—notably the United States, where eugenics influenced public policies such as restrictions on immigration by certain ethnic groups. Virginia passed a law that allowed health officials to forcibly sterilize people that had been judged to be genetically unfit. Supported by geneticists and physicians, upheld by the U.S. Supreme Court, this legislation paved the way for more involuntary sterilization laws in other states.

Evolutionary Theory Goes to Court

The idea of an evolving natural world did not originate in the 19th century with Charles Darwin. Thinkers at least as far back as Aristotle saw in rock formations and fossils the evidence of ancient times in which

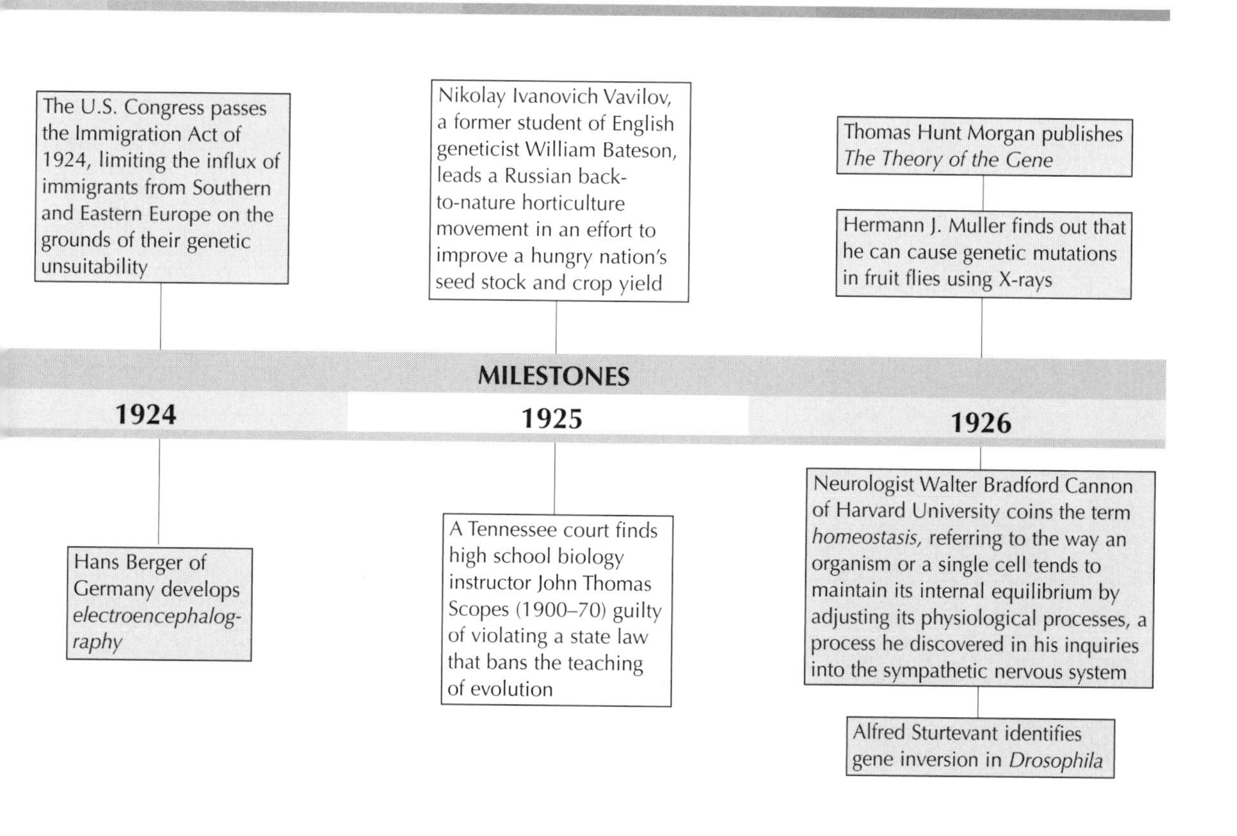

the landscape and the animals that roamed it were vastly different from those that share the Earth with human beings. Renaissance philosophers such as Germany's Georg Bauer (1494–1555) inquired into archaic life in books such as his *On the Nature of Fossils.* In the Renaissance, however, one was well advised not to follow this line of thought too far. Scholars who developed theories about lost (that is, extinct) species and a much older Earth than suggested by scripture risked the charge of heresy. Church authorities tied Italian philosopher and priest Lucilio Vanini (1584–1619) to a stake and set him afire after he suggested that human beings might be descended from apes.

Darwin's mid-19th-century theory of evolution also sparked furious (if less lethal) opposition from those who saw in his science-based thinking a challenge to established religious ideas. In America, such opposition took political form in the 20th century after a group of evangelical church leaders published 10 pamphlets called "The Fundamentals" in 1910. The pamphlets articulated conservative reaction against what the ministers saw as immoral excesses of modern life—among them, freethinking science. Asserting the literal truth of the Bible, "The Fundamentals" appealed especially to rural Christians, people who led their lives far from

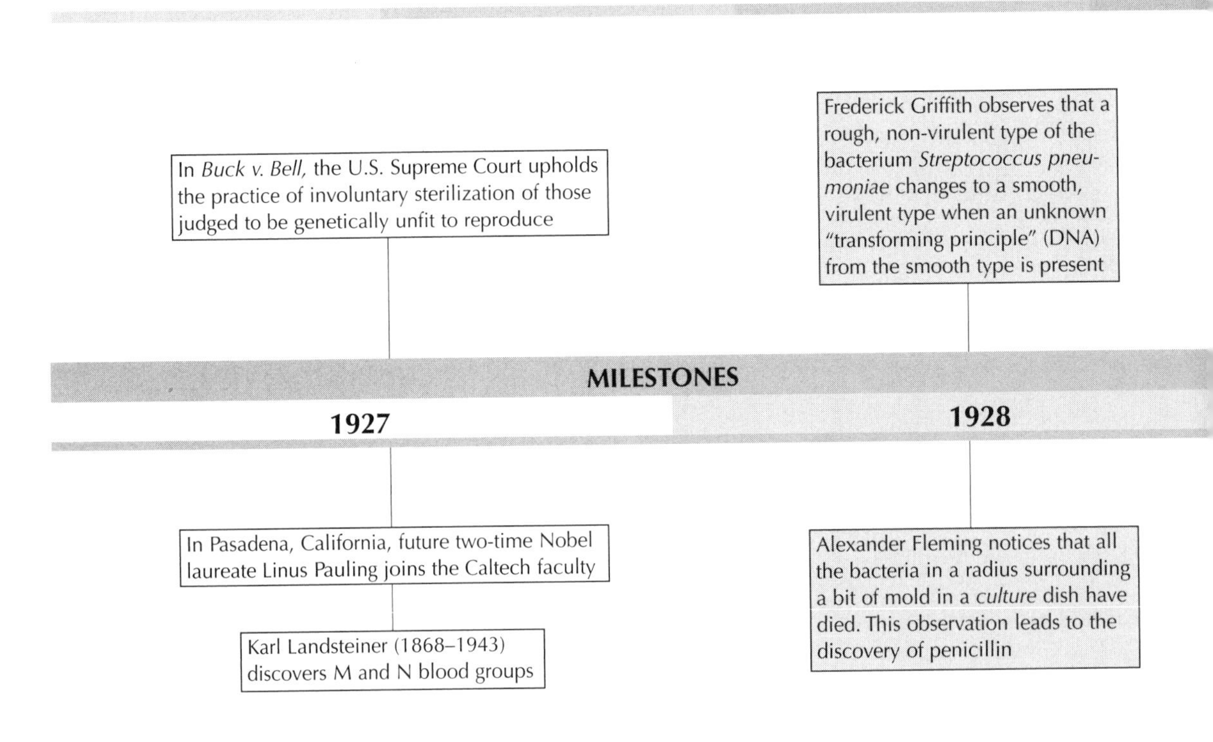

universities and intellectual trends. This was especially so after the war, when many people craved a return to old ways.

In that spirit, former U.S. Secretary of State William Jennings Bryan (1860–1925) mounted a state-by-state campaign to ban the teaching of evolution in public schools. Bryan, who had been a U.S. senator from Nebraska and a newspaper editor, was one of the best-known public figures of his time, three times nominated as the Democratic Party's presidential candidate. Despite having lost to William McKinley in 1896 and 1900 and to William Howard Taft in 1908, Bryan remained a hero to cultural conservatives, especially in what was then the solidly Democratic South.

By the mid-1920s, he and his fundamentalist allies had succeeded in getting antievolution legislation introduced in 15 states. On March 21, 1925, Tennessee's governor signed into law the Butler Act, which made it illegal "to teach any theory that denies the story of divine creation as taught by the Bible and to teach instead that man was descended from a lower order of animals."

The American Civil Liberties Union, in its role as defender of free speech, responded by offering free legal defense to anyone challenging

MILESTONES

1929

German chemist Hans Fischer figures out the structure of hemin, a crystalline complex iron compound found in blood

Phoebus Levene finds the sugar deoxyribose in nucleic acids that do not contain ribose; those nucleic acids are now known as deoxyribonucleic acids, or DNA

Polish microphysicist Manfred Joshua Sakel first uses electroshock to treat schizophrenia

1930

British statistician and geneticist Ronald Aylmer Fisher publishes *The Genetical Theory of Natural Selection*

Paleontology's Indiana Jones?

In his later work as a commercial geologist, scouting for potential petroleum deposits, John Scopes employed scientific expertise built on an understanding of the Earth's great age, its complex and evolving natural history. Geology may seem a discipline wholly separate from biology, yet—as in virtually every area of science—borders blur.

Geologists since England's William Smith (1769–1839) have used fossils—preserved remains of ancient organisms—to help them identify and date the Earth's strata. Conversely, in paleontology, biologists use the Earth's strata to help them identify and date archaic organisms. By the 1920s, paleontology, which had originated among amateur fossil hunters and comparative anatomists in the 19th century, was thoroughly established as a field with a record of eye-opening discoveries (famously, the dinosaurs). Because of the nature of field research—a hunt for fossil treasures, often carried out in remote locations—the discipline also carried an aura of dusty glamour. This glow shone especially bright from well-publicized American expeditions in 1921–22 and again in 1925 into the Gobi Desert of central Asia.

Organized by the American Museum of Natural History (AMNH) in New York, the expeditions made several important finds. Most significant, a paleontology field assistant named George Olson (d. 1939) found a nest of oblong eggs about six inches (15 cm) long and arranged in a circular cluster. These proved to be dinosaur eggs, the first scientifically certified evidence that dinosaurs were egg-layers. The party found additional such dinosaur nests, which they dated to the Cretaceous period and identified (errone-

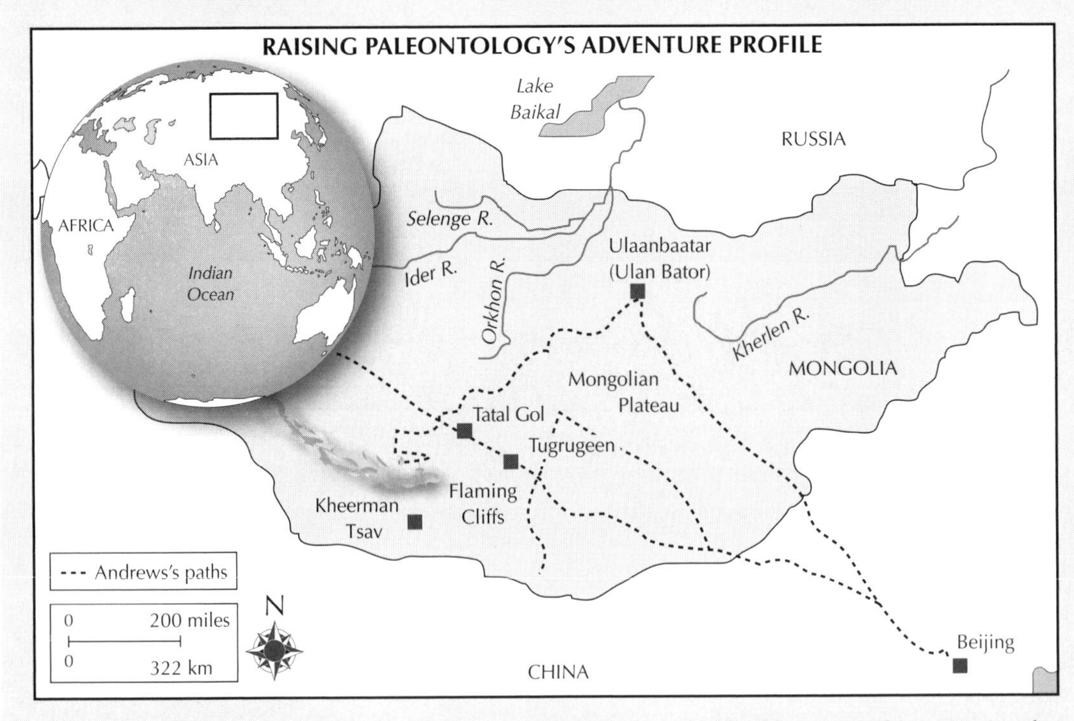

For the American Museum of Natural History, Roy Chapman Andrews led a series of fossil-hunting expeditions into Mongolia.

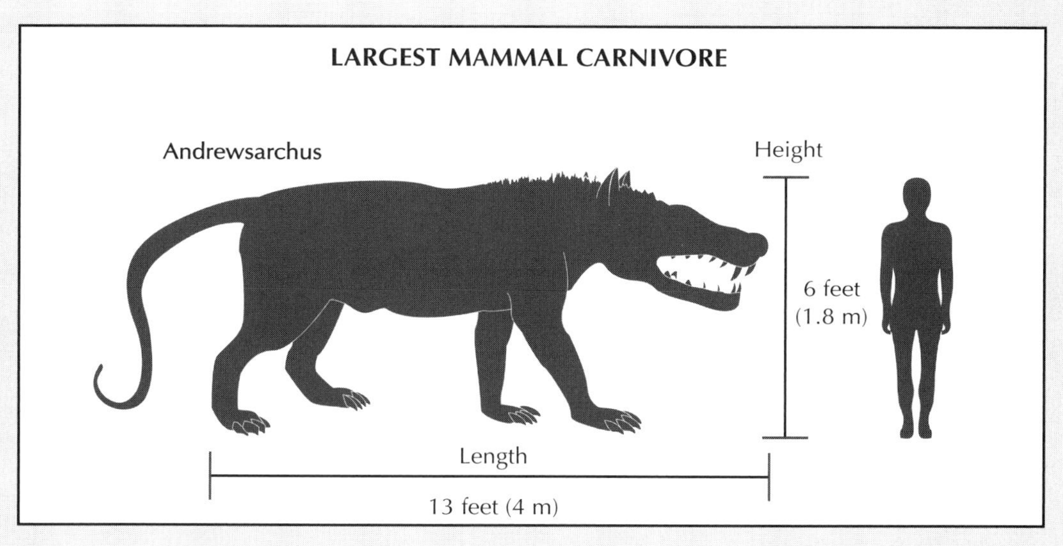

Andrewsarchus mongoliensis, *despite its lupine appearance, was not a close relative of modern carnivores.*

ously, it turned out) as belonging to Protoceratops (*Protoceratops andrewsi*), an ancestor of the horn-faced dinosaurs such as Triceratops (*Triceratops horridus*). The searchers found a skeleton of a small bipedal dinosaur atop another such nest and assumed it to be preying on the eggs. They named the find *Oviraptor philoceratops,* which means "ceratops-loving egg robber." Later researchers discovered that the poor *O. philoceratops* was falsely convicted. It turned out to be the mother, guarding its eggs.

The first of these AMNH treks also found the skeleton of the largest mammal ever to walk on land—a long-necked, hornless rhinoceros that stood 18 feet (5.5 m) at the shoulder and weighed 30 tons (27.22 metric tons). Henry Fairfield Osborn (1857–1935) director of the museum and chair of its Department of Vertebrate Paleontology, named the beast, which lived between 30 and 16.6 million years ago, *Balucatherium grangeri,* after discoverer Walter Granger, the expedition's chief paleontologist. The name did not stand, as later paleontologists disagreed over whether the former *B. grangeri* belonged in either the genus *Indricotherium* or the related genus *Paraceratherium.*

Another spectacular mammal find was *Andrewsarchus mongoliensis,* the largest-ever land carnivore. An inhabitant of the early Eocene epoch, about 45 million years ago, it was 13 feet (4 m) long with a skull over three feet (1 m) in length. Although it had clawed feet and teeth similar to a wolf's, it is more closely related to modern whales and cloven-hoofed mammals than to any modern land carnivore. Its name, which means "Andrews beast of Mongolia" is a tribute to Roy Chapman Andrews, the leader of the AMNH expeditions and their de facto publicist. Andrews was a dashing, rifle-toting wanderer with a gift for self-promotion. As a popular fund-raiser, speaker, and author, he presented the central Asia expeditions in the most dramatic light possible.

Assigned to the museum's Department of Mammalogy, Andrews had early in his career sailed to Alaska, China, and Japan while studying whales, but, eventually, his travels took precedent over research. In a ranger hat and bullet-studded ammunition belt, Andrews became the museum's adventurer at large, collecting all manner of

(continues)

(continued)

animals as well as taking photographs for the museum. Natural history museums of the time still employed hunters to kill exotic animals and taxidermists to mount them for display. Andrews had mastered both of those skills as a youth in southern Wisconsin, where he earned his Beloit College tuition mounting deer heads and other hunting trophies.

In 1919, while collecting specimens in China, Andrews had learned from Swedish paleontologist Johann Gunnar Andersson (1874–1960) about the likelihood of major fossil finds in central Asia—especially in the Gobi Desert. Andersson confided to Andrews that he was trying to secure support from the Swedish government for a large-scale field research expedition.

Returning to New York later that year, Andrews reported what he had learned to the museum director. A proponent of ambitious field work, Osborn had 20 years earlier suggested central Asia as a likely place to find evidence of pre-*Cenozoic* development of *placental* mammals, and he still thought so. He agreed with Andrews that the American Museum of Natural History could achieve a coup by preempting Andersson's expedition, which it did.

Perhaps the greatest coup, however, was in the way Andrews told the story of the expeditions to the public. His popular addresses—especially in a 1923 speaking tour between Asiatic jaunts—stressed the adventure of the trail rather than the tedium of fossil hunting or the scientific rigor of research. He told of the way he fended off attacks by bandits on horseback, of scores of poisonous snakes that invaded the scientists' camp on cold nights, and of blinding sandstorms that blew away tents and sandblasted the expedition's vehicles so that the windshields were pitted and opaque. He underscored these stories in his many books about his travels, including *New Conquest of Central China* (1932) and his autobiography *Under a Lucky Star* (1943).

Andrews's popular appeal benefited the American Museum of Natural History and paleontology at large, but his approach sometimes had unsought consequences. Along with the speaking engagements, Andrews turned auctioneer, promoting the museum's sale of a fossil egg (thought to be Protoceratops but really Oviraptor) for $5,000 to help finance the 1925 return expedition. Word of the sale got back to Chinese and Mongolian officials, reinforcing their suspicions that the Americans were stealing valuable native treasures.

East Asia became increasingly tumultuous and politically unstable over the 1920s, especially after Mongolia became a Marxist "People's Republic" in 1924 and after the death of Sun Yat-sen (b. 1866), China's de facto leader, in 1925. Andrews was unable to secure permissions for a third central Asia expedition in the late 1920s. He did return to the Gobi Desert for a smaller-scale fossil hunting trip in 1930, but after that, the region became closed to Western scientists, who did not return for 60 years.

the new Tennessee law. In the small town of Dayton, Tennessee, local boosters decided that this might be a low-risk, high-visibility way to publicize their economically challenged community. They asked Rhea County High School science teacher and football coach John Thomas Scopes (1900–70) if he would stand up to the ban. Scopes, who taught from a standard biology textbook espousing the well-accepted theory of evolution, agreed to be prosecuted for violating the new law.

In what was clearly going to be a national test case, Bryan—who had last practiced law 30 years earlier—publicly offered his services to the district attorney's office. Had he refused, the district attorney would have imperiled his own political future. Famous defense attorney (and well-known agnostic) Clarence Darrow (1857–1938) volunteered to lead the defense team.

Conducted in the steamy Tennessee summer, the trial drew huge crowds of sweating spectators—antievolution, pro-evolution, and just curious—and reporters from far-flung newspapers. Its most dramatic moments came when Darrow called Bryan to the stand as an expert witness and then grilled him until the great orator said that not every word in the Bible must be taken literally.

The court convicted Scopes, as Darrow had requested (anticipating appeal before a higher court), and the judge fined the teacher $100. Despite that verdict (later overturned on a technicality), the case was a setback for antievolution forces. Under Tennessee law, Darrow's request for a guilty verdict robbed the eloquent Bryan of a chance to deliver his carefully prepared closing statement. That was a great disappointment to him and a moral defeat for his supporters. Still in Dayton five days after the trial ended, Bryan died in his sleep during an after-supper nap. Of the other 14 states considering a ban on the teaching of evolution, only Arkansas and Mississippi proceeded to pass such laws. Scopes, with the help of sympathetic newspaper reporters who had covered his case, went back to college to study geology.

The Scopes trial by no means ended the controversy. An Arkansas law banning the teaching of evolution remained on the books until it was struck down by legal challenge in 1968. In the case of *Epperson v. Arkansas*, the U.S. Supreme Court ruled against "creationist laws" on grounds that they required the teaching of a particular religious doctrine—in violation of the U.S. Constitution's prohibition against governmental establishment of religion, often called the establishment clause. In a 1981 law, Arkansas legislators took a slightly different approach, requiring that public schools balance evolution science with "creation science." In the landmark 1982 case *McLean v. Arkansas Board of Education*, U.S. District Court Judge William R. Overton ruled against the state and in favor of a group of plaintiffs—including prominent clergy—who had contended that the law was in violation of the establishment clause. Overton ruled that creation science was religion, not science.

U.S. courts have consistently struck down similar requirements for the teaching of creationism, creation science, or intelligent design in public schools, yet the issue continues into the 21st century. In 2004, the school board in Dover, Pennsylvania, a rural community in the south-central part of the state, ruled that its science teachers must teach intelligent design, a philosophy holding that the workings of nature are too complex to have come about without the planning and guidance of a supreme intelligence. Parents and community leaders opposed to the move filed a federal lawsuit against the school board.

The following year, eight members of the Dover school board—all of them that had sought reelection—were defeated. Voters preferred a slate of candidates opposed to the intelligent design rule. In December 2005, Federal District Judge John E. Jones III ruled that intelligent design is not science and cannot be taught as science in public schools.

Such clashes have not been restricted to the United States. In 2004, Letizia Moratti, Italy's education minister, decreed that creationism would be taught in that country's schools. After more than 50,000 Italians signed a petition of protest drafted by Italian scientists, Moratti withdrew the decree.

A Giant Misstep for Genetic Science

Scopes taught from the textbook *A Civic Biology: Presented in Problems* by George William Hunter (1873–1948). Published in 1914, it stated that "millions of years ago life was very simple and that gradually more and more complex forms appeared," explaining Darwin's theory that "simple forms of life . . . gave rise to those more complex and that thus ultimately the most complex forms came into existence." On the next page, it listed those most complex forms as "five races or varieties of man, each very different from each other in instincts, social customs, and, to an extent, in structure." The list concluded with "the highest type of all, the Caucasians, represented by the civilized white inhabitants of Europe and America."

Darwin's theory of evolution was being used in the 1920s to teach racism to American high school students. Hunter's was a common and accepted interpretation of human genetic theory. Public health officials and politicians used such views, considered scientific, to justify discriminatory and cruel policies in the United States and, soon, downright murderous policies would follow in Europe.

Francis Galton (1822–1911), Charles Darwin's cousin, coined the term *eugenic*, meaning well born, or of good heritage. Galton believed that all human traits—including industriousness, intelligence, and honesty—were strictly the result of inheritance. Eugenics proponents believed that the human species could be improved, even perfected, through careful genetic management. But the movement came to embody more prejudice than science. It latched onto the mistaken belief that certain kinds of people are inherently superior to others. This thinking led to the idea that inferior strains ought to be prevented from mixing, that is from mating, with superior nationalities and classes. If possible, went this line of thought, inferior classes ought to be prevented from reproducing at all.

With support from "scientific" arguments, U.S. politicians enacted eugenics-based laws. Congressional testimony by Harry Laughlin (1880–1943), superintendent of the Eugenics Record Office at Cold Spring Harbor, New York, helped pass the U.S. Immigration Act of 1924. The law limited the number of immigrants from southern and eastern Europe on the grounds of their genetic unsuitability. It placed no such limits on those coming from western and northern Europe. Laughlin, an outspoken anti-Semite, would go on to serve as an honored consultant to Germany's Nazi Party in developing its so-called race cleansing policies of the 1930s and 1940s.

Another Test Case

Eugenics-minded public officials also took it upon themselves to rule that certain individuals considered genetically inferior should be surgically sterilized against their will—for their own good and for the good of society. The Commonwealth of Virginia passed a law to that effect in 1924. Not long after, state officials, aware that the involuntary sterilization law would be challenged on constitutional grounds, found a test case and put it to trial.

The plaintiff, assigned an attorney by the state, was teenager Carrie Buck (1908–83), of Charlottesville. A cousin of her foster family raped and impregnated Carrie when she was 16. Her foster parents blamed the girl. Carrie's birth mother was a prostitute who had been confined to the Virginia Colony for Epileptics and the Feebleminded in Lynchburg, and the pregnancy apparently convinced her foster father that Carrie belonged there too. He petitioned that the pregnant teen be institutionalized. And so she was, in 1923.

When Carrie's daughter, Vivian, was seven months old, the state ordered that Carrie be surgically prevented from having more children. The case for sterilization was based on the fact that Carrie's mother, Emma, had been found deficient in intelligence and moral sense, that Carrie had supposedly inherited those deficiencies, and that a social worker had judged Vivian a sluggish baby.

As state health officials intended, the case of *Buck v. Bell* found its way to the U.S. Supreme Court. (Bell was the name of the colony's superintendent.) A representative of the Eugenics Record Office testified in favor of the sterilization law, and the Court upheld it, finding the law within the constitutional functions of the state. Justice Oliver Wendell Holmes, Jr. (1841–1935), writing the majority opinion, stated that "It is better for all the world if instead of waiting to execute degenerate offspring for crimes, or to let them starve for their imbecility, society can prevent those who are manifestly unfit from continuing their kind. . . . Three generations of imbeciles are enough."

Doctors performed a *tubal ligation* to sterilize Carrie five months later. Virginia went on to sterilize 8,000 more "undesirables"—a category including the developmentally disabled and those with birth defects, but also alcoholics, drug addicts, habitual lawbreakers, and even the chronically unemployed. With the way cleared by the high court, 35 other states passed sterilization laws. U.S. doctors sterilized as many as 60,000 over the next four decades, 20,000 in California alone.

Carrie Buck did not spend her life institutionalized. She won release, worked for a living, and married. In middle age, she took an IQ test and scored in the normal range. Vivian died of an infection in the second grade. Before she did, the little girl—unaware that she had been called an imbecile by the U.S. Supreme Court—earned a place on her school's honor roll.

Meanwhile, Back at the Lab

Like the eugenicists, Hermann J. Muller (introduced in chapter 2) believed that it should be possible to improve humanity through genetic selection. Muller, however, realized when he was still a student at Columbia University that before scientists could do anything like guiding human evolution for the better, they needed to understand much more about the process of physical inheritance.

After his stint as one of Thomas Hunt Morgan's Fly Boys of the *D. melanogaster* experiments and a few years at the Rice Institute in Houston, Muller in 1920 joined the faculty of the University of Texas. In Austin, he theorized about complex structures that would one day be found to function inside individual genes.

Hermann J. Muller examines a fruit fly in a bottle. (Caltech Archives)

Much of Muller's work, like that of his mentor Morgan, involved identifying mutations and tracking their frequency through generation after generation of fruit flies. It frustrated him that even in fruit flies, with their rapid rate of reproduction, mutation was relatively rare. Attempting to speed up the process, he hit upon an original idea: What would happen if he bombarded the *Drosophila* with X-rays before allowing it to mate?

First, Muller had to get the fly to sit still long enough to be x-rayed. His solution was to place the tiny insect inside a gelatin capsule, similar to the semitransparent capsules that one swallows to take some medicines. Then he directed a concentrated ray at the container. Some flies died and others were rendered sterile before Muller correctly calculated the effective dose of radiation, which was tiny. The first time Muller successfully mated an irradiated but fertile *Drosophila* to a normal fly, in 1926, the resulting generation sported an astonishing rate of variation—including such features as curled wings, stubby wings, and even no wings at all. He had proved that it was possible to induce genetic mutations—an invaluable tool for his fellow

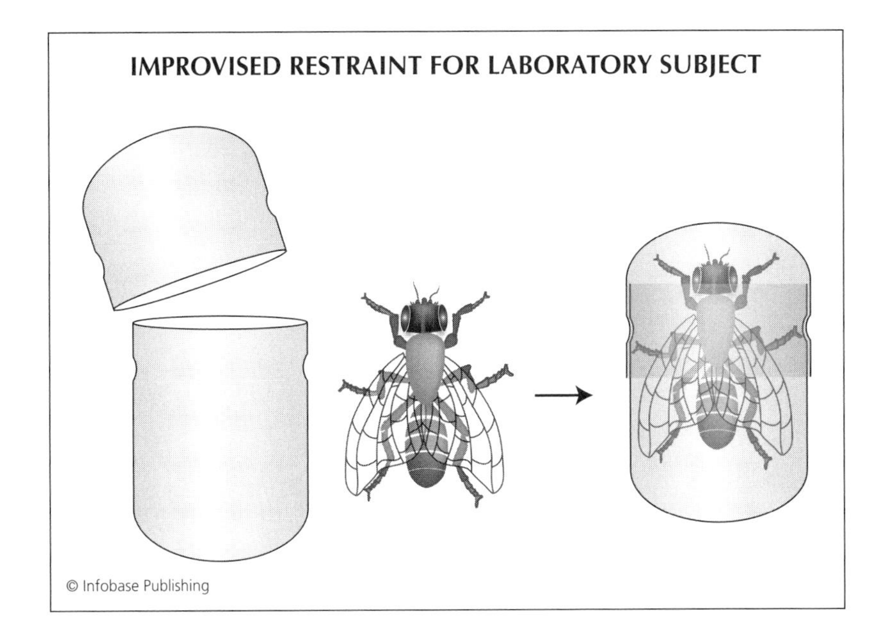

Muller used a gelatin capsule to hold the fruit fly in place so that he could expose the insect to X-rays.

geneticists—and he could demonstrate from his results that broken chromosomes and changes in individual genes bring about mutations. The experiments also showed that the overwhelming majority of mutations are, if not lethal, highly unfavorable for species survival.

A Transforming Principle

Geneticists were making great strides toward understanding how genes behaved. In addition to Muller's work in Texas, there was also his old lab mate Alfred Sturtevant's mid-1920s research back in New York, showing that some genetic abnormalities must result from a chromosome segment that breaks off during meiosis and then reattaches upside down.

Scientists still did not know exactly what it was that transferred the genetic information from parent to offspring. They were, however, reasonably certain that it happened at the molecular level.

Remarkable clues emerged during this decade. British bacteriologist Frederick Griffith (ca. 1880–1941) hit upon a fascinating phenomenon in which one strain of bacteria seemed to be transformed into another. As a medical corps officer, Griffith had been frustrated by pneumonia epidemics that broke out in England just after the war, killing hundreds. After the war, he concentrated his research on better understanding pneumonia and the microorganisms that can cause it.

In experiments in 1928, Griffith transformed one strain of *Streptococcus pneumoniae*, a bacterium that causes pneumonia, into another. He did it by injecting a group of mice with a smooth-surfaced strain (S strain) of the bacterium that was virulent—that is, it was very aggressively infec-

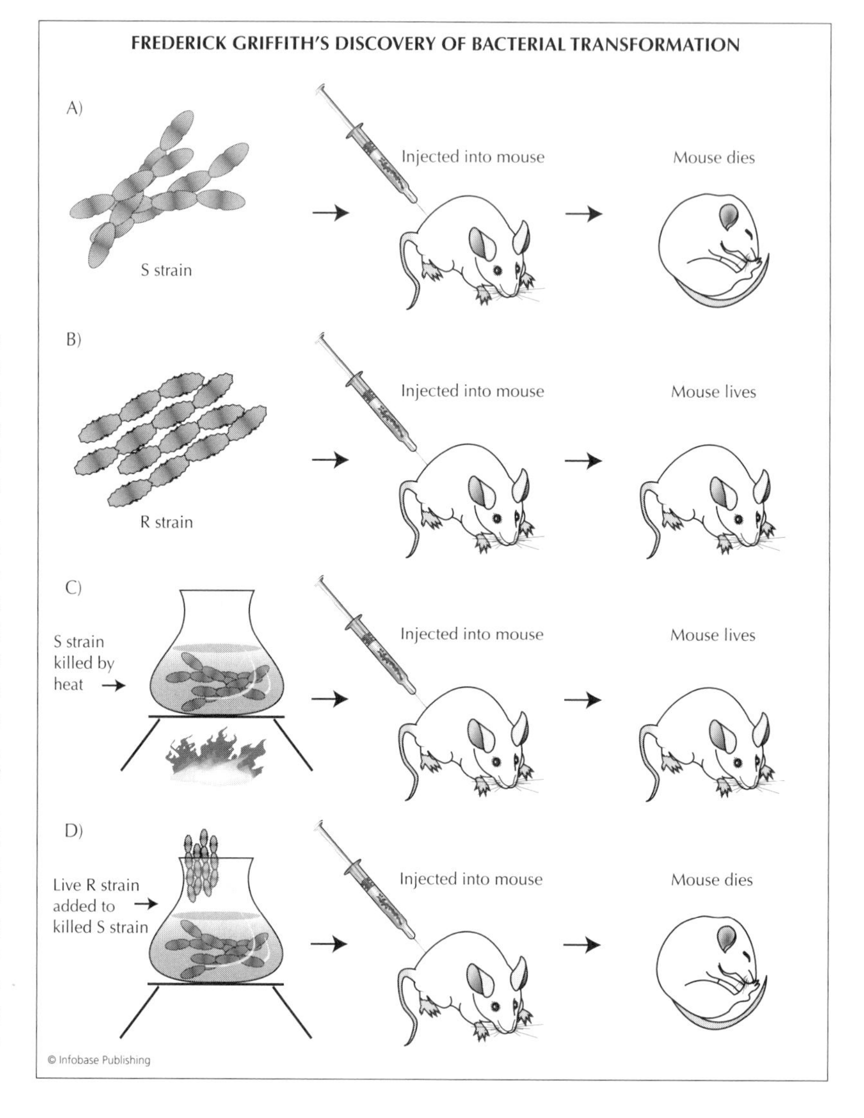

In a classic experiment, Griffith injected mice with the deadly smooth strain of Streptococcus pneumoniae *to show its virulence. Next, he injected mice with the non-virulent rough strain of the bacterium, to show that it was not deadly. Griffith then killed smooth-strain* S. pneumoniae. *When the killed bacteria were injected into mice, the mice were not affected. Finally, he added the non-virulent rough strain to the killed smooth strain of the* S. pneumoniae. *This mixture of previously harmless bacteria, when injected into mice, killed the subjects. Griffith concluded that something from the killed strain had changed the living bacteria, causing them to become virulent. This became known as the "transforming principle," which later was discovered to be DNA.*

tious and overwhelmed a body's defenses. The mice died. Then Griffith injected a rough-surfaced strain (R strain) of the bacterium, one that was not virulent, into some other mice. They were fine.

Then Griffith took some of the deadly S strain bacteria that had been killed by heat and injected them into mice. Those rodents also were fine. Next, he mixed heat-killed S strain with the non-virulent R strain. Surprisingly, the mixture killed mice. Their blood was full of virulent, S strain *S. pneumonia.*

Griffith's hypothesis was that a *transforming principle* had turned one strain of the bacteria, the harmless one, into the other, deadly one. More than a decade would pass before other scientists showed that Griffith's transforming principle was DNA.

Griffith might have benefited from a consultation with New York biochemist Phoebus Levene, the same researcher who had previously discovered the nucleic acid RNA (although no one yet knew what it did). In 1929, Levene found a previously unknown sugar, *deoxyribose*, in a nucleic acid that did not contain *ribose*. That sugar's name became part of the term *deoxyribonucleic acid*, which would be shortened to DNA.

To understand DNA at the molecular level, biologists were going to need to go smaller—to the sub-molecular, atomic, and even subatomic levels. That is the path taken by a young chemist from Oregon, who earned his Ph.D. in 1925 at Caltech in Pasadena. There, Linus Pauling joined the faculty and became one of the first scientists to use the principles of quantum mechanics (a science of subatomic matter and energy) to describe how atoms form molecules. In the following decade, Pauling would begin applying what he had learned to the molecules that make up living tissues.

Another Magic Bullet

Like his fellow researcher Griffith, the Scotland-born immunologist Alexander Fleming (1881–1955) served in Britain's wartime medical corps. And like Griffith, he returned to his research determined to better treat disease.

At a frontline hospital in France, Fleming had grown frustrated by all the wartime death he had seen. He was most disturbed that more soldiers died of secondary infections—staphylococcus and other deadly microbes that took hold in exposed tissue—than from their wounds directly. With his colleagues from St. Mary's Hospital in London, the genial Scot had devised new treatments for bullet and shrapnel wounds, ways to prevent and limit infection through sanitary surgical procedures and dressings. What he really wanted, however, was a new bacteria-fighting substance, something that would aggressively kill bacteria without harming the delicate tissues of the body where those bacteria took hold. Harsh chemical antiseptics in use at the time sometimes did more harm than good, especially when they killed leukocytes, the white blood cells that Fleming knew could remove bacteria from pus.

Although he was a qualified surgeon, Fleming specialized in inoculation and bacteriology research. As a friend and professional peer of German immunologist Paul Ehrlich, he had become one of the first doctors in England to administer Ehrlich's discovery Salvarsan, the "magic bullet" for treating syphilis. Fleming wanted something that would work as Salvarsan did, but against a whole range of infections.

His first discovery in this quest came in 1921, after Fleming caught a nasty cold and decided to treat it as a research opportunity. He put a drop of mucus from his running nose on a glass plate and looked at it under a

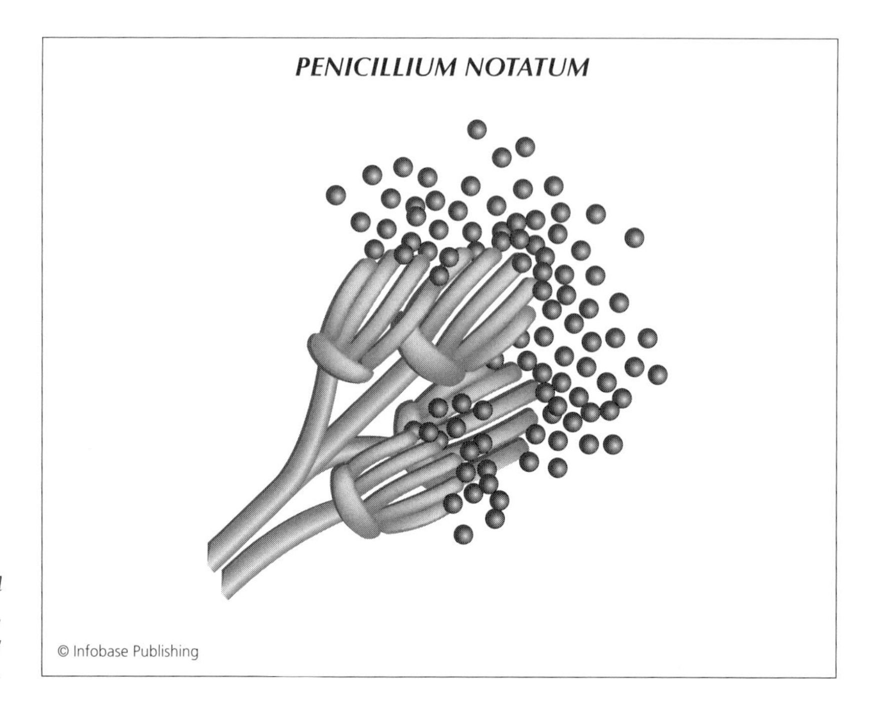

Simplified diagram of the mold fungus, source of penicillin, shows spores supported by microscopic stemlike structures.

microscope. He did this daily as the cold lasted, and the smeared plates piled up until it was time to clean the laboratory glassware—something Fleming was notorious for putting off. As he went through the dirty plates, he noticed a yellow colony of microbes growing on one. He saw nothing unusual in that. Microbes are everywhere.

Something did strike the doctor as unusual about this particular plate, because the microbes apparently were steering clear of the drop of nasal mucus—or the nasal mucus was repelling, even killing them. Fleming had discovered lysozyme, an enzyme found not just in mucus but also in tears, gastric juices, and egg whites. Lysozyme, it turned out, causes the *cell walls* of some infectious bacteria to break down. Fleming hoped it would prove his magic bullet against infections, but it was not strong enough. (It did later prove useful in certain medical applications and even as a preservative.)

In 1928, Fleming stumbled upon another, much better antimicrobial agent, one that would eventually revolutionize the practice of medicine. Again, the discovery was an accident involving dirty glassware. Fleming had been experimenting on cultures of staphylococcus bacteria. As usual, his lab was a casual mess, strewn with used petri dishes. When at last he got around to cleaning, the doctor saw that mold spores had landed on one of the dishes, and a mold had grown. Around the mold was a clear, bacteria-free spot. The fungal growth had apparently killed off part of Fleming's staphylococcus culture.

Scientist of the Decade: Alexander Fleming (1881–1955)

It took Chain and Florey to turn penicillin into what Fleming knew it could be. Yet they never would have begun that effort were it were not for the discoverer himself. Investigating naturally occurring antibacterial chemicals, the Oxford team's original focus was Fleming's earlier discovery, lysozyme, which they successfully isolated and purified.

Chain then ran across a copy of Fleming's paper on penicillin. The paper and the substance it described sparked his interest. Soon the team at Oxford was trying to purify and stabilize penicillin in hopes of manufacturing it for medical use. Their success would lead to a Nobel Prize in physiology or medicine shared by Fleming, Chain, and Florey.

Some critics have argued that Fleming did not deserve as much credit as he got as the discoverer of antibiotics, that he was merely the beneficiary of a happy accident. This was hardly the case. Although there was serendipity to Fleming's discoveries, they reflected precisely what Fleming was seeking. He knew how to recognize an antibacterial agent, and he knew how to proceed in investigating what he had found.

That said, there was also a certain serendipitous quality about many aspects of Alexander Fleming's life and career. In some ways, his medical career, and his specialty, seemed chosen for him—as if by fate—rather than by him.

Known as "Alec" to siblings and friends, the biologist began life on a remote Scottish farm. At age 14, he came south to London because his father had died and an older brother was starting a medical career in the English capital. Fleming became a physician, in part, because of his brother. There was also the fact that young Fleming, who attended London's Polytechnic Institute, then tried working at entry-level jobs in business and disliked them. An uncle died, leaving him enough money to afford medical school, so Fleming decided to enroll.

He chose medical school at London's St. Mary's Hospital for no better reason than that, as an athlete for the Polytech, he had played water polo against St. Mary's. After earning his medical degree and training as a surgeon, he stayed at St. Mary's because the captain of the rifle team

(continues)

Fleming linked the antibacterial property to a substance in the liquid around the mold, a substance given off by the organism itself. After determining that the mold culture was *Penicillium notatum*, he named his discovery for it, calling the liquid "penicillin." With experimentation, he defined a range of harmful microorganisms that were sensitive to penicillin and found that range to be fairly wide. The substance struck him as precisely what he had been seeking. Anticipating its importance, he deposited a culture of *p. notatum* with the British Medical Research Council. Certain that penicillin had great potential against infection and bacterial disease, Fleming published his early findings in a 1929 article, "On the Antibacterial Action of Cultures of a Penicillium with Special Reference to Their Use in the Isolation of B. Influenzae" in *The British Journal of Experimental Pathology*.

Fleming knew that for penicillin to live up to its potential, he must first purify it and then find a way to stabilize it. The liquid that he could isolate from mold cultures proved effective on minor infections, including a case of conjunctivitis, an inflammation of the tissue around the eye,

(continued)

there wanted to keep Fleming, a crack shot, on the squad. No opening available in surgery, the rifle master found the young surgeon a job in the inoculations department. Thus, the surgeon became an immunologist who spent his career at St. Mary's.

The haphazardness about the soft-spoken Fleming's life and employment did indeed extend to his 1920s discoveries—first lysozyme and then penicillin—both found on dirty laboratory glassware. Yet there was nothing haphazard about his intellect or his commitment to research. He excelled at academics despite his limited early schooling in rural Scotland and received top marks on the entrance exam for medical training at St. Mary's. Lysozyme and penicillin could have happened to any immunologist or bacteriologist studying cultures in a less-than-tidy lab. Yet they happened to Fleming, whose war experience had inspired him to seek an agent against infection.

It took Fleming to recognize the "mold juice," as he called it, contained a powerful potential weapon for physicians. Without the financial and institutional support that would later enable his successors, he immediately set out to find a way to turn his discovery into the drug it would become. Another scientist may have dropped that dish in the cleaning solution with hardly a second thought.

If that had been the case, it may have taken far more than another decade for somebody to discover this incredible substance and follow up on the discovery. Many thousands more could have died from the everyday bacterial infections that used to kill routinely. Alexander Fleming had help doing it, certainly, but he vastly improved medicine and the world at large. His discovery cannot be undervalued. How many other biologists have achieved such a widespread, positive result? How many other physicians have saved so many lives?

In the years after World War II, as penicillin became widely available for clinical use, Fleming lived the life of a scientific celebrity—traveling around the world to seminars and speaking engagements. The popular press praised him as the man behind the medical miracle—as if he had done it alone. He could have left it at that, but Fleming carefully reminded audiences and interviewers, again and again, about the invaluable work of Florey and Chain.

in one of Fleming's fellow scientists at St. Mary's, but the substance was unstable. It lost its antibacterial properties rather quickly. Fleming was not going to urge that physicians grow fresh mold cultures in their offices and examining rooms.

In his quest to purify and preserve, Fleming failed. Biochemistry was neither his field nor that of St. Mary's bacteriology department. Yet he did not give up. He continued to push for wider research, especially by biochemists. Fleming sent samples of penicillin to any lab that would have it. At last, in the 1930s, a team of Oxford University researchers led by pathologist Howard Walter Florey (1898–1968) and biochemist Ernst Boris Chain (1906–79) took up Fleming's challenge. Inspired by a paper the immunologist had written, and starting with a sample of penicillin Fleming provided, they found a way to purify and preserve the invaluable substance—the first antibiotic—for medical use. This advance is discussed in chapter 4.

Further Reading

Andrews, Roy Chapman. *New Conquest of Central China.* New York: American Museum of Natural History, 1932. Andrews's popular account of 1920s fossil-hunting expeditions.

———. *Under a Lucky Star: A Lifetime of Adventure.* New York: The Viking Press, 1943. Autobiography of the dashing leader of fossil-hunting for the American Museum of Natural History.

Bausum, Ann. "On the Trail of Roy Chapman Andrews." *Beloit College Magazine,* Spring 2001. Available online: URL: http://www.beloit.edu/~belmag/spring01/html/RCA.html. Accessed September 4, 2004. Magazine article looks back on Andrews's career and exploits.

Brush, S. G. "How Theories Became Knowledge: Morgan's Chromosome Theory of Heredity in America and Great Britain." *Journal of the History of Biology* 35, no. 3 (Autumn 2002): 471–535. In a context of comparative studies of theory acceptance, author examines reasons that Morgan's chromosome theory caught on.

Discovery Channel.com. "Answers from Expert Mikael Forteliu." Available online. URL: http://dsc.discovery.com/convergence/beasts/know/fortelius.html. Accessed April 3, 2006. In question-answer format, paleontologist addresses misconceptions about dinosaurs and prehistoric mammals.

Fleming, Alexander. "On the Antibacterial Action of Cultures of a Penicillium with Special Reference to Their Use in the Isolation of B. Influenzae." *British Journal of Experimental Pathology* 10 (1929): 226–236. Discoverer discusses properties and potential of landmark antibiotic.

Gallencamp, Charles, and Michael J. Novacek. *Dragon Hunter: Roy Chapman Andrews and the Central Asiatic Expeditions.* New York: Penguin, 2001. Biography of Andrews focuses on his fossil-hunting trips.

Gillham, Nicholas W. *A Life of Sir Francis Galton: From African Exploration to the Birth of Eugenics.* Oxford: Oxford University Press, 2001. Biography of Victorian polymath who coined the word *eugenic.*

Kevles, Daniel J. *In the Name of Eugenics: Genetics and the Uses of Human Heredity.* New York: Knopf, 1985. Historical and philosophical discussion of eugenics movement.

Larson, Edward J. *Summer for the Gods: The Scopes Trial and America's Continuing Debate over Science and Religion.* New York: Basic Books, 1997. Account of long-standing disagreement between evolutionists and creationists in the United States.

Lawrence Livermore National Laboratory Science and Technology Education Program. "Transformation." Available online. URL: http://ep.llnl.gov/bep/science/10/tLect.html. Accessed September 4, 2004.

National laboratory's resource explains Frederick Griffith's landmark experiment that led to understanding of DNA's role in heredity.

Morgan, Thomas Hunt. *The Theory of the Gene.* New Haven, Conn.: Yale University Press, 1926. Genetics pioneer's influential book based on years of *Drosophila* research.

Morgan, Vincent L., and Spencer G. Lucas. "Walter Granger, 1872–1941, Paleontologist." *The Granger Papers*, Project 19, 2002. New Mexico Museum of Natural History and Science. Available online. URL: http://users.rcn.com/granger.nh.ultranet/bulletin/MorganLucas1.pdf. Accessed September 4, 2004. Authors illuminate important role of a 1920s fossil-hunter who was often overshadowed by flamboyant colleague Roy Chapman Andrews.

Muller, H. J. "Variation Due to Change in the Individual Gene." *American Naturalist* 56 (1922): 23–50. Geneticist's speculation on the structures within the gene looks forward to DNA molecular research.

Nardo, Don. *The Scopes Trial.* San Diego, Calif.: Lucent Books, 1997. Accessible account of landmark trial over the issue of teaching evolution in schools.

Otfinoski, Steven. *Alexander Fleming: Conquering Disease with Penicillin* (Makers of Modern Science series). New York: Facts On File, 1992. Accessible profile of antibiotics pioneer.

Smith, J. David, and K. Ray Nelson. *The Sterilization of Carrie Buck.* Far Hills, N.J.: New Horizon Press, 1989. Account of Virginia case in which the U.S. Supreme Court upheld a state law justifying involuntary sterilization of "genetic defectives."

U.S. Supreme Court. *Buck v. Bell, Superintendent of State Colony Epileptics and Feeble Minded.* 274 U.S. 200 (1927). Available online. URL: http://caselaw.lp.findlaw.com/cgi-bin/getcase.pl?court=us&vol=274&invol=200. Accessed September 4, 2004. Landmark case in which the U.S. high court ruled in favor of involuntary sterilization.

Wainwright, Milton. *Miracle Cure: The Story of Penicillin and the Golden Age of Antibiotics.* Oxford: Basil Blackwell, 1990. History recounts story of penicillin discovery, development, and impact.

White, G. Edward. *Justice Oliver Wendell Holmes: Law and the Inner Self.* New York: Oxford University Press, 1993. Biography puts jurist's decisions, including opinion in *Buck v. Bell*, in context of Holmes's life, work, and philosophy.

4 1931–1940: Hard Times and Hard Lessons

Depression and Discovery

The 1930s was a difficult decade marred by a worldwide economic slump, the Great Depression, and by repressive, dictatorial, and militaristic governments in several parts of the world. As Joseph Stalin (1879–1953) inflicted his agricultural, industrial, and political "reforms"—involving mass imprisonment and wholesale slaughter—upon the Soviet Union, Japan and Italy launched military conquests (of Manchuria and Ethiopia, respectively) that led toward the horrors of World War II.

Adolf Hitler (1889–1945)—who would by decade's end start that war—seized power in Germany, where his Nazi Party quickly enacted laws against those considered either politically or genetically undesirable. Into the genetic category fell the disabled, Romany (gypsies), and above all, Jews. The Nazis sterilized or executed the disabled. The regime took from Jews and Romany their civil liberties, livelihoods, property, and, ultimately, millions of lives. Hitler and his officials, physicians among them, committed mass murder because of irrational, prejudicial hatred combined with political expediency, yet they were able to point to biological pseudoscience for justification of their policies—specifically to that unfortunate offshoot of genetics called eugenics. As discriminatory laws took effect, many top German scientists—especially those of Jewish heritage—fled Germany, setting back that country's research programs.

Nazi policies caused many scientists, educators, and public health officials in the rest of western Europe and North America to reexamine ideas about race and ethnicity and to back away from eugenics. When properly followed, the scientific method rejects prejudicial assumption in favor of hard data. Among biologists who kept that in mind, the 1930s was a fruitful decade.

In Britain, pathologist Howard Florey assembled and led the Oxford University team that isolated, purified, and eventually developed methods for manufacturing penicillin in quantity—a breakthrough that would revolutionize medicine and pharmacology.

At Cornell University, Barbara McClintock (1902–92) helped invent the new field of *cytogenetics* with her observations of corn chromosomes. Her peers at California's Stanford University illuminated the relationship between genes and enzymes in biochemistry. Another new field, molecular biology, grew in part from X-ray diffraction experiments in Britain as physicists turned their attention to biology. Linus Pauling married the new theories of quantum mechanics to biochemistry. His approach informed a wide range of biological inquiry—including genetics and immunology.

Another American, medical researcher Wendell Meredith Stanley (1904–71), advanced understanding of the molecular nature of viruses and discovered that a nucleic acid, soon found to be RNA, was an important part of their makeup.

Taking a broader view of life-forms, population geneticists advanced new theories such as genetic drift and gradual genetic differentiation, called a *cline*, as opposed to firm lines between species. A small but growing group of research biologists began to emphasize the interrelationships of organisms with each other and the natural resources of their natural habitats. No species, these scientists argued, could properly be understood in isolation from its environment.

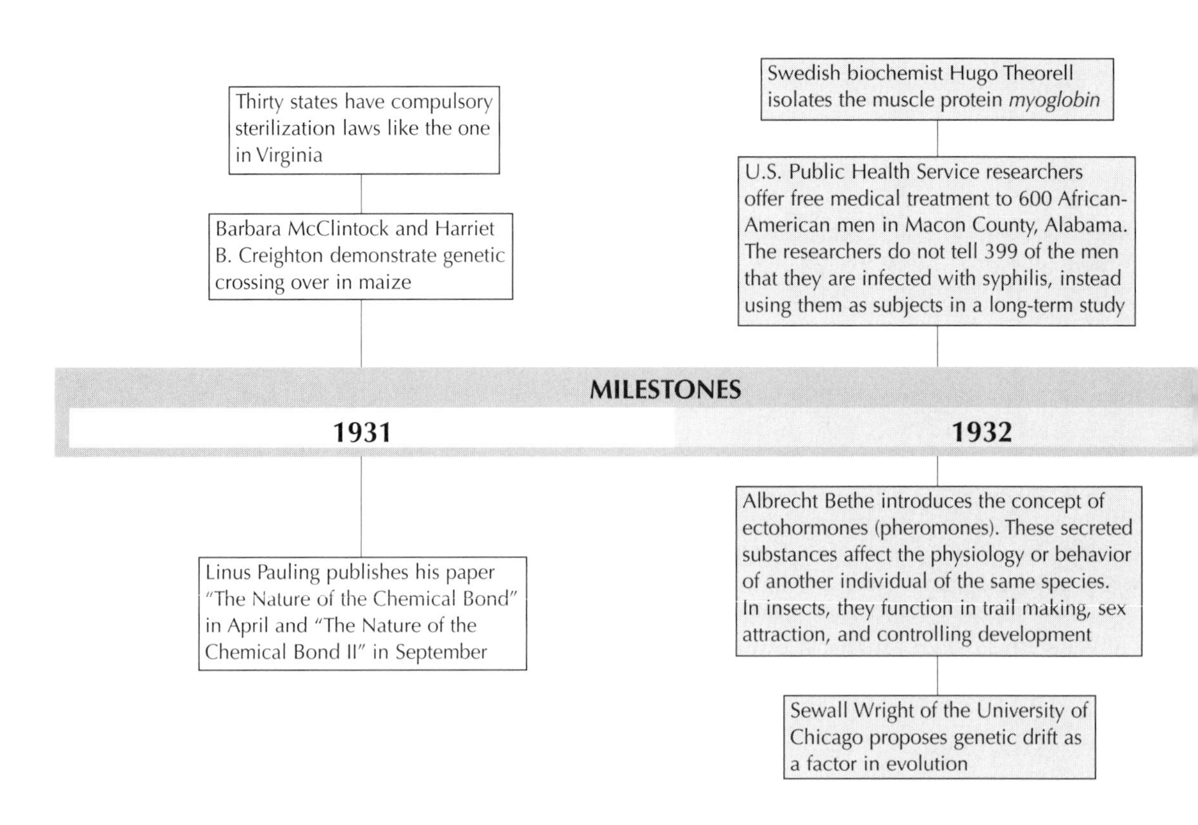

This was not necessarily a new idea, as naturalists—many of them passionate amateurs—long had observed plants and animals in nature. In South Africa, a naturalist who was also a museum director spotted among a commercial fishing trawler's catch the zoological find of the century, a coelacanth. It was a representative of an order of life that ichthyologists thought had gone extinct 80 million years earlier.

Peering Deeper into the Cell

Early in the century, groundbreaking work on the hereditary traits of the common fruit fly *D. melanogaster* (and some other, closely related members of the *Drosophila* genus), largely conducted by Thomas Hunt Morgan and his associates, and on generations of American corn, or maize, by such pioneers of scientific hybridization as Edward Murray East and Donald F. Jones, had already made genetics perhaps the most exciting field within biological study. It held such promise. Many saw the likelihood that inquiries into maize genetics could bring rapid economic advantages for farming and related industries. The mysteries of trait heredity and mutations pursued by the fruit fly breeders seemed somewhat more remote but held

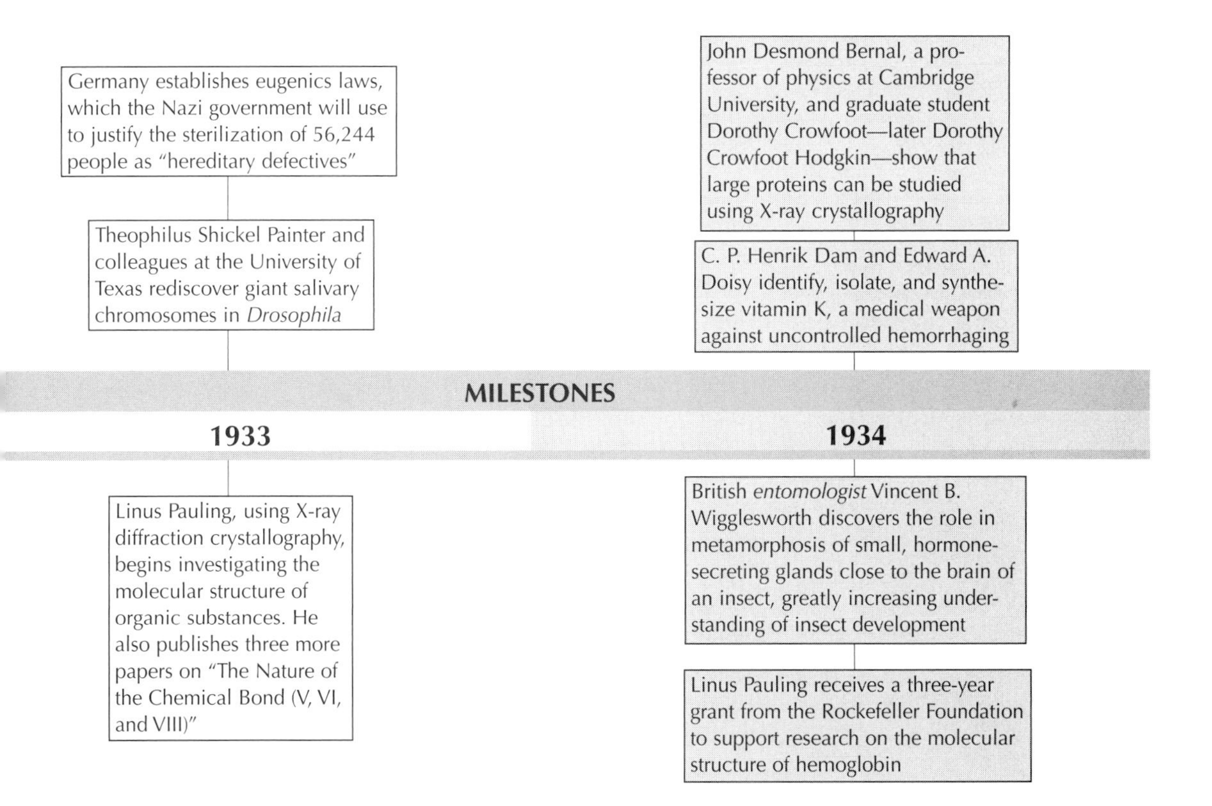

out potential in areas ranging from selective breeding of livestock to, as many thought, improvement of the human race.

Barbara McClintock entered Cornell University, in Ithaca, New York, in 1919 to study biology. In 1921, she had taken the only course in genetics offered to Cornell undergraduates. It was in the School of Agriculture and taught by a professor of plant breeding. At the same time, she was studying cytology under a botany professor. She found that she shared his keen interest in the role of chromosomes. At the end of that semester, her genetics professor called McClintock on the phone and invited her, still an undergrad, to enroll in a graduate-level course on the subject.

"Obviously, this telephone call cast the die for my future. I remained with genetics thereafter," she wrote in a brief autobiography in 1983, after being named that year's Nobel laureate in the category of physiology or medicine.

After earning her Ph.D. in 1927, McClintock remained for a time at Cornell as an instructor. She stayed, in part, so she could brainstorm with two like-minded graduate students from the Great Plains—George W. Beadle (1903–89) and Marcus M. Rhoades (1903–91). Kansan Rhoades arrived from the California Institute of Technology (already becom-

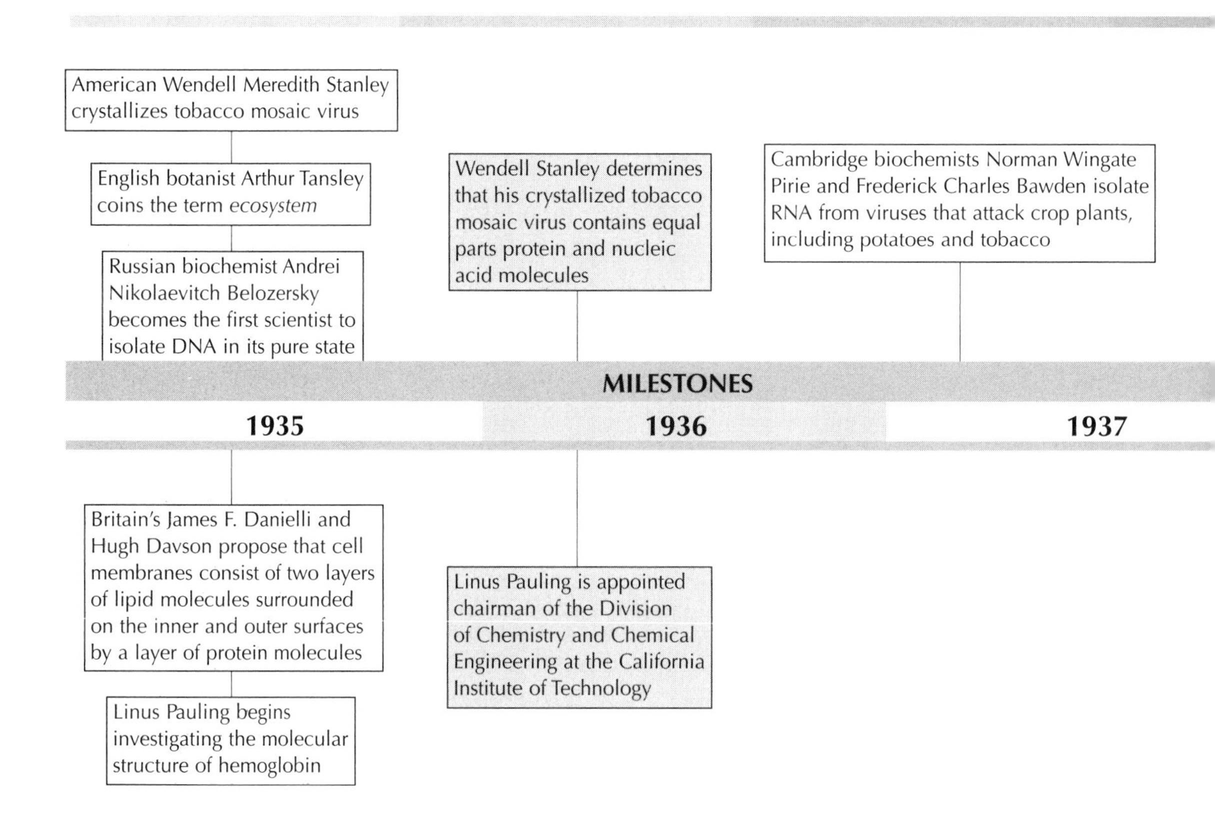

ing known as Caltech), where he had studied under Alfred Sturtevant. He was up to date on the latest ideas in the Thomas Hunt Morgan school of *Drosophila* genetics. (Morgan had accepted a 1928 invitation to organize a department of genetics at the university in Pasadena.) Like McClintock, Rhoades would spend much of his career as a maize cytogeneticist. Beadle, who had studied plant genetics in his native Nebraska, would make Caltech his next stop after Cornell, on his way to a Nobel Prize–winning career in biochemistry. Not long after his association with McClintock, Beadle would come to realize that the influence of genes upon heredity must happen by means of chemical reactions.

During what she called in her Nobel autobiography "an extraordinary period" of intellectual cross-fertilization, McClintock observed direct visual evidence of the crossing over of genes between pairing chromosomes.

McClintock enlisted graduate student Harriet Creighton (1910–2004) in experiments, conducted between 1928 and 1931, that tracked crossing-over within maize cells. Chromosomes are paired, one inherited from each parent. Biologists thought, but had not yet confirmed, that during meiosis, parts of the chromosome inherited from one parent could

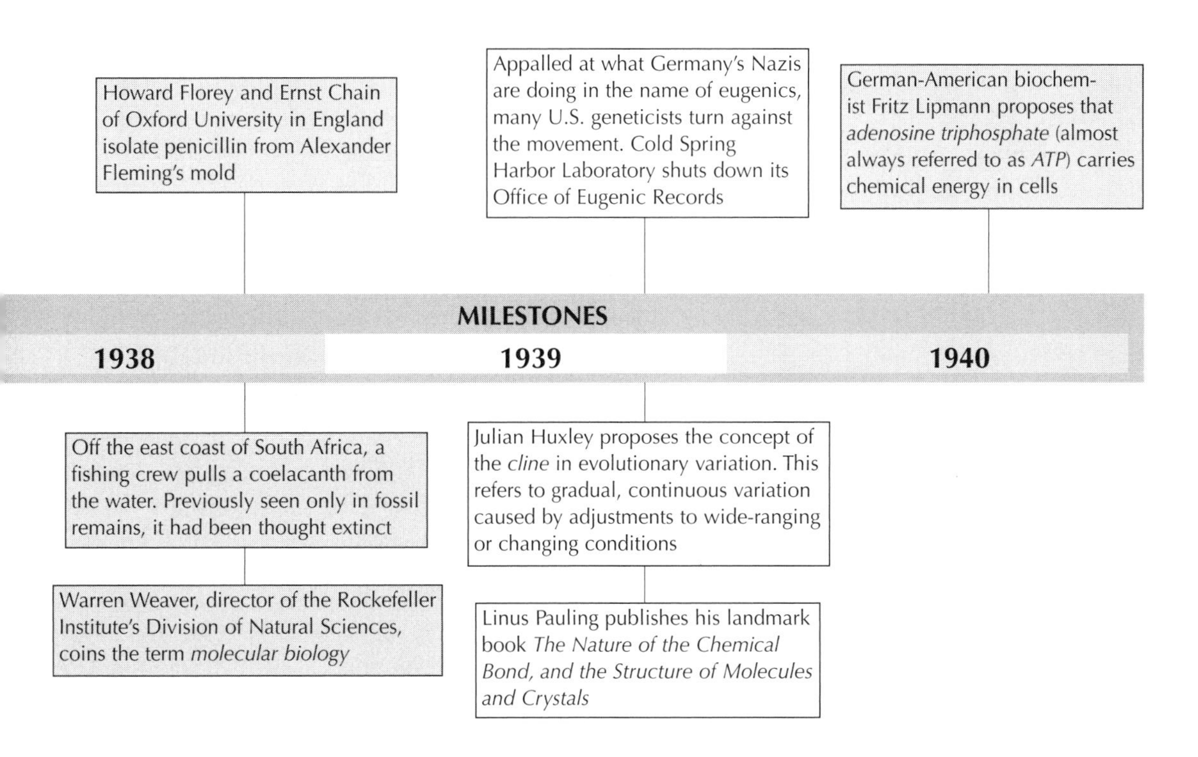

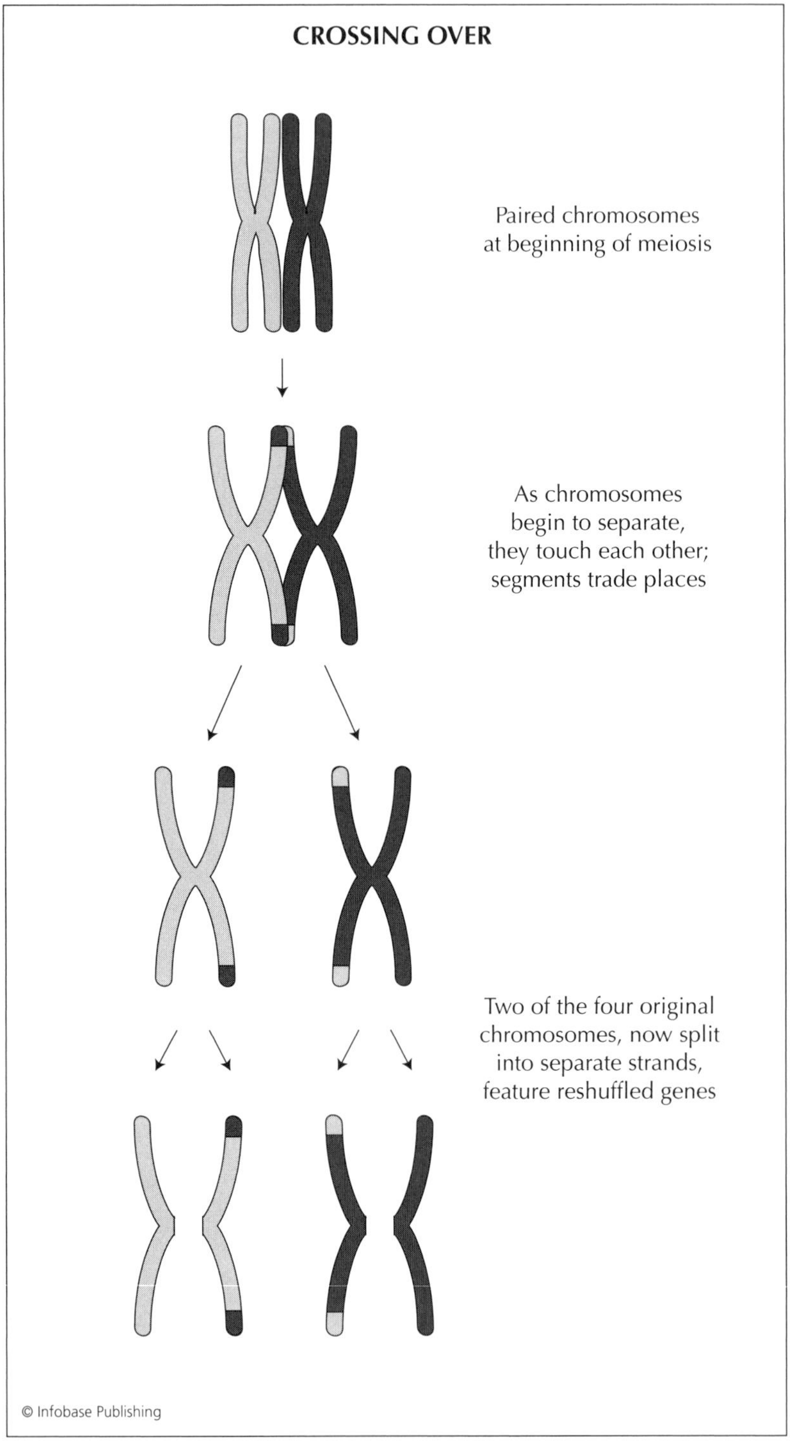
CROSSING OVER
Paired chromosomes at beginning of meiosis
As chromosomes begin to separate, they touch each other; segments trade places
Two of the four original chromosomes, now split into separate strands, feature reshuffled genes
© Infobase Publishing

The phenomenon results in an exchange of genetic material between maternal and paternal chromosomes.

change place with its corresponding part on the chromosome from the other parent. McClintock and Creighton used a new technique whereby they applied a stain to the *germ cells* of the plant. The stain allowed them to link a specific genetic trait with a part of the chromosome that they could see under a microscope. Thus, they followed and confirmed genetic crossing-over. The women published their findings in a 1931 landmark paper, "Correlation of Cytological and Genetical Crossing-over in Zea Mays," in *Proceedings of the National Academy of Sciences.* Top genetics researchers such as Sturtevant and other graduates of Morgan's programs at Columbia and Caltech welcomed the breakthrough, which bolstered their own findings.

Such well-received work led to broader opportunities for McClintock, including a summer research fellowship at the University of Missouri in Columbia. Lewis J. Stadler (1896–1954), who also specialized in the cellular genetics of maize, introduced McClintock to X-rays as a tool for genetic research—the same mutation-inducing technique that Hermann Muller had pioneered at the University of Texas.

The 1930s was an exciting time to be an ambitious, imaginative cytologist. While McClintock and colleagues were peering into the phenomenon of crossing-over, zoology researcher Theophilus Shickel Painter (1889–1969), at the University of Texas, realized that he could use the unusually large chromosomes contained within the cells of *Drosophila* salivary glands to get a better look at chromosomes under a microscope. In 1933, Painter announced in the journal *Science*, in a paper titled "A New Method for the Study of Chromosome Rearrangement and the Plotting of Chromosome Maps," that he had tracked perceptible differences among these chromosomes under the microscope and then correlated the crossing over of genes with individual physical traits. He included a drawing of a section of a *Drosophila* chromosome showing more than 150 bands, pinpointing the precise positions of individual genes.

McClintock's friend Beadle was soon to collaborate, in 1935, with Boris Ephrussi (1901–79) at the Institut de Biologie Physico-Chimique in Paris. There, they designed a method to determine the nature of the chemical effects exerted by individual genes in *Drosophila.* They found that a trait that seemed simple—eye color, for example—resulted from a complex chain of chemical reactions that genes somehow triggered.

Back in the United States, Beadle continued to work at the puzzle, first at Harvard University and then at Stanford University. There, in 1937, he and Edward L. Tatum (1904–75) used X-rays to bring about mutations in *Neurospora crassa*, a pink bread mold. Some of the mutants lost the ability to produce an essential amino acid or vitamin. The researchers then crossed these mutant strains of *N. crassa* with normal strains. The resulting molds inherited the metabolic defect as a recessive trait, showing that mutations were genetic defects. More important, Beadle and Tatum's experiments showed that when a genetic mutation can be shown to affect a specific chemical reaction, the enzyme catalyzing that reaction will be altered or missing. It followed that each gene determines the structure of a specific enzyme. That enzyme then allows a specific chemical reaction to proceed. This concept, called one gene–one enzyme, would bring the two scientists a share of the 1958 Nobel Prize in physiology or medicine.

McClintock's career, meantime, hit a snag. A Guggenheim fellowship in 1933 sent her to Berlin to work with Curt Stern (1902–81), a German geneticist who, like Sturtevant and Muller, had studied under Morgan at Columbia University. Stern had returned to his native country in 1926. At Berlin's Kaiser Wilhelm Institute, his research on Y chromosome fragmentation in *Drosophila* supported McClintock's findings in maize. She eagerly looked forward to working alongside Stern, but it was not to be.

"I could not have picked a worse time," McClintock later wrote to Stern and his wife about her fellowship stay in Germany. She arrived in Europe in the same year that the Nazi Party, which held anti-Semitism as a cornerstone of its philosophy, rose to power under Hitler. Politically aware Jewish-German scientists, Stern among them, rapidly realized that they would be wise to leave the country. Many departed for France and England. Stern had arranged a six-month appointment for himself at Caltech. Officially, he was supposed to return to Germany when that period was over. Instead, he found a job at the University of Rochester, New York, and never saw his native country again.

When McClintock arrived in Germany, it was zoologist Richard B. Goldschmidt (1878–1958), instead of Stern, who greeted her. Goldschmidt, director of Berlin's Kaiser Wilhelm Institute and an inventive genetics researcher in his own right, was himself a Jew. Although distracted by the growing threat to himself and his family, he made the young American woman welcome. (Goldschmidt immigrated to the United States and obtained a position at the University of California, Berkeley, in 1936.) A minor thyroid imbalance added to McClintock's discomfort and unease over the political and social tensions of Berlin. She traveled on to Saxony, where she found the low morale of researchers at that city's botanical institute discouraging.

Barbara McClintock at Cold Spring Harbor Laboratory, her research home for most of her career (Barbara McClintock Papers, American Philosophical Society)

After returning to Ithaca in the spring of 1934, she worked for two years as a Cornell

Science Misused to Justify the Unjustifiable

War criminal Josef Mengele (1911–79) considered himself a biologist, as did his employer, the German government. With a medical degree from the University of Frankfurt am Main, Mengele became a researcher at Berlin's Institute for Hereditary Biology and Racial Hygiene upon its founding in 1934. That work and Mengele's service with the Nazi SS (elite guard) led to his position as chief medical officer at the Auschwitz extermination camp in German-occupied Poland during World War II.

The Nazi Party, which came to power in 1933, passionately embraced eugenics—the field of human genetic improvement—as a scientific justification for Chancellor Adolf Hitler's anti-Semitism, a tenet of Nazi political philosophy. Germany was far from exceptional in adopting eugenics laws. Its mandates for involuntary sterilization of "genetic undesirables" were based on similar U.S. legislation (discussed in chapter 3). Norway, Sweden, Denmark, and Switzerland also passed such laws in the early 1930s. The idea that people are divided into inferior and superior strains—most often defined by ethnic and racial distinctions—of course dates back to ancient times. Diverse societies have used such thinking to justify unjust, cruel, and often murderous practices that ranged from slavery to brutal wars to 20th-century medical experiments on human subjects.

A troubling example of the latter was the U.S. Public Health Service's 40-year study, begun in 1932, of the effects of long-term syphilis on African-American men. The 399 subjects, all of them poor and most of them sharecroppers, were selected because the study's doctors had diagnosed them with syphilis. The doctors, based at the Tuskegee Institute in Alabama, never told the men that they had syphilis or that it was spread by sexual intercourse. Instead, they told the subjects, along with another 201 healthy African-American men selected as *controls,* that they had qualified for free medical care. Early in the study, doctors gave medication to some of the patients, but none received an adequate dose to treat the disease effectively. (There was no true cure for syphilis at the time.) No steps were taken to prevent the infected men from spreading the disease to their wives or to prevent their children from contracting congenital syphilis. (In the 1940s, when penicillin, a real cure for syphilis, became available, Public Health officials prevented the subjects from getting it.) An investigative reporter finally exposed the secret study in the 1970s. (This book will revisit the Tuskegee Syphilis Study in chapter 8.)

So the Nazis were not unique in their prejudices, but in the 1930s and 1940s, their racist ideas combined with what was then widely considered to be a *scientific* truth about genetic determinism. The deadly mixture lead to the Nazi Holocaust, a mass extermination of Jews, Roma, and others in German-ruled lands. It was state-sanctioned murder of anyone judged by the German regime to be unfit.

Beginning with 1933's Law for Protection Against Genetically Defective Offspring (modeled after the state of Virginia's 1924 law permitting coerced sterilization of the genetically imperfect) and continuing with 1935's Blutschutzgesetz (Blood Protection Law) forbidding marriage or sexual relations between Germans and Jews, the Nazis pursued genetic "improvement" with extremes that would finally, belatedly plunge the field of eugenics into worldwide disgrace.

Surely Hitler could have carried out his genocidal agenda without pseudoscientific rationalization. The fact remains, however, that well-meaning, serious-minded biologists worldwide made it easier for Germany's leader to turn his irrational hatreds into national policy. Nazi philosophers and scientists used and twisted the theories of English, American, and other geneticists in concocting their ugly brand of neo-Darwinism.

Nazi research programs, in turn, helped sadistic charlatans to pose as legitimate researchers. In 1936, the University of Heidelberg, acting at

(continues)

(continued)

the behest of the Nazi government, awarded an honorary degree to Harry H. Laughlin (1880–1943), superintendent of the Eugenic Records Office at Cold Spring Harbor, New York, for his services on behalf of racial hygiene. Although his background was as a Missouri high school agriculture teacher with an interest in animal husbandry, the anti-Semite Laughlin, with help from better-qualified biologists, presented himself as a world authority on human betterment. In a letter of acceptance to Carl Schneider, professor of *racial hygiene* at the University of Heidelberg, Laughlin wrote of his pride at receiving recognition "from a nation which for many centuries nurtured the human seed stock which later founded my own country and thus gave basic character to our present lives and institutions."

Harry H. Laughlin, left, with geneticist Charles Davenport, at the Eugenic Records Office. Davenport founded the office with support from corn flakes inventor John Harvey Kellogg and philanthropist Mrs. Averell Harriman.

In 1939, the year the war began, Germany instituted its T-4 program, administered by physician Philip Bouhler, under which children disabled from birth (and thus "defective") were systematically poisoned or starved to death. Soon doctors were eliminating disabled adults by the same means.

Although some scientists resisted the Nazis and many, especially those of Jewish background, fled Germany after Hitler came to power, other scientists both advocated and participated in the Holocaust, which killed 6 million people. Mengele, nicknamed "Angel of Death," and other Nazi doctors carried out barbaric experiments on prisoners—mostly Jews—whom the researchers treated with virtually the same regard as researchers elsewhere extended to bottle-grown fruit flies. These Nazi researchers included physicians Bruno Weber and Joachim Mrugowsky of the Institute for Hereditary Biology and Racial Hygiene; neuropathologist Julius Hallervorden of the Kaiser Wilhelm Institute; gastroenterology professor Kurt Gutzeit of the University of Breslau; Erwin Gohrbandt, director of surgery at the University Clinic of Berlin; anatomists Hermann Voss of Posen University and Hermann Stieve, director of the Institute of Anatomy at Berlin University; and professor and surgeon August Hirt of the University of Strasbourg. Their experiments included castrations, X-ray sterilization, infecting prisoners with diseases, removing organs and other body parts from living subjects, and injecting various chemicals, usually lethal, into subjects to observe the excruciating results.

One may dismiss Nazi research as both unspeakably unethical and unscientific—fatally flawed by the presuppositions behind it—but it would be irresponsible, especially in a survey of 20th-century biology, to gloss over the fact that so much torture and murder could hide behind so-called scientific principles.

research associate, until Stadler invited her back to the University of Missouri, this time as an assistant professor. At the university in Columbia, Missouri, she again conducted inquiries in which she exposed maize chromosomes to X-rays. McClintock threw herself into this work. The unprepossessing-looking academic—a small woman wearing owlish, round-lens spectacles and a short, no-fuss hairstyle—became known around campus, and among her scientific peers elsewhere, for her enthusiastic dedication to research.

She found that in some cases, the damage that X-ray exposure inflicted on a chromosome would split a single strand into two. She recorded the ways that the broken ends found one another and fused, creating newly configured chromosomes. Some connected with their own ends, to create rings.

McClintock discovered certain plants among those she had previously x-rayed whose chromosomes kept breaking and breaking again, even as the plant grew—without further irradiation. In 1938, she described what she called a *breakage-fusion-bridge cycle*, which involves the way damage and fusion repeat through successive cell cycles. With this work, McClintock set upon a path that would lead to a much deeper and more complex concept of how chromosomes pass along genetic information.

In the 1940s, she became a researcher at Cold Spring Harbor Laboratory in New York, an arm of the Carnegie Institution of Washington, D.C. There is more about McClintock's continuing career in chapter 8.

Making Penicillin Practical

Biochemist Ernst Boris Chain was one of the Jewish scientists who fled Germany as soon as Hitler came to power in 1933. Chain's valuable work in his adopted country, England—like that of so many of his fellow refugees—would eventually strengthen Germany's enemies. Yet his achievements under the direction of Australian-born pathologist Howard Florey proved much more than a wartime edge. As a team, Florey, Chain, and their associates at Oxford University reached the goal that had eluded penicillin discoverer Alexander Fleming. After Chain read an article about penicillin and its potential, written by Fleming, this team was able to isolate, purify, and conduct the first clinical trials of the first antibiotic miracle drug.

Although his family had fallen on hard times after the death of his industrial chemist father when Ernst was only 13, the boy's intellect and talents in mathematics, chemistry, and also music—he was a brilliant pianist—had helped him win admission to the Friedrich Wilhelm University of Berlin, where he studied chemistry and physiology. After graduation, he conducted research at the Kaiser Wilhelm Institute for Physical Chemistry and Electrochemistry, under director Fritz Haber, and then at the Institute of Pathology, Charité Hospital, Berlin. As soon as Hitler became chancellor in 1933, however, doors of opportunity began slamming shut on German Jews. Almost immediately, the government revoked the licenses of Jewish physicians.

Chain realized he had to leave the country. Tragically, he did not realize that the extremes of anti-Semitism in Germany would result in his mother and sister, both of whom stayed in Germany, dying in the coming Holocaust.

In England, Chain considered becoming a professional pianist, but he found a research post in the chemical pathology department at University College Hospital Medical School, London. He was not happy there, however. A malcontent with a quick temper, Chain complained about the lack of first-class laboratory equipment. He resigned in favor of a position at Cambridge under Frederick G. Hopkins, the prolific and inventive biochemist famous for his work on vitamins. Hopkins inspired Chain, as he had an earlier student, Howard Florey.

Florey was by then director of the Sir William Dunn School of Pathology at Oxford, where he was embarking upon something new at the time: assembling an interdisciplinary team of researchers to study diseases and seek cures through several different scientific specialties simultaneously. Their approaches would range, in his design, from conventional physiological and pathological studies down to the chemical and molecular levels. Highly recommended by Hopkins, Chain became one of Florey's first team members in 1936. Chain's volatility continued to bother those with whom he worked, but Florey had a temper, too, and the two scientists—though perhaps ill-matched temperamentally—cooperated well enough.

The son of an English emigrant who had prospered as a shoe manufacturer in Australia, Florey had studied science and medicine at the University of Adelaide, but in the early 20th century, that institution had no program to prepare a student for a career as a researcher. His top-notch grades, combined with success at collegiate tennis, brought him a prestigious Rhodes Scholarship to earn a master's degree at Oxford.

After a postgraduate adventure as a physician for an arctic expedition in the 1920s, a research fellowship had taken Florey to the University of Pennsylvania before he returned to England and earned a Ph.D. in pathology at Cambridge. At Cambridge, he had worked not only with Hopkins but also with Albert Szent-Györgyi (1893–1986), a Hungarian-born biochemist whose many years of investigation into the biochemical nature and role of vitamin C would lead to a 1937 Nobel Prize in physiology or medicine.

At Oxford, Florey asked Chain to assemble a biochemical squad within the new pathology unit. Chain also directed an early project, crystallizing the enzyme lysozyme (also discovered by Fleming) and analyzing its chemical attachment to bacteria. In 1938, as this work neared completion, Florey and Chain decided to study biochemical and biological properties of other enzymes that demonstrated antibacterial properties. Among his gifts, Chain possessed a keen memory, and he recalled having read Fleming's 1929 paper on penicillin. The scientists decided to include the product of mold in the study, thinking that it, like lysozyme, was an enzyme.

Florey's predecessor as director of the Dunn School, during a study of bacteriophages several years before, had gotten a culture of penicillium, the mold that produces penicillin, from Fleming. The school had kept the culture growing. Thus, Chain and Florey already had the raw material for that part of their work. With fellow biochemist Edward Penley Abraham (1913–99), Chain devised a technique to purify and concentrate the substance, something Fleming had not been able to do. By controlling the pH of the liquid that the mold produced and lowering its temperature, then freeze-drying the concentrate, Chain could start with many gallons of raw penicillin and produce a tiny amount, perhaps enough of the purified version to spread over one-half an inch (12.7 mm) of a petri dish bottom.

Early in 1940, Chain directed team researcher Norman Heatley (1911–2004) to inject two laboratory mice with a sample of the purified penicillin. The mice survived without apparent harm. Next, Heatley injected eight mice with a streptococcus infection. An hour later, he gave four of the mice doses of penicillin. As Heatley watched, hour-by-hour, until almost 4 A.M. the next day, the bacteria killed the untreated mice, but not those that had received penicillin. After further testing on hundreds of mice confirmed these results, Chain and Florey reported the group's findings in a paper titled "Penicillin as a Chemotherapeutic Agent," published in the British medical journal *Lancet*. The experimental success of refined penicillin was especially welcome news to military physicians. World War II had begun the previous year and, as Fleming and other frontline surgeons had witnessed in World War I, infection and bacterial illness killed more soldiers than did bullets, shells, bombs, and bayonets combined.

The first human test subject, a man in whom a simple scratch on a rose thorn had become infected with staphylococcus, improved with penicillin treatments but died after the scientists ran out of the drug. Before the team could effectively test their refined penicillin on humans, they had to learn how to make more of the stuff, much more. Young Heatley suggested a chemical method to increase output. The process involved something the researchers already knew, which was that if one takes a solution of water that has been treated to make it acidic (with a pH value greater than 7), mixes it with ether and shakes it, the penicillin will pass into the ether. If the chemist does this with a solution of penicillin in normal, pH-neutral water, the penicillin will not pass into the ether. Heatley discovered that if he first caused the penicillin to pass into the ether, then shook the ether extract with water stabilized at neutral pH, the penicillin would return to a watery state, purified. Heatley also designed a special ceramic container to speed growth of the lab's penicillium cultures.

As Florey's team improved production, its member scientists achieved successes in treating infections in people, first in Britain and then in a

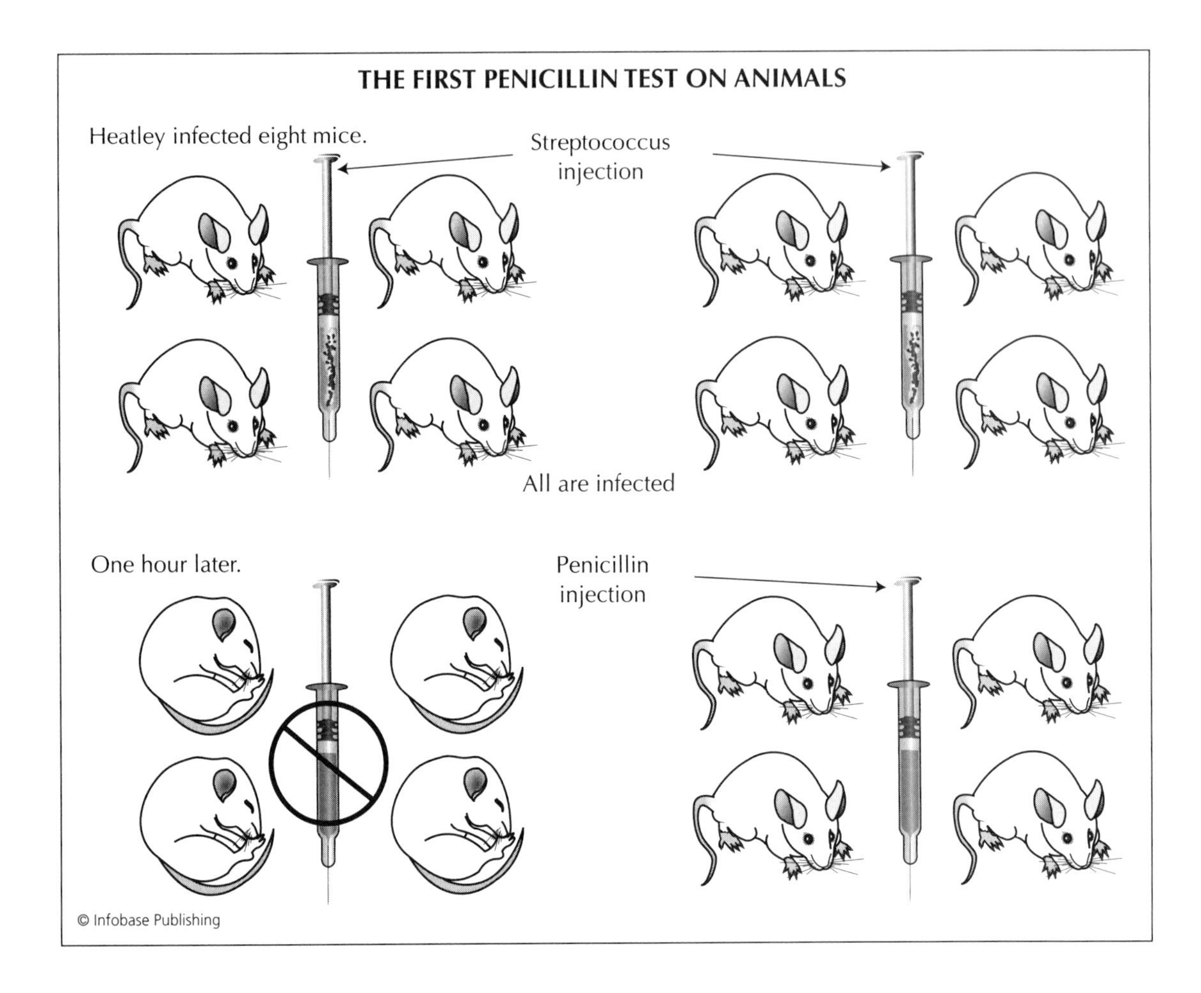

Researcher Norman Heatley tested purified penicillin by infecting eight mice with deadly bacteria. One hour later, he injected half of the subjects with penicillin. Those that received the penicillin survived, but the untreated mice died.

North African battlefield hospital. With each success, it became apparent that Florey's team needed help to produce penicillin in enough quantity to make a real difference. Because British pharmaceutical companies were overwhelmed by the task of producing conventional medicines in quantities required for wartime, Florey turned to the United States government and U.S. industry. He and Heatley made the dangerous flight to America in a blacked-out British plane to plead their case with contacts Florey had made during his earlier, U.S.-based research. It was in America that the penicillin-making process was further refined and improved. By 1943, several companies made penicillin in commercial quantities.

From Minerals to Complex Molecules

X-ray crystallography, the field pioneered by another team in England—W. Lawrence Bragg and his father, William Henry Bragg—belonged first under the umbrella of physics, yet its impact on biology could hardly have been greater.

Beginning in the late 1920s, researchers competed to learn more about the structure of complex molecules using X-ray crystallography. In the 1930s, many researchers turned their ionization spectrometers (an X-ray diffraction device invented by William Bragg) from the structure of inorganic minerals to that of organic compounds, progressing to proteins and amino acids in a line of inquiry that would later lead to the all-important nucleic acids.

A formal portrait of the young chemist Linus Pauling, who applied his understanding of chemical bonds to the molecules that make up living matter. (Ava Helen and Linus Pauling Papers, Oregon State University Library)

Lawrence Bragg competed in the race to understand the nature of large inorganic molecules such as silicates, pitting himself against Linus Pauling, the dazzling young Caltech researcher. Pauling got there first. The competition then turned into a long-distance race to understand fully the molecular structure of proteins. (Pauling prevailed again, well over a decade later.) Meanwhile, John Desmond Bernal (1901–71), a protégée of William Bragg, helped steer crystallographic studies toward investigations of organic and living matter. A student of Bernal—Dorothy Crowfoot, later Dorothy Crowfoot Hodgkin (1910–94)—became one of the first scientists who would use the technique to examine proteins.

Pauling trained in chemistry—first at Oregon Agricultural College (now Oregon State University) in Corvalis and then at Caltech, where he used X-ray crystallography in his doctoral studies on the molecular structure of minerals. While on a mid-1920s Guggenheim Fellowship to Munich, he encountered the fascinating new realm of particle physics expressed in the theories of German physicists Werner Heisenberg (1901–76) and Erwin Schrödinger (1887–1961). Heisenberg's purely mathematical approach, called *matrix mechanics*, and Schrödinger's somewhat-easier-to-grasp *quantum mechanics*, were essentially two ways of getting at the same understanding of the way matter behaves at the subatomic level. This new science effectively demolished the idea that electrons orbit an atom's nucleus like planets around the Sun. It also upset rather simplistic notions about how and why certain atoms bonded with others—Pauling's field.

Back at Caltech, where he joined the faculty in 1927, Pauling applied his background in practical chemistry, his skill at crystallography, and

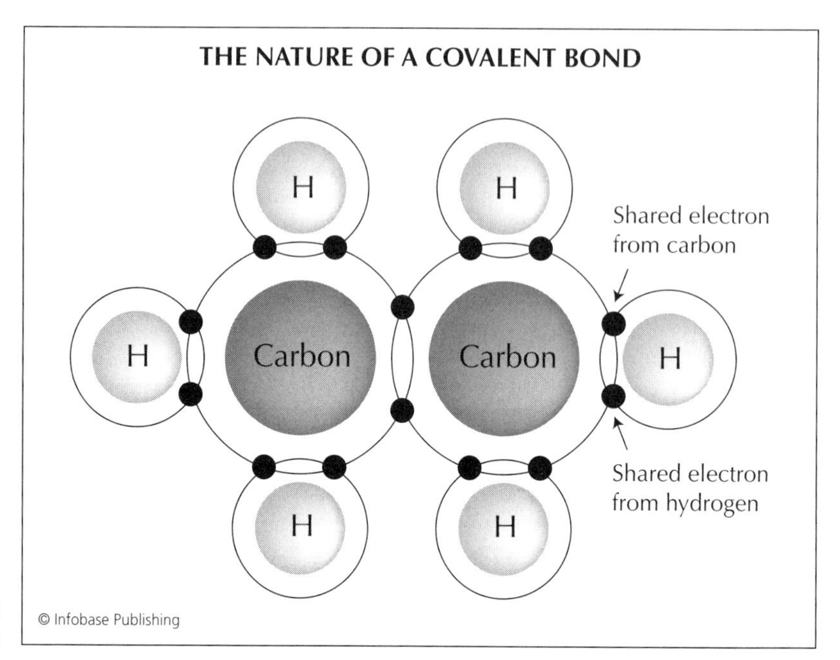

Covalent bonds happen when two atoms share an electron pair.

his newly expanded, theoretical physicist's approach to atomic structure, all toward the mechanics of atoms linking into molecules. Over the course of the 1930s, Pauling produced a series of papers and a landmark book explaining, as his title (for all of the papers and the book) states, *The Nature of the Chemical Bond.* Now a classic, the book works out the ways that bonds arise from the attraction of unlike electric charges. For example, *ionic bonds* are a type of linkage formed from electrostatic attraction between oppositely charged *ions.* They form when the outermost (or valence) electrons of one atom transfer permanently to another atom. *Covalent bonds* happen when two atoms share an electron pair. Most chemical bonds are a hybrid of both of these phenomena.

By exploring and understanding such forces, specific to each compound, Pauling got at the specifics of the angles at which atoms connect, thus pointing toward the 1953 discovery of the double-helix structure of DNA (a discovery he would try to make himself), arguably the greatest breakthrough in 20th-century biology.

In the 1930s, he also became a cofounder of the field of molecular biology, a cross-disciplinary science that did not have a name until 1938, when Warren Weaver (1894–1978) of the Rockefeller Institute gave it one. Weaver, a cross-disciplinarian himself (he had taught math at the University of Wisconsin before concentrating on life sciences), saw in Pauling the young scientist he was looking for, someone to apply the newest breakthroughs in molecular science to the study of living things. He influenced Pauling's direction by recommending Rockefeller Foundation funding for the Californian's research into organic molecules and proteins. One Rockefeller grant specifically paid for Pauling's inquiries, beginning in 1935, into the molecular structure of hemoglobin. That study would lead him to identify sickle-cell anemia as a molecular disease.

Another multifaceted scientist and teacher, John Desmond Bernal, also turned from examinations of mineral molecules toward organic molecules in the 1930s. Bernal, who had served on the elder Bragg's research staff at the Royal Institution in London in the 1920s, was one of the more colorful figures in 20th-century science. Although a devout Catholic in his boyhood, he became an outspoken atheist, socialist, and sometime Communist Party member who over his career concerned himself with matters that included the molecular structure of proteins, the role of science in an enlightened society, military strategies for Britain in the World War II invasion of Normandy, the origin of life on Earth, and ahead-of-his time ideas about how humans could and must colonize outer space.

From Tipperary, Ireland, Bernal had displayed a wide-ranging and precocious intellect from childhood. At age two, he could converse easily in French as well as English. He arrived at Cambridge University in 1919, bent on studying mineralogy and the mathematics of symmetry. Soon the young Irishman was known to friends and associates as "the Sage of Cambridge," or simply "Sage."

Dorothy Crowfoot also was precocious, captivated by chemistry from age 10. She was born in Cairo, where father was a school administrator and later an archaeologist and her mother a botanist. The girl spent summers with them in Egypt and later British Palestine but grew up largely in England, at boarding schools. At her school in Suffolk, she was one of only two girls allowed to join the chemistry class, usually open only to boys.

At Somerville College, Oxford, Crowfoot learned crystallography, still an experimental, tedious procedure. She used the technique to study the structural arrangement of the atoms in simple salts and minerals. The young woman so impressed her professors that one of them secured a fellowship that sent her to work with Bernal at Cambridge, where he was making a name for himself with his crystallographic examinations of the molecular structure of metals. In 1933, as Crowfoot joined him to begin working toward her Ph.D., Bernal was just turning his attention from metals to organic compounds.

Under Bernal's tutelage, she took diffraction photos of sterols, a subgroup of steroids. (Steroids encompass a broad category of compounds with a basic ring structure in common. Cholesterol is one of many sterols. Sterols often occur in cell membranes.) She also took the first X-ray diffraction photograph of pepsin, a digestive enzyme that breaks down proteins. Enzymes are themselves proteins, and this research delved into proteins' molecular structure, which is more complex than that of other biological molecules. Proteins are polymers, long chains of repeating units. Pauling would later work out the way they fold over on themselves into specific three-dimensional molecular shapes. The

Dorothy Crowfoot Hodgkin, while a graduate student, pioneered a technique for studying the molecules of proteins and nucleic acids. (AIP Emilio Segrè Visual Archives, Physics Today Collection)

relative complexity of these molecules, larger than other biological molecules, led many early molecular geneticists to believe that a protein, not a nucleic acid, carried the mechanism by which hereditary traits pass from generation to generation.

Using pepsin, Bernal and Crowfoot discovered that wet protein crystals—that is, those crystals still surrounded by the natural fluid in which they occur—give off far better X-ray diffraction patterns than do dried crystals. Up until that time, crystallographers had used dried crystals in probing organic compounds. By discerning the diffraction pattern of a wet, globular protein, Bernal and Hodgkin pointed the way toward a historic photograph. It would be taken in the early 1950s by a student trained by Bernal at his next professorial post, at Birbeck College of the University of London. That later student's name was Rosalind Franklin (1920–58), and she would provide a crucial clue to the structure of DNA.

Dorothy Crowfoot continued her research after her 1934 return to Oxford, where she spent much of an academic career that would greatly advance molecular biology and lead to her 1964 Nobel Prize in chemistry (under her married name, Dorothy Crowfoot Hodgkin) for determining the structure of vitamin B_{12}. After raising money for new X-ray crystallography equipment, she soon crystallized insulin, another protein, by devising a technique whereby she replaced one atom within the insulin molecule with another, heavier, atom—in this case, an atom of zinc. The method helped her better interpret her diffraction images. She was soon able to report the molecular structure of insulin, only the second protein after pepsin to yield its secrets to such research.

Dorothy Crowfoot, still at the beginning of what would be a 34-year course of crystallographic experiments, had emerged as a rising star of science. Still, the Oxford faculty chemistry club barred her from its meetings because she was a woman. It would be several years before she would break down that barrier. In 1937, she married historian Thomas Hodgkin, a specialist in the history and politics of Africa and the Arab world. That year, Dorothy Crowfoot Hodgkin also received her doctorate.

Tracking Disease to the Molecular Level

Well before the electron microscope (which came into general use around 1940), immunologists knew of the existence of disease agents much smaller than bacteria. Russian bacteriologist Dimitri Ivanovski (1864–1920) blamed such an agent in 1892 for tobacco mosaic disease—named for the crazy-quilt patterns that the blight left in *Nicotiana tabacum* leaves on Ukrainian plantations. Between 1915 and 1917, Frederick William Twort and Félix d'Hérelle had discovered (and d'Hérelle named) bacteriophages, the sometimes helpful viruses that infect and kill bacteria. To study viruses that sickened people, immunologists tried for decades to find animal hosts that were susceptible to the same viral infections, but these efforts often failed.

It was not until the mid-1930s that scientists began thinking of viruses in molecular terms. Viruses are large molecules, far simpler than living agents better known at the time, yet able to invade the cells of other living things and thus replicate themselves. A major breakthrough came in 1935 as U.S. biochemist Wendell Meredith Stanley, at the Rockefeller Institute for Medical Research's labs in Princeton, New Jersey, first crystallized the same type of virus—tobacco mosaic—that Ivanovski had identified more than 40 years earlier. A virus crystal contains several thousand virus molecules. In this purified form, it provides a better subject for chemical analysis than the virus in its unaltered state.

Stanley, from the eastern Indiana village of Ridgeville, had excelled in school, entering Earlham College, a small Quaker institution, at age 16. He majored in chemistry and math and was a football star at the college in Richmond, Indiana. He was contemplating a career as a football coach when he visited the University of Illinois in 1929. A chemistry professor in Urbana convinced Stanley that he should pursue a graduate degree in science. Three years at Illinois, followed by a year of study at the University of Munich (with fellow researcher and new wife, Marian Jay Stanley) led to the Rockefeller Institute and its medical research arm in New Jersey, which had just established a laboratory of plant pathology.

Stanley had thought that viruses consisted completely, or largely, of protein. At the Rockefeller lab, he and colleagues followed the feat of crystallizing the tobacco mosaic virus—demonstrating that it was a large molecule—by an analysis that showed the molecule contained equal parts protein and nucleic acid. Around this time, Stanley's laboratory colleague John Howard Northrop (1891–1987) speculated that a nucleic acid was the agent of bacteriophage activity. Northrop's view gained credence from the work of two British biochemists, Norman Wingate Pirie (1907–97) and Frederick Charles Bawden (1908–72), who in 1937 isolated RNA from a virus that causes disease in potatoes. Pirie and Bawden further showed that the nucleic acid in the tobacco mosaic virus and other viruses was RNA. Northrup, a graduate of Columbia University

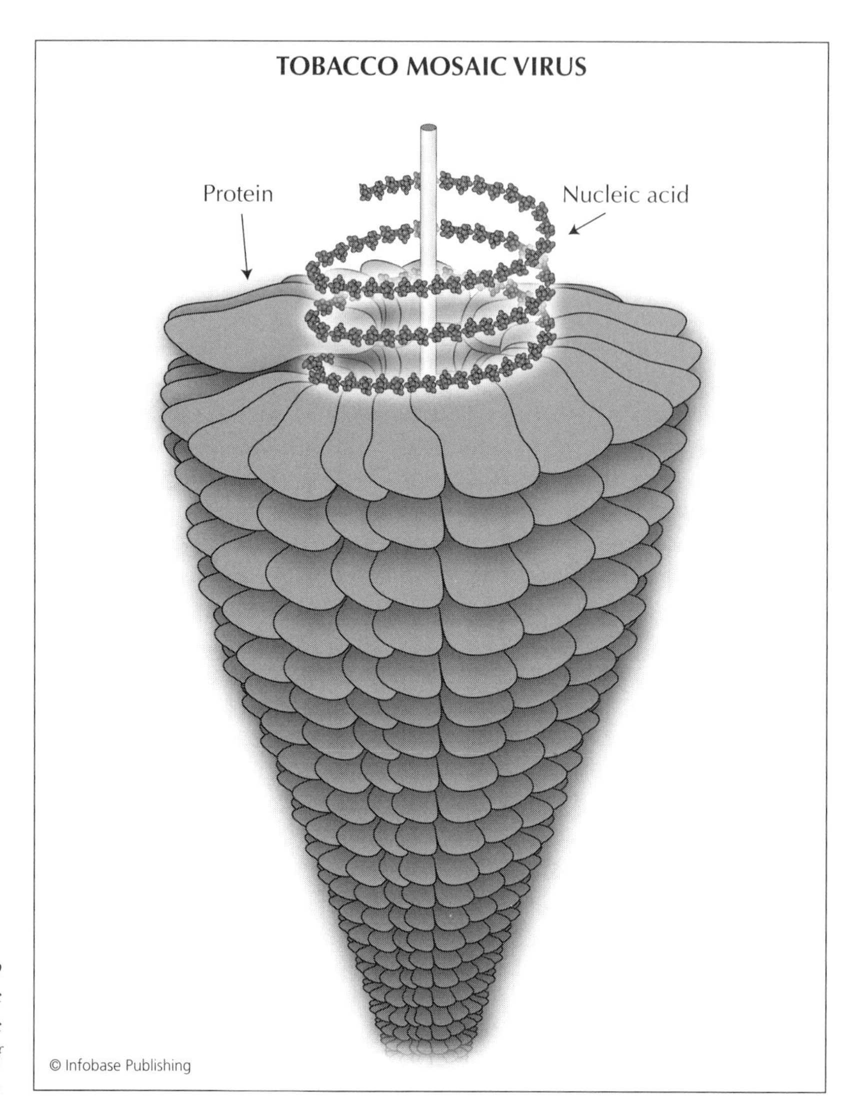

By crystallizing the tobacco mosaic virus, Stanley was able to reveal its molecular structure and show that it was made of nucleic acid as well as protein.

and a former U.S. Army captain (in a chemical warfare unit) would share the 1946 Nobel Prize in chemistry with Stanley (and James B. Sumner (1887–1955), who had crystallized an enzyme, urease, in 1926).

The crystallization of tobacco mosaic virus made it possible for crystallographers to begin probing its molecular structure. Stanley's continued studies of viruses led to vaccines against influenza and polio (although his vaccine was not the one adopted for general use). He also brought the discipline of virology to the University of California, Berkeley, where he continued to shape the growing field of biophysics and became chairman of the school's Department of Biochemistry.

Population Genetics

Mathematics—so vital to crystallography—plays a role in every area of biological research (and science in general). Gregor Mendel began the field of experimental genetics with carefully kept records and resulting ratios of hereditary traits. A subarea, the field of population genetics, depended on an algebraic equation, the Hardy-Weinberg principle, formulated in the first decade of the century. This field took on an important new perspective in the 1930s because of the work of University of Chicago population geneticist Sewall Wright (1895–1988). He was a keen statistician who was able to take numbers gleaned from research and project the rate of trait distribution among organisms, especially mammal populations.

Named after codiscoverers Godfrey H. Hardy (1877–1947), a Cambridge mathematician, and Wilhelm Weinberg (1862–1937), a German physician, the principle applies to a large, stable, random mating population. It states that, in general, the proportion of dominant and recessive genes in that group stays the same from generation to generation—unless outside forces such as migration or habitat exert an influence. This means that even the rarest genes do not disappear, as might seem likely, but stay distributed among the population. Within a hypothetical population of mice in which 80 percent of the gametes carry a dominant allele for black coat (B) and 20 percent the recessive allele for gray coat (b), random mating will produce a generation with 64 percent homozygous for BB ($0.8 \times 0.8 = 0.64$), with 32 percent Bb heterozygotes ($0.8 \times 0.2 \times 2 = 0.32$), and 4 percent homozygous (bb) for gray coat ($0.2 \times 0.2 = 0.04$). The resulting generation will have a ratio of 96 percent black coats to 4 percent gray, making it seem that gray-coated mice will eventually disappear.

That assumption fails to figure in the fact that, although all the gametes formed by homozygous BB black mice will contain allele B, only one-half of the gametes formed by heterozygous black (Bb) mice will contain allele B. All the gametes of the gray (bb) mice will contain b, as will one-half of the gametes of the heterozygous mice.

Hardy and Weinberg's formula showed why selective, rather than random, mating must occur for there to be natural selection. If genetic traits are selected for or selected against as organisms choose mates, their choices will alter the proportion of certain dominant genes to their recessive counterparts.

In 1935, Wright put forward his new perspective on this matter. Born in Maine, Sewall Green Wright was of old New England stock but grew up in Galesburg, Illinois, where his father had taken a position teaching mathematics, astronomy, surveying, economics, English composition, and physical education at the very small Lombard College. An intellectually precocious though shy boy, Sewall was fascinated with both math and the natural world from an early age.

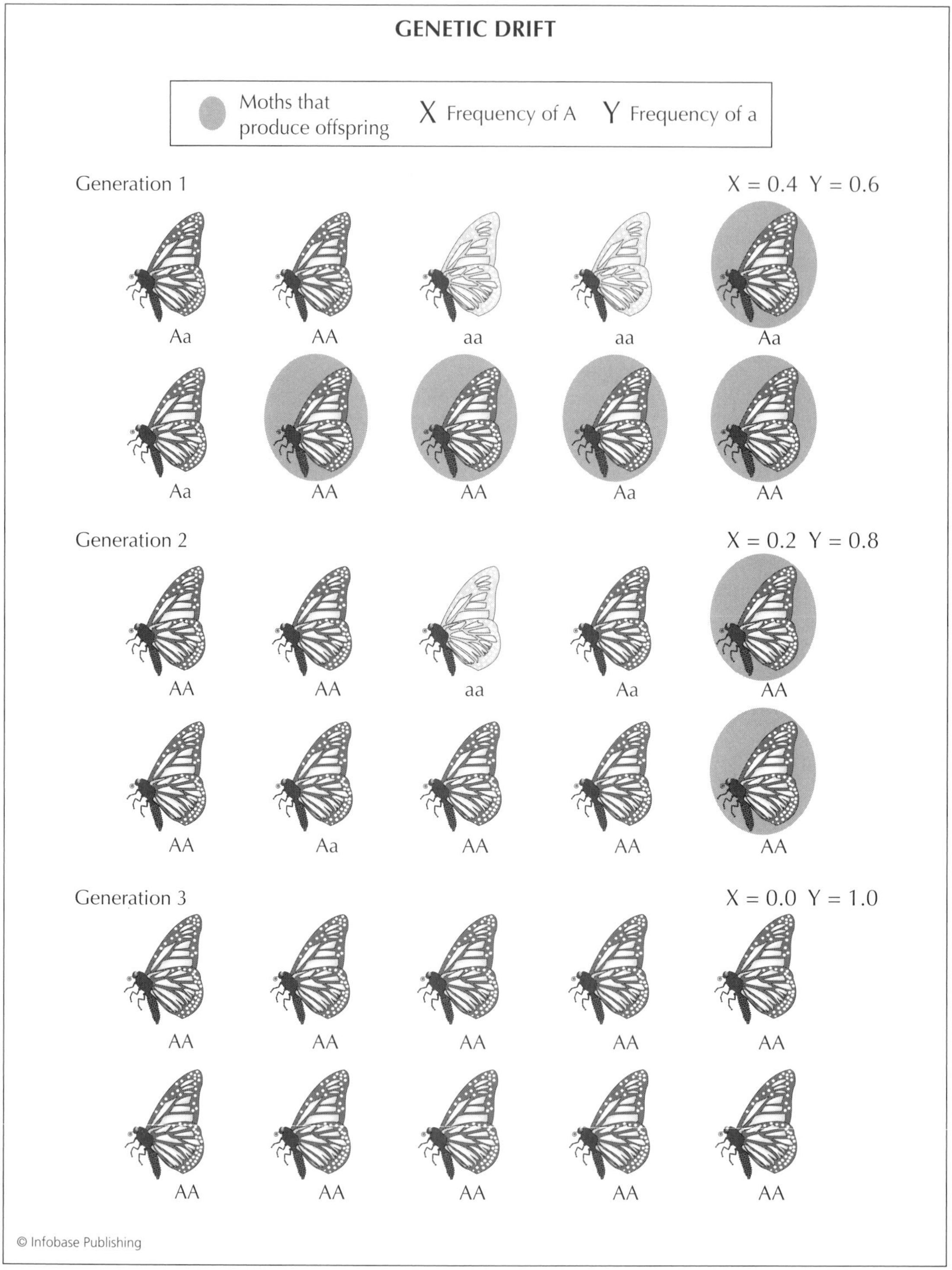

GENETIC DRIFT

Moths that produce offspring
X Frequency of A
Y Frequency of a

Generation 1
X = 0.4 Y = 0.6
Aa AA aa aa Aa
Aa AA AA Aa AA

Generation 2
X = 0.2 Y = 0.8
AA AA aa Aa AA
AA Aa AA AA AA

Generation 3
X = 0.0 Y = 1.0
AA AA AA AA AA
AA AA AA AA AA

(Opposite page) Wright showed statistically that chance events can cause relatively rare traits—in this instance, the recessive gene for the transparent wing—to disappear, resulting in a population carrying only the dominant gene.

Although he began a double major in mathematics and surveying at Lombard (and spent a summer working as a railroad surveyor), he won a fellowship to pursue a master's degree in biology from the University of Illinois, which led to a doctorate in zoology from Harvard. His thesis focused on the genetics of fur colors in guinea pigs.

After working for the U.S. Department of Agriculture, Wright came to the University of Chicago. There his statistical studies (based on his own breeding experiments and on numbers collected from other researchers) led him to put forward his new theory, genetic drift. It is not contrary to the Hardy-Weinberg principle, but rather a complementary addendum to the rule. Also called genetic sampling error or the Sewall Wright effect, genetic drift tends to apply to a small population of a species, especially when isolated—for example, by geography, as on an island or on one side of a deep canyon. In such a case, the few individuals who carry relatively rare genes may fail to transmit them—purely by chance. Those genes then may disappear. The loss of those rare genes may subsequently lead to the emergence of new species, even though there was no sexual selection or survival advantage at work.

This will occur in a small rather than in a large population, just as a tossed coin may come up tails every time in a small number of throws, despite the statistical odds of heads and tails being exactly even.

Genetic drift can also result in certain genetic traits becoming widespread in a small population, regardless of the survival advantage or reproductive value of the alleles responsible for those traits. After Wright identified this effect, geneticists accepted it as part of an increasingly sophisticated understanding of heredity. His work helped move theoretical genetics further beyond the relatively simple "survival of the fittest" Darwinism of the previous century.

In a 1938 article in *Science*, British biologist Julian Huxley (1887–1975) introduced the concept of a *cline* to the study of genetic variation. The cline refers to a gradual genetic-morphological variation within a single species spread over a broad geographical area. The idea contrasted with

Julian Huxley was a grandson of biologist T. H. Huxley and brother of novelist Aldous Huxley. (Fondren Library, Woodson Research Center, Rice University)

traditional taxonomy, which tended to separate species strictly on the basis of morphology (color, size, structure, and so on), in that it led to the consensus that two animals, even when they look considerably different, belong to the same species as long as they are genetically compatible. If their mating regularly produces a fertile offspring, the two populations are subcategories of a larger species. The cline also applies to evolution, with gradual genetic change over time blending one population into another, seemingly different population.

Toward a Science of Ecology

Like his grandfather—the 19th-century giant T. H. Huxley—Julian Huxley was an educator and philosopher as well as a scientist. He came from a naturalist's tradition that encouraged general thought as well as specific observation. As the 20th century progressed and as theoretical geneticists, cytologists, biochemists, and physicists probed ever deeper into the microscopic mysteries at the core of the life process, biologists such as Huxley continued to look at a bigger picture.

Since Aristotle, naturalists had been examining plants and animals as whole organisms and, beyond that, observing the relationships between these organisms. Their subjects included relationships between members of a species, between different species, and, ultimately, between living things and the environments in which they lived. This observation gave rise to the rather obvious consensus that all life is interconnected and that organisms are not just dependent upon the natural systems in which they occur but essential parts of such systems.

As early as 1873, German zoologist Ernst Haeckel (1834–1919), a dedicated proponent of evolutionary theory, had coined the term *Ökologie* to refer to the interrelationship of organisms and their environment. The term soon found its way into English as *ecology*. In 1875, Australian geologist Eduard Suess (1831–1914) had suggested the term *biosphere* for the interlocking conditions—ranging from minerals and gases to flora and fauna—promoting life on Earth.

By the 1920s, the Russian geologist Vladimir Ivanovich Vernadsky (1853–1945) had correctly recognized that living things produce the oxygen, carbon dioxide, and nitrogen in the atmosphere. Considered a founder of the interdisciplinary science of *biogeochemistry*, Vernadsky also studied the ways that living things and their by-products help build the chemical components of Earth's crust.

This growing recognition of organisms' diverse and numerous roles in an interdependent biosphere eventually resonated throughout biological research, but environmental biology was a field slow to gain widespread respect. (It is revisited in chapter 7.) The perspective of such scientists as those mentioned above, however, popped up in the 1930s in a context less cerebral-seeming: the 1933 book *Game Management* by Iowa-born,

Yale-educated naturalist Aldo Leopold (1887–1948), codirector of the U.S. Forest Products Laboratory in Madison, Wisconsin.

Game Management was (and remains) a practical guide for foresters, game wardens, and park rangers. Yet in it, Leopold put forth his distinctive view of a natural community, a personal perspective developed during his years in the Forest Service. In this handbook, he described techniques for protecting and restoring wildlife populations. Interweaving forestry, agriculture, biology, zoology, and ecology, among other scientific fields, while putting a strong emphasis on communication and education, Leopold pointed toward his philosophy of *land ethic* that he would articulate in his later, highly influential book *A Sand County Almanac.*

Around the same time, in 1935, British ecologist Arthur Tansley (1871–1955), a botanist by training who had founded and been longtime editor of the magazines the *New Phytologist* and *Journal of Ecology*, coined the word *ecosystem*, with a meaning quite close to that of Leopold's natural community. The term encompasses a complex of organisms within a particular geographical boundary, along with every aspect of their physical environment—biological, behavioral, chemical, geological, and any combination thereof—emphasizing the interrelationships between these aspects. *Ecosystem* can mean a delta wetland, a forest, a pond, or even a decaying log. Again, despite such forward-looking groundwork, the science of ecology would have to wait until the later decades of the century before taking its place as a major area of study.

A Visitor from the Ancient Past

As new fields arose within biology, as new disciplines increasingly linked biology with other specialties such as chemistry, physics, and geology, the work of that original breed of biologist—the naturalist—went on as before. Naturalists—ranging from sophisticated professional field researchers to self-trained amateurs—continued to examine and evaluate the natural world by observing nature and collecting specimens from it. This approach could produce fascinating examples of living things. It still can.

Marjorie Courtenay-Latimer (1907–2004) trained as a nurse, not a field biologist, before she landed a job that better suited her intense interest in nature study. As curator of a tiny museum in a small South African port city northeast of Cape Town, she was able to return to her girlhood fascination with birds and other animals and plants. She built up the museum's nature and science collection with collecting jaunts into the South African countryside. For example, in 1935 she and a fellow enthusiast unearthed an almost complete fossil skeleton of a dinosaur from the Triassic, *Kannemeyeria simocephalus.*

History remembers Courtenay-Latimer for another discovery, often called the zoological find of the 20th-century. Just before Christmas in

1938, she picked out a freshly caught fish from a local trawler's haul at the port of East London, South Africa. The creature belonged to a genus that ichthyologists and paleontologists thought had been extinct for 80 million years.

The 32-year-old curator's interest in marine life had made her a familiar figure to East London–based fishing boat crews. The men enjoyed talking with her about their more exotic catches. Hendrick Goosen, captain of the trawler *Nerine*, liked to help her out by having the dock attendant telephone the museum when he pulled up anything that he thought Courtenay-Latimer might find interesting. When the dockman called that day in December 1938, the curator was busy mounting an exhibition and almost decided not to go down to the waterfront for a look. With the holiday coming up, she later reported, she decided it would be impolite to decline, so she hailed a taxicab and went down to give Goosen and his crew her best wishes for Christmas and the New Year.

Hurried, she paid less attention than usual to the pile of fish on the deck of the *Nerine*, but she could not ignore a glimpse of a luminescent blue-and-silver fin buried among the haul. Pulling aside other fish, she discovered one unlike any creature she had seen before: five feet (2.5 m) long with fins—including the middle section of the tail fin—that seemed to grow on the ends of short, bony stalks. She did not know what it was, but she thought it best to save the specimen.

After an argument with the cab driver, who did not want the monster in his vehicle, especially on a hot December day (December is high summer in the Southern Hemisphere), she talked him into transporting her prize back to the museum. Then she turned to her limited library of reference books, trying to figure out what it was. She knew it was not a rock cod, as the president of the museum board of directors thought, but could it be what it appeared? One of her books depicted and described an extinct fish, a coelacanth. It had a trilobed tail like her specimen, and the rest of the fin configuration also seemed to match.

Seeking an informed opinion, Courtenay-Latimer wrote to James L. B. Smith (1897–1968) at Rhodes University in Grahamstown, South Africa. She enclosed a rough sketch. Although a chemistry professor, Smith was also a self-educated ichthyologist. When he saw the sketch, he recognized it as belonging to the order *Coelacanthiformes*, that is, a coelacanth. No naturalist had ever recorded one except as an ancient fossil. He cabled her back immediately, asking that she preserve the skeleton and viscera.

It was already too late for the curator to do as he asked. Refrigeration was not common in 1938 South Africa. The only facilities in East London with sufficient refrigerator space to preserve the big fish were a hospital morgue and a commercial cold-storage business. Neither wanted anything to do with this strange creature. The curator soaked cloths in formaldehyde and wrapped the coelacanth in them. She did not have enough of the chemical in which to sink a 150-pound (68.8-kg) specimen.

Scientist of the Decade: Linus Pauling (1901–1994)

Linus Pauling won the first of his two Nobel Prizes in 1954, for chemistry. In the words of the Royal Swedish Academy of Sciences (which chooses the Nobel awardees in chemistry, physics, and economics) he was recognized "for his research into the nature of the chemical bond and its application to the elucidation of the structure of complex substances."

Specifically, that referred to the work that Pauling had begun in the late 1920s, the work that he had spent much of the 1930s expanding upon, refining, and explaining in the series of writings that culminated with his 1939 book *The Nature of the Chemical Bond.*

The academy's deliberately broad language, however, embraced much more than Pauling's marrying of theoretical particle physics to biochemistry, with its complex substances. It applied to the scientist's research into immunology and genetics, which were essentially continuations of his explorations into the chemical bond. For example, Pauling's 1930s investigations of sickle-cell anemia led him to announce that it is a genetic disease occurring at the molecular level. Many of his scientific peers thought he merited a Nobel Prize in physiology based on that discovery alone.

For that matter, Pauling's insights into the forces that bond atoms into molecules can be seen as vital underpinnings for the entire field of molecular biology—the field that led other scientists to the structure of DNA and amazing developments that have followed in fields from medicine to agriculture to crime solving. That fact may not have been apparent to the 1954 selection committee of the Swedish Academy, as it was only the previous year that James Watson and Francis Crick had edged past Pauling to finish first in the race to discover DNA's structure. Watson and Crick's discovery, however, could not have escaped the notice of academy members, who surely knew that the two Cambridge researchers had reached their conclusion by building a three-dimensional model of the DNA molecule, a technique that Pauling had shown valuable as early as 1927. The academy understood that Pauling was one of the giants upon whose shoulders the new DNA wizards stood.

Born in Portland, Oregon, Linus Pauling grew up poor. His father, Herman, was a self-educated pharmacist, hardworking but not prosperous. His mother, Belle, came from a remote small town and had little education. Young Pauling read voraciously, with the encouragement of his father, who also taught him Latin phrases.

A perforated ulcer killed Herman Pauling around the time of Linus's ninth birthday. Young Belle had little idea of how she could afford to feed, clothe, and house her son and his two younger sisters. She managed to open a boardinghouse, a steady source of modest income. However, her health was not good, and she suggested Linus quit school so that he could help support the family.

He resisted. Linus picked up extra money for his mother with odd jobs such as delivering milk and running a projector in a Portland movie house as he accelerated through his classes, reaching high school two years ahead of other children his age. He also found time for his own reading and science, pursuits that Belle thought frivolous. He began collecting insects, using library books to identify his finds. He developed a deep interest in minerals. After a friend showed him some simple chemical reactions, Linus became hooked on chemistry. He built a lab in the boardinghouse basement, using industrial chemicals he found in a shed at an abandoned foundry.

Pauling took all the classes in physical science and mathematics that his high school offered, receiving excellent grades. He was less interested in history and put off registering for two required courses until his final semester. School rules forbade taking the two courses simultaneously, so Pauling dropped out without graduating. With his mother's blessing, he took a job in a machine shop. The family of a friend, however, convinced Linus that he must go to college.

Pauling started at Oregon Agricultural College in Corvallis in 1917. Apparently, no high school

(continues)

(continued)

diploma was required. (The high school awarded him one decades later, after he had won his second Nobel Prize.) At first, Belle sent him $25 a month. When she was no longer able to do that, Pauling found several ways to earn money. His jobs included chopping wood for the cookstove and other kitchen tasks for the girls' dormitory. He later noted that the need to work so hard while studying trained him not to waste time. Soon he was able to cover his own expenses and send a little money home.

In fall 1920, the chair of the chemistry department offered Pauling a job teaching quantitative analysis. Still an undergraduate, Pauling had taken the course only the previous spring. While teaching a class of freshmen, he met Ava Helen Miller (1903–81), who would in 1923 become his wife. He later called it the most important encounter of his life.

Pauling received his degree in industrial chemistry in 1922. Ignoring Belle's renewed pleas that he get a full-time job—perhaps as a high school teacher—he chose between Harvard, which had offered him a half-time teaching post, and the California Institute of Technology, a small but excellently staffed and ambitious institution where Arthur Amos Noyes (1866–1936) had only recently established a first-rate chemistry faculty. Pauling chose Caltech, where he arrived in 1922. By the end of that decade, the institution had earned a worldwide reputation as a scientific research center, partly on the strength of Pauling's work.

Noyes assigned Pauling to work with Roscoe Gilkey Dickinson (1894–1945), a specialist in the new field of X-ray crystallography. As a graduate student, the tall, genial young chemist from Oregon developed a reputation for a peculiarly intuitive way of approaching scientific problems—a method that made some other scientists uneasy. Pauling would make an educated guess about something such as the molecular makeup of a compound and then go to work on arranging the data and working calculations to support his idea. Perhaps what most bothered some of his peers, who saw this approach as procedurally backward, arrogant, and potentially wasteful, was that Pauling's intuitions so often proved right.

Noyes arranged Pauling's Guggenheim Fellowship to Germany in 1925, as soon as the young scientist had earned his Ph.D. Noyes's motive was, at least in part, to prevent Pauling from accepting an assistant professorship at the University of California, Berkeley. Noyes had built a reputation as a keen recruiter of talent, both at MIT, where he had been acting president, and at Caltech. Determined not to lose Pauling to another university, the department head let Pauling know that he would be a welcome addition to the faculty in Pasadena after he returned to the United States.

The fellowship sent Pauling to the University of Munich, where he worked with theoretical physicist Arnold Sommerfeld (1868–1951) and met both Heisenberg and Schrödinger. By 1926, he had adopted the latter's quantum mechanics in his approach to chemical bonds and the structure of molecules. This orientation was still so new that Pauling was among a handful of Americans who both understood the new physics and saw how it could be applied to chemistry.

Pauling found a jumping-off point for his own work in the research of Walter Heitler (1904–81) and Fritz London (1900–54). These associates of Schrödinger applied his *wave equations,* a crucial part of quantum mechanics, to the bond between two hydrogen atoms. Using the concept that Heisenberg called *exchange energy,* they proposed that as two atoms near each other, the positively charged nucleus of one attracts a negatively charged electron from the other. An electron from the second atom, meanwhile, feels the pull from the first. This proceeds, according to their theory, until the electrons are hopping back and forth between the two nuclei, as if neither belonged to one single atom but both were shared between them. The two nuclei, meanwhile, being both positively charged, repel each other. The result of these competing electrical forces is a stable chemical attachment.

Heitler and London had explained the simplest chemical bond in nature. Pauling embraced their work and, as a chemist, set out to expand upon it. By 1928, he was able to announce, in a note to the National Academy of Sciences, that quantum mechanics could explain the *tetrahedral* binding of carbon. The makings of life—proteins, starches, and fats—are all formed upon carbon atoms.

Pauling was talking about the chemistry underlying biology. He proceeded to show that the physicist's view of this crucial element—that its four binding electrons occur in two slightly different energy levels, with only two in the outermost level able to bind with other atoms—and the chemist's view—that carbon offers four strong bonds to other atoms (forming a tetrahedron, or three-sided pyramid)—were compatible.

Pauling proposed that the electron exchange energy that came from forming four tetrahedral bonds actually took carbon's four binding electrons out of their *subshells*—as the physicist saw it.

Pauling immersed himself in the problems of solving molecular structures. Taking off from William Lawrence Bragg's assertion that basic structural patterns are often repeated in different crystals, he assembled simple rules indicating which basic molecular patterns were most likely in complex crystals. These guidelines allowed Pauling to develop a relatively simple procedure for eliminating scores of unlikely crystal structures and predicating the most likely ones. He delineated his guidelines in a 1929 article for the *Journal of the American Chemical Society*. Soon researchers were calling them "Pauling's rules."

Around this time, he also began building models of crystal and molecule structures using wire, wooden balls, and other material. With Pauling's rules to guide him and his intuitive grasp of the way electrical attraction and repulsion ruled the behavior of electrons and atomic nuclei, he could indulge more fully in his favorite working method—starting with the likely structure and then filling in the mathematical blanks, which in those precomputer times took many, many long hours of mental-manual calculations.

In 1931, the American Chemical Society awarded Pauling the Langmuir Prize for "the most noteworthy work in pure science done by a man [sic] under 30 years of age," and MIT offered him a full professorship. Preferring Pasadena, he instead negotiated with the prestigious Cambridge, Massachusetts, institution to come for a one-year visiting professorship. Two years later, at 32, he became the youngest person ever appointed to the National Academy of Sciences. In 1939, he became chair of Caltech's Division of Chemistry and Chemical Engineering.

Linus Pauling hiking with son Linus, Jr., on his back. (Ava Helen and Linus Pauling Papers, Oregon State University Library)

Pauling's mid-1930s work on hemoglobin began a period of intense inquiry into the chemistry of life, including most of a decade during which he and colleagues established the structures of many small peptides, which are organic substances made of linked amino acids, as are proteins, but much smaller than proteins. That

(continues)

(continued)

is, a peptide may contain as few as two amino acids linked together. A simple protein molecule is a very large polypeptide chain, a sequence of about 20 different amino acids repeated over and over. It was not until 1948—while bedridden with a kidney infection—that Pauling worked out the alpha helix structure of a polypeptide, using folded paper to make a model of a protein molecule.

During and especially after World War II, Pauling took up causes of social justice. He joined wife, Ava Helen, and other Californians in protesting the wartime internment of Japanese Americans. Pauling, who had declined an invitation to work on the Manhattan Project but contributed to other military weapons research during the war, came to see nuclear bombs—especially after the bombing of Hiroshima and Nagasaki—as having made war an outmoded and fruitlessly tragic way to solve international disputes. With the Scientists Movement, he worked for regulation of nuclear power. He joined Ava Helen, a member of the Women's International League for Peace and Freedom, in favor of a ban on nuclear testing. As anticommunist fear rose in the postwar United States, Pauling disagreed with those who called for teachers and others to sign loyalty oaths. Subpoenaed to appear before the 1950 Senate Investigating Committee on Education of the State of California, he explained his opposition in terms of freedom of thought and freedom of expression.

When Pauling applied for a passport to attend a 1952 scientific conference in England, the U.S. State Department denied his request as "not in the best interests of the United States." Pauling appealed and was turned down a second time on grounds that his anticommunist statements were not sufficiently strong. Had he gone to England that year, he would likely have seen X-ray diffraction photos of DNA—sharper and clearer than any captured before—that were being taken by crystallographer Rosalind Franklin at the Biophysical Laboratory at King's College, London. One such photo guided James Watson and Maurice Crick to their accurate model of the structure of DNA the next year. In 1954, after his Nobel Prize was announced, the State Department granted him a passport to attend the December award ceremony in Sweden.

Pauling continued to lobby for a ban on nuclear testing. Along with cellular biologist Barry Commoner (1917–) and physicist Edward Condon (1902–74) he prepared and distributed the Scientists' Petition to Stop Nuclear Testing, a document that cited the dangers of radioactive fallout, especially to children and the unborn, as a major reason to stop bomb testing worldwide. A total of 11,021 scientists representing 49 countries signed. Thirty-seven of them were Nobel laureates. In 1958, the same year he presented the petition to the United Nations, Pauling published *No More War!,* in which he argued that in the nuclear age, humankind must "move into a new period . . . of peace and reason, when world problems . . . are solved by the application of man's power of reason. . . ."

Such activism brought Pauling more critical scrutiny from the U.S. government and from the Caltech trustees, who openly sought to dis-

Despite this effort, the fish began rotting. Seeking to keep its outward appearance intact, if not its inward morphology, the curator resorted to hiring a taxidermist to mount her curiosity. As standard practice, he threw away most of the bones and tissue within the skin. After receiving Smith's cable, Courtenay-Latimer sifted through garbage bins for fish bones but found none. The professor arrived to find only a stuffed coelacanth. He was thrilled and astonished anyway.

Smith named the new species *Latimeria chalumnae* in honor of the discoverer and the place it had been caught, near where the Chalumna River flows into the Indian Ocean. When the museum offered the South

miss him. Again under subpoena, he testified before the U.S. Senate Internal Security Committee, politely refusing to name petition organizers beyond Commoner, Condon, and himself. Soon after, the National Science Foundation and the National Institutes of Health cut funding for his research. The trustees, unable to find grounds for dismissal, relieved him of the department chairmanship he had held for 22 years.

The activism, however, also helped spur the Limited Test Ban Treaty between the United States and the Soviet Union. On the day the ban was signed, the Norwegian Nobel Committee announced that it had selected Pauling as winner of the 1962 Nobel Peace Prize, making him the only person in history to have been awarded two unshared Nobel Prizes.

Not long after accepting the award, Pauling resigned from Caltech. He later joined the faculty of Stanford University; taught at the University of California, San Diego; and established the Linus Pauling Institute for Medical research at Big Sur, California (now at Oregon State University). Later projects included investigations into the chemistry of the brain and further pursuit of the cause of sickle-cell anemia. Over the last two decades of his life, he publicly advocated extremely large doses of vitamin supplements, especially vitamin C. This work put him at odds with the medical and biological establishment, which disputed his claims as overblown and unproven. The disagreement did not detract from Pauling's earlier contributions to biochemistry, molecular biology, and medicine, all rooted in his 1930s breakthroughs.

Linus Pauling pickets the White House as part of a mass demonstration against aboveground nuclear bomb tests. After World War II, Pauling became a passionate advocate for peace. (NARA, AIP Emilio Segrè Visual Archives)

African public a glimpse at *L. chalumnae*, many thousands of people lined up at the door.Newspapers around the world published the news and a photo of Courtenay-Latimer with her find.

Not only was the catch rare, it was difficult to duplicate. Fourteen years would go by before Smith would be able to examine an intact specimen, caught off the Comoro Islands, which lie in the Indian Ocean between Mozambique and Madagascar. Between 1952 and 1970, more than 60 examples of *L. chalumnae* would be caught around these islands at depths of 65 to 1,000 feet (200 to 300 m). Afraid of depleting the population, scientists eventually stopped offering rewards for specimens. In the

1990s, a closely related species of coelacanth would be found thousands of miles away in the western Pacific.

For decades, ichthyologists and paleontologists speculated that the coelacanth, with its limb-like fins and evidence of a vestigial air sac in the head, was a direct ancestor of the first amphibians. DNA studies have shown, however, that the lungfish appears more closely related to the earliest land vertebrates.

Further Reading

Academy of Achievement. "Interview: Linus Pauling." Available online. URL: http://www.achievement.org/autodoc/printmember/pau0int-1. Accessed April 5, 2006. Frank and informative 1990 interview with two-time Nobel Prize winner.

Annas, G. J., and M. A. Grodin, eds. *The Nazi Doctors and the Nuremberg Code: Human Rights in Human Experiments.* New York: Oxford University Press, 1992. Essays on medical experimentation on human subjects by physicians during Nazi rule in Germany.

Beadle, George W., and Edward L. Tatum. "Genetic Control of Biochemical Reactions in Neurospora." *Proceedings of the National Academy of Sciences* 27 (1941): 499–506. Research paper sets forth principle of one-gene–one-enzyme.

Bernal, John Desmond. *Science in History.* Cambridge, Mass.: MIT Press, 1969. Polymath Irish crystallographer examines role of science in shaping world events.

Carlson, Elof Axel. *The Unfit History of a Bad Idea.* Cold Spring Harbor, N.Y.: Cold Spring Harbor Laboratory Press, 2001. Available online. URL: http://www.netLibrary.com/urlapi.asp?action=summary&v=1&bookid=66639. Accessed September 4, 2004. Title summarizes author's approach toward eugenic theory and its misuse.

Chain, E., H. Florey, A. D. Gardner, N. G. Heatley, M. A. Jennings, et al. "Penicillin as a Chemotherapeutic Agent." *Lancet* 2 (August 24, 1940): 226–228. Antibiotic research team at Oxford reports results of landmark study.

Clark, Ronald William. *The Life of Sir Ernst Chain: Penicillin and Beyond.* London: Weidenfeld and Nicolson, 1985. Biographer puts isolation and purification of first antibiotic in context of researcher's remarkable life.

Creager, Angela N. H. *The Life of a Virus: Tobacco Mosaic Virus as an Experimental Model, 1930–1965.* Chicago: University of Chicago Press, 2002. Author evaluates the uses and value of organism in cytology and genetics research.

Creighton, Harriet B., and Barbara McClintock. "The Correlation of Cytological and Genetical Crossing over in Zea Mays." *Proceedings of the National Academy of Sciences* 17 (1931): 492–497. Landmark paper in which McClintock and graduate student established genetic crossing-over.

———. “The Correlation of Cytological and Genetical Crossing over in Zea Mays: A Corroboration.” *Proceedings of the National Academy of Sciences* 21 (1935): 148–150. Authors address critics by providing more data to corroborate 1931 conclusions.

Dronamraju, Krishna R. *If I Am to Be Remembered: The Life and Work of Julian Huxley with Selected Correspondence.* Singapore; River Edge, N.J.: World Scientific, 1993. Biography of polymath scholar who made great contribution to population genetics.

Ferry, Georgina. *Dorothy Hodgkin: A Life.* London: Granta, 1998. Biography of Nobel Prize–winning crystallography pioneer.

Friedlander, Henry. *The Origins of Nazi Genocide: From Euthanasia to the Final Solution.* Chapel Hill: University of North Carolina Press, 1995. Author traces ideas and ideology behind shameful historical events.

Goldsmith, Maurice. *Sage: A Life of J. D. Bernal.* London: Hutchinson, 1980. Biography of crystallography pioneer and wide-ranging intellect.

Hagar, Thomas. *Force of Nature: The Life of Linus Pauling.* New York: Simon & Schuster, 1995. Biography of Pauling examines interplay between character, personality, science.

Hillel, Marc, and Clarissa Henry. *Of Pure Blood.* New York: McGraw-Hill, 1976. Well-researched account of Nazi atrocities before and during World War II.

Huxley, Julian. “Clines: An Auxiliary Taxonomic Principle.” *Nature* 142, no. 7 (1938): 219–220. Biologist advances the idea that species are less clearly defined than previously assumed.

Keller, Evelyn Fox. *A Feeling for the Organism: The Life and Work of Barbara McClintock.* New York: W. H. Freeman, 1983. Sympathetic, detailed biography of influential maize cytogeneticist.

Laughlin, Harry. “Letter to Carl Schneider, May 28, 1936.” *Laughlin Papers*, Missouri State University, Kirksville. Letter from American eugenics leader accepting Nazi honor.

Leopold, Aldo. *Game Management.* New York: Charles Scribner’s Sons, 1933. The forester’s practical guide foreshadows ecology pioneer’s “land ethic.”

———. *A Sand County Almanac and Sketches Here and There.* New York: Oxford University Press: 1949. Natural history classic has been compared to writings of Thoreau and John Muir.

Lifton, Robert Jay. (1986). *The Nazi Doctors: Medical Killing and the Psychology of Genocide.* New York: Basic Books, 1986. Author seeks to illuminate mental states of researchers who participated in Nazi atrocities.

“Linus Pauling. The Nature of the Chemical Bond—A Documentary History.” Oregon State University Library Special Collections. Available online: URL: http://osulibrary.oregonstate.edu/specialcollections/coll/pauling/bond/index.html. Accessed April 5, 2006. Online resource includes narrative, documents, and timeline of Nobel Prize–winning scientist’s life and work.

Loribiecki, Marybeth. *Aldo Leopold: A Fierce Green Fire.* New York: Oxford University Press, 1999. Biography of great American environmentalist and naturalist.

McClintock, Barbara. Autobiography from *Les Prix Nobel. The Nobel Prizes 1983.* Stockholm: The Nobel Foundation, 1984. Available online. URL: http://nobelprize.org/medicine/laureates/1983/mcclintock-autobio.html. Accessed April 5, 2006. Nobel winner looks back on her life and achievements.

———. "The Fusion of Broken Chromosomes Ends of Sister Half-Chromatids Following Chromatid Breakage at Meiotic Anaphasis." *Missouri Agricultural Experiment Station Research Bulletin* no. 290 (1938): 1–48. McClintock explores and elucidates chromosome behavior.

———. "Letter to Curt Stern and Evelyn Stern." March 4, 1934. *Profiles in Science*, National Library of Medicine. Available online: URL: http://profiles.nlm.nih.gov/LL/B/B/M/J/_/llbbmj.pdf. Accessed April 14, 2005. McClintock reflects with some regret on her fellowship in Europe.

———. "Letter to Curt Stern and Evelyn Stern." Undated (1934?). *Profiles in Science*, National Library of Medicine. Available online: URL: http://profiles.nlm.nih.gov/LL/B/B/M/K/_/llbbmk.pdf. Accessed April 14, 2005. More on the above topic, state of science in prewar Nazi Germany.

———. "The Production of Homozygous Deficient Tissues with Mutant Characteristics by Means of the Aberrant Behavior of Ring-Shaped Chromosomes." *Genetics* 23 (1938): 315–376. Scholarly paper finds unexpected structures and functions within germ cells of maize.

McFarlane, Gwen. *Howard Florey, the Making of a Great Scientist.* Oxford: Oxford University Press, 1979. Biography of Nobel Prize–winning pathologist who led penicillin effort.

Painter, Theophilus Shickel. "A New Method for the Study of Chromosome Rearrangement and the Plotting of Chromosome Maps." *Science* 78 (1933): 585–586. Zoologist and cytologist discusses approach to study of chromosomes using salivary glands of *D. melanogaster.*

Pauling, Linus. *The Chemical Bond.* Ithaca, N.Y.: Cornell University Press, 1967.

———. *The Nature of the Chemical Bond and the Structure of Molecules and Crystals: An Introduction to Modern Structural Chemistry.* Ithaca, N.Y.: Cornell University Press, 1939.

———. *No More War!* New York: Dodd, Mead, 1958.

———. "The Principals Determining the Structure of Complex Ionic Crystals." *Journal of the American Chemical Society* 51, no. 1010 (1929): Chemist sets forth rules regarding ion bonds in crystal structure.

———. "Theoretical Prediction of the Physical Properties of Many Electron Atoms and Ions; Mole Refraction, Diamagnetic Susceptibility, and Extension in Space." *Proceedings of the Royal Society, London* A119 (1927): 181–211. Scholarly paper is example of Pauling's intuitive bent for theory.

Provine, William B. *Sewall Wright and Evolutionary Biology.* Chicago: University of Chicago Press, 1986. Biography of influential American population biologist.

Reville, William. "John Desmond Bernal—Sage." *Irish Times* 11 October 2001. Available online. URL: http://understandingscience.ucc.ie/pages/sci_johndesmondbernal.htm. Accessed January 6, 2004. Profile of eccentric polymath scholar who played important role in crystallography.

Serafini, Anthony. *Linus Pauling: A Man and His Science.* New York: Paragon House, 1991. Accessible biography of Pauling.

Smith, Charles H. "Some Biogeographers, Evolutionists and Ecologists: Chrono-Biographical Sketches. Tansley, Arthur George." Available online. URL: http://www.wku.edu/~smithch/chronob/TANS1871.htm. Accessed October 10, 2006. Biographical sketch of influential British botanist.

Summers, William C. *Félix d'Herelle and the Origins of Molecular Biology.* New Haven, Conn.: Yale University Press, 1999. Biography of researcher who named bacteriophages.

5 1941–1950: A Transformative Time for Microbiology

On the Research Front

Microbiology may never have more urgent application than in wartime. Throughout history, pestilence has accompanied war. Microorganisms infect wounds, contaminate foodstuffs, and spread disease. Far more than glory or honor, war brings sickness and death—not only sudden death, but also the painful, lingering kind.

Only 21 years separated the end of World War I from the beginning of World War II. When Germany invaded Poland in 1939, the memories of the worldwide influenza epidemic of 1918, a plague that will always be associated with the earlier war, were still fresh. Yet as the 1940s opened, so did the promise of new ways to defeat microorganisms that cause disease. Penicillin—discovered in the 1920s and developed in the 1930s—was about to come into production. Many researchers, such as Selman Abraham Waksman's team at Rutgers University, concentrated directly, and with success, on the problem of finding more such substances to fight more kinds of infections.

Other experimentation appeared far less applicable to wartime need. For example, Stanford University researchers Beadle and Tatum (introduced in the previous chapter) linked specific genes to the production of specific enzymes in cultures of bread mold. This may not have yielded a timely improvement in military ration preservation but it did open the field of chemical genetics, pointing the way for such 21st-century fields as gene replacement therapy.

American laboratories were particularly productive during the 1940s—before, during, and after direct U.S. involvement in the conflict. European countries during this period devoted what research resources they could afford toward weapons and defense application. In the Soviet Union, meanwhile, a major area of biological research—the study of genetics—fell victim to a political power game in which unproven, crackpot theories were sanctioned by the state as truth.

Many fine European scientists found refuge from Nazi anti-Semitism by coming to the United States. Two of them—Salvador Luria (1912–91) and Max Delbrück (1906–81)—discovered that bacteria evolve, as do more complex organisms, through random genetic mutation. Again, such knowledge did not win the war, but it did speed the way toward a more sophisticated view of microscopic life and what it shares with all life, including humans. At Yale University, Joshua Lederberg (1925–) joined Tatum in experiments showing that bacteria can and do combine genes and emerge in hybrid forms. Their peers at Vanderbilt and Washington universities discovered that even viruses could swap genetic material.

The most surprising information to come out of wartime microbiology was the identity of that genetic material—the mysterious substance that could transform an organism's traits from one generation to the next. Oswald T. Avery (1877–1955) and fellow medical researchers at the Rockefeller Institute worked out the answer to that central question through research on pneumococcus bacteria. Put forward in a modestly unassuming paper in 1944, their surprising finding—that DNA was the stuff of life—would ultimately advance the study of biology at every level. In the 1940s, however, most scientists simply were not ready to accept the idea that a nucleic acid could do so much and be so central to everything that lives.

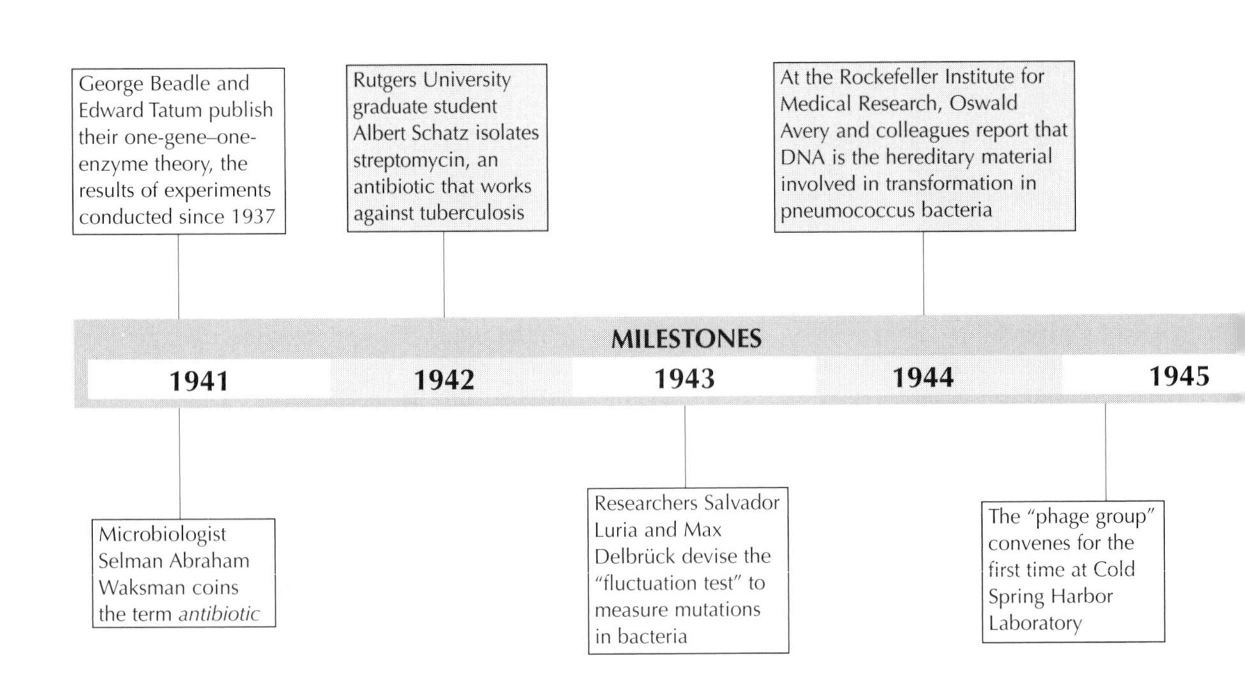

Asking How Genes Do What They Do

By the 1940s, biologists knew quite a bit about genes—such as how they must be grouped along the chromosomes of certain organisms in order to produce specific combinations of traits—but researchers still lacked answers to some basic questions. They did not understand how a gene produces a trait. They understood that a specific gene combination on a pair of chromosomes of a pea plant resulted in a wrinkled seed (as opposed to a smooth one), but they did not understand the mechanism by which the gene performed this function.

George Beadle, the same geneticist from Nebraska who had traded ideas with Barbara McClintock at Cornell University and trained in Thomas Hunt Morgan's Pasadena laboratory, was among biologists convinced that genes influence heredity through biochemical processes. He found inspiration in the work of British physician Archibald Garrod, who in the first decade of the 20th century had identified a rare disorder of the human urinary tract as a biochemical genetic mutation. (Garrod's work is described in chapter 1.) Working in Paris with Russian-born geneticist Boris Ephrussi, Beadle had already linked eye color in fruit flies

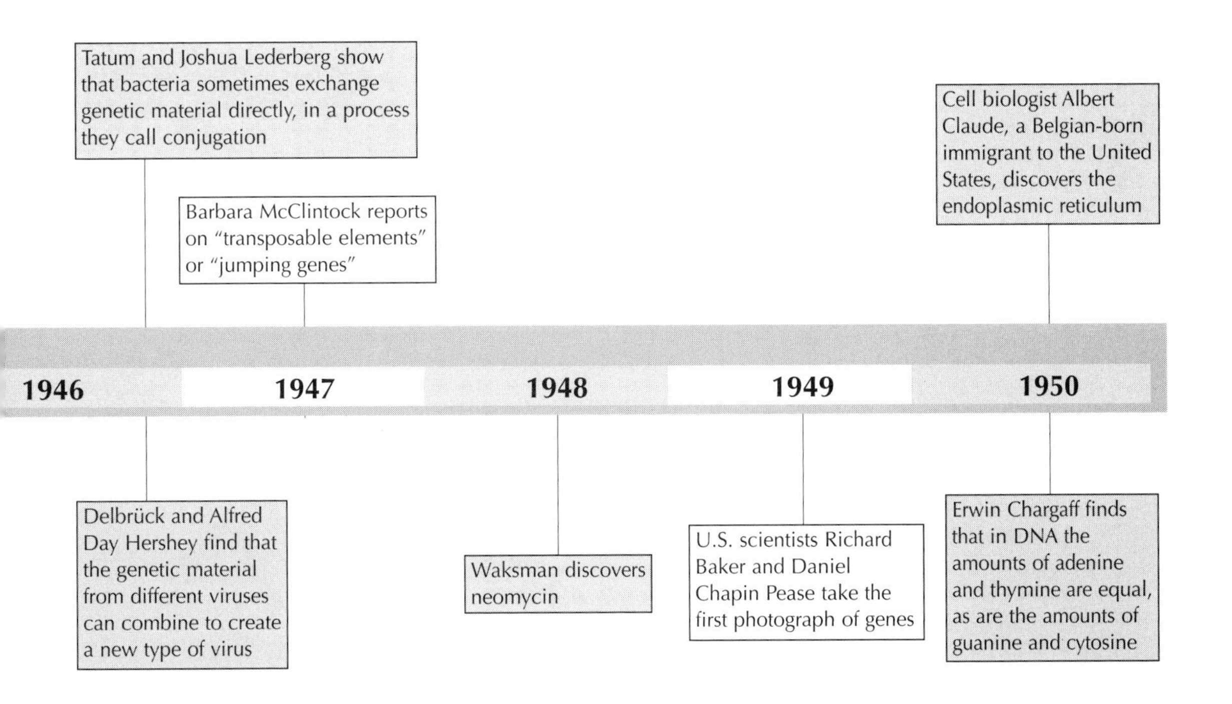

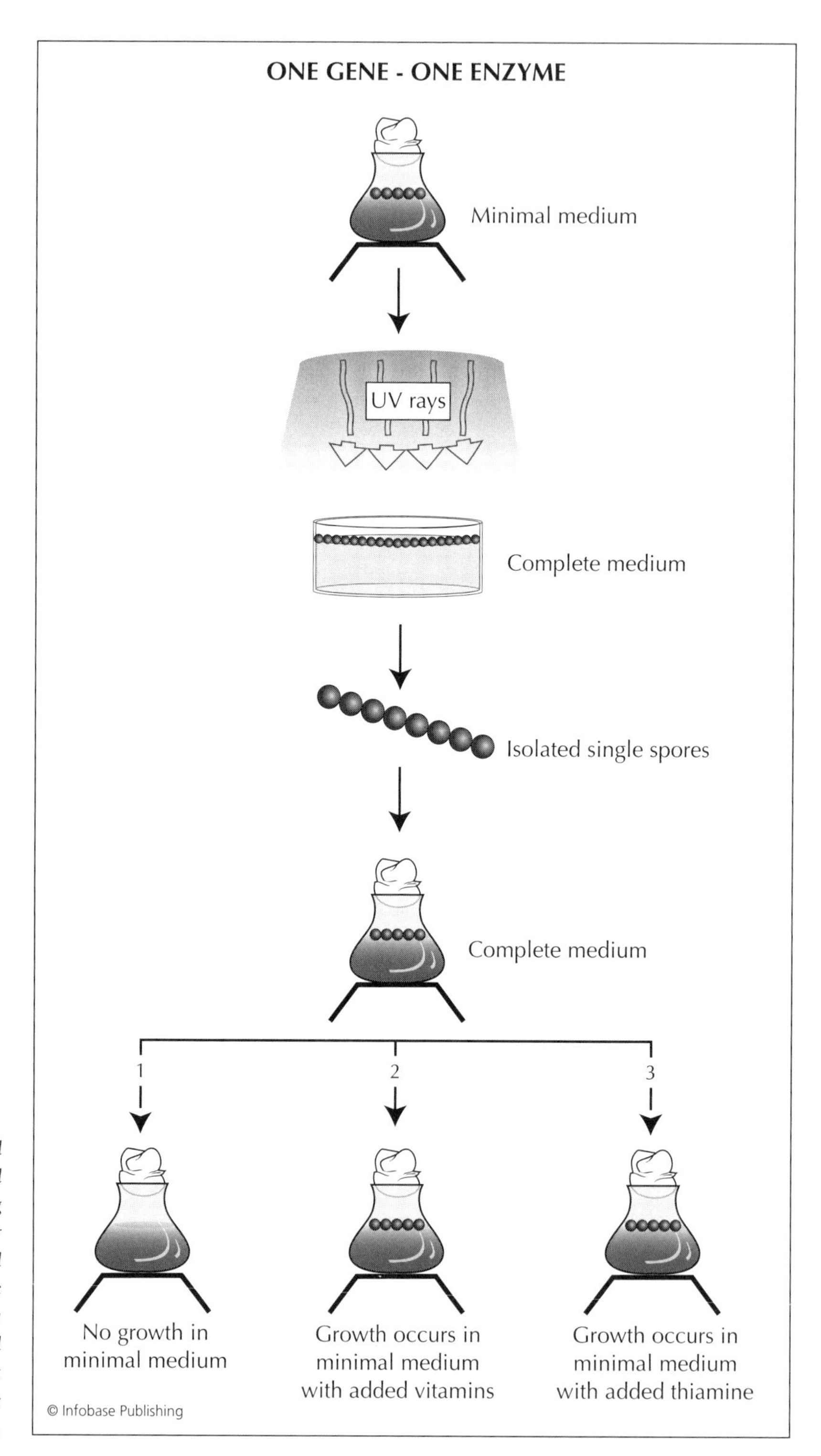

A gene mutation in the mold Neurospora crassa *(induced in the laboratory by exposing the organism to X-rays or ultraviolet rays) can be linked to a metabolic defect, the inability to synthesize a key nutrient. Thus, Beadle and Tatum showed that a specific disabled gene resulted in the absence of a specific enzyme.*

to a series of chemical reactions. He wanted to learn how genes direct these reactions.

At Stanford University at the end of the 1930s, Beadle teamed with research associate Edward Tatum, using the bread mold *Neurospora crassa* in a series of experiments that led them to the concept of one-gene–one-enzyme. As mentioned in the previous chapter, this work linked specific genetic mutations to corresponding metabolic defects.

Born in Boulder, Colorado, Tatum was the son of a pharmacology professor. He grew up in Madison, Wisconsin, where his father was on the medical school faculty at the University of Wisconsin. Tatum earned his Ph.D. in biochemistry from that institution in 1934 with a thesis on the nutrition of bacteria. It was good preparation for his work with Beadle.

At Stanford, the research partners sought to create genetic mutants that would be unable to produce specific enzymes. They exposed spores of *N. crassa* to radiation and found among the resulting mutant strains of mold an assortment of special nutritional needs. Mutant strains died unless the scientists added particular amino acids or vitamins to the nutrient culture in which the mold grew. These were amino acids or vitamins that normal *N. crassa* was able to manufacture by its own metabolism. By crossing these mutants with their normal counterparts, Beadle and Tatum demonstrated that each metabolic defect was a recessive trait. They further showed that when a genetic mutation interferes with a biochemical reaction, the enzyme catalyzing that reaction has been altered or left out as a result of the mutation.

As Beadle and Tatum announced in a 1941 paper, "Genetic Control of Biochemical Reactions in Neurospora," they found each mutant varied from normal *N. crassa* by just one gene. Each gene determines the structure of a specific enzyme. With each altered gene, a metabolic pathway had been arrested at a specific point, determined by a single missing enzyme.

Later research led biologists to understand that a gene may code for another *polypeptide*, a specific structural protein rather than an enzyme. The principle brought forward by Beadle and Tatum stands, however. It became a foundation for gene replacement therapy in decades to come.

The Fluctuation Test

In 1941, Max Delbrück, a Berlin-born physicist, met Salvador Luria, an Italian biologist, in Philadelphia, Pennsylvania. The two scientists, attending a meeting of the American Physical Society, hit it off immediately. This was a beneficial meeting for the fields of bacteriology, virology, and especially genetics.

The charismatic Delbrück and the sociable Luria had much in common. Both were citizens of Axis powers and had fled fascism in Europe for what was still an isolationist United States. (Delbrück emigrated in 1937, Luria in 1940.) When the United States entered the war, a year

Max Delbrück, standing, and Salvador Luria, center, relaxing with Luria's colleague from Columbia University, Frank Exner, during the Cold Spring Harbor Symposium of 1941. (National Institutes of Health)

after the two scientists met, the German and the Italian would both be classified by the U.S. government as enemy aliens, which actually worked out well for their research. Lacking federal security clearances, neither scientist was assigned to defense-related projects. That freed them to concentrate on pure research.

Delbrück and Luria shared an interest in applying the methodology and ideas of physics to the problems of biological research. After they met in Philadelphia, they traveled together to New York City, where they ran experiments together in Luria's lab at Columbia University. The scientists found themselves so much in tune as regarded their interests and working methods that they resolved to meet again the following summer at Cold Spring Harbor Laboratory.

Their research rendezvous led to what came to be called the "phage group," an informal network of scientists from a wide assortment of universities and laboratories. Sharing experiments and ideas, the group—with Delbrück as de facto leader—would gather at Cold Spring Harbor starting in 1945 and every summer thereafter for decades. Coming from a variety of specialties—most in biology, but also including physics and chemistry—they shared a quest to understand viral self-replication.

Apart from the wider group, Delbrück, of Vanderbilt University in Tennessee, and Luria, who would soon leave Columbia for Indiana University in Bloomington, forged a partnership of discovery. The work of this duet, which became a scientific trio with the 1944 addition of Washington University's Alfred Hershey (1908–97), would yield a shared Nobel Prize in physiology or medicine in 1969.

To better study bacteriophages, Luria and Delbrück decided to focus on bacteria—upon which phages prey. They wanted to know how mutations occur among these microbes. They understood that among multicelled organisms the rare mutation that improves a species' ability to survive a threat does not arise in response to that threat. Instead, the mutation arises at the molecular level and leads to a trait—an ability to digest a certain plant material, for example—that is preserved through reproduction because those animals with the trait are able to survive, reproduce, and pass it on.

Yet it was still widely thought that bacteria developed resistance to viral attack, to phages, as a direct reaction against a phage attack. Delbrück and Luria wanted to test if this was so. According to his autobiography, inspiration hit Luria as he was watching a colleague at a faculty dance play a dime slot machine. The return every time the player pulled the handle was usually zero and then, rarely, a big jackpot. The machine was clearly designed to do that, rather than to pay out frequent small handfuls of dimes.

The pattern made Luria think of gene distribution. If bacteria could develop an immunity to a phage in reaction to phage attack, he realized, then the rate of immunity should be roughly even over a wide population of bacteria. However, if the bacteria developed the immunity as the result of a random mutation, then only a very few bacteria would prove immune, and only their offspring, out of a general population, would

If bacteria mutated in response to outside stimuli, such as a hostile bacteriophage, then the change would happen at a constant rate in separate contaminated cultures, as in the top example. Delbrück and Luria demonstrated that changes occur at different rates in different cultures, indicating random mutation.

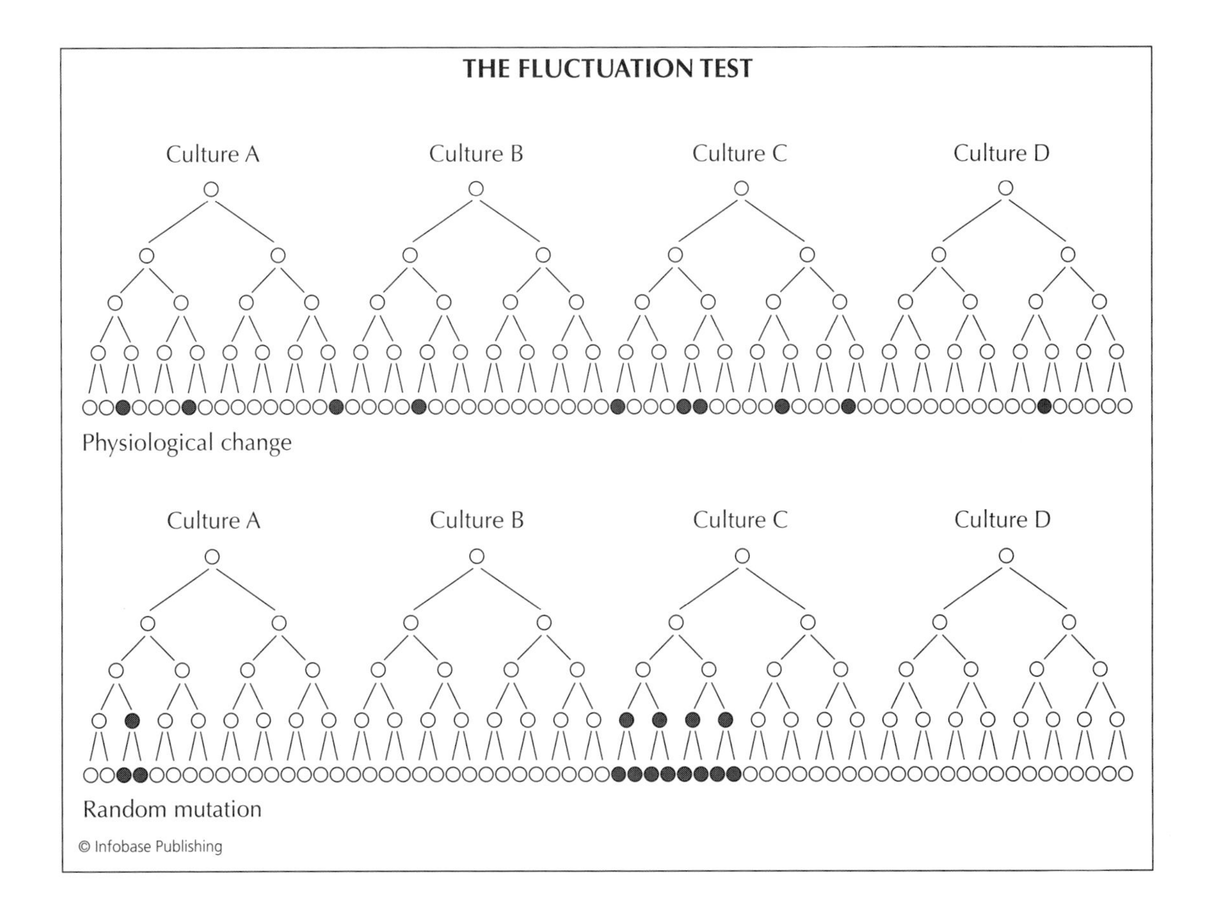

Delbrück and Luria working together in the lab. Their collaboration led to a better understanding of how bacteria evolve genetic resistance. (National Institutes of Health)

be likely to carry on that trait. The trait would become general to the population only as the immune bacteria withstood the infection and thus reproduced at a higher rate than their susceptible kin.

Luria and Delbrück set up an experiment in which they took a culture of phage-sensitive *E. coli* bacteria—uniformly of a single strain—and divided it into many small cultures of only a very few cells. After each small culture had been allowed to reproduce through several generations, they tested it for resistance to bacteriophage attack. What they found was that the trait for immunity did not appear at a uniform rate through the descendant cultures. In most cultures, there was no immunity at all. In some, there was a little, and in a very small number of cultures, there was a great deal of immunity. The scientists clearly had not induced phage immunity by introducing a bacteriophage to the separate cultures. Instead, the unevenly distributed immunity had arisen from a small number of ancestor bacteria that were mutant in this beneficial way.

Why was this discovery important? Aside from adding to biologists' understanding of bacteria, it also proved that these one-celled creatures are like more complex, multicelled organisms in their genetic mechanisms. That meant that bacteria—easily grown and managed in a laboratory—began to be seen as useful research subjects for genetics researchers.

The Transformative Role of DNA

As early as 1932, Oswald Avery, a veteran microbiology researcher concentrating on the *Streptococcus pneumoniae* bacterium, had become interested in identifying the *transforming principle.* This was the theoretical term for a biochemical agent believed to cause a surprising change in *S. pneumoniae*, as described by Britain's Frederick Griffith in the 1920s. Griffith had shown that he could transform a non-virulent strain of the bacterium into a virulent form by exposing the non-virulent strain to virulent bacteria that had been killed. In other words, the killed bacteria contained something—the mysterious transforming principle—that could change one strain of the living, reproducing bacteria into another. This experiment is covered in chapter 3.

Working at Rockefeller Institute Hospital in New York, Avery had originally been skeptical of Griffith's results. Eventually, he accepted the idea of a transforming principle and began working on methods to isolate and identify it.

Avery had learned a great deal about pneumococcal bacteria over the years since World War I. Having earned his medical degree in 1904, he had worked as a clinical physician for only a few years before turning to bacteriological research. He joined the medical research staff at the Rockefeller Institute in 1913. There, he and fellow researchers had developed a way to diagnose which strain of the bacterium was infecting a pneumonia patient. His team had developed a serum treatment against its most common form and had worked out details about the microorganism's nutritional requirements. With organic chemist Michael Heidelberger (1901–90), Avery had determined that the difference between smooth, virulent strains of *S. pneumoniae* and rough, non-virulent strains was an outer capsule on the rough strain, a capsule made of a complex polysaccharide. In common language, the capsule was made of a sugar. Avery began referring to this pneumococcus as "the sugar-coated microbe."

In 1940, Avery began to focus his research on Griffith's troublesome transforming principle. That was the year that geneticist Colin MacLeod (1909–72), a fellow Rockefeller researcher, worked out a technique for isolating the mysterious substance by eliminating matter that did not effect the change from the rough strain of the bacterium to the smooth. MacLeod then left the institute for the medical school of New York University (NYU), but his departure did not leave Avery without a collaborator. NYU provided a substitute. William S. Tillett (1892–1972), chairman of the bacteriology department at NYU and a streptococcus researcher himself, tapped young Maclyn McCarty (1911–2005) to join Avery in his quest. Born in Indiana and educated at Stanford University and at Johns Hopkins Medical School, McCarty had arrived in New York to pursue bacteriology research earlier that year.

Avery had come to believe that the agent they sought was not, as had at first seemed likely, a protein. He and McCarty proved this when they showed that proteases, which are enzymes that break down proteins, did not deactivate the transforming principle. Neither did lipases, which are enzymes that destroy lipids, or fats. They eliminated carbohydrates, such as the material making up the polysaccharide capsule of rough-strain *S. pneumoniae*, as a suspect. That process of elimination led them to the nucleic acids. Another enzyme, ribonuclease, which acts upon RNA, did not prevent the transforming principle from working. The list of suspects had been narrowed down to one: DNA. Indeed, a new test aimed at detecting the presence of deoxyribonucleic acid confirmed that this was the agent at work, the substance that could carry permanent, heritable, genetic change.

The researchers published their results in a 1944 paper titled "Induction of Transformation by a Desoxyribonucleic Acid Fraction Isolated from Pneumococcus Type III," but the idea that DNA alone could do what the paper said it could was very difficult for many other scientists to accept. Most thought of DNA as little more than a structural element of the cell, a simple chain of repeating nucleotides. Alfred E. Mirsky (1900–74), a prominent molecular biologist who was also at the Rockefeller Institute, was among those who hung onto the belief that Avery's team must have missed something. Through the 1940s, Mirsky and others continued to suspect that a tiny amount of protein was likely to have been attached to the DNA that Avery tested. It was not until the next decade that DNA's role as the transforming agent of genetic inheritance was generally accepted.

Chargaff's Rules

Other scientists embraced Avery's finding and found inspiration in it. Columbia University Researcher Erwin Chargaff (1905–2002) read it and decided to investigate the chemical makeup of DNA.

Born in what was then the Austro-Hungarian Empire and educated in Vienna, Chargaff had studied at Yale as well as at European universities before coming to Columbia as an assistant professor in 1935. Having published findings on the chemical properties of several biological substances, including blood proteins, plant *chromatin*, and lipids, Chargaff was a well-respected researcher before he began to study DNA.

His analysis found something striking about the chemical makeup of the nucleic acid. DNA contains the organic chemical bases adenine and guanine, classified as *purines*, and cytosine and thymine, which are *pyrimidines*. Chargaff discovered that not only is the amount of purine base about the same as the amount of pyrimidine but that the amount of the purine *adenine* is always roughly equal to the amount of the pyrimidine *thymine*. And, it followed, the amount of the purine *guanine* always matches (within a very small variance) the amount of the pyrimidine *cytosine*.

This, it turned out, was the chemical rule behind DNA *base pairs*—although, of course, no one had yet thought of DNA base pairs. That would come a few years later (and in the following chapter), when biologist James Watson (1928–) and biophysicist Francis Crick (1916–2004) proposed a model for the DNA molecule. Watson and Crick, working on the problem at Cambridge University, would receive a visit from Chargaff. He later downplayed the idea that his chemical rule led to their breakthrough, but it certainly established in the minds of Watson and Crick a requirement to which any model molecule must, to be plausible, adhere.

Chargaff arrived at a second rule about DNA. This was that the relative amounts of adenine and thymine and guanine and cytosine vary in the DNA of different species. Until Chargaff, biochemists had assumed that all DNA was alike. This second rule suggested that DNA was more complex than previously thought and thus a better candidate for carrying genetic information than had been previously thought. Like Avery and company's discovery about DNA, both of Chargaff's rules fit with what Watson and Crick would establish in the 1950s.

Conjugation

Biologists, and especially other bacteriologists—whether they accepted the Avery team's finding or not—were coming to realize that no one had yet approached understanding the genetics of bacteria. Delbrück and Luria's finding of genetic mutation in these prokaryotes, combined with Griffith's demonstration that a biochemical agent from one bacterium can change the genetic makeup of another, caused researchers to wonder whether bacteria routinely exchange genetic material.

The idea that bacterial reproduction, through mitosis, produced nothing but clone after genetic clone was coming to seem simplistic and naive. Tatum, who left Stanford for Yale University in 1946, decided to look into the issue. Through his work with bacterial nutrition, he had discovered a double-mutant bacterium, which required two supplemental nutrients to survive. Lederberg, a medical student from New York City, teamed with Tatum to develop experiments that used the double-mutant bacteria to trace genetic recombination, if any, in these organisms.

Lederberg and Tatum combined two strains of double-mutant bacteria to see if "mating" would occur. The experiment can be understood, in simplified form, as starting with a bacterium that needs nutrients *w*, *x*, *y*, and *z* to survive but that is able to metabolize all four of these substances. One mutant strain of this bacterium, however, is unable to metabolize its own *w* and *x* and must have supplements of those nutrients added to its culture. The other mutant strain cannot make *y* and *z*. The researchers bred many generations of each and found that descendants of the bacteria

Joshua Lederberg in 1946, the year that he and Tatum announced their discovery of bacterial conjugation. (University of Wisconsin–Madison Archives)

Soviet Science Subverted

In 1943, the great plant geneticist Nikolay Ivanovich Vavilov (1887–1943), died in a Soviet prison camp. He had been locked away for the crime of doing scientific research.

Was science a crime in the Soviet Union? It was if the scientist's methods and results ran counter to official Soviet policy—especially if the scientist published those results. Unfortunately for Vavilov—a former student of Britain's William Bateson and a well-respected member of the European research community—the study of genetics was governed by political philosophy rather than by demonstrated fact under the long reign of dictator Joseph Stalin. All of biological inquiry became a closed system in which the lessons of Gregor Mendel and Thomas Hunt Morgan—the line of thought that was so rapidly advancing the field of genetics in the United States and western Europe—were systematically banned. From the mid-1930s through most of the 1940s, as biologist Trofim Denisovich Lysenko (1898–1976) rose to political power in the nation's scientific establishment, the label "Mendelist-Morganist" became an epithet to be hurled against politically incorrect Soviet geneticists.

One explanation of Lysenko's rise, and the fall of legitimate science, in Stalin's USSR has to do with ideology. Somehow genetic theory—the idea that genes, carried upon chromosomes, contain heritable data that direct the formation of organisms—was misunderstood so grossly within the Soviet establishment that it was held to be incompatible with the official Marxist philosophy of *dialectical materialism*. Some Soviet policymakers distrusted the gene as too much like one of the philosopher Plato's "ideas." Platonic ideas are philosophically perfect forms. The philosopher imagined these forms casting shadows, so that a table (chair, flower, or bumblebee) in the

unable to manufacture their own nutrients *w* and *x* also were not able to make those nutrients. So, too, descendants of the mutants unable to make *y* and *z* were like their ancestors in that respect.

Next, the researchers mixed the two separate mutant strains and allowed the resultant culture to grow. They found among the descendants of the mixed culture some bacteria that needed no nutritional supplements. These bacteria were clearly a genetic mix of the two mutant strains.

Lederberg and Tatum's findings, published in 1946, suggested that bacteria mated, although it was not yet clear what the mechanism was for this to happen. Many bacteriologists imagined that this bacterial *conjugation*, as its discoverers called it, required cell walls to break down so that the genetic material could come in contact and recombine.

That same year, Delbrück and Hershey found that viruses, too, can mix genes. A few years earlier, Hershey's papers on his bacteriophage research at Washington University in St. Louis had impressed Delbrück. The German scientist invited Hershey to join him and partner Luria in phage investigations. In a 1946 experiment, Delbrück and Hershey infected bacteria with two different strains of a virus. They discovered that the culture then contained bacteriophages with infective properties that were different from either of the viruses they had introduced. Repetitions of this experiment suggested that the two different phages were exchanging

material world was but a shadow of the idea of a table (chair, etc.). People with even a casual grasp of genetics know that it has nothing to do with Platonic idealism, but in this misinterpreted form, the discipline could be attacked as contradictory to Marxist "truth."

That said, Lysenko's power was surely rooted in politics more than it was in ideology. He was skilled at advancing himself and his supporters while undermining those who disagreed with him. Once he was powerful enough, his opponents—those foolish enough to speak up—ended up in prison camps or dead. Lysenko became director of the Institute of Genetics of the Soviet Academy of Sciences in 1940. By 1948, his hold over Soviet genetic theory was absolute. This was despite the disastrous effects of his ideas about agronomy when applied to Soviet farming.

Rejecting decades of genetic research and knowledge, Lysenko advanced theories that hearkened back to the early 19th century and Lamarck. Lysenko held that environmental changes imposed upon an organism will be inherited by that organism's offspring. He said that chilling sprouts of spring wheat would make the crop, and succeeding generations, more cold-tolerant. (It did not.) Much worse, he argued that wheat plants could be manipulated to yield seeds of rye (a different species) and that a hen who had mated with several roosters would produce chicks that were hybrids of those roosters. He supported these views by manipulating outcomes of experiments, altering data, and throwing out any result that contradicted his beliefs.

After Stalin's death in 1953, Soviet authorities began to allow other scientists to criticize Lysenko. It was far too late for Vavilov and others like him, but standard genetics did regain a foothold. Lysenko remained as director of Moscow's Institute of Genetics, however, until 1965. Even afterward, he continued teaching his discredited ideas.

genetic material. The reproductive cycles of microbes were coming to look far more complicated than scientists had previously suspected.

An Antibiotic Effective against Tuberculosis

The war years in the West saw a rising public regard for the study of microbes and their biochemistry. This was due less to the investigations of people like Tatum, Lederberg, Delbrück, and Hershey than to penicillin. Chain and Florey's success yielded, within a relatively short time, enormous practical benefits for physicians and their patients. In June 1944, after Allied forces stormed the beaches of Nazi-occupied France, U.S. and British medical teams were able to save hundreds of lives with the new medicine.

The power of penicillin, derived from such a humble source—a common mold—suggested to microbiologist Abraham Waksman (1888–1973) that there were other, similar, substances in nature. Waksman, who was chairman of the microbiology department at New Jersey's Rutgers University, organized a research effort to find these substances among actinomycetes, which are an order of filament-shaped bacteria that live in soil. Waksman coined a term for substances like penicillin. He called them *antibiotics*. By 1940, he thought he had something with potential,

Credit Where Credit Is Due

Selman Abraham Waksman won the 1952 Nobel Prize in physiology or medicine as discoverer of streptomycin, the first antibiotic effective against tuberculosis. There was no colaureate. There was no mention of Albert Schatz, whose name had been listed first—as primary author—on the 1944 paper announcing the discovery, titled "Effect of Streptomycin and Other Antibiotic Substances upon Mycobacterium Tuberculosis and Related Organisms." Waksman did not credit the younger scientist in his Nobel lecture; neither did he mention Schatz in his 1953 autobiography.

Many have cited this as an example of a research supervisor taking credit for his student's breakthrough. Schatz did the hands-on work that brought a new antibiotic into being. Waksman's defenders argue that the student, then 23, employed standard research methods while building on the department chair's decades of actinomycete research. According to that line of reasoning, the creative part of the discovery was in Waksman's cumulative body of work.

After Rutgers awarded Schatz a Ph.D. in 1945, based upon his dissertation on the streptomycin discovery, it became clear to him that Waksman had begun taking sole credit for the experiments. Unwilling to be eclipsed, Schatz sued the university. An out-of-court settlement in 1950 put his name alongside Waksman's on the patent for the drug. Under terms of the settlement, Schatz and other microbiology graduate students who had been involved in antibiotic research also received small shares of the income from the patent. Those included Elizabeth Bugie (1920–2001), another coauthor of the original streptomycin paper. (Bugie, who later became a medical librarian, was not a plaintiff in Schatz's lawsuit and never publicly claimed to have been a codiscoverer.)

The legal action was an extremely unusual step, widely seen at the time as a slap directed at Waksman, a renowned scientific authority. Such open defiance may have hurt Schatz's subsequent research career. After a number of short-term affiliations with other science facilities, one in Chile, Schatz in 1969 secured a tenure-track faculty position at Temple University in Philadelphia. The suit and the ill will it brought to him may also have spoiled, rather than enhanced, any chance he might have had at sharing the 1952 Nobel Prize.

With passing years, however, especially after Waksman's death in 1973, Schatz's version of the streptomycin breakthrough gained broader acceptance from academics and science historians. Schatz and his account of the discovery figure in Frank Ryan's 1993 book *The Forgotten Plague*, a story of the scientific fight against tuberculosis. In 1994, 50 years after the discovery of streptomycin, Rutgers awarded to Schatz a medal and citation honoring him as codiscoverer.

a liquid that he called actinomycin. When veterinary researchers tested actinomycin on animals, however, it proved highly toxic.

Waksman was at the time one of the world's top soil microbiologists. His 1927 book *Principles of Soil Microbiology* was the authoritative text on the subject. Born in 1888 in Ukraine (then part of the Russian Empire), Waksman had come to Rutgers, in New Brunswick, New Jersey, in 1911 and had become a U.S. citizen in 1916. Aside from two years completing his Ph.D. at the University of California, Berkeley, he had spent his career at Rutgers.

Among the graduate students working under Waksman, young Albert Schatz (1920–2005)—recently discharged from the Army Air Corps—had a particular interest in the disease tuberculosis, for which there was

Scientist of the Decade: Oswald T. Avery (1877–1955)

Joshua Lederberg, the Nobel Prize laureate who in 1978 became president of Rockefeller University (the former Rockefeller Institute), told the *New York Times* in 2005 that the 1944 paper in which Oswald Avery and colleagues named DNA as the "transforming principle" had been the "pivotal discovery of twentieth century biology." Lederberg, whose own work is discussed earlier in this chapter, estimated that as many as 25 Nobel Prizes had been awarded to scientists whose findings were built on that of Avery, Maclyn McCarty, and Colin MacLeod. Such an evaluation raises a question: Why were Avery, McCarty, and MacLeod never awarded a Nobel Prize, despite several nominations?

Several factors have been suggested to explain this lapse. The timing of the discovery may have been a factor. The scientific community, along with the public at large, may have been distracted by World War II, then raging at its height. The war did disrupt international communication between scientists. Also, the paper announcing DNA's unexpected property appeared in a publication, the *Journal of Experimental Medicine,* that was more closely followed by physicians and immunologists than by geneticists. Still, the initial paper, discussed in the part of this chapter, titled "The Transformative Role of DNA" (page 10), was widely read and widely cited.

Oswald Avery, known to friends as "Fess," took a systematic approach to the study of pneumonia-causing microbes. (History of Medicine Division, Prints and Photographs Collection)

Nobel winner Hershey, who in 1962 became director of the Genetics Research Unit at Cold Spring Harbor, told the *Times* that Avery and his teammates never received the top award in science because they were too modest. The initial paper's tone has been called tentative, diffident. And Avery, in charge of the project, was simply not the kind of man to crow about his achievements or campaign for recognition. Colleagues and friends spoke of the lifelong bachelor as slightly shy and very modest.

McCarty lived until 2005, well into a world changed by DNA research and technology. Even by the time of MacLeod's death, in 1972, it had become widely apparent how significant the three Rockefeller scientists' contribution was. But team leader Avery, acknowledged by his partners as the one most deserving of recognition, died in 1955, when science was still slowly waking up to the 1953 discovery of DNA's structure and what it might mean. Nobel Prizes are never awarded posthumously.

Avery had not seemed destined for a career in science. Born in Halifax, Nova Scotia, he was the

(continues)

(continued)

son of an English couple who had immigrated to Canada. His father, a Baptist clergyman, brought the family to New York City in 1987, when Oswald was almost 10. The boy and his two brothers grew up in and around the Mariner's Temple, a mission on Manhattan's Lower East Side. Later, at Colgate University in Hamilton, New York, then a Baptist-affiliated institution, he majored in humanities with an emphasis on literature.

Earning his bachelor's degree, Avery enrolled in New York's College of Physicians and Surgeons (later the medical school of Columbia University). A student could do that in those days, without having first followed a premed regimen heavy on biology and chemistry courses. He earned a medical degree in 1904 and practiced medicine briefly before becoming a bacteriology and immunology researcher.

Maclyn McCarty, on the podium, greets James Watson, center, and Francis Crick at an awards ceremony at the Scripps Institute in La Jolla, California. McCarty's 1940s work with Avery and Colin MacLeod paved the way for later DNA breakthroughs. (U.S. National Library of Medicine)

no effective cure at the time. Schatz later explained that he had seen cases of tuberculosis while growing up in Passaic, New Jersey, and wanted very much to fight the disease, one of the world's most deadly. No form of penicillin works against the *Mycobacterium tuberculosis*, the infectious agent. Also called consumption—because of the way its victims, wracked by painful coughing, lost weight and wasted away—tuberculosis claimed more victims in 19th-century North America than all other infectious illnesses put together. During the early 1940s, the disease had reached epidemic proportions in war-ravaged Europe.

Accounts from the time differ as to whose idea it was to assign Schatz the task of seeking a new antibiotic against the disease. Schatz's memory was that veterinary biologist William Hugh Feldman (1892–1974) and medical researcher H. Corwin Hinshaw (1902–2000), both of Minnesota's Mayo Clinic, urged Waksman to take up the challenge. Waksman reportedly worried about having the infectious tubercle bacillus in the lab, because of the chance that it could escape. Schatz volunteered for the hazardous duty and was given a basement research space of his own, away from other scientists and laboratory assistants.

There he isolated and tested hundreds of substances derived from cultures of actinomycetes. After three months, in the fall of 1943, Schatz isolated a substance that was able to inhibit growth of the deadly bacillus.

At the Hoagland Laboratory in Brooklyn, where he joined the staff in 1907, Avery learned research techniques and gained a nickname, "The Professor," often shortened to "Fess." (He taught courses for student nurses.) In 1913, he received an invitation to join the pneumonia research staff of the Rockefeller Institute for Medical Research. Except during his brief stint as an army immunologist during World War I (which earned him U.S. citizenship), the laboratories of Rockefeller remained his professional home until he retired in 1948.

Over most of those years, Avery concentrated on pneumonia-causing bacteria, mostly the species *Diplococcus pneumoniae,* which, like *S. pneumoniae,* occurs in rough non-virulent and smooth virulent strains. The aim was to develop treatment, perhaps even a preventive cure, for pneumonia, which at that time killed more than 50,000 people in the United States every year. However, as fellow microbiologist Réne J. Dubos (1901–82) noted in his biography of Avery, *The Professor, the Institute, and DNA,* Avery did things in a thorough and systematic way. His approach to a microorganism was to understand it by investigating, step-by-step, its biochemical processes—processes that other researchers were showing as directly linked to genetics. When he turned his full attention to *S. pneumoniae* and the transformative principle, Avery's approach was precisely the correct way to reach the correct conclusion that this agent of biological specificity was none other than the unsuspected DNA.

Avery was technically already retired when he and his partners made their big discovery. Having reached the institute's mandatory retirement age of 65 in 1942, he was given emeritus status because of the ongoing work on the transforming principle and also because of a wartime shortage of bacteriologists. It was not until 1948 that he left his laboratory and New York, his home of 61 years, for Nashville, Tennessee. There, in a house near that of his brother Roy, a biology researcher at Vanderbilt University, Oswald Avery enjoyed his final years quietly among family members.

In Minnesota, Hinshaw and Feldman tested the new substance, which Schatz had named streptomycin, on guinea pigs and found it was not toxic. Effective as well against diseases including cholera, brucellosis (discussed in chapter 2), *tularemia*, and bubonic plague, the new broad-spectrum antibiotic was put into clinical use in 1947, dramatically reducing the incidence of tuberculosis in developed countries.

Further Reading

Altman, Lawrence K. "Maclyn McCarty Dies at 93; Pioneer in DNA Research." *New York Times*, 6 January 2005, p. B7. Available online. URL: http://www.nytimes.com/2005/01/06/obituaries/06McCarty.html. Accessed April 7, 2006. Obituary of McCarty, who worked with Oswald Avery.

Avery, Oswald T. "Portion of Letter to His Brother, Roy O. Avery." May 13, 1943. National Institutes of Health. Available online. URL: http://profiles.nlm.nih.gov/CC/A/A/B/V/_/ccaabv.pdf. Accessed April 7, 2006. Oswald Avery describes DNA work to Roy Avery, also a biological researcher.

———, Colin M. MacLeod, and Maclyn McCarty. "Induction of Transformation by a Desoxyribonucleic Acid Fraction Isolated from

Pneumococcus Type III." *Journal of Experimental Medicine* 79, no. 1 (January 1944): 137–158. Available online. URL: http://images.google.com/imgres?imgurl=http://osulibrary.orst.edu/specialcollections/coll/pauling/dna/papers/avery. Accessed August 16, 2005.

Beadle, George, and Edward L. Tatum. "Genetic Control of Biochemical Reactions in Neurospora." *Proceedings of the National Academy of Science* 27 (1941): 499–506. Landmark paper in biochemical genetics set forth one-gene–one-enzyme principle.

Berg, Paul, and Maxine Singer. *George Beadle, An Uncommon Farmer: The Emergence of Genetics in the 20th Century.* Cold Spring Harbor, N.Y.: Cold Spring Harbor Laboratory Press, 2003. Berg, a Nobel Prize–winning biochemist (in 1983) is coauthor of biography of biochemical geneticist Beadle.

Chargaff, Erwin. *Heraclitean Fire: Sketches from a Life before Nature.* New York: Rockefeller University Press, 1978. Great biochemist's insightful, entertaining memoir illuminates personalities and human-scale motives behind scientific research.

Davis, Rowland H. *Neurospora: Contributions of a Model Organism.* Oxford: Oxford University Press, 2000. Scholarly history treats research uses of *N. crassa*, subject of Beadle-Tatum work.

Dubos, René J. *The Professor, the Institute, and DNA.* New York: Rockefeller University Press, 1976. Microbiology colleague's biography of DNA pioneer Oswald "The Professor" Avery.

———. *The White Plague: Tuberculosis, Man, and Society.* New Brunswick, N.J.: Rutgers University Press, 1987. Microbiologist's account of science's quest to cure tuberculosis.

Fox, Margalit. "Albert Schatz; Microbiologist, Dies at 84." *New York Times*, 2 February 2005. Available online. URL: http://www.nytimes.com/2005/02/02/obituaries/02schatz.html?ex=1265086800&en= 42cb05d3ca083852&ei=5088&partner=rssnyt. Accessed April 7, 2006.

Kay, Lily E. "Selling Pure Science in Wartime: The Biochemical Genetics of G. W. Beadle." *Journal of the History of Biology* 22, no. 1 (March 1989): 73–101.

Lederberg, Joshua, and Edward L. Tatum. "Gene Recombination in *Escherichia Coli*." *Nature* 158, (October 19, 1946): 558. Microbiologists' paper announcing further work supporting finding that bacteria trade genetic material.

Luria, S. E. *A Slot Machine, a Broken Test Tube: An Autobiography.* New York: Harper & Row, 1984. Well-written, entertaining autobiography by Nobel Prize–winning microbiologist.

Oswald T. Avery Collection, Biographical Information. Profiles in Science. National Library of Medicine. Available online. URL: http://profiles.nlm.nih.gov/CC/Views/Exhibit/narrative/biographical.html. Accessed September 8, 2005. Accessible account of life and work of microbiologist, immunologist, and DNA pioneer.

Roll-Hansen, Nils. *The Lysenko Effect: The Politics of Science.* Amherst, N.Y.: Humanity Books, 2005. History of tragic politicization of biological research in Stalinist USSR.

Ryan, Frank. *The Forgotten Plague: How the Battle against Tuberculosis Was Won—And Lost.* Boston: Little, Brown, 1993. Pessimistic history of immunology and public health challenge.

Schatz, Albert. *My Experience in World War II.* Available online. URL: http://fas-history.rutgers.edu/oralhistory/Docs/memoirs/schatz_albert/schatz_albert_memoir.html. Accessed September 7, 2005. Researcher recounts research that led to antibiotic breakthrough.

———, and Selman A. Waksman. "Effect of Streptomycin and Other Antibiotic Substances upon Mycobacterium Tuberculosis and Related Organisms." *Proceedings of the Society for Experimental Biology and Medicine* 57 (1944): 244–248. Paper reporting effectiveness of streptomycin against tuberculosis.

———, Elizabeth Bugie, and Selman A. Waksman. "*S. Streptomycin,* a Substance Exhibiting Antibiotic Activity against Gram-Positive and Gram-Negative Bacteria." *Proceedings of the Society for Experimental Biology and Medicine* 55 (1944): 66–69. Early paper reporting discovery of antibiotic properties of streptomycin.

Soyfer, Valery N., Leo Guliow, and Rebecca Gruliow. *Lysenko and the Tragedy of Soviet Science.* New Brunswick, N.J.: Rutgers University Press, 1994. History of the way state-sanctioned ideology derailed scientific research in the USSR.

Tatum, E. L., and J. Lederberg. "Gene Recombination in *Escherichia Coli.*" *Journal of Bacteriology* 53, no. 6 (June 1947): 673–684. Microbiologists announce exchange of genetic material in microorganisms once thought to have reproduced strictly by mitosis.

University of Hawaii, Department of Botany. "The Aftermath of Penicillin." Available online. URL: http://www.botany.hawaii.edu/faculty/wong/BOT135/Lect23.htm. Accessed September 7, 2005. Online resource recounts powerful medical and social changes wrought by antibiotics.

Wainwright, Milton. *The Miracle Cure: The Story of Penicillin and the Golden Age of Antibiotics.* Cambridge, Mass.: Blackwell, 1990. Readable account of how penicillin was discovered, isolated, and mass-produced and the way it changed medical practice.

Waksman, Selman A. *The Antibiotic Era: A History of the Antibiotics and of Their Role in the Conquest of Infectious Diseases and in Other Fields of Human Endeavor.* Tokyo: Waksman Foundation of Japan, 1975. Nobel winner's account of antibiotics revolution and his role in it.

———. *My Life with the Microbes.* New York: Simon & Schuster, 1953. Autobiography by codiscoverer of streptomycin's effectiveness against tuberculosis.

———. *Principles of Soil Microbiology.* 2nd ed. Baltimore: Williams & Wilkins, 1932. Authoritative textbook by Nobel Prize–winning microbiologist.

6 1951–1960: The Double Helix Decade

A Crossroads

The world changed in 1953, when James Watson and Francis Crick hit upon the correct structure for the DNA molecule. Or so it seems from the perspective of history. Actually, there was no immediate public acclaim, little realization beyond the small world of molecular biologists and biophysicists of how important the discovery was. That would not come until almost a decade after Watson and Crick announced what they had found.

The double-helix molecule stands as the most prominent historical landmark in biological research between Gregor Mendel's 19th-century discoveries about pea heredity and the present-day world of *recombinant DNA* and *bioengineering*. Yet it was also just one scientific advance in a continuum of discovery. Watson and Crick have acknowledged many who inspired and aided them. History must view the partners in the context of a 1950s community of researchers who were closing in on the elementary physics and chemistry of life. Shortly before the Watson-Crick breakthrough, an ingenious experiment at Cold Spring Harbor, New York, confirmed the central role of DNA in heredity. In related 1950s work, researchers in Berkeley, California, showed that the nucleic acid in a virus was not only the active infectious agent but that it could direct the assembly of the virus itself. In Pasadena, young scientists inspired by the double helix found a way to test whether DNA really did make copies of itself as the model-builders had theorized. They found that it did.

Small units of life were becoming ever more important test subjects for biologists. In London, a former military immunologist demonstrated how one bacterium could physically transfer a bit of its genetic material into another. In Madison, Wisconsin, bacteriologists found that a bacteriophage can incorporate genetic material from one bacterium and then add it to the chromosomes of the next host cell.

Medical researchers were learning more about cell-to-cell interaction, discovering the role of the neurotransmitter l-dopa in mammalian brains and the function of interferons in a wide range of tissue. Along more immediately applicable and anxiously anticipated lines, immunology research delivered a vaccine against the growing peril of infantile paralysis, better known as polio.

Perhaps the greatest legacy of the double helix, and of 1950s biological research, is that scientists, and soon informed people at large, began to understand how alike all living matter is—from protozoa to pronghorn antelope to people—at the most basic, molecular level. Meanwhile, a complementary perception was just beginning to catch on, in the form of ecological research. It was the idea that all living things are linked and interlinked on a much larger scale—at macrobiological as well as microbiological levels. Long overlooked by much of biological science, this commonsensical perspective would soon gain widespread credence.

Confirmation in a Blender

At the beginning of the 1950s, many biologists had yet to accept the role of DNA as the agent of genetic heredity. As discussed in the previous chapter, leading geneticists—notably Alfred Mirsky of the Rockefeller

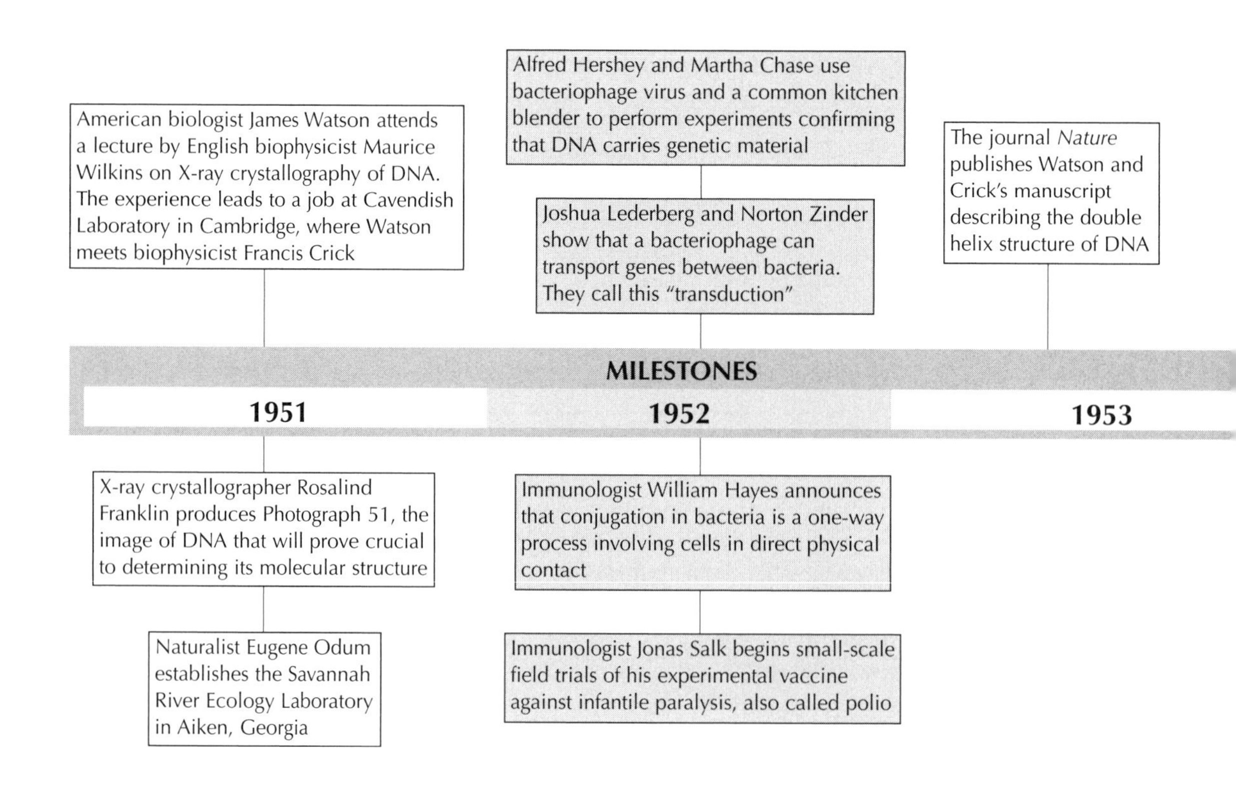

Institute—continued to suspect that the work of Oswald Avery and colleagues in the early 1940s, work that reported DNA to be the transforming principle in bacteria, was flawed. They thought that the chemical agent that transfers genetic material from a bacterium to another—and by extension, from any cell or organism to its progeny—must be either a protein or a combination of nucleic acid and protein.

That was until 1952, when an experiment conducted by Alfred Hershey and his laboratory assistant, Martha Chase (1928–2003), confirmed DNA's importance. Hershey, who had spent much of the 1940s investigating genetic changes in bacteriophages—a quest he shared with Salvador Luria and Max Delbrück, among others—had accepted a genetics research position in 1950 at the Carnegie Institution's Cold Spring Harbor Laboratory. There, he decided to tackle an elementary question about bacteriophages, the viruses that attack bacteria. What was it that allowed the phage, after attaching itself to a bacterial cell, to manufacture duplicates of itself? Was the active agent the protein—largely contained in the outer shell, or capsid, of the virus—or was it the DNA carried within? It had to be one or the other, because the bacteriophage is such a simple organism that it consists of virtually nothing else.

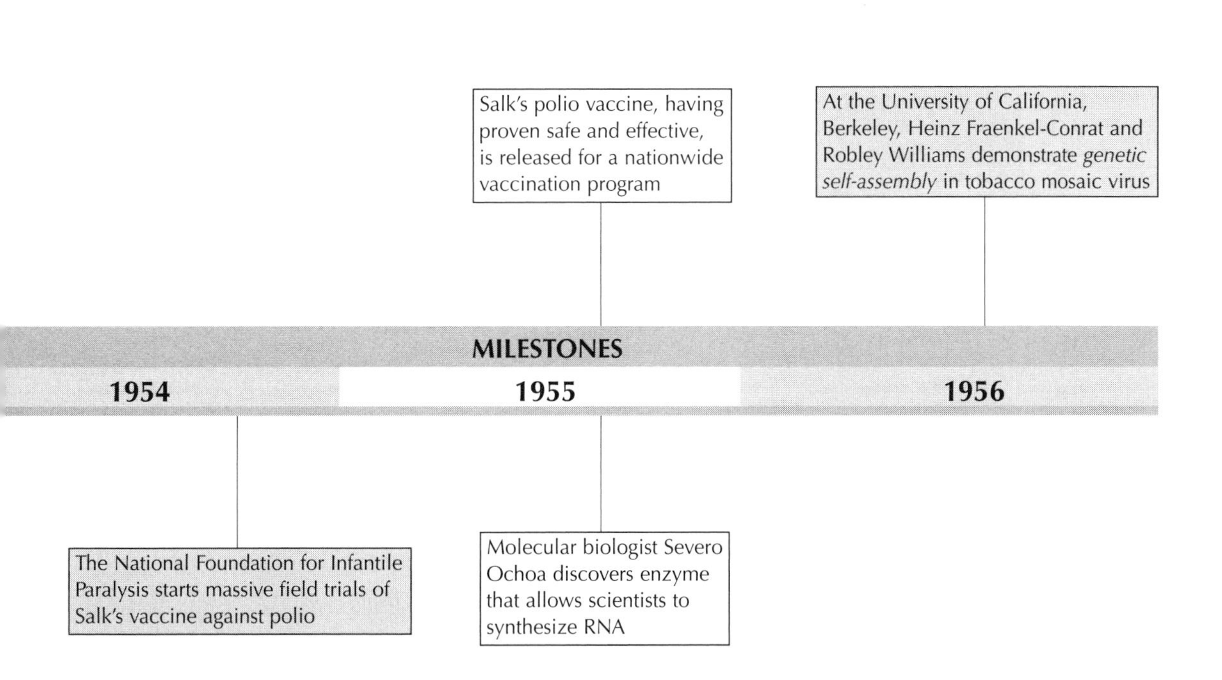

When the virus infects a bacterium, it takes over. The occupied bacterium becomes a reproductive machine for making more viruses. Hershey and Chase devised a way to answer their either-or question about what triggered the takeover.

They knew that protein contains sulfur while DNA does not. Further, they knew that DNA contains a great deal of phosphorus while protein contains only a small amount. So Hershey and Chase grew some bacteriophages in cultures that contained radioactive sulfur. The phages took the radioactive sulfur into their protein. At the same time, they grew other bacteriophages in a culture that contained radioactive phosphorus. Those phages incorporated a very small amount of the radioactive phosphorus into their protein, but they took most of it into their DNA.

Now Hershey and Chase had two kinds of bacteriophage. One kind had a radioactive capsid. The other had a bit of radioactivity in its capsid but much more radioactivity in its DNA. Under Hershey's direction, Chase added some of the first kind of phage to one culture of bacteria and some of the second kind to another culture of bacteria. After the viruses had infected the bacteria, she whirled each culture in a common kitchen blender. Why a blender? They had tried it out and found that it produced

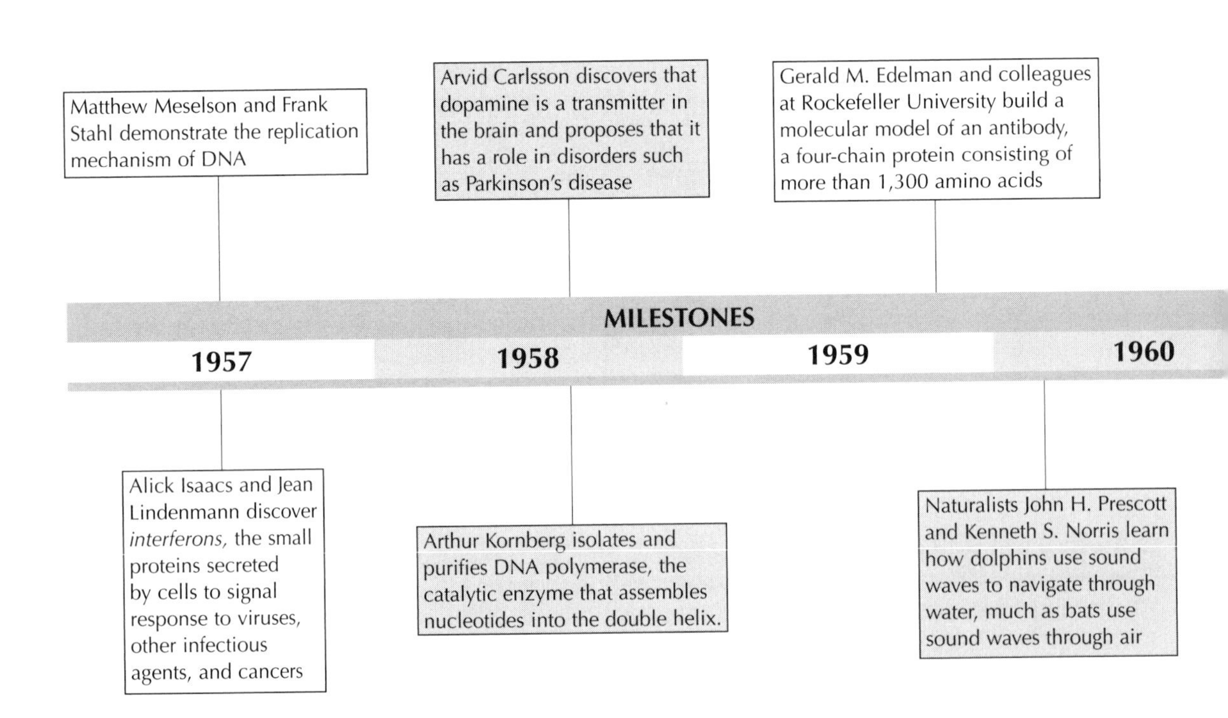

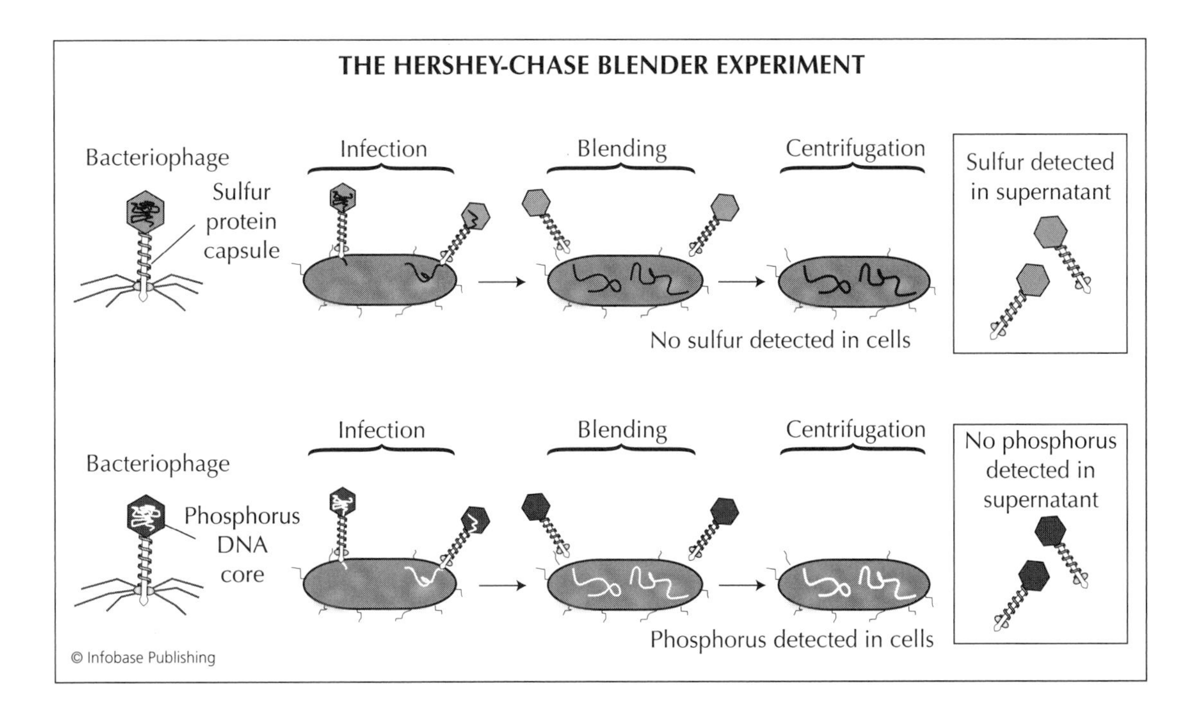

In the top sequence, the protein in the outer capsule of the phage has been tagged with radioactivity. In the lower sequence, the DNA within has been tagged. After phage particles are dislodged and separated from infected bacteria cells, the experiment shows that the viral DNA, not the viral protein, has entered the cell. This indicates that DNA, not protein, is the agent of reproduction.

enough force to shear phage particles away from a bacterial wall but not enough to rupture bacteria.

As the blender blades spun, any part of the attached bacteriophage that had not penetrated the bacterium fell away. The scientists took the resultant liquid and spun it again, this time in a centrifuge, which causes heavier particles—in this case the bacteria—to fall to the bottom. The bacteriophages and pieces of bacteriophages were left suspended in the liquid.

In the cultures that had been infected by bacteriophages with radioactive sulfur in their protein, the radioactivity was still with the phages and pieces. In those cultures infected by phages whose DNA carried high levels of radioactive phosphorus, most of the radioactivity was with the bacteria that had fallen to the bottom.

This showed that protein—the capsid and tail of the bacteriophage—had not entered the infected bacterium. The DNA from the interior of the phage had entered the bacterium, where it took over the cell's reproductive function.

Further, the offspring of the bacteriophages with radioactive phosphorus in their DNA also carried radioactive DNA but no radioactivity in their protein. It was clear that the DNA had been the agent to effect reproduction. The *Journal of General Physiology* that September published Chase and Hershey's paper "Independent Functions of Viral Protein and Nucleic Acid in Growth of Bacteriophage."

This experiment, added to his earlier bacteriophage investigations, led to Hershey's share of the 1969 Nobel Prize in physiology or medicine,

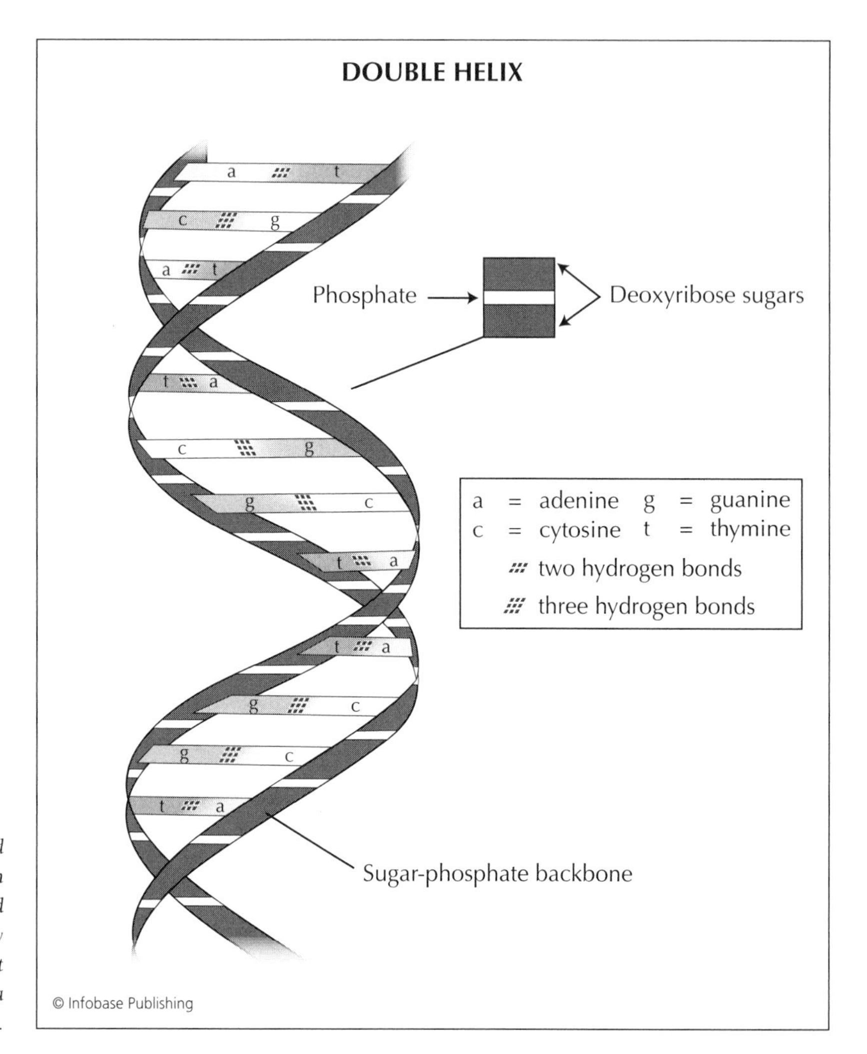

Watson and Crick envisioned two strands of DNA wound in a spiral around each other and connected by complementary base-pairing—an arrangement that has been compared to a spiral staircase.

which he received along with Luria and Delbrück. Martha Chase did not reap such rewards from her work in biology. The young woman, who had grown up in Shaker Heights, Ohio, and graduated from Wooster College, continued in lab work at the Oak Ridge National Laboratory in Tennessee and at the University of Rochester. She later moved to Los Angeles, where she married. She earned a Ph.D. from the University of Southern California in 1964, but personal setbacks, including the failure of her marriage, mounted through the 1960s. Chase descended into decades of dementia, which robbed her of short-term memory and made it impossible for her to return to science.

The Hershey-Chase experiment effectively ended any dissent from the idea that DNA was the physical agent of genetic heredity. In its elegant simplicity and its apparent finality, it proved an inspiration to other researchers, including biochemist Heinz Fraenkel-Conrat (1910–99) and biophysicist Robley Williams (1908–95), who in 1956 reported that the nucleic acid and protein from the tobacco mosaic virus, after being disassembled and purified, would actually reassemble themselves into a fully functional, that is infectious, virus. Further, Fraenkel-Conrat was able to show that the nucleic acid—which in the tobacco mosaic virus is RNA—can infect a tobacco plant by itself, after it has been separated from its protein plasmid.

The blender experiment inspired young James Watson. A Chicago native, Watson was working at the Cavendish Laboratory of Cambridge University in the fall of 1952, when the Hershey-Chase paper was published. He later credited that paper with spurring his determination to figure out the molecular structure of DNA.

The Secret of Life

Watson was bound to be interested in the Hershey-Chase blender experiment. The American had earned his Ph.D. from Indiana University with a study of bacteriophage reproduction. As a postdoctoral fellow in Denmark, Watson conducted studies with an aim similar to those that Hershey and Chase were doing at the same time in Cold Spring Harbor. He had been trying to trace what happened to the DNA of phages once they infected bacteria.

In the spring of 1951, Danish biochemist Herman M. Kalckar (1908–91), one of Watson's research supervisors in Copenhagen, brought the young Ph.D. to a symposium in Naples, Italy. There, Watson attended a presentation given by Maurice Wilkins (1916–2004), who as assistant director of the Medical Research Council Unit of King's College, London, was involved in a biophysics project probing the molecular structure of nucleic acids. Wilkins displayed a photo showing an X-ray diffraction pattern derived from crystalline DNA. Watson was hooked. He decided he wanted to do what Wilkins was doing.

Watson was not able to land a job at King's College, but with the help of Salvador Luria, who had been his mentor at Indiana University, he came close. On Luria's recommendation, the American was hired by the Cavendish Laboratory of Cambridge University, where director Lawrence Bragg had pioneered crystallography. Officially, Watson was assigned to study the structure of the protein myoglobin, but he could not stop thinking about genes, about DNA. Neither could another researcher at Cavendish, Francis Crick, a former physicist who had turned to biology after his service as a weapons researcher during World War II. Although still a graduate student in biology, Crick was already among a new breed of biophysicists, intensely interested in the molecules of genes. He was also in correspondence with some of the world's top

James Watson, left, and Francis Crick with their model of the DNA molecule at the Cavendish Laboratory (A. Barrington Brown/Science Photo Library)

DNA researchers. Crick first learned of the Hershey-Chase experiment through a personal letter from Alfred Hershey.

Almost immediately upon Watson's arrival in Cambridge, in October 1951, he and Crick became nearly inseparable, constantly talking about genes and the role of DNA. Both self-confident to the point of arrogance and obsessed, they talked about DNA so much that other researchers, tired of the chatter, got the pair moved into an office together, away from the rest of the lab.

Aware that the brilliant Linus Pauling, in Pasadena, was about to turn his attention to the structure of DNA, Watson and Crick decided to imitate Pauling's method—the building of molecular models based on a grasp of chemical bonding—and beat the master at his own game. They lacked more than Pauling's famous intuition, however. They also lacked his chemical expertise and his resources. While the Californian was in charge of his own research agenda at Caltech, including crystallographic studies of DNA, Watson and Crick worked for a lab where neither of them was assigned to the problem of DNA structure. In fact, nobody at the Cavendish Lab was working on DNA. That was the exclusive territory—in England, anyway—of Wilkins's unit at King's College.

The partners needed help from the King's College crystallographers, who were only a little more than an hour south by train. Crick knew he could talk to Watkins, an acquaintance who had also been a weapons physicist during the war. (In fact, Wilkins had been part of a California-based unit that contributed to the U.S. development of the atomic bomb.) Wilkins also shared Crick's conviction that the pattern suggested in many crystallographic photos of DNA could indicate a helical structure.

Yet Wilkins had only limited access to the latest and best in crystallographic research on DNA. Another researcher at King's College, Rosalind Franklin, believed that she was the sole researcher whose responsibility it was to study the elusive molecule. Although Wilkins was assistant director of the research unit, the soft-spoken, New Zealand–born scientist disliked confrontation. Franklin, by contrast, was volatile and outspoken—fierce some said—in defending what she saw as her scientific turf. She had confronted Wilkins several times about his pursuit of DNA structure. At one point in the summer of 1951, according to Franklin biographer Brenda Maddox, Franklin waited for Wilkins after he had given an upbeat talk on DNA research in which he confidently predicted that the lab's crystallographic photos pointed toward a helix. Not only did she disagree, but she also told him he was out of bounds.

"Go back to your microscopes," is what he remembered her saying. Who was Rosalind Franklin to say such a thing? Primarily, she was a brilliant crystallographer, perhaps the best of her time. A careful, methodical physicist, she believed in empirical results, derived from experiments. She knew that Pauling could achieve remarkable insights through his informed intuition and scaled-up models of molecules. That Watson and Crick might achieve similar results struck her as improbable at best. The pair from Cavendish did little to change her mind when they based their first DNA model on data that Watson had picked up when he attended a lecture delivered by Franklin. Recklessly confident, he had neglected to take notes, assuming he could remember what was important. He was wrong.

Franklin paid Watson and Crick the courtesy of coming with Wilkins to Cambridge to view the model in late 1951, but at first sight, she pointed out that the imaginary molecule was chemically impossible. She had already been less than fond of Crick, whose interest in DNA she did not welcome, and she came away with little respect for Watson. The Cavendish pair returned the sentiments. Watson, still in his early twenties, was particularly uncomfortable around assertive, intelligent women. It did not smooth matters over that both he and Crick insisted on calling Franklin—their superior in experience and scientific achievement—by the nickname "Rosie," which she hated.

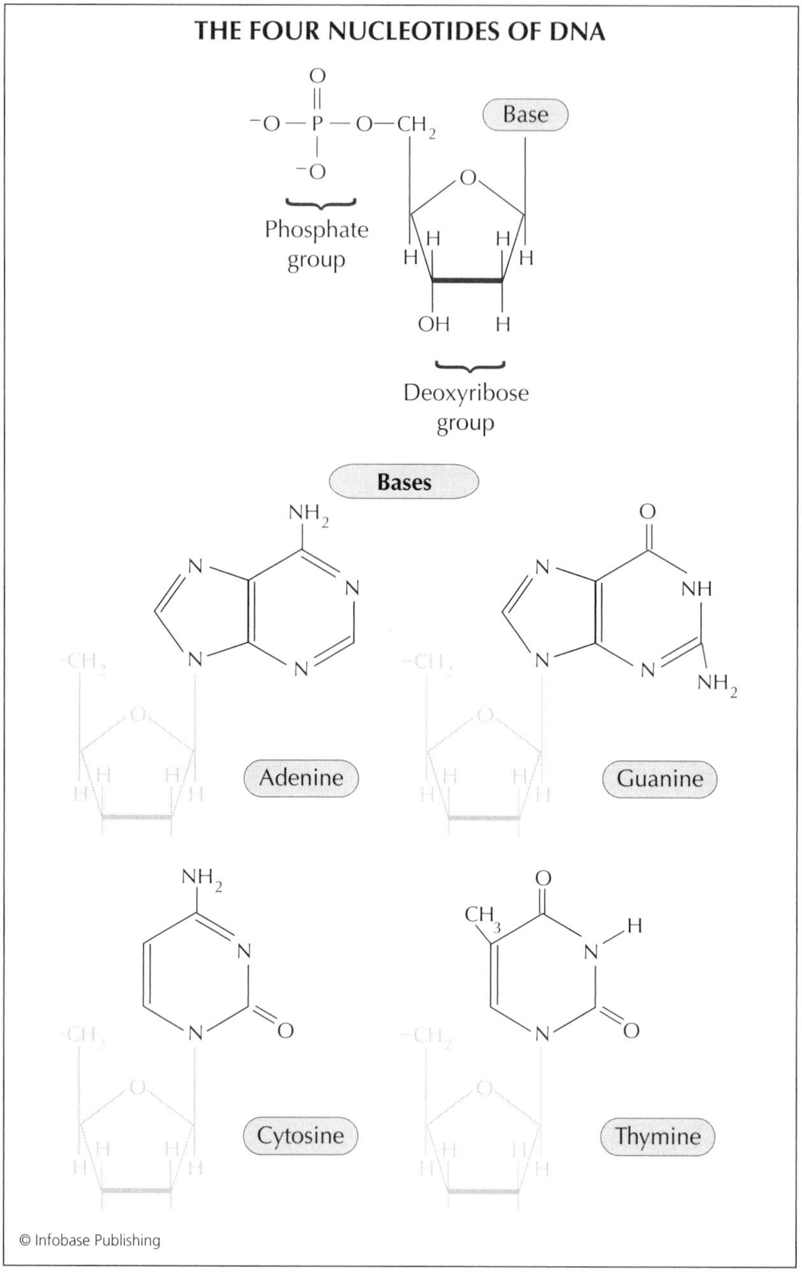

THE FOUR NUCLEOTIDES OF DNA

© Infobase Publishing

Nucleotides are organic compounds in which the molecular structure is made up of three parts: a simple sugar called deoxyribose, a phosphate, and a special molecule called a nitrogen base. DNA is built of nucleotides based on adenine and guanine (both derivatives of purine), thymine, and cytosine (both derivatives of pyrimidine).

Shortly thereafter, Bragg, who was Watson and Crick's boss at Cavendish and who did not appreciate their failure to stick to what he had assigned them, decided enough was enough. After consulting with the lab director who oversaw Wilkins's and Franklin's work at King's

College, Bragg forbade his staffers from working any further on DNA. For a while, Watson and Crick obeyed.

In London, the rift between Wilkins and Franklin widened over the next several months, but the work went on. Franklin made an important breakthrough when she found that by increasing the humidity in her apparatus she could produce another form of DNA, a wet form in which the molecule stretched and became thinner. By photographing this *B form* of DNA, as she called it, she produced sharper images, and in May 1952, she produced the sharpest one yet. Labeled Photograph 51, it looked to Wilkins like strong support for the theory that the molecule was helical in shape.

Wilkins's interest led to another clash with Franklin. After the worst row yet between the colleagues, the director of the King's College lab played referee. He formally assigned to Franklin sole responsibility for studying the crystalline, or A form of DNA. To Wilkins, he assigned the B form.

Linus Pauling, who pioneered the use of models to test his ideas about the chemical bond, remained in the 1950s the most likely scientist to puzzle out the molecular structure of DNA. Francis Crick and James Watson viewed the famous chemist, here shown in a Caltech laboratory, as their chief rival. (Ava Helen and Linus Pauling Papers, Oregon State University Library)

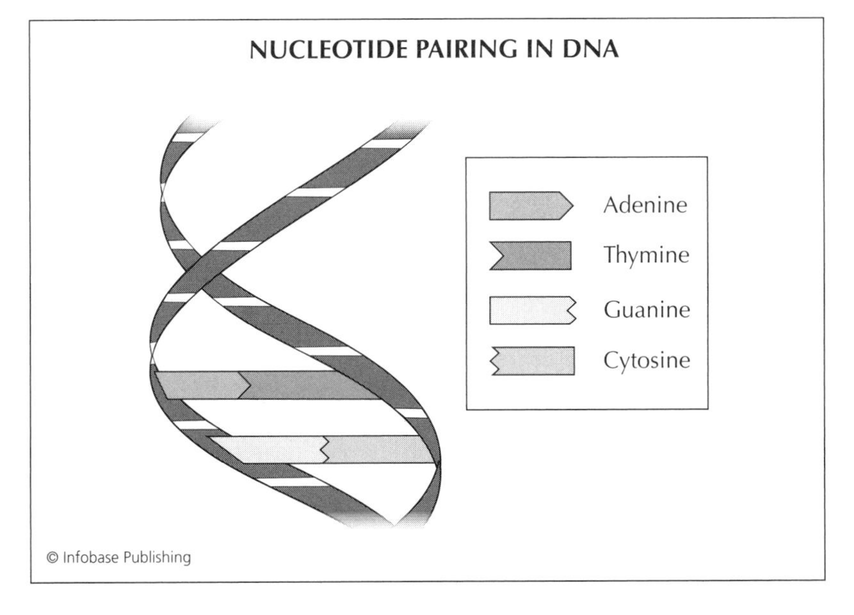

A key to understanding the structure of DNA is the fact that each of these bases can attach itself to only one of the other three. Adenine can link only to thymine, and guanine can hook up only with cytosine.

"We Have Also Been Stimulated . . ."

In the acknowledgments at the end of their 1953 paper in *Nature,* Watson and Crick wrote: "We have also been stimulated by a knowledge of the general nature of the unpublished experimental results and ideas of Dr. M. H. F. Wilkins, Dr. R. E. Franklin and their co-workers at King's College, London." A decade later, Wilkins shared the Nobel Prize in medicine or physiology with the two authors. Franklin, who died in 1958 at age 37, did not.

It has been suggested that Rosalind Franklin, whose now-famous photograph pointed the way to this great discovery, was cheated of credit for her contribution. Watson and Crick certainly treated her shabbily. Watson, in particular, was unkind to the late Franklin in his best-selling 1968 book, *The Double Helix.* He criticized her preference for wearing little makeup and dismissed her style of dress—which appears conservatively elegant in photographs—as showing "all the imagination of English bluestocking adolescents." As a professional, he judged her unnecessarily belligerent, stubborn, and short-sighted. "Clearly Rosie had to go or be put in her place," he wrote, recalling the discord at King's College.

Watson cut or tempered such passages about Franklin in subsequent editions of *The Double Helix.* He also apologized to his readers and to women in general for his sexist attitude toward the crystallographer. Speaking to *Time* magazine's Michael Lemonick in 2003, he framed Franklin's limitations in much more generous terms. Remembering her resistance to the idea that the molecule was helical, he cited her firm belief in hard data. Until the X-ray crystallography clearly showed a helical structure—and she believed that had not yet happened—she was unwilling to make an assumption about DNA. He also said that her preference for working alone deprived her of the kind of back-and-forth intellectual stimulation that gave him and Crick an edge. ". . . Rosalind was so intelligent that she rarely sought advice. If you're the brightest person in the room, you're in trouble," Watson told Lemonick.

From a well-to-do London family, Rosalind Elsie Franklin studied physical chemistry at Newnham College, Cambridge. A specialist in the physical properties of carbon, she worked for the British Coal Utilisation Research Association

The following January, Watson and Crick got word that Pauling had built a speculative model of DNA and was about to publish a paper on it. To their great relief, they realized that Pauling's model, as described in a letter to his son Peter Pauling (a Cambridge graduate student), was wrong. Watson took the train to London to talk with Wilkins about this turn of affairs, and while at the King's College lab, he provoked an argument with Franklin. She put him out of her office. Afterward, as they commiserated about the unpleasantness, Wilkins shared with Watson the startlingly clear photo of B-form DNA that Franklin had taken the previous spring. Watson immediately saw in Photograph 51 a double helix.

The missing bit came to Watson late the next month, as a rather Pauling-like piece of insight. After struggling to fit together the chemical bases of DNA—adenine, guanine, thymine, and cytosine—in a way that made chemical sense and supported an evenly spaced double helix, he realized that if he paired adenine with thymine and only thymine and if he paired guanine exclusively with cytosine, then the pairs, held

and then for the State Chemical Laboratory in Paris. That work led to practical advances in Europe's energy and steel industries.

In 1951, Franklin, bowing to the wishes of her close-knit family, reluctantly returned from France—a country she preferred—to London, where she joined the Biophysical Laboratory at King's College. According to biographer Maddox, she disliked the lab, the facilities, and her labmates. This no doubt colored her uneasy relationship with Maurice Wilkins and his associates from the Cavendish Laboratory at Cambridge.

Although colleagues sometimes found her argumentative and abrasive, her many friends remembered Franklin as fun-loving and gracious. Maddox and others have noted that she tended to lose patience with men who underestimated her. Yet Franklin's impatience also extended to her work habits. In an era when safety standards were less than thorough, she was one of many X-ray crystallographers who often neglected to wear a lead-lined apron. It is likely that the radiation to which she exposed herself contributed to the ovarian cancer that killed her.

As for whether she was cheated of her share of credit for the discovery of DNA's structure, Franklin never seemed to think so. After Crick and Watson's breakthrough, she maintained a much less combative—even friendly—relationship with the pair. It probably helped that in the spring of 1953, about the time they announced their achievement, she left King's College for a job she much preferred, studying viruses at the University of London. The crystallographer was happier in what turned out to be her last years.

Yet she never knew quite what Watson and Crick had meant by including her in their acknowledgments. No one told her how central her Photograph 51 had been to their discovery. On her own, Franklin had not interpreted the photo in the way that Wilkins and Watson had. She had never—despite her superior grasp of chemistry—been inclined to make the leap of logic that Watson and Crick made. Leaps were not her way of reasoning.

As for whether she should have shared in the Nobel Prize, the point is moot. The prizes are for living scientists. No one receives a Nobel posthumously.

in place by hydrogen bonds, matched in shape. Thus, the order of bases along one strand determined the complementary order of bases along the other—suggesting a mechanism for reproduction. Watson and Crick had arrived at two intertwining spiral strands that could do, in theoretical terms, what DNA would have to do if it were indeed the very stuff of life. They described their finding in a short manuscript titled "Molecular Structure of Nucleic Acids," published by the journal *Nature* on April 25, 1953. It was illustrated with a diagram of the double helix drawn by Odile Crick and by Franklin's Photograph 51.

Tackling the Code

Watson and Crick's discovery stands as a monumental turning point in biological research. They had opened the door to a new age of molecular genetics. Yet, as so often in the history of science, their peers were slow to recognize the significance of what they had accomplished.

George Gamow's achievements included the first successful explanation for the mechanism of radioactive decay. (AIP Emilio Segrè Visual Archives)

The double helix, in its elegant symmetry, seemed perfectly suited for self-replication, as Watson and Crick said in their 1953 announcement of the discovery. "It has not escaped our notice," they concluded, "that the specific pairing we have postulated immediately suggests a possible copying mechanism for the genetic material." Yet the biochemical details by which this process manufactured proteins and assembled them into organisms remained unknown. What was the genetic code, and how could that code build a bacterium or a beluga whale? Nobody—not Watson, not Crick, not Wilkins—knew the answers to such questions.

It was an already-famous physicist, George Gamow (1904–68), who began the race to crack the genetic code when he wrote a provocative letter to Watson and Crick later in 1953. In the letter, the Russian-born Gamow, of George Washington University, proposed a genetic code determined by the order of recurring triplets of *nucleotides*, which consist of the base (such as adenine or guanine) linked to a sugar (deoxyribose) and a phosphate, the latter two making up the backbone of the helix. The sequence of nucleotides, he thought, specifies the amino acid sequence in protein formation. Gamow—widely known as the author of astrophysics' *big bang* theory, an explanation of the formation of the universe—elaborated on his mathematics-based proposal for a genetic code in a 1954 article titled "Possible Mathematical Relation between Deoxyribonucleic Acid and Proteins," for *Nature*.

Gamow's letter and article prompted Crick, in particular, to begin working on the coding problem. Along with Gamow, he and Watson believed that genetic information can flow from DNA to messenger RNA to protein, but never in reverse. This rule, although later found to have exceptions, became a tenet of molecular genetics doctrine, referred to as the "central dogma."

Other biophysicists and biologists, and a number of physicists like Gamow, found the problem of the genetic code a fascinating challenge. Nuclear physicist Edward Teller (1908–2003), an associate of Gamow and best known as the father of the hydrogen bomb, took up the quest for a while in the 1950s.

Crick and others at Cavendish did some of the most illuminating early work toward understanding the mechanics of the genetic code. No one succeeded at cracking that code, however, until the early 1960s. That story continues in the next chapter.

Semiconservative Replication

Gamow worked on the assumption that Watson and Crick were right about the physical process by which DNA replicates—that each strand of the double helix serves as a template for a new opposite strand. In the summer of 1954, however, two young Ph.D.'s at Woods Hole Laboratory set out to prove or disprove that notion, which had become known as *semi-conservative replication.*

Matthew Meselson (1930–), a Denver native, was a crystallography researcher working under Linus Pauling at Caltech. He had come to Woods Hole that summer as a teaching assistant, largely because he knew that Watson and Crick would be in residence. Meselson recalled later that he was with a group of scientists when Watson pointed out Franklin W. Stahl (1929–), a postdoctoral fellow from the University of Rochester, and said that they should throw a tough experiment at Stahl and see how he performed.

Wanting to warn Stahl, Meselson approached him where Stahl was sitting on a lawn, in the shade, with bottles of gin and tonic and fresh limes. He had been mixing drinks and selling them to passersby. As they talked, Meselson learned that Stahl, a Boston native, would join the molecular biology research staff at Caltech in the fall. The two struck up a friendship, decided to room together in Pasadena, and began discussing experiments they could do together. One was a test of Watson and Crick's theory of semiconservative replication—the idea that entwined strands of the double helix replicate themselves in a process that involves unwinding from one another, with each strand able to direct the formation of a new complementary opposite, creating two double helixes, each of which conserves one-half of the original.

The partners arrived at a way to do this at Caltech in 1957. Using a heavy isotope of nitrogen, they were able to grow cells with a higher-than-normal density DNA. Cells descended from those with this dense DNA, when then grown in a culture including nitrogen of the more usual isotope, contained DNA of intermediate density. The two researchers used a high-speed centrifuge to separate out DNA molecules of varying density. By tracing the nitrogen content of succeeding generations of DNA, Meselson and Stahl established in 1958 that DNA does indeed separate according to the Watson and Crick model, with each helical strand serving as a template for its complementary opposite.

DNA Polymerase

Meselson and Stahl confirmed the manner in which DNA replicates itself, but there was still a question as to the mechanism. How did the cell make DNA molecules? What caused the nucleotide bases that comprise the nucleic acid to string together into the double helix?

Such a molecule as DNA, a repeating structure made of smaller molecules strung together, is a polymer. To form, it requires that its constituent pieces polymerize—a chemical process generally brought about by a catalyst. In 1958, Arthur Kornberg (1918–), head of the microbiology department at Washington University in St. Louis, figured out how that polymerization process for DNA works.

Two years earlier, Kornberg had begun this work by tagging nucleotides with radioactive isotopes and adding them to extracts prepared from *E. coli.* Following the isotopes allowed him to see evidence of polymerization reaction. With a background in enzyme research, Kornberg and his wife, Sylvy R. Kornberg (d. 1986), also a researcher, were able to isolate and purify the enzyme (DNA polymerase) that catalyzed the reaction. Further, they were able to combine nucleotide building blocks and DNA polymerase in a test tube and actually make precise copies of short DNA molecules.

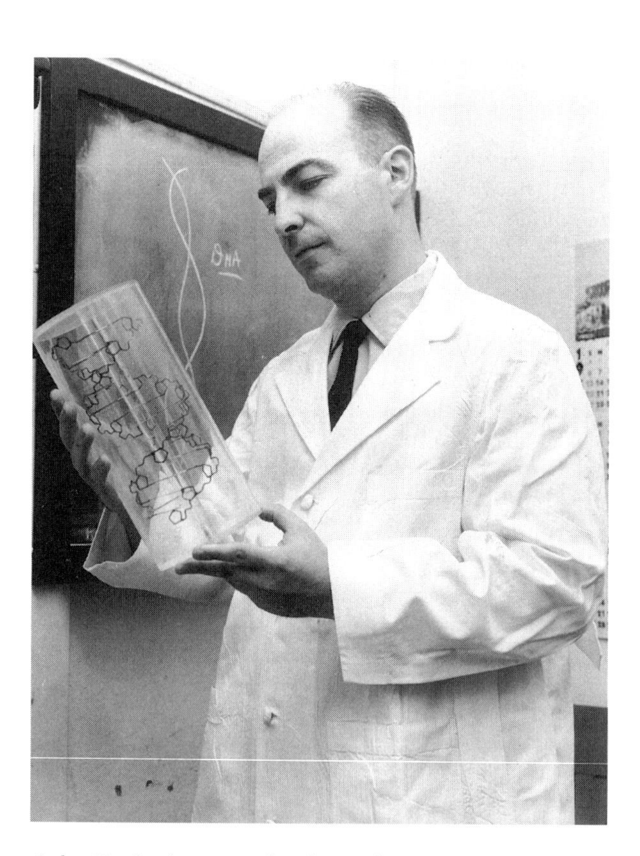

Arthur Kornberg's curiosity about his own benign genetic disorder, Gilbert's syndrome, steered him toward a career in research. (Bernard Becker Medical Library, Washington University)

Born in New York City, Kornberg was the son of a garment worker who had come to America from Galicia (an area of eastern Europe then in Austria, now in Poland). The son grew up in Brooklyn and earned his bachelor's degree from City College. With an M.D. from the University of Rochester, he became a coast guard ship's doctor during part of World War II and worked as a nutrition researcher for the National Institutes of Health in Maryland before joining the laboratory of Spanish biochemist Severo Ochoa (1905–93) at New York University.

There, Kornberg learned to isolate and purify enzymes. Subsequent work with the National Institutes of Health (NIH), where he became head of the Enzyme and Metabolism Section in 1947, led toward Kornberg's discovery of DNA polymerase. For the NIH, he concentrated on adenosine triphosphate (ATP), a molecule essential in the metabolism of all living cells. Cells constantly break down ATP, which is made of adenine, ribose, and three phosphates, but ATP forms during cell respiration, mostly by means of a specific enzyme.

In 1955, after Kornberg had moved to St. Louis, his former mentor at New York University made a crucial discovery relevant to the polymerization of that other mysterious nucleic acid, RNA. Ochoa found a way to synthesize RNA using a specific enzyme, polynucleotide phosphorylase. Later research revealed that this enzyme's function in a cell is actually to break apart RNA molecules. In a test tube, its biochemical process runs in reverse, assembling the single-strand nucleic acid. For that reason, scientists have found polynucleotide phosphorylase to be an important tool for understanding and replicating gene translation.

For their discoveries, Kornberg and Ochoa shared the 1959 Nobel Prize in physiology or medicine. Kornberg's wife, Sylvy, who had contributed significantly to her husband's work, commented, "I was robbed."

Kornberg was still active as a researcher at Stanford University in 2006, when his son, Roger D. Kornberg (1947–   ), won the Nobel Prize in chemistry for a discovery built upon the work of his father and other molecular biologists. Roger Kornberg, a professor of structural biology at Stanford, used extremely sophisticated crystallography techniques to discover and describe the process whereby genetic information is copied from DNA into messenger RNA, so that the information can be carried to the ribosomes where proteins are built.

Back to Bacteria

Using the species *E. coli*, Joshua Lederberg and Edward Tatum had shown in the previous decade that a bacterium could combine its genetic material with that of another bacterium. This phenomenon has been compared to sexual reproduction, as in multicelled organisms. The transfer, however, is not sexual, and the combined genetic material that results from it is not made up of equal parts from each of the parent cells.

The parallel with sexual reproduction became a common way to explain the process, called bacterial *conjugation*, after London immunologist William Hayes (1913–94) announced in 1952 his discovery that the transfer happens in only one direction between cells that are in physical contact with each other. Most microbiologists and geneticists had thought that any gene transfer between bacteria involved a breakdown of the cell wall or a merging of cells. Hayes, an Irish-born physician who had spent World War II as a major in the Royal Medical Corps, was not in the mainstream of genetic research, and he surprised the establishment with his finding that neither assumption was so.

He said that instead, certain bacteria have the ability to inject a portion of their own DNA through the cell wall of another bacterium. The donor gives a short piece of DNA but does not receive genes in return. The receptor takes but does not give. Scientists began referring to the donors as male and the receptors as female. (Later researchers dropped the terminology as inaccurate, as there is no true gender in *E. coli* or other species of bacteria.)

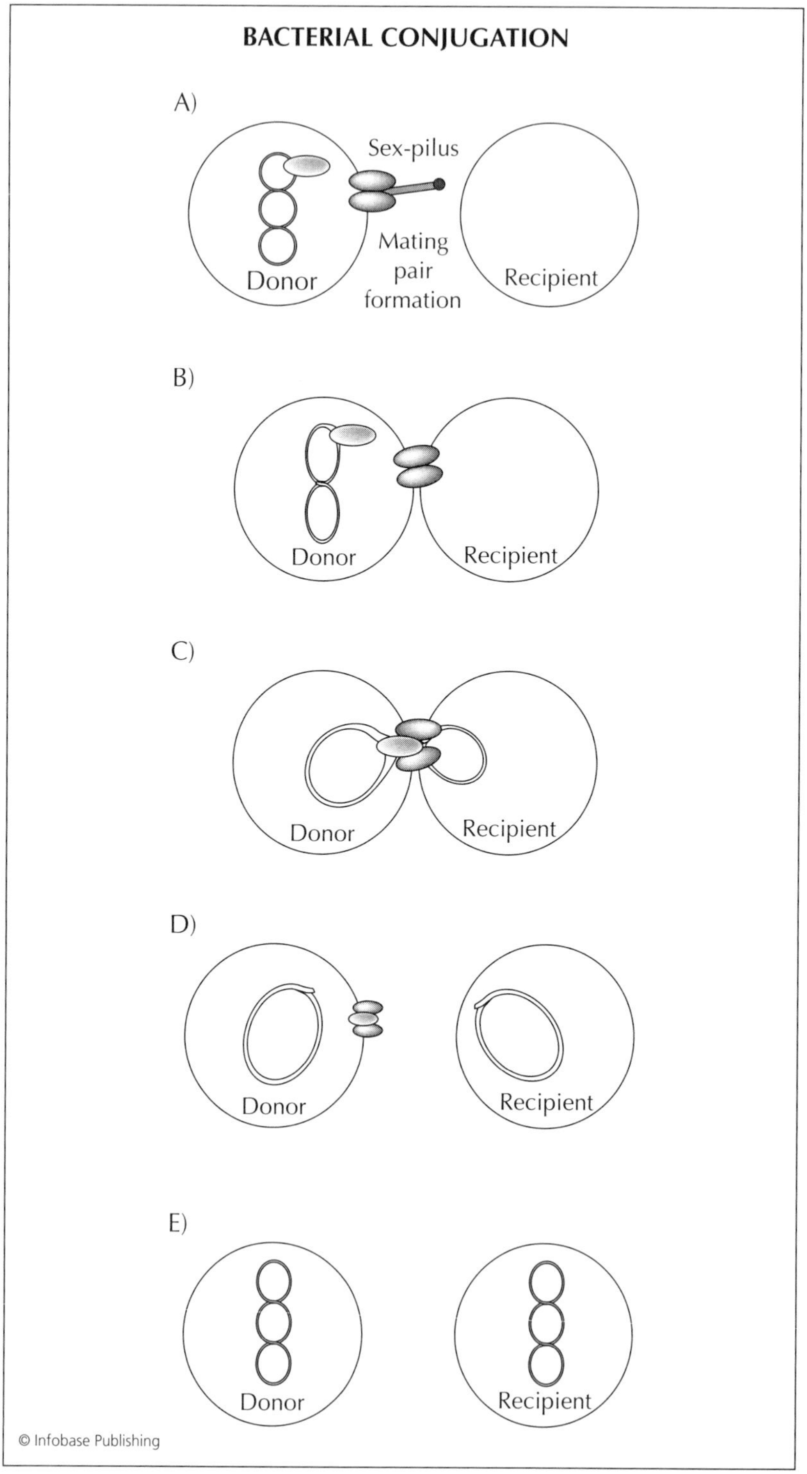

BACTERIAL CONJUGATION

A)

Sex-pilus

Donor

Mating pair formation

Recipient

B)

Donor

Recipient

C)

Donor

Recipient

D)

Donor

Recipient

E)

Donor

Recipient

William Hayes explained the one-way transfer of genetic materials between cells. A) The donor cell forms a specific plasmid-coded pilus, which is a hairlike structure on the cell's surface. B) Sometimes called a "sex pilus," this structure makes contact with the surface of an adjacent recipient cell and pulls it close, so that the two cells are in direct contact. Then it forms a conjugal passage. An enzyme cleaves one strand of plasmid DNA. C) The strand of DNA travels through the passage from donor to recipient. D) The conjugal passage closes, and the pilus disengages. E) DNA from the donor cell integrates into the recipient cell, which thus becomes a donor cell.

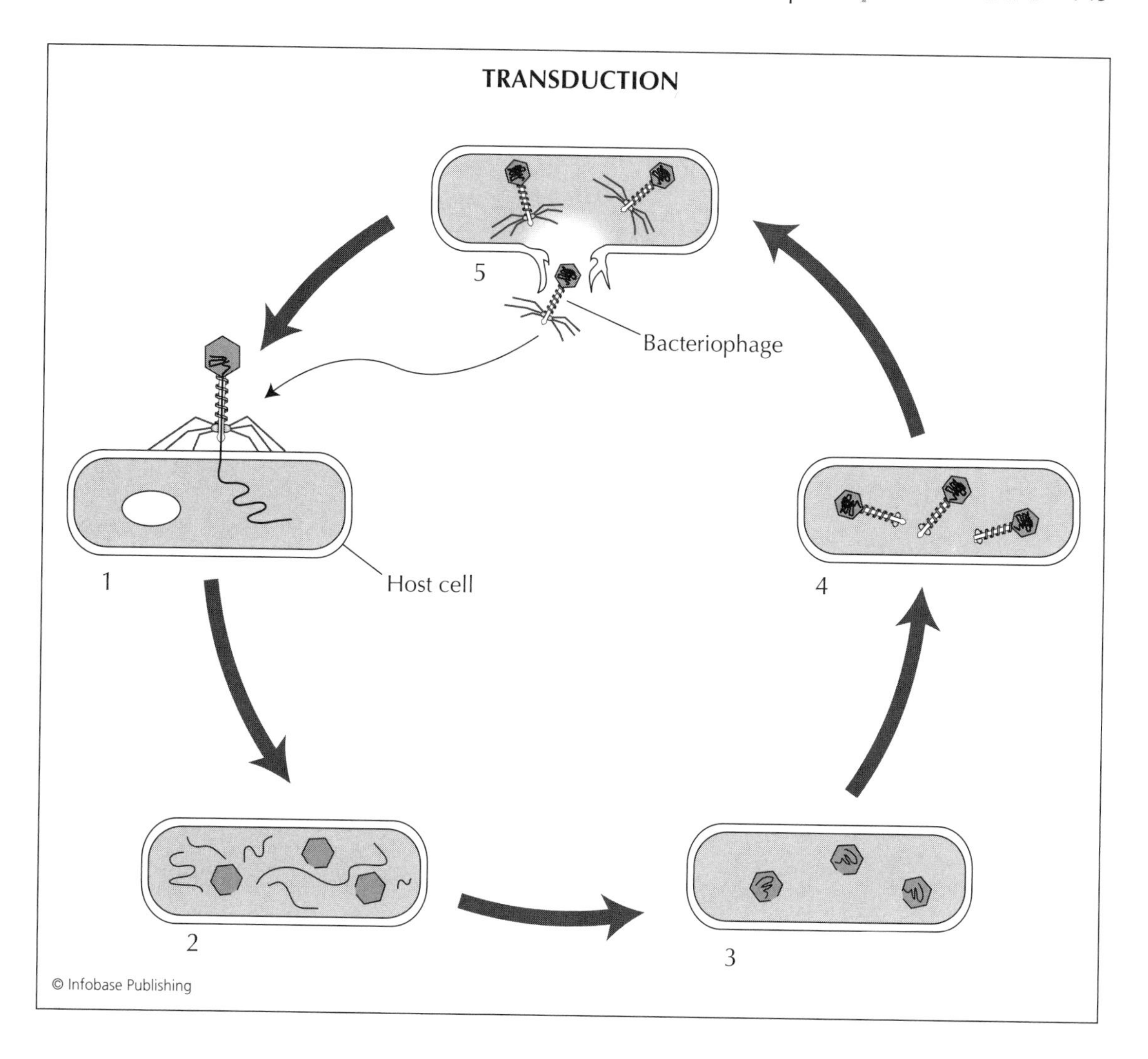

Bacteria sometimes exchange genes indirectly, through a bacteriophage virus that snares bits of DNA from one cell and transports them to the next cell infected.

Hayes, on the faculty of the Postgraduate Medical School of London (then associated with Hammersmith Hospital), also discovered that the donor cells contained a piece of DNA that the receptors did not. He called this the F (for fertility) factor.

These discoveries joined a rapid series of findings about bacteria that were shaping the fields of microbial genetics and molecular biology. At the University of Wisconsin in Madison, for example, Lederberg and his graduate student Norton D. Zinder (1928–) in 1952 reported that a bacteriophage of the bacterium *Salmonella typhimurium* can carry genes from one cell to another. The DNA is taken into the genome of the phage and then, as the virus moves on to infect another *S. typhimurium* cell, carried to that new host. They called this process, which also takes place in other species of bacteria, *transduction*.

These discoveries by Hayes, Lederberg, and others showed that genes could be inserted directly into cells, where they would be incorporated into the cell's own DNA. Scientists began to see that they might also be able to insert foreign genes, thus recombining DNA artificially.

Race to Cure Polio Tops Medical News

As certain bacteria and viruses became ever more valuable to researchers studying genetic mechanisms, others continued to spread pain, disability, and death as infectious agents. Among the most feared in the early 1950s was the virus that caused poliomyelitis, or polio.

Also called infantile paralysis, the neuromuscular disease could strike adults. It had robbed 39-year-old Franklin Delano Roosevelt of the use of his legs in 1921 (more than a decade before he became U.S. president). Polio was far more common in children, however. It caused skeletal muscles, such as those in the limbs, to atrophy and become useless. Sometimes polio left people permanently disfigured.

Cases had been increasing decade by decade through the 20th century. In 1952, there were 58,000 new infections reported and 3,000 deaths in the United States alone. That was also the year that a University of Pittsburgh medical researcher, Jonas Salk (1914–2005), began small-scale field trials on a vaccine he had developed.

With support from the National Foundation for Infantile Paralysis (best known at that time for its fund-raising arm, the March of Dimes), immunologist Salk had begun in 1947 to disprove the accepted theory that any effective polio vaccine must use live virus. Salk, who had earlier developed flu vaccines, thought the use of live virus in a polio vaccine would be unacceptably dangerous.

The son of Russian-Jewish immigrants to the United States, Salk had been the first in his family to attend college. Even before completing medical school at New York University, he went into virus research there, working under Thomas Francis, Jr. (1900–69), an immunologist who developed breakthroughs in flu vaccines. When his mentor accepted a position at the University of Michigan, Salk followed, taking a job as a public health immunologist on Francis's staff. In 1947, Salk left Ann Arbor to become head of the virus research laboratory at Pittsburgh, where he began his polio research.

With the disease spreading at an alarming rate, Salk continued collaborating with his former colleagues in Michigan and with immunologists elsewhere as they raced to perfect a vaccine. After isolating three separate strains of the virus, he showed that killed virus of each strain, though it could not infect tissue with the disease, could nevertheless cause monkeys to produce *antibodies* against polio. After the tests in monkeys, Salk won approval to conduct the first small-scale field tests of his vaccine. The virus was first tested on children who had recovered from polio and thus already had antibodies against the disease. After it was shown that an injection of Salk's virus significantly raised the level of those antibodies, Salk and fellow researchers went on to test the vaccine on subjects who had never been exposed to polio.

In 1954, the National Foundation for Infantile Paralysis asked Francis to conduct a large-scale test of the vaccine. On April 12, 1955, Francis announced the test's success as the Salk vaccine was released for use in the United States. New cases of polio declined dramatically, becoming virtually unheard of in those who had been vaccinated by a massive public health campaign across the nation.

Hailed as a hero, Salk became one of the most famous men in the world. Admiration for him grew as he refused to patent the vaccine, passing up what surely would have been great wealth. He said he simply wanted to see the vaccine in use by as many people over as wide an area as possible.

Salk's vaccine continues to be widely used, although it has been superseded in the United States and many other countries by a live virus vaccine which is administered orally, rather than by injection. Polio was considered eradicated from the Western Hemisphere by the mid-1990s. Salk, who opened the Salk Institute for Biological Studies in La Jolla, California, in 1963, continued his research, in addition to lecturing and writing books. At the time of his death, he was working on an AIDS vaccine.

The decade saw another medical research breakthrough in 1958, when Swedish pharmacologist Arvid Carlsson (1923–) reported the role of the organic compound dopamine as an important neurotransmitter in the brain.

Born in Uppsala, Sweden, Carlsson earned a medical degree from the University of Lund in 1951 and stayed on as a teacher and researcher through most of the 1950s. There, he looked into the then-accepted belief that dopamine's job was merely to trigger brain cells in their production of the neurotransmitter *noradrenalin.* Carlsson invented a test that found very high levels of dopamine in a part of the brain that controls voluntary movements such as walking. By depriving animal research subjects of dopamine, he was able to impair their movement. Then he administered the amino acid levodopa, commonly called L-dopa. The brain converts L-dopa to dopamine. The test subjects treated with L-dopa regained the ability to move normally.

Carlsson's work led to the use of L-dopa as a treatment for Parkinson's disease. It also led scientists to understand neurotransmitters better—a first step toward the development of modern antidepressant drugs. For Carlsson, who became a professor of pharmacology at Göteborg University (in Göteborg, Sweden), these and continuing studies into the actions of neurotransmitters led to a share of the 2000 Nobel Prize in physiology or medicine.

Among further progress in medical research during the 1950s, there was the discovery in 1957, by British bacteriologist Alick Isaacs (1921–67) and Swiss microbiologist Jean Lindenmann (1924–), of the small proteins called interferons, which are an important part of the body's immune system.

While studying viral infections on tissue cultures, the pair found that any cell, when it detects attack by a virus, can issue a type of interferon. (These proteins were later classified into three major groups and many subtypes.) The interferon will then signal nearby cells to produce a protein that, in turn, prevents the virus from reproducing.

Stepping Back

Any evaluation of advances in biological research from 1951 to 1960 must center on the work of Watson, Crick, and others like them—scientists concerned with life's mechanisms on a scale smaller than the cell. To some extent, the same can be said for any consideration of biological research in the 20th century. It was indisputably the DNA century, when science discovered and demonstrated how alike all life is at its most basic—down in its molecules, its nucleotides, its atoms.

That approach makes it too easy to slight the many other fields of biology that look at the whole organism, at species, and—increasingly through the second half of the century—at interconnected systems of diverse species.

Among these scientists, Eugene Odum (1913–2002) set the tone for an important, growing movement within biology in the later decades of the century. Rather than a physicist-turned biologist, like Crick and Wilkins, or a chemist concerned with biology, as was Linus Pauling, Odum more resembled the natural philosophers of the 19th century. Born in New Hampshire, he was the son of sociologist Howard W. Odum, whom he credited with helping him to think about individuals (and by extension, individual organisms) as part of an interactive community. Eugene Odum received his Ph.D. in zoology from the University of Illinois in 1939, not long after British botanist Arthur Tansley had coined the term *ecosystem.*

As a professor of zoology at the University of Georgia, in Athens, Odum observed life through an entirely different lens from that of the molecular biologists—from the opposite perspective. Unlike some zoologists of his time, he put the emphasis of his studies not simply on an animal as a whole but on the interrelationships of animals and other organisms—from single-celled plants to large vertebrates—and the natural systems that sustain them. At the time, ecology was still a minor subdivision of biology. Its research criteria were little understood, even among scientists. Odum helped change that.

In 1951, he founded the Savannah River Ecology Laboratory in Aiken, Georgia. Its inception grew from Odum's desire to study how a nuclear weapons plant had affected the *riparian* environment around it. At the time, few researchers worldwide had seriously looked into the impact of human activity on natural systems.

Scientists of the Decade: James Watson (1928–) and Francis Crick (1916–2004)

At Cambridge University in the early 1950s, Francis Crick and James Watson made a matched set. Each was intense, lean, tall, energetic, talkative, brash, and obsessed with the same scientific problem. Their similarities, especially that shared obsession, led them to what may fairly be called the biological discovery of the 20th century, described earlier in this chapter.

The two researchers were also, obviously, different. Crick was in his mid-30s, married for the second time, a father, and English. Watson was in his early 20s, single, and American. Crick had a brother. Watson was an only child. They took rather different paths to reach the Cavendish Laboratory at Cambridge, where they met in 1951. Watson's path was the faster and more direct.

The son of a Northampton shoe manufacturer, Crick was born in 1916. He had been on his way to a Ph.D. in physics when World War II interrupted his studies. His wartime work for the British Admiralty, designing circuits for acoustic and magnetic mines, could have led to an appointment as head of Britain's scientific intelligence, had he not decided to change careers.

Watson, born in 1928 in Chicago, had been 11 years old when the war broke out in Europe and only 13 when the United States got into the fight. An amateur birdwatcher and an academic prodigy, Watson entered the University of Chicago at 15 (after zipping through the city's South Shore High in only two years) and majored in zoology.

During his junior year there, Watson read *What Is Life?*, a book by physicist Erwin Schrödinger. In it, Schrödinger posited that a physical genetic code, at the molecular level, is a basic tenet of life—in other words, that life, by definition, must have a *physiochemical* method of reproduction that adheres to the general tenets of science.

That was approximately where Watson's path began to intersect with Crick's.

After the war, Crick's life was in flux. His marriage to Ruth Dodd, mother of his son, Michael, failed, and they divorced in 1947. Crick was not sure he wanted to continue with physics, despite a secure job with the Admiralty. The quest for more efficient ways to kill enemy seamen had lost its charm for him. While casting about for a new direction, he read Schrödinger's *What Is Life?* and found it as inspiring as had young Watson. The book convinced Crick that the principles and methods of physics must be applied to biology.

Crick particularly disagreed with a doctrine called vitalism, which had been around in various forms for millennia. Vitalism held that living matter and living processes are fundamentally different from other matter and processes and that life's vital force is beyond rational explanation. "I think what led me into biological research was really because I felt there was a mystery which I thought ought to be explained scientifically," he said decades later, in an interview published on the National Health Museum Web site.

While working at another laboratory at Cambridge, still as a physicist, Crick had begun to fill in the gaps in his knowledge of basic biology and biochemistry. With collaborators, he worked out a general theory of X-ray diffraction by a molecular helix. In 1949, he came to the Cavendish Lab, where he was assigned to study the structure of myoglobin. Also in 1949, he married again, this time to Odile Speed, an artist.

Watson had more guidance toward his area of discovery. Focusing on viruses at Indiana University, in Bloomington, he had the good fortune to study under Hermann Muller, the same Muller who had trained in Thomas Hunt Morgan's laboratory at Columbia University and who had devised groundbreaking experiments using X-rays to induce mutations in fruit flies. Another of Watson's mentors, Salvador Luria, helped him land the fellowship that took him to Copenhagen. The fellowship, in turn, led him to

(continues)

(continued)

hear Wilkins's lecture about DNA structure, which convinced him to seek a job doing biophysical research as close to Wilkins as possible. As close as possible (again with Luria's help) turned out to be the Cavendish lab, where Watson met Crick. As friends and partners in pursuit of discovery, they clicked immediately, with Crick playing big brother to the often mischievous Watson.

The differences between the men grew more pronounced after they arrived at the structure of the double helix in 1953. Watson returned to the United States, becoming for a short time a senior research fellow at Caltech in Pasadena. After another brief stint at the Cavendish, he settled in at Harvard in 1956, where as a professor and administrator he helped build the university's stature as a center for molecular biology research. In 1968, he became director of the Cold Spring Harbor Laboratory, and from 1988 to 1992, he was director of the Human Genome Project.

His reputation for abrasiveness followed him, as demonstrated when Crick was offended by the

James Watson followed his precocious early research with decades of success as a science administrator and fund-raiser. (Cold Spring Harbor Laboratory)

In 1953, Odum published *Fundamentals of Ecology*, which stood for a decade as the only textbook in its field and remains in the 21st century an important resource. The book, and Odum's other writings, helped convince generations of biologists that the workings of nature, although they begin at the sub-molecular level, must also be studied on a larger scale, all the way up to a global perspective.

Further Reading

Bett, Kristin. "Arvid Carlsson: 'The Nobel Prize Did Change My Life!'" *ECNP* no. 4 (December 2002). Available online. URL: http://www.ecnp.nl/Matters/number4/interview.htm. Accessed April 8, 2006. Question-answer interview with pharmacologist who established role of dopamine as an important neurotransmitter.

Carter, Richard. *Breakthrough: The Saga of Jonas Salk*. New York: Trident Press, 1965. Biography of scientist who developed successful polio vaccine.

Chase, Martha, and Alfred Day Hershey. "Independent Functions of Viral Protein and Nucleic Acid in Growth of Bacteriophage." *Journal*

way Watson depicted him in an early draft of *The Double Helix*. Despite rubbing friends and peers the wrong way on occasion, Watson, who never married and has no children, also became known as an excellent fund-raiser, to the great benefit of Harvard, Cold Spring Harbor, and the Human Genome Project.

Crick, meanwhile, took a completely different course. He did not teach. He did not administer or throw himself into raising money. He turned down hundreds of invitations to lecture. Instead, Crick continued as a researcher until his death in 2004. What is more, he was an extraordinarily successful researcher. With other collaborators at the Cavendish laboratory, he made fundamental contributions toward the unlocking of the genetic code. In 1956, he put forward an "adaptor hypothesis" that led to understanding of the role of messenger RNA in the synthesis of proteins. There is more about Crick's achievements in this area in the next chapter.

In 1966, Crick began theoretical research into the nature of consciousness. He left Cambridge in 1976, moving with wife, Odile, to La Jolla, California, and the Salk Institute. There, he remained working through the rest of his life.

Francis Crick's long research career led him to investigations of the nature of consciousness. (Francis Crick)

of General Physiology 36, no. 1 (September 20, 1952): 39–56. Available online. URL: http://osulibrary.orst.edu/specialcollections/coll/pauling/dna/papers/hersheychase.html. Accessed August 12, 2005. Account of blender experiment confirming role of DNA.

Crick, Francis. *Of Molecules and Men*. Seattle: University of Washington Press, 1966. Author attacks vitalism, discusses the line between organic and inorganic, and makes prescient predictions about what was then the future of science.

———. *What Mad Pursuit: A Personal View of Scientific Discovery*. New York: Basic Books, 1988. Crick's uniquely informed and invaluably insightful thoughts about predecessors and peers.

———, and James Watson. "Molecular Structure of Nucleic Acids—A Structure for Deoxyribose Nucleic Acid." *Nature* 171, no. 4356 (April 25, 1953). Available online. URL: http://osulibrary.orst.edu/specialcollections/coll/pauling/dna/papers/msna.html. Accessed August 11, 2005. Landmark paper unveils the double-helix structure of DNA.

Davis, Tinsley H. "Meselson and Stahl: The Art of DNA Replication." *Proceedings of the National Academy of Sciences* 101, no. 52 (December 28, 2004): 17,895–17,896. Available online. URL: http://www.pnas.org/cgi/

content/full/101/52/17895. Accessed August 13, 2005. Author revisits classic experiment confirming Watson and Crick's theory of semiconservative replication.

Dawson, Milly. "Martha Chase Dies: With Alfred D. Hershey, She Established DNA as the Genetic Material." *Scientist.* August 20, 2003, p. 4. Appreciative short obituary of important researcher whose life turned tragic.

Ecology Hall of Fame: Eugene Odum. Available online. URL: http://www.ecotopia.org/ehof/odum. Accessed August 13, 2005. Profile of leader in U.S. ecology movement.

Fraenkel-Conrat, H., and Robley C. Williams. "Reconstitution of Active Tobacco Mosaic Virus from Its Inactive Protein and Nucleic Acid Components." *Proceedings of the National Academy of Sciences* 41 (1955). Researchers establish viral self-assembly.

Gamow, George. *My World Line: An Informal Autobiography.* New York: Viking Press, 1970. Physicist whose work ranged from the big bang to DNA looks back.

———. "Possible Mathematical Relation between Deoxyribonucleic Acid and Proteins." *Nature* 173 (1854): 318. Nuclear physicist suggests formula for genetic code.

Grady, Denise. "A Revolution at 50: Rosalind Franklin's X-Ray Fuels Debate." *New York Times*, 25 February 2003, p.1. Available online. URL: http://query.nytimes.com/gst/fullpage.html?sec=health&res=9907E3DA1F3DF936A15751C0A9659C8B63. Accessed April 8, 2006.

Grosman, Lev. "Rosalind Franklin—Mystery Woman: The Dark Lady of DNA." *Time*, 17 February 2003, pp. 56–57. Profile of Franklin and her role in discovery of DNA structure.

Grunberg-Manago, P. J. Ortiz, and S. Ochoa. "Enzymatic Synthesis of Nucleic Acidlike Polynucleotides." *Science* 122 (November 11, 1955): 907–910. Severo Ochoa and colleagues announce discovery of enzyme that proves able to assemble RNA under test-tube conditions.

Harper, Eamon. "Getting a Bang out of Gamow." *GW Magazine*, Spring 2000. Available online. URL: http://www.gwu.edu/~physics/gwmageh.htm. Accessed August 13, 2005. Concise, celebratory biography of physicist with wide-ranging interests, including biophysics.

Hayes, William. "Recombination in Bact. Coli. K-12: Unidirectional Transfer of Genetic Material." *Nature* 169 (1952): 118–119. Immunologist explains one-way process whereby some bacteria share genetic matter.

Isaacs, A., and Lindenmann, J. "Virus Interference I. The Interferon." *Proceedings of the Royal Society, London* series B, vol. 147 (1957): 258–273. Available online. URL: http://www.garfield.library.upenn.edu/classics1989/A1989AX53100002.pdf. Accessed April 8, 2006. Paper discusses experiments showing existence and action of interferons.

Kornberg, Arthur. *Enzymatic Synthesis of DNA.* New York: Wiley, 1961. Nobel Prize winner discusses his breakthrough discovery of DNA polymerase.

———. *For the Love of Enzymes: The Odyssey of a Biochemist.* Cambridge, Mass.: Harvard University Press, 1989. Kornberg looks back at his stellar research career.

———, et al., eds. *Reflections of Biochemistry: In Honor of Severo Ochoa.* Oxford: Pergamon Press, 1976. Collected writings a memorial to Spanish biochemist, mentor to many.

Lemonick, Michael D. "Francis Crick: Beyond the Double Helix." *Time,* 17 February 2003, p. 55.

———. "Interview: 'You Have to Be Obsessive.'" *Time,* 17 February 2003, p. 52.

———. "A Twist of Fate: Two Unknown Scientists Solved the Secret of Life in a Few Weeks of Frenzied Inspiration in 1953. Here's How They Did It." *Time,* 17 February 2003, pp. 48–58.

Maddox, Brenda. *Rosalind Franklin: The Dark Lady of DNA.* New York: HarperCollins, 2002. Detailed and sympathetic biography of an uncompromising X-ray crystallographer.

Maley, F., and S. Ochoa. "Enzymatic Phosphorylation of Deoxycytidylic Acid." *Journal of Biological Chemistry* 233 (1958): 1,538–1,543. Ochoa and colleague extend RNA phosphorylation studies into DNA research.

Meselson, Matthew. "Topic: On Meeting Frank Stahl." Cold Spring Harbor Laboratory Digital Archives. Available online. URL: http://www.cshl.edu/cgi-bin/ubb/library/ultimatebb.cgi?ubb=get_topic;f=1;t=000021. Accessed August 3, 2005. Memoir about the beginning of important research partnership.

———, and Franklin W. Stahl. "The Replication of DNA in *Escherichia Coli.*" *Proceedings of the National Academy of Sciences* 44 (1958). Available online. URL: http://www.pnas.org/cgi/search?qbe=pnas;0407540101&journalcode=pnas&minscore=5000. Accessed August 13, 2005. Researchers confirm Watson and Crick's theory of semiconservative replication.

Odum, Eugene Pleasants. *Fundamentals of Ecology.* 3rd ed. Philadelphia: Saunders, 1971. First textbook on ecology was for its first decade the only such text. This is the later edition. Original, a rare find.

Rowland, John. *The Polio Man: The Story of Dr. Jonas Salk.* London: Butterworth Press, 1960. Accessible account of Salk's quest for a polio vaccine.

Salk, Jonas. *Infectious Molecules and Human Disease.* Albany, N.Y.: Health Education Service, 1962. Salk, as prominent authority, lays forth an overview of disease-causing viruses.

Sayre, Anne. *Rosalind Franklin and DNA.* New York: W. W. Norton, 1975. Biography of X-ray crystallographer who figured in quest to learn DNA structure.

Schrödinger, Erwin. *What Is Life? The Physical Aspect of the Living Cell.* New York: Macmillan, 1946. Physicist's book steered both James Watson and Francis Crick toward quest to understand DNA structure.

"Visit with Dr. Francis Crick." Access Excellence @ The National Health Museum Activities Exchange. Available online. URL: http://www.accessexcellence.org/AE/AEC/CC/crick.html. Accessed August 14, 2005. Crick talks about his work and its impact over succeeding decades.

Wade, Nicholas. "A Revolution at 50: Watson and Crick, Both Aligned and Apart, Reinvented Biology." *New York Times*, 25 February 2003, p. 1.

Watson, James D. *The Double Helix: A Personal Account of the Discovery of the Structure of DNA.* New York: New American Library, 1969. Watson's best-selling account of his Nobel Prize–winning partnership with Francis Crick.

———. *Genes, Girls and Gamow: After the Double Helix.* New York: Knopf, 2002. Playful memoir by codiscoverer of molecular structure of DNA.

Wilkins, Maurice. *The Third Man of the Double Helix.* Oxford: Oxford University Press, 2003. Wilkins reflects on Nobel-winning discovery and his role, in context of his life.

Zinder, N., and J. Lederberg. "Genetic Exchange in Salmonella." *Journal of Bacteriology* 64, no. 8 (November 1952): 679–699. Researchers show genetic recombination in bacteria.

7 1961–1970: Code Breakers and Ecologists

A Tumultuous and Pivotal Decade

Historians who study social and cultural history look back at the 1960s as a time of turmoil, rebellion, and rapidly changing values. The United States rang with protests—for civil rights and free speech and against the war in Vietnam—and the world rocked with unrest. The tragic and ill-conceived Cultural Revolution ripped through China. French workers and students rioted in the streets of Paris.

Biological science also saw rapid shifts in attitude and understanding during a short span of years. Molecular geneticists, molecular biologists, and biochemists, working to unlock the deepest secrets of physical heredity, learned to use the newly identified enzymes that allowed them to synthesize ribonucleic acid and DNA itself. As details of the genetic code emerged, the promise of Watson and Crick's 1953 discovery of DNA's molecular structure began to appear very large indeed, and rather alarming. On the horizon loomed a future in which scientists would be able to manipulate life processes at their most basic.

Swift social and cultural changes saw counterparts in research as independent-minded scientists struck out in new and contrary intellectual directions. From the badlands of Montana, by way of Yale, came a fresh perspective on dinosaurs. It challenged the orthodox evolutionary view of the beasts as sluggish, overgrown lizards. From Boston University came a startling new way to think about the origin of plant and animal cells—as cooperative unions of primitive microorganisms.

More biologists, rather than probing ever deeper into the molecular and sub-molecular roots of life processes, drew back for a larger view of organisms, a broader perspective that stressed living things' interconnectedness with each other and with the environment. There were more ecological studies, and ecologists were able to add enlightening, real-world context to specialized bioscience studies. A concern with ecology also overlapped with and contributed to one of the decade's many shifts in public attitude—a widespread concern with environmental pollution and its effects on living things, especially people.

The Cryptographers

Scientists striving to unlock the genetic code in the wake of Watson and Crick's 1950s discovery of DNA's molecular structure had some solid leads by the end of that decade, but central mysteries remained. The leads had come largely from biochemical inquiries into DNA and RNA, especially the enzyme polymerization breakthroughs of Kornberg and Ochoa.

Such 1950s advances, discussed in the previous chapter, confirmed details of DNA's molecular structure and illuminated how nucleic acids form but had not yet provided a key to the code by which DNA communicates genetic instructions.

Francis Crick, emerging as not just codiscoverer of DNA's double helix but also a forward-looking genetic theorist—had suggested that since proteins are the basic building blocks of living matter, and since proteins are made of combinations of amino acids, the role of genes—that is, DNA—must be to direct amino acids into the formation of proteins that form living matter. His suggestion would prove correct.

Yet how could the four bases in DNA—guanine, cytosine, adenine, and thymine—specify the amino acids that combine to build proteins?

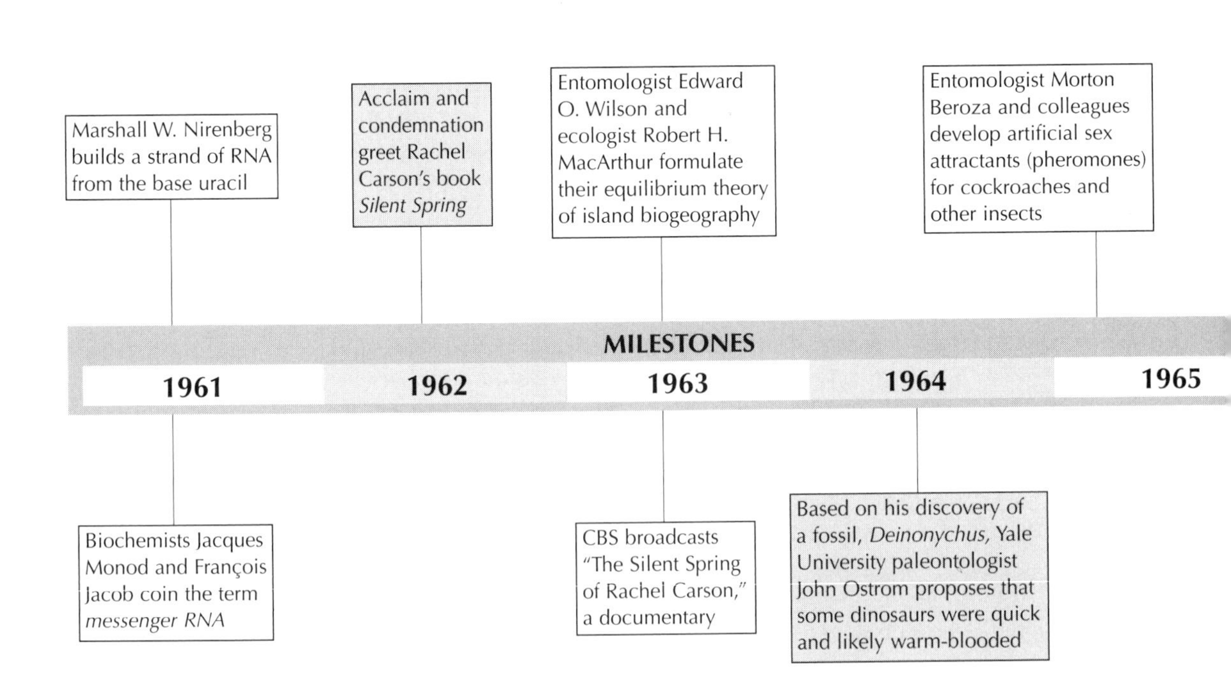

Scientists knew that guanine always pairs with cytosine and adenine with thymine, but if there were just two bases in each "code word," which Crick and colleagues called a *codon*, then there would be only two-times-two-times-four ways to "spell" such a word specifying an amino acid—theoretically designating only 16 amino acids. Any such formula could not be right, because there were 20 known amino acids that could combine into the very large number of known protein types.

Along with physicist George Gamow, Crick thought the correct number of nucleotide "letters" in a codon must be three. At Cambridge, Crick and his South African–born colleague Sidney Brenner (1927–) devised a series of experiments using genetic crosses of bacteriophages. By tracking amino acid production, they found evidence supporting the theory that a codon is a combination of three nucleotide bases, which they referred to as a *triplet*. Three times three letters, multiplied by four nucleotide bases, would result in a "vocabulary" of 64 genetic words.

Scientists also needed to know how the instructions for the process of protein assembly gets from the DNA of chromosomes—contained in the nucleus of a eukaryotic cell—to the *ribosome*, a tiny granule within the cytoplasm where proteins are synthesized.

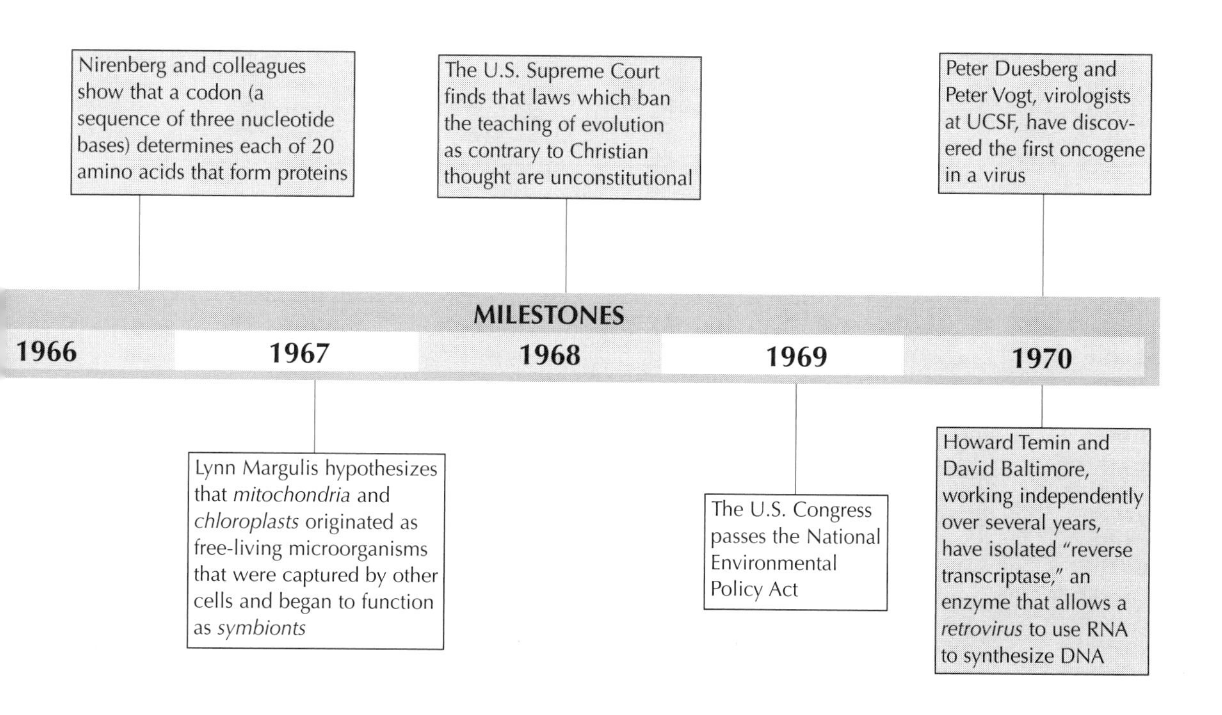

A clue had come in the 1950s from the Oak Ridge National Laboratory in Tennessee, where biochemists Elliot Volkin (1921–) and Lazarus Astrachan (1925–2003) discovered a previously unobserved kind of RNA production in *E. coli* bacteria infected with a bacteriophage. The unexpected RNA resembled the cell's DNA in its nucleotide composition—as if it were taking on characteristics of the DNA, as if the new nucleic acid had formed as a sort of copy of another nucleic acid. Volkin and Astrachan called their discovery "DNA-like RNA." Its significance was not understood until the 1960s, although Brenner did speculate in 1959 that DNA-like RNA could be the agent transferring the genetic code from chromosome to ribosome.

In 1961 at the Pasteur Institute in Paris, biochemists Jacques Monod (1910–76) and François Jacob (1920–) coined the term *messenger RNA* (quickly shortened to "mRNA") for the same substance, which they proposed was indeed the carrier of genetic information from DNA. They examined mRNA's role as part of their investigation into how specific genes regulate cell metabolism. This metabolic regulation, they found, takes place through the synthesis of enzymes, which are proteins, the product of genetic coding. Monod and Jacob received shares of the 1965 Nobel Prize in physiology or medicine for this work.

Scientists working on the genetic code problem had a rudimentary picture of the chemical pathway from DNA to RNA to amino acid to protein. Yet they still lacked the key to deciphering the code itself.

The young biochemist Marshall W. Nirenberg (1927–) at the National Institutes of Health (NIH) in Bethesda, Maryland, was among the many scientists (biophysicists, cytologists, molecular geneticists, and more) working simultaneously in the early 1960s on the problem. Nirenberg, born in New York City, had come to biological research by a fairly common path—through an appreciation of and curiosity about nature.

After he was stricken with rheumatic fever as a boy, his parents had moved the family to Orlando, Florida. In that pre-Disney era, the central Florida landscape boasted undisturbed wetlands and subtropical savanna as well as farmland. Exploring swamps, climbing trees, collecting snakes and insects, the boy became fascinated by the workings of the natural world. That set him on a path toward degrees in zoology and chemistry from the University of Florida and a Ph.D. in biochemistry from the University of Michigan. At the NIH, where he arrived in 1957, he set out to identify codons and ultimately to read them.

Nirenberg and J. Heinrich Matthaei (1929–), a postgraduate student on a fellowship from Germany, devised a simple but clever experiment in which they used a mortar and pestle to grind up cells of *E. coli* bacteria. This was to break apart cell walls and free the cytoplasm within. Nirenberg had shown that cytoplasm can synthesize protein, even outside of its cell walls. It can do this, however, only when triggered by the right kind of nucleotide template.

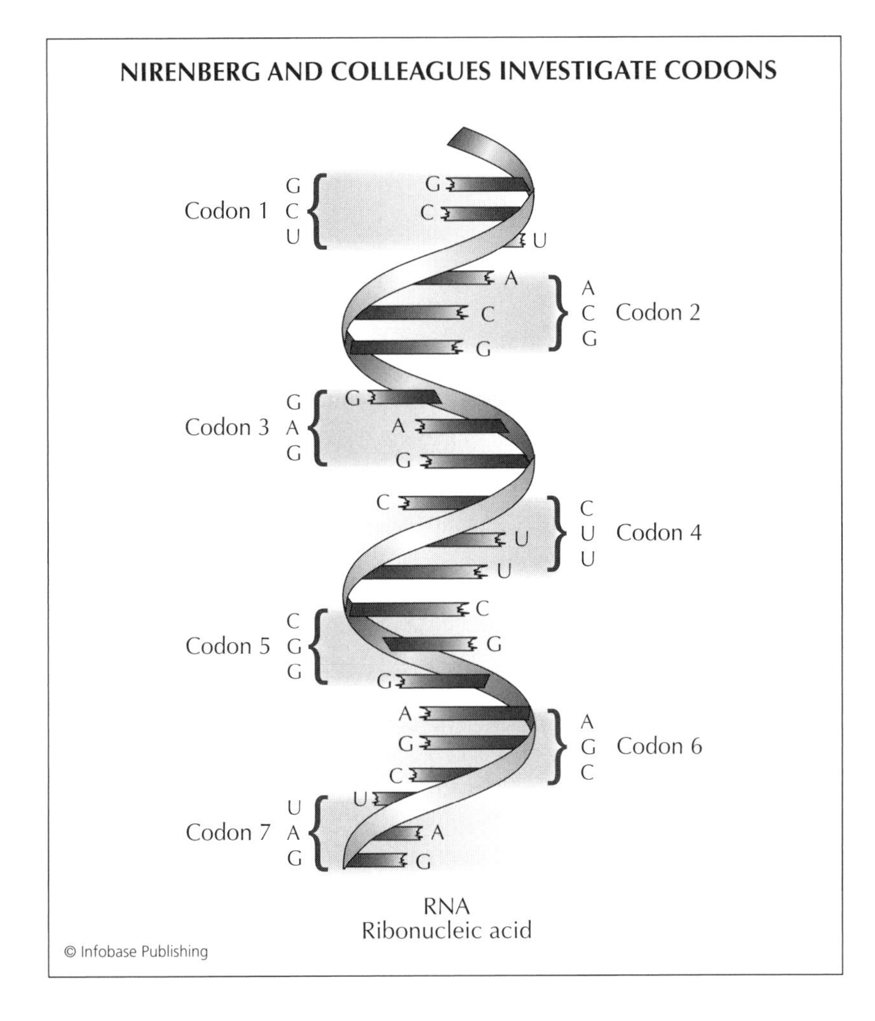

By the mid-1960s, researchers at the National Institutes of Health were beginning to read DNA code, having figured out dozens of three-nucleotide "words" that designated amino acids and specific combinations of amino acids, building enzymes and other proteins.

Using polynucleotide phosphorylase, the enzyme discovered by Ochoa, they synthesized a simple RNA strand to use as their nucleotide template. Nirenberg and Matthaei's synthetic RNA was made of nothing but the base uracil.

Very early in the morning of May 27, 1961, Matthaei, who had been working in the lab through the night, combined the synthetic RNA (they called it *poly-U*) with *E. coli* cytoplasm and added it to each of 20 test tubes, each containing a different amino acid. After an hour, the amino acid phenylalanine was shown to have formed a protein chain. It was a simple protein chain of one amino acid, forced by a single-nucleotide RNA. Simple though it was, it showed that a sequence of the base uracil in RNA designated the amino acid phenylalanine in protein production. A few months later, the researchers found that a synthetic RNA made exclusively of cytosine could designate the amino acid proline. They were on their way to deciphering the code.

Matthaei completed his fellowship at the end of 1961 and returned to Europe, but Nirenberg worked on with many other collaborators at the NIH. After announcing his breakthrough that year at a late-summer scientific conference in Russia, Nirenberg had found that Ochoa, a recent Nobel Prize winner (1959), was working with his team in New York on the genetic code. The quest had become a race.

It was Nirenberg's National Institutes of Health team that ultimately won the competition to work out the sequences and the amino acids that each codon designates. By 1966, the NIH researchers had worked out more than 60 codons. These were three-nucleotide "words" that, both alone and together (as in sentences), designated not just individual amino acids but specific combinations of amino acids—and thus specific enzymes and structural proteins.

The work of other scientists—beyond Crick, Brenner, Ochoa, Nirenberg, and so on—also proved essential to a general understanding of codons and how genetic information gets from DNA to RNA to amino acids and ultimately proteins.

Biochemist Har Gobind Khorana (1922–) was another important contributor. Born to a poor, though literate, family in the Indian state of Punjab, he benefited from his father's insistence that he be educated. Khorana earned a Ph.D. from the University of Liverpool, England, before coming to North America for research positions first in British Columbia, Canada, and then at the University of Wisconsin, Madison. At the latter, he devised new ways to make much more complex synthetic RNA than the type Nirenberg and Matthaei had first used. With this fuller, more precisely arranged complement of nucleotides, Khorana was able to confirm Nirenberg's findings and fill out details of the complex biochemical picture.

The scientists established that Crick and Brenner had been right about the codon; it is a sequence of three bases, assembled into messenger RNA (mRNA) that is copied from DNA—one single strand of RNA from one-half of DNA's double strand. Because each nucleotide base matches only one possible base on the opposite DNA strand, the sequence can be read from that single strand. With four bases—cytosine, guanine, adenine and thymine (the last of which translates into RNA's uracil)—and three letters per codon word, there are 64 codons. Sixty-one of them, either individually or in combination, code to direct the 20 amino acids into forming proteins. The other three indicate the beginning and end of a sequence coding for a protein.

At Cornell University, researcher Robert W. Holley (1922–93) added more perspective to this developing picture by discovering transfer RNA and then working out its structure. Often called tRNA, this nucleic acid is another link in the chain of transcription—again, one that Crick had hypothesized before it was actually discovered. It is the molecular agent that actually orders the amino acids as instructed by the mRNA that carries the code from the DNA in a cell's nucleus.

A native of Urbana, Illinois, and a graduate of the University of Illinois and Cornell, where he had earned his Ph.D. in 1947, Holley was another biochemist who had been inspired by a love of nature to study life processes. With Nirenberg and Khorana, he shared the 1968 Nobel Prize in physiology or medicine for their work in interpreting the genetic code and its function.

Reverse Transcriptase

Among the ideas that Francis Crick had advanced, and that had been widely accepted by his scientific peers of the 1950s and 1960s, one stood above the rest, to the point that it was widely accepted among biologists as the central dogma of molecular genetics. This was the statement that genetic information travels a one-way street. It flows from DNA to RNA to (by way of amino acids) proteins. It never travels the other way.

The central dogma turned out to have exceptions. This possibility arose around 1960, when Howard M. Temin (1934–94), a postdoctoral fellow at the California Institute of Technology, advanced a hypothesis about how the Rous sarcoma virus causes cancers in birds. Temin observed that cancer cells in tissue that had been infected by the virus exhibited characteristics that seemed determined by the genetic information in the virus.

Temin had come to Caltech from Swarthmore College near Philadelphia, where he had majored in biology. The middle of three sons of a Philadelphia lawyer, Temin had found fascination early in biology. He spent teenage summers in a special high school study program at Jackson Laboratory in Bar Harbor, Maine. At Caltech, he majored first in experimental biology and then switched to virology, under the tutelage of Max Delbrück and the Italian virologist Renato Dulbecco (1914–).

Howard Temin pioneered the study of retroviruses. This work led to his discovery of reverse transcriptase. (University of Wisconsin Board of Regents)

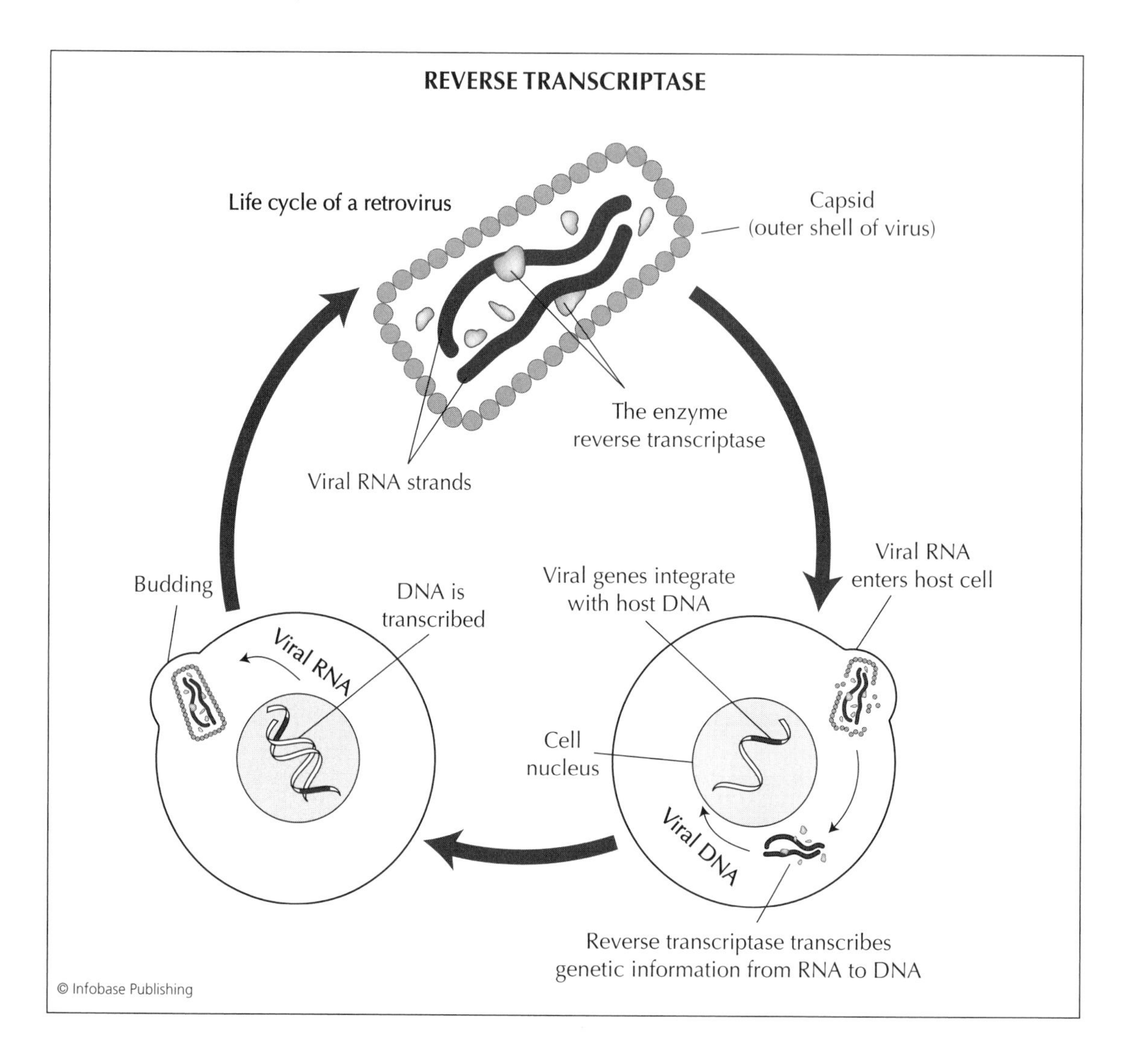

The enzyme is produced by retroviruses that use it to transcript viral RNA into DNA, which is then incorporated into the genetic material of a host cell.

After finishing his postdoctoral fellowship, Temin joined the faculty of the University of Wisconsin Medical School in Madison. There, he continued the line of research he had begun in Pasadena.

Rous sarcoma virus consists essentially of RNA, which serves as its genetic component. Yet when Temin impeded the production of DNA in a cell that was exposed to the virus, Rous sarcoma was not able to infect that cell. Temin proposed that the virus operated by translating genetic code from its RNA into the cell's DNA. The DNA then redirected the cell's reproduction mechanism, making it a cancer cell that would reproduce to make more cancer cells.

Called the pro virus DNA hypothesis, Temin's idea seemed an impossible reversal of cell biology to most microbiologists, but by 1970, both

Detours on the Way to a Research Career

Many scientific researchers in the 20th century led relatively stable lives—marked by academic achievement and steady employment at universities or other research facilities. They went from undergraduate to graduate student to assistant professor and from there up the ladder of promotion, depending on the quality and importance of their research.

Renato Dulbecco's life—especially his early adulthood—stands in stark contrast to such a measured career. He served both in dictator Benito Mussolini's army and in the Italian resistance. He nearly died of a wound suffered along Russia's Don River, and he finally found his way to Indiana University—and a virology research career that led to a Nobel Prize—helped along by a former college classmate.

Born in Catanzaro, in southern Italy, Dulbecco was the son of a World War I soldier who moved his family to Imperia, in northwestern Italy, where the boy grew up. A prodigious student who finished high school at 16, he went to the University of Turin, where a fellow student and acquaintance was future Nobel laureate Salvador Luria.

Shortly after he earned a medical degree at Turin in 1936, Dulbecco was drafted into the Italian army as a staff physician. He served two years and was discharged, but he spent only a year as a civilian—working as a medical pathologist—before the beginning of World War II. The army called him to service again. Dulbecco's war service took him to combat zones in France and in Russia, where he was severely injured in 1942. He spent several months in a hospital bed before being sent home.

Mussolini's government turned against the dictator in the war-torn summer of 1943. Mussolini was arrested, only to be rescued by German troops who installed him in a German-controlled puppet government in his country's north. In the fall of that year, Germany invaded Italy, its former ally.

Recovered from his wounds, Dulbecco found himself again swept into wartime drama. He joined the Italian resistance, serving as physician to partisan units in the region around Turin. He became a member of the city's underground Committee for National Liberation until war's end in 1945 and even served briefly in city government after the war.

Renato Dulbecco was a soldier and a political rebel before starting his research career. (© Salk Institute for Biological Studies)

In 1946, Luria returned from America to Turin for a visit and offered his former schoolmate a modest research position at Indiana University. Dulbecco accepted. His research in Bloomington, focused on bacteriophages, caught the attention of Luria's friend and frequent research partner Max Delbrück, who had gone from Vanderbilt to Caltech in 1947. Delbrück brought Dulbecco to Pasadena, where the Italian plunged into studies that would bring him a share of the 1975 Nobel Prize.

Temin and fellow virologist David Baltimore (1938–) had discovered independently the enzyme that transcribes genetic information from RNA to DNA—running the normal process of genetic transcription backwards. The enzyme is called reverse transcriptase. A virus that uses it, such as the Rous virus and the Rauscher murine leukemia virus (used in Baltimore's 1960s research) came to be called a retrovirus. Around the same time, German-born virologist Peter Duesberg (1936–) and his research partner Peter Vogt (1932–), both at the University of California, San Francisco, identified an *oncogene*, a cancer-causing gene, in a retrovirus.

Temin and Baltimore had much in common. Like Temin, Baltimore had as a teen traveled to Jackson Memorial Laboratory in Maine for a summer of biological research. Further, Baltimore, who had grown up in New York City, shared an alma mater with Temin: Swarthmore, where Baltimore had majored in chemistry. Finally, Baltimore also counted his virology work with Renato Dulbecco as a major influence. After earning a Ph.D. from Rockefeller University (the former Rockefeller Institute), Baltimore spent more than two years working with Dulbecco at the Salk Institute in La Jolla, California. Dulbecco had left Caltech for the institute in 1962. It was at the Salk Institute that Baltimore conducted most of the research on viral genetics that led him to isolate and identify reverse transcriptase. He joined the faculty of MIT in 1968.

Temin and Baltimore would share the 1975 Nobel Prize in physiology or medicine with Dulbecco. The 1960s research at Caltech and the Salk Institute that led to Dulbecco's share of the Nobel Prize went hand in hand with that of his erstwhile associates. While Temin and Baltimore had focused on RNA-based viruses, Dulbecco had investigated and explained chemical and biophysical paths by which DNA-based viruses take control of the DNA of cells that they infect.

Terrible Claw

In the 1860s, English biologist Thomas Henry Huxley (1825–95)—a close friend and colleague of Charles Darwin—argued that all birds are descended from small, carnivorous dinosaurs. Huxley used skeletal similarities to make his *phylogenetic* case. His view was not well accepted, however. For the next century, the consensus among scientists was that dinosaurs had been cold-blooded reptiles. That began to change only in 1964, with a fossil find by John Ostrom (1928–2005) of Yale University's Peabody Museum of Natural History.

In the Bighorn Basin of Montana, Ostrom found the skeleton of a previously unknown species. Almost nine feet (2.74 m) long from its nose to the tip of its outstretched tail, this carnivore of the late Cretaceous period apparently was built for speed and agility. In a talk to an audience of fellow paleontologists that year in Chicago, Ostrom described a predator that ran on its slender, four-toed hind limbs, probably using that long tail as a balance against its thrust-forward posture. Each hind foot featured an enormous hook of a claw. It looked like a killing weapon. To use this claw, Ostrom hypothesized, the dinosaur, which he named *Deinonychus antirrhopus* (terrible claw, counterbalanced), was capable of leaping upon its prey, grasping with its long-fingered front limbs and muscular jaw, while slashing with deadly feet.

It was the behavior, he said, of a warm-blooded animal—a hunting style more like that of a wolf or an eagle than of a cold-blooded alligator. After further field work and extensive analysis of the specimen, Ostrom published a 1969 paper, "Osteology of *Deinonychus antirrhopus*, an Unusual Theropod from the Lower Cretaceous of Montana," that challenged the established view and put forward his contention that this animal should not be classified among *ectothermic* lizards. As Huxley had 100 years earlier, he suggested a close evolutionary relationship between dinosaurs and birds.

Ostrom's discovery of Deinonychus antirrhopus, *a predator dinosaur with switchblade-like claws on its feet, helped spark a revision of scientific opinion about what dinosaurs were and how they lived.*

Born in New York City, Ostrom had grown up hiking and fishing in the Adirondack Mountains near his boyhood home in Schenectady, New York. A premedicine major at Schenectady's Union College, he switched to geology after reading *The Meaning of Evolution*, a book written by pale-

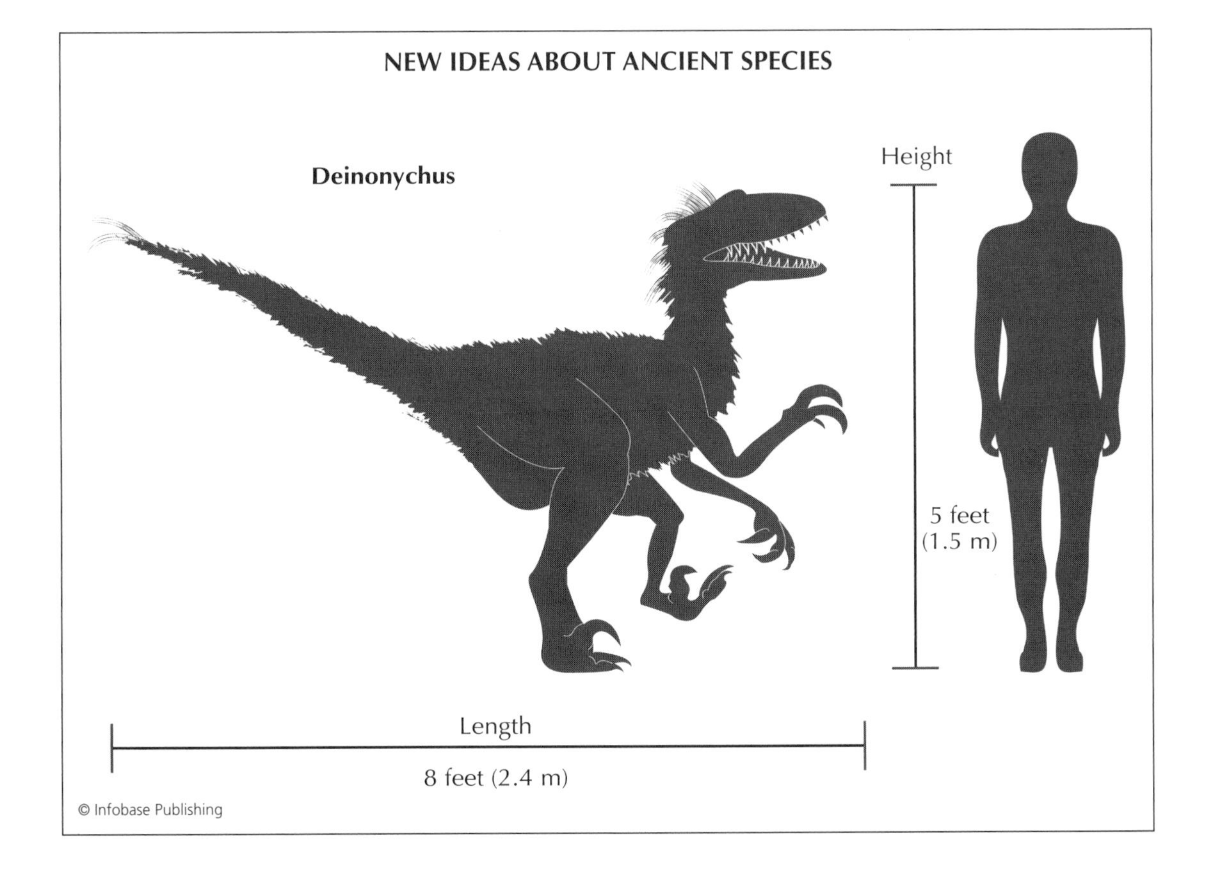

ontologist George Gaylord Simpson (1902–94) of the American Museum of Natural History.

Ostrom was able to learn firsthand from Simpson on a postgraduate field expedition to New Mexico and then as a research assistant at the Museum of Natural History. After earning a master's degree in geology from Columbia University, Ostrom taught at Beloit College in Wisconsin. Once he had completed his Ph.D., also from Columbia, he joined the geology faculty at Yale and became a curator of paleontology at the university's Peabody Museum. He made the *D. antirrhopus* find on the first of his annual field expeditions for the Peabody.

One of Ostrom's paleontology students, Robert T. Bakker, became especially interested in the warm-blooded dinosaur hypothesis. Raised in a conservative Christian family in Ridgewood, New Jersey, Bakker had developed a fascination with dinosaurs as a boy. At Yale, the undergraduate quickly took Ostrom's idea of dinosaur *endothermy* beyond ancient bipedal carnivores, with their bird-shaped skeletons. He also claimed warm-bloodedness (or hot-bloodedness, as he liked to call it) for a much wider range of dinosaurs. During his junior year, Bakker decided that the Peabody's *Apatosaurus* skeleton was incorrectly mounted. The long-necked, 30-ton behemoth (once known as *Brontosaurus*), must have had legs arranged directly under its body, as in a modern elephant, rather than splayed to the sides like those of a crocodile, he thought.

In an article titled "The Superiority of Dinosaurs," published in Yale's journal *Discovery* in 1968 (the year that he received his bachelor's degree), Bakker put forward the argument that even the huge *Apatosaurus* was active, upright, and probably even warm-blooded. He based his argument in part upon his examinations of dinosaur skeletons and comparisons with the bones of modern reptiles, birds, amphibians, and mammals. Newspapers and broadcast news reports carried Bakker's assertions, beginning the long-haired, bearded rebel's rise to scientific celebrity in the late decades of the century.

The ideas of Ostrom and Bakker would gain further momentum in the 1970s (see the next chapter). Bakker would publish a controversial article titled "Dinosaur Renaissance" in *Scientific American*, challenging assumptions of mainstream paleontology. Ostrom would boldly reclassify a fossil that had been found a century earlier, showing it to be a phylogenetic link between dinosaurs and birds.

A Bigger Picture

Ostrom trained as a geologist to prepare for a career that changed the course of paleontology. His student Bakker, educated as a paleontologist, would become known not just for his contrarian hypotheses about dinosaur anatomy and evolution but also for looking at the ancient beasts from an interdisciplinary perspective, in the broader context of the world they inhabited. He became one of a new breed of *paleoecologists.*

Like Ostrom and Bakker, like Linus Pauling and biophysicists Francis Crick and Max Delbrück—in fact, like most scientists included in this history—chemist Adolf Butenandt (1903–95) crossed arbitrary boundaries between disciplines. The German researcher isolated estrone, androsterone, and progesterone—the first sex hormones identified in humans. This work shaped biologists' understanding of growth in mammals, the development of secondary sex characteristics, and even gender identity. Those studies also led to Butenandt's half-share of the 1939 Nobel Prize, not in the category of chemistry, his specialty, but in physiology or medicine. His subsequent work isolating and identifying enzymes controlling eye color in fruit flies led him into genetics and entomology—extending the one-gene–one-enzyme findings of Beadle and Tatum to a more complex species.

In 1959, another of Butenandt's lines of research—this time into the life chemistry of the silkworm moth (*Bombyx mori*)—led him to be first to isolate and identify a *pheromone*, bombykol. Naturalists had long observed insect behavior spurred by chemical communication—as when a single bee's sting seems to signal other bees also to sting. Pheromones provide the language for such communication.

As Butenandt and other chemists learned more about the physical properties of substances that send such signals, entomologists such as Morton Beroza (1917–) of the U.S. Department of Agriculture were sorting out the ways that such substances regulated insect behaviors. In the 1960s, Beroza suggested that it would be possible to manipulate insects' breeding behavior, thus achieving a measure of agricultural pest control, by applying artificial sex pheromones.

Strictly speaking, Edward O. Wilson (1929–) of Harvard University began his research career as a myrmecologist, an entomologist who specializes in ants. Far more than most scientists, however, the Alabama-born Wilson would cross and even transcend the lines that separate disciplines.

By 1960, Wilson had determined that not only are pheromones important to ants, but they are also the primary mode of communication within these insects' highly regulated societies—directing the specialized behaviors by which ant species survive. His studies of ants were by necessity, studies of social systems. No species of ant gets its living on an individual-by-individual basis. From studying how ants within a society communicate and cooperate with each other, it was not a great leap to study how ants interact across species boundaries. This course of inquiry led to investigations of how animals evolve social behaviors, even in larger, interconnected communities of organisms. Wilson's greatest prominence would begin in the 1970s (see chapter 8) as he introduced the concept of *sociobiology*.

From his earliest career, Wilson was among biologists bringing a new focus—informed by advances in biochemistry, genetics, and even experimental psychology—to the study of how species live and adapt in

An Evolving View of Cell Evolution

The idea behind sociobiology, also important to ecology, is that organisms shape each other in behavior and evolution. It seems somewhat self-evident. Beyond the ubiquitous predator-prey relationship, there are many examples in nature of parasite and host, and far more benign symbiotic relationships—as in lichen (which consist of mutually beneficial algae and fungi joined together) or the bond between the black rhinoceros (*Diceros bicornis*) and the tick-eating yellow-billed oxpecker (*Buphagus africanus*) that rides upon its back. In 1967, a Boston University geneticist advanced a surprising theory regarding symbiotic relationships that struck many of her peers as bizarre—at first, anyway.

Lynn Margulis (then using her married name, Lynn Sagan) published a paper titled "On the Origin of Mitosing Cells," in which she argued that eukaryotic cells (the ones that have nuclei) began as a symbiotic merger of prokaryotic bacteria. Under this *endosymbiotic* theory, mitochondria—important *organelles* within the cell—descended from once-independent species of bacteria.

The endosymbiotic hypothesis was not without precedent. Russian botanist Konstantin Mereschkowsky (1855–1921) had proposed in the 1920s that chloroplasts, which are the organelles responsible for *photosynthesis* in plant cells, began as *cyanobacteria* (blue-green algae cells) that had been captured by protozoa, with each microorganism having evolved to complement the functions of the other.

Lynn Margulis's endosymbiotic theory gained support from later studies showing the DNA of mitochondria and chloroplasts to be different from nuclear DNA. (Lynn Margulis and Bates College)

A Chicago native, Margulis (1938–) is a graduate of the University of Chicago, the University of Wisconsin–Madison, and the University of California, Berkeley, from which she earned her Ph.D. in genetics in 1965. When she formulated her endosymbiotic theory, she was married to the astronomer Carl Sagan (1934–96). They later divorced.

Her work through succeeding decades—at the University of Boston and then the University of Massachusetts, Amherst—has continued to look at symbiosis as a major force in cell evolution and in the wider process of evolution as well—a force equal to or greater than that of Darwinian natural selection. Initially rejected by the biology establishment, her theories (especially about cell evolution) gradually gained a significant measure of acceptance, especially as cytologists have found that mitochondria and chloroplasts contain their own DNA, separate from that in the cell's nucleus.

Margulis's application of symbiotic cooperation to the broader process of evolution remains controversial.

the wild. In 1963, he and ecologist Robert H. MacArthur (1930–72) put forward what became known as the equilibrium theory of island biogeography. Based upon their field research, which they conducted on mangrove islands off southern Florida, this theory posits a balance between the rate at which new species colonize an island and the rate at which populations of established species become extinct. Still in use by ecologists and wildlife biologists, the equilibrium theory has proved useful not just on islands but also in studying other isolated environments—such as a nature preserve that consists of woodland or prairie surrounded by human development.

Wilson's work with MacArthur began his transition from entomologist to ecologist. It also began his interest in nature conservation—informed by research. Meanwhile, MacArthur's appointment to the biology faculty of Princeton University in 1965 showed that ecology was, in the 1960s, claiming its place among biological specialties—a specialty that combined specialties. The word *interdisciplinary* was not yet as popular as it later became, but it applied. The influential Eugene Odum, who founded the University of Georgia's Institute of Ecology in 1961, was perhaps America's leading pioneer in the field. He advocated that biologists take ever-broader views of the diverse interconnected forces—biochemical, environmental, genetic, behavioral, and social—that shape the lives of organisms.

The Silence That Echoed

It was and is obvious—not just to ecologists and other biological field researchers but also to the casual observer—that the species able to exert the most percussive influence over the widest range of ecosystems was and is *H. sapiens.* Human activities—from hunting and fishing to farming to land development—involve using other species or their habitats. They always have. With the Industrial Revolution and ever more sophisticated technologies, however, humans have not merely gained better and more efficient ways to feed, clothe, house, defend, transport, and amuse themselves. They have also developed new ways to alter the natural environment, often with little thought about consequences such as smog-thickened air and waste-fouled rivers. The United States's use of atomic bombs in warfare in 1945, followed by its development of the much more destructive hydrogen bomb in 1952, underscored for many people the species' spectacular capacity to disrupt environments.

As physicists developed nuclear weapons for use against human enemies, so immunologists developed vaccines and, ultimately, antibiotics against microbial enemies. What other enemies were there? High on the list were many species of insect. Mosquitoes, fleas, lice, locusts, flies, and termites were, and are, among the most hated—justifiably so. These are species that have spread destruction, famine, and deadly disease. In

1948, Swiss chemist Paul Hermann Müller (1899–1965) was awarded the Nobel Prize in physiology or medicine. His discovery: the insect-killing properties of the chemical compound DDT. This synthetic pesticide worked against a wide variety of insects. The bugs did not have to ingest DDT; it killed on contact. Proven effective against disease-carrying mosquitoes during World War II, the insecticide was quickly hailed as a great lifesaver.

Through the 1950s, DDT and related organic halogen compounds came into widespread use against all manner of arthropod pests, with many positive results in public health and crop yield. Yet some scientists—zoologists, ecologists, wildlife biologists, and even entomologists such as Wilson—worried that the new pesticides were being used too indiscriminately and in too much volume. As early as the mid-1940s, scientists and laypeople had begun reporting mass bird deaths following DDT spraying.

C. J. Briejer of the Netherlands's Plant Pest Control Service, had reported that the new generation of contact pesticides were already diminishing in effectiveness—even by the mid-1950s—as successive generations of insects developed a genetic resistance against the chemicals. The solution for many farmers and pest control agencies was to apply higher concentrations of DDT. Meanwhile, evidence was mounting in the United States that the miraculous new pesticides were not as safe as had been advertised—especially not in high doses. Robert Rudd (1924–), a zoologist at the University of California, Davis, had worked on a number of studies through the late 1950s that found pesticides could disrupt wild systems by killing fish, birds, and other unintended targets. At wildlife refuges near the California-Oregon border, dead and sick pelicans, grebes, herons, and other fish-eating species were found to have high concentrations of toxaphene and DDE—chemical residues of pesticides—in their tissues. Ornithologists such as George J. Wallace (1907–86) at Michigan State University and Joseph Hickey (1907–93) at the University of Wisconsin linked high concentrations of pesticide in the environment with high mortality rates and reproduction problems in several species of birds. DDT can persist in the environment for up to a decade after its application. It can enter the food chain. The pesticide or its by-products can accumulate in the fatty tissues of birds and other animals. In high enough concentrations, these substances have been found to cause thinning of eggshells in certain bird species—resulting in fewer hatchlings.

In 1957, ornithologist Robert Cushman Murphy (1887–1973) of the American Museum of Natural History led a group of his Long Island neighbors in filing suit against the U.S. Department of Agriculture and the New York Department of Agriculture. The Long Islanders sought a ruling that would restrain government agencies from spreading a messy mixture of DDT and fuel oil over private property. Government planes had been spraying vigorously to fight the gypsy moth (*Lymantria dispar*) and the European elm bark beetle (*Scolytus multistriatus*), among

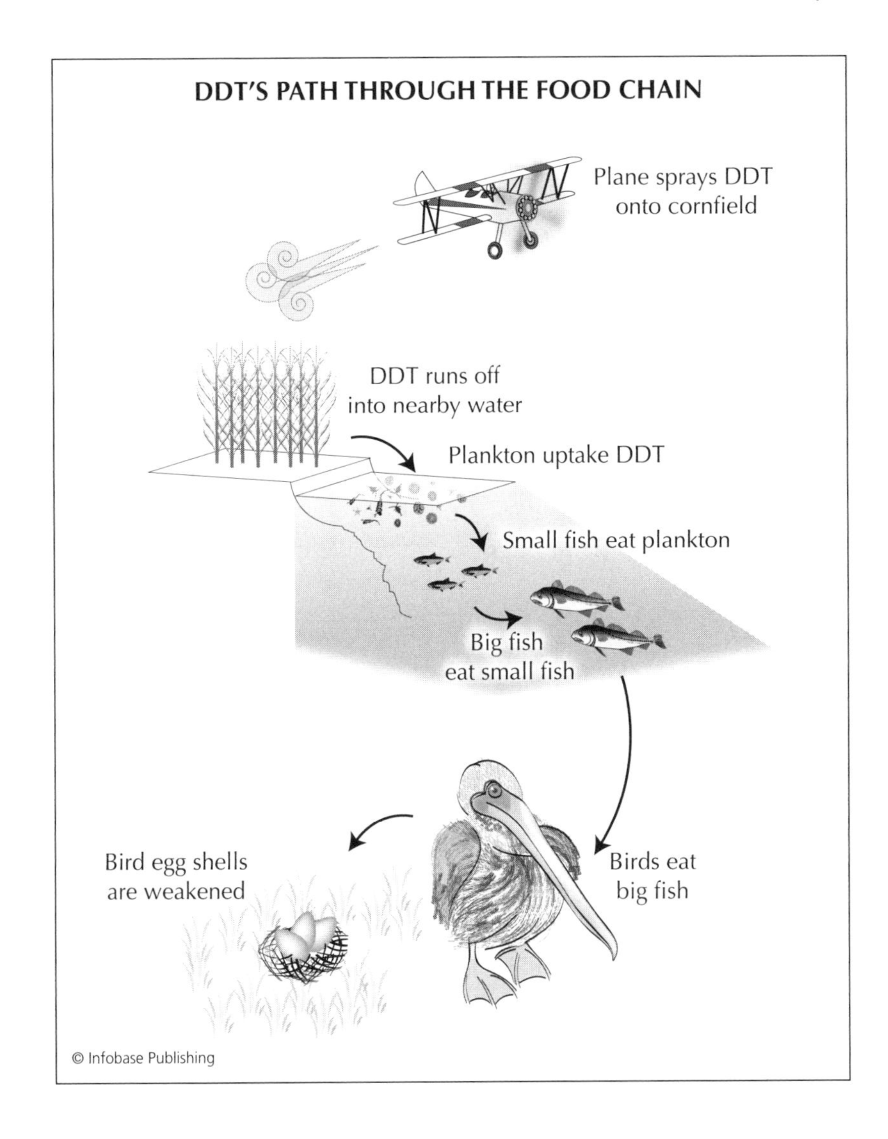

The pesticide or its by-products can accumulate in the fatty tissues of birds and other animals.

other destructive pests. In that suit and one that followed, also filed by Murphy and his neighbors, federal judges ruled against the plaintiffs, dismissing their concerns about harm to birds, gardens, pets, livestock, organic farms, and people. The suit, however, signaled shifting public sentiment.

It would be incorrect to identify the environmental movement as a scientific enterprise rather than a change in societal attitudes, a change with a number of causes. Among the causes were highly publicized scares. Just before Thanksgiving in 1959, for example, a portion of the U.S. cranberry crop had to be pulled from the market because the fruit had been contaminated with the weed killer aminotriazole. Consumers were startled at the idea of such a seemingly wholesome part of the holiday meal becoming adulterated with a potential poison. Then, in 1961, physicians began to realize that a rash of tragically severe birth defects, mostly in Britain and Germany, had been the result of the drug thalidomide, taken by the babies' mothers during pregnancy. Most of the affected children died. Others were born without arms and legs. What had been expected to be a routine approval for thalidomide's introduction into the United States had been delayed the previous year by U.S. Food and Drug Administration inspector Frances Oldham Kelsey (1914–), who wanted to see more thorough testing. Such incidents as these prompted worry and suspicion about the safety of chemical products.

Environmentalism was, however, inspired, informed, and shaped in large measure by biological research conducted by scientists such as Rudd, Wallace, Hickey, MacArthur, Wilson, and many others. Building on a tradition that included Scottish-American conservationist John Muir as well as naturalist Aldo Leopold and ecologist Odum, the movement found its catalyst in a book. Published in 1962, it was titled *Silent Spring.*

Author Rachel Carson (1907–64), who had come to prominence in 1951 and 1952 with her best-selling *The Sea around Us*, was the rare scientist who could write both compellingly and accurately for an educated general audience. That ability was her interdisciplinary gift. Trained at Johns Hopkins University, she had conducted research at the Marine Biological Laboratory in Woods Hole, Massachusetts, and taught biology at the University of Maryland before becoming an aquatic biologist for the U.S. Bureau of Fisheries (later the U.S. Fish and Wildlife Service). Unlike most biologists, however, she had won magazine story-writing contests when she was a girl. Once her bosses at the federal agency recognized her talent as a writer, they assigned Carson almost exclusively to public information duties—writing and editing official publications and radio scripts. That work led her to an independent career as the author of magazine articles and books.

Much of Carson's earlier writings were eloquent contemplations on the wonders of aquatic life and the workings of nature. *Silent Spring* was a departure in that it argued for critical awareness and action. It also used a frank rhetorical device—the silent spring of the title—to jar readers into envisioning a world without birds, her imagined consequence of unchecked pesticide abuse. The best-selling and extremely controversial book presented and interpreted the results of many scientific studies as well as naturalists' more casual observations. At the heart of the author's argument was the idea—central to ecological science—that living things are inextricably connected at every level, from the molecular to the global, and that any action against one form of life should take into account possible unintended effects on other organisms and systems of organisms.

Silent Spring is not, and was never intended as, a dispassionate scientific treatise but a persuasive argument. At that, it succeeded—despite

Scientist of the Decade: Rachel Carson (1907–1964)

Quiet and neat, organized in thought and deed, the conservatively attired Rachel Carson seemed an unlikely rebel, an unlikelier scourge. Yet this unassuming woman—a biologist by training and a writer by talent—changed the world. Her admirers credit her with giving voice to the modern environmental movement. Among her detractors, some extremists—those who decry all environmental regulation—have gone so far as to call her a mass murderer.

Both sides point to Carson's 1962 book *Silent Spring* as a turning point in social attitudes toward pesticides and other environmental chemicals. Although Carson performed private research through much of her career as a nature writer, she did not conduct the many experimental and scientific survey programs cited in *Silent Spring*—research that found dangerous problems caused by reckless and excessive applications of chemicals such as DDT. She did, however, organize and present scientific data in a literary context (also including personal and anecdotal observation) that persuaded readers to change the way they thought about casual chemical use. Many see *Silent Spring* as the crucial spur toward rigorous environmental studies and laws to protect the natural environment. Others have claimed that without Carson's argument, without her "interference," DDT and similar pesticides would have been used to wipe out deadly malaria in the Tropics, saving millions of lives. Carson—although she passionately and eloquently attacked the misuse of chemical poisons—never called for an outright ban on any pesticide. She died in 1964, years before any country banned DDT. (Although restricted or prohibited by many governments and intergovernmental treaties, DDT use against the *Anopheles* mosquito, carrier of malarial protozoa, continues in the 21st century to be allowed under World Health Organization regulations.)

Rachel Carson learned to love nature and language as a little girl in Springdale, Pennsylvania. Much younger than her sister and brother, she was the cherished baby daughter of a semirural household. In the World War I era, Springdale was not yet a suburb of Pittsburgh but a town making the transition from farming to a factory center.

The Carsons lived on a large parcel of undeveloped land that Rachel's father, Robert, sought to subdivide into house lots. There were no close neighbors. Her mother, Maria, a former schoolteacher, often guarded Rachel's fragile health by keeping her home from school for private lessons and nature walks through the wooded property. They read together, and Rachel became a lover of books. When she was 10, the children's magazine *St. Nicholas* accepted the first of several stories by young Rachel that would see publication.

While at Pennsylvania College for Woman (later Chatham College) in Pittsburgh, Carson, an English major, found a mentor and role model in Mary Scott Skinker (1889–1948), acting head of the biology department. The undergrad switched her major to biology, with the forward-looking explanation that the study of biology would give her valuable subject matter about which to write. Biology would also lead her to a research fellowship at Woods Hole (where she saw the ocean for the first time) and to a master's degree in marine zoology from Johns Hopkins University in 1932.

Carson's family and its chronic financial need profoundly shaped her adult life. While she was in graduate school, her parents came to live with her in suburban Maryland. Robert Carson's plan to reap a profit by selling off his Pennsylvania land had not borne fruit. The Great Depression made times tough for virtually everyone. Rachel worked as a laboratory assistant and teaching assistant at Johns Hopkins and a zoology instructor at the University of Maryland to pay the bills. By the time she was 30, she was the sole financial support of a household that included her widowed mother (Robert died in 1935) and her two preteen nieces, effectively orphaned by the

(continues)

(continued)

death of Carson's divorced sister. (Later, when she was 50, Carson would adopt five-year-old grand-nephew Roger Christie, orphaned son of one of those nieces.)

Need prompted Carson to seek work with the U.S. Bureau of Fisheries in Washington, D.C., where she became a junior aquatic biologist in 1936. She stayed with the agency (renamed the Bureau of Fish and Wildlife) a decade and a half, becoming editor in chief of its information service. Although she earned small sums of extra money from writing newspaper and magazine articles over those years, it was the success of the National Book Award–winning *The Sea around Us,* published in 1951, that finally afforded her the financial freedom to quit her government job.

She had at first planned to write no more than a magazine article about DDT. In fact, she had proposed such a piece to *Reader's Digest* as early as 1945. The magazine's editors rejected the idea. As she gathered information and talked to scientists about pesticides, the project that became *Silent Spring* grew from a proposed magazine article (*The New Yorker's* editor William Shawn was eager to publish it), to what she thought of as a short book, to the full-length book as it emerged in 1962.

Biologist and writer Rachel Carson was posthumously awarded the Presidential Medal of Freedom. (Beinecke Rare Book & Manuscript Library, Yale University)

Carson's health, never robust, deteriorated as she turned 50 and began working in earnest on *Silent Spring.* In 1960, Carson underwent surgery to remove an abnormal mass from her breast. The diagnosis was cancer.

She spent her final months not just ill but also embroiled in controversy. The National Agricultural Chemicals Association mounted an expensive publicity campaign to discredit *Silent Spring* and its author. The Manufacturing Chemists Association put out bulletins attacking the studies she cited. The public relations department of Monsanto Corporation parodied the opening of Carson's book by publishing its own fable about an insect-devastated "world without bug spray."

Carson did not enjoy public speaking; it made her nervous. She had never been comfortable drawing attention to herself, but for as long as she could, she agreed to interviews and accepted invitations to speak about her book. She refuted her critics calmly, citing facts and correcting misconceptions. As the book's sales soared and her fame grew, television appearances showed the public a woman of quiet, unruffled grace—in contrast to her loud, angry, and even abusive critics.

As she weakened, Carson showed up for public appearances in a wheelchair pushed by her literary agent. The writer did not want anyone to know how ill she was. She let audiences think it was arthritis that made it painful for her to walk. In March 1964, Carson's doctors found that the cancer had spread to her liver. She died quietly at home the next month, not quite two years after the publication of *Silent Spring.* Her death came as a surprise to her many thousands of readers and admirers.

ferocious attacks on the book and its author from the chemical industry, scientists financed by chemical companies, and the USDA, which had eagerly embraced the new pesticides.

Carson accumulated powerful supporters too. William Shawn (1907–92), the influential editor of *The New Yorker*, published *Silent Spring* as a series of articles in his prestigious magazine before it appeared in book form. By the end of 1962, there were bills introduced in the legislatures of 40 American states to regulate pesticide use. CBS television aired a sympathetic documentary, "The Silent Spring of Rachel Carson," in 1963, the same year that President John F. Kennedy's Science Advisory Committee supported the book's conclusions.

Through the 1960s and 1970s, growing environmental awareness throughout the developed world led to private and government grants for environmental studies. It led to new ecology research positions at universities and scientific field stations. The U.S. Congress in 1969 passed the National Environmental Policy Act, using the word *biosphere* for the first time in a federal law and establishing a Council on Environmental Quality. President Richard Nixon proposed the creation of a new government agency devoted to the enforcement of environmental laws and standards. Approved by Congress, the Environmental Protection Agency began operations in late 1970. That was also the year of the first Earth Day, sponsored by U.S. senator Gaylord Nelson of Wisconsin and Representative Paul McCloskey of California.

Also in 1970, both Norway and Sweden banned the use of DDT. The United States enacted its own DDT ban in 1971. Over subsequent years and decades, many other nations followed suit.

Further Reading

Anderson, Daniel, and Joseph Hickey. "Chlorinated Hydrocarbons and Eggshell Changes in Raptorial and Fish-Eating Birds." *Science*, 162 (October 1968): 271–273. Evidence of harm caused to bird species by pesticide contamination.

Bakker, Robert T. "The Superiority of Dinosaurs." *Discovery* 3, no. 2 (1968) 11–22. Yale undergraduate speculates that even huge *Apatosaurus* was active, upright, and probably warm-blooded.

Baltimore, David. "Viral RNA-dependent DNA Polymerase: RNA-dependent DNA Polymerase in Virions of RNA Tumour Viruses." *Nature* 226 (June 27, 1970): 1,209–1,211. Available online. URL: http://www.nature.com/nature/20thcentury/1baltimore.pdf. Accessed October 25, 2005. Baltimore announces his discovery of reverse transcriptase.

Beroza, M., B. H. Alexander, L. F. Steiner, W. C. Mitchell, and D. H. Miyashita. "New Synthetic Lures for the Male Melon Fly." *Science* 131

(1960): 1,044. Entomology researchers focus on alternatives to chemical pesticides.

Breijer, C. J. "The Growing Insensitivity of Insects to Insecticides." *Atlantic Naturalist* 13 (July–September 1958): 17–18. Early report of genetic mutations toward pesticide resistance.

Brenner, S., L. Barnett, E. R. Katz, and F. H. Crick. "Third Nonsense Triplet in the Genetic Code." *Nature* 213 (February 4, 1967): 449–450. Crick, Brenner, and colleagues, working on genetic code, find evidence of triplets serving as spacers between coding sequences.

Carson, Rachel. *Silent Spring*. New York: Houghton Mifflin, 1962. Landmark book that alerted the nation to the dangers of uncontrolled use of chemical pesticides.

Crick, Francis, H., L. Barnett, S. Brenner, and R. J. Watts-Tobin. "Central Dogma of Molecular Biology." *Nature* 227 (August 8, 1970): 561–563. Available online. URL: http://www.euchromatin.org/Crick01.htm. Accessed April 10, 2006. Crick updates his central dogma, a rule about genetic information flow from DNA to RNA to protein.

———. "General Nature of the Genetic Code for Proteins." *Nature* 192, no. 409 (December 30, 1961): 1,227–1,232. Crick, Brenner, and colleagues describe experiments showing that nucleotide triplet codes for a protein.

DeWitt, James. "Chronic Toxicity to Quail and Pheasants of Some Chlorinated Insecticides." *Journal of Agriculture and Food Chemistry* 4 (April 1956): 833–866. Further study reveals poisonous effect of select insecticides on quail.

———. "Effects of Chlorinated Hydrocarbon Insecticides upon Quail and Pheasants." *Journal of Agriculture and Food Chemistry* 3 (March 1955): 672–676. Research paper discusses harm to game birds caused by pesticide overexposure.

Duesberg, Peter H., and Peter K. Vogt. "Differences between the Ribonucleic Acids of Transforming and Nontransforming Avian Tumor Viruses." *Proceedings of the National Academy of Sciences* 67 (December 1970): 1,673–1,680. University of California research team identifies oncogene in retrovirus.

Dulbecco, Renato. "Cell Transformation by Viruses." *Science* 166, no. 908 (November 21, 1969): 962–968. Virologist discusses viral cause for tumors.

Edwards, J. Gordon. "The Lies of Rachel Carson." *21st Century Science and Technology Magazine*. Summer 1992. Available online. URL: http://www.21stcenturysciencetech.com/articles/summ02/Carson.html. Accessed September 21, 2005. Example of campaign against Carson still being waged in 21st century.

Gartner, Carol B. *Rachel Carson*. New York: Frederick Ungar, 1983. Biography of environmental writer Carson.

Genelly, Richard E., and Robert L. Rudd. "Effects of DDT, Toxaphene, and Dieldrin on Pheasant Reproduction." *The Auk: A Quarterly Journal of Ornithology* 73, no. 4 (November 1956): 529–539. Available online. URL: http://elibrary.unm.edu/sora/Auk/v073n04/p0529-p0539.pdf. Accessed April 1, 2006. Author's discussion of impact by specific pesticides upon unintended species was among scientific papers that led to Rachel Carson's *Silent Spring*.

Genetics and Genomics Network. 1960. Available online. URL: http://www.genomenewsnetwork.org/resources/timeline/1960_mRNA.php. Accessed October 7, 2005. Article on Web site of J. Craig Venter tells history of discovery of messenger DNA, with focus on work of Brenner, Crick, and Jacob.

Hazlett, Maril. "'Woman vs. Man vs. Bugs': Gender and Popular Ecology in Early Reactions to *Silent Spring*." *Environmental History* 9, no. 2 (October 2004). Available online. URL: http://www.historycooperative.org/journals/eh/9.4/hazlett.html. Accessed April 10, 2006. Social history discussion of controversy surrounding Rachel Carson's 1962 book.

Holley, Robert W., Jean Apgar, George A. Everett, James T. Madison, Mark Marquisee, Susan H. Merrill, John Robert Penswick, and Ada Zamir. "Structure of a Ribonucleic Acid." *Science* 147 (March 1965): 1,462–1,465. Authors explore chemical bonds that shape RNA helix.

Jacob, F., and J. Monod. "Genetics Regulatory Mechanisms in the Synthesis of Proteins." *Journal of Molecular Biology* 3 (March 1961): 318–356. Research partners at Pasteur Institute discuss their work with messenger RNA and its function.

Josse, John, J. A. Kaiser, and A. Kornberg. "Enzymatic Synthesis of Deoxyribonucleic Acid. VIII. Frequencies of Nearest Neighbor Base Sequences in Deoxyribonucleic Acid." *Journal of Biological Chemistry* 236 (March 1961): 857–863. Arthur Kornberg and colleagues discuss role of enzymes in polymerization of DNA nucleotide bases.

Karlson, P., and A. Butenandt. "Pheromones (Ectohormones) in Insects." *Annual Review of Entomology* 4 (1959): 39–58. Entomologists discuss expanding knowledge about importance of chemical communication between insects.

Kay, Lily E. *Who Wrote the Book of Life? A History of the Genetic Code.* Stanford, Calif.: Stanford University Press, 2000. Author illuminates the story of research to crack the genetic code by placing this work in the context of its era, interweaving subjects that include the biological sciences, communication technology, computer development, and the social history of the United States and Europe.

Khorana, H. Gobind. *Chemical Biology: Selected Papers of H. Gobind Khorana.* Singapore: World Scientific Publishing Company, 2000. Biochemist's papers contain accounts of his work with nucleic acids and enzymes.

Kornberg, Arthur. *DNA Synthesis.* San Francisco, Calif.: W. H. Freeman, 1974. Updated discussion of principles and procedures involved in enzymatic synthesis of DNA.

Lear, Linda. *Rachel Carson: Witness for Nature.* New York: Henry Holt, 1997. Accessible biography of science writer who changed history.

Lehman, I. R., M. J. Bessman, E. S. Simms, and A. Kornberg. "Enzymatic Synthesis of Deoxyribonucleic Acid. I. Preparation of Substrates and Partial Purification of an Enzyme from *Escherichia coli.*" *Journal of Biological Chemistry* 233 (July 1958): 163–170. First in series of papers by Kornberg and colleagues discussing studies of enzymatic polymerization of DNA.

MacArthur, Robert H., and E. O. Wilson. "An Equilibrium Theory of Insular Zoogeography." *Evolution* 17 (1967): 373–387. Useful and enduring theory was step in the rise of ecological research.

———. *The Theory of Island Biogeography.* Princeton, N.J.: Princeton University Press, 1967. Wilson and MacArthur's theory at length, in book form.

Margulis, Lynn. *Origin of Eukaryotic Cells.* New Haven, Conn.: Yale University Press, 1970. Author advances her hypothesis that eukaryotic cells trace to a symbiotic relationship in which formerly free-living cells, captured within larger cells, evolved to function in partnership with hosts.

Matthaei, J. Heinrich, and Marshall W. Nirenberg. "Some Characteristics of a Cell-Free DNAase Sensitive System Incorporating Amino Acids into Protein." *Proceedings of the Federation of American Societies for Experimental Biology* 20 (1961). In a scholarly paper, researchers explain experiments in which they demonstrated a cell-free system's incorporation of amino acids into protein.

Metcalf, R. L., ed. *Advances in Pest Control Research*, vol. 3. New York: Interscience Publications, 1960. Collection of writings by entomologists includes piece by Morton Beroza and colleagues (129–179) regarding the strategic use of chemical attractants as alternative to pesticides.

Murphy, Robert Cushman. *Fish-Shape Paumanok: Nature and Man on Long Island.* Philadelphia: American Philosophical Society, 1964. Naturalist's breadth includes impact of pesticide spraying.

Ostrom, J. H. "New Therapod Dinosaur from the Lower Cretaceous of Montana." *Postilla* 128 (1969): 1–17. Paleontologist announces his find and its importance in terms of dinosaur phylogeny.

———. "Osteology of *Deinonychus antirrhopus*, an Unusual Theropod from the Lower Cretaceous of Montana." *Bulletin, Peabody Museum of Natural History* 30 (1969): 1–165. In second paper on *D. antirrhopus*, Ostrom discusses bone structure and interpretation.

Ratcliffe, D. A. "Decrease in Eggshell Weight in Certain Birds of Prey." *Nature* 215, no. 97 (July 8, 1967): 208–210. Paper examines environmental impact on raptors.

Rudd, Robert L. "The Irresponsible Poisoners." *Nation* 188, no. 022 (May 30, 1959): 57–61. Article calls attention to instances of severe chemical contamination of water and instances of unintentional animal deaths.

———. *Pesticides and the Living Landscape.* Madison: University of Wisconsin Press, 1964. Rudd continues his information campaign about dangers of pesticide overuse.

Sagan, L. "On the Origin of Mitosing Cells." *Journal of Theoretical Biology* 3 (March 1967): 255–274. Geneticist later known as Lynn Margulis posits that eukaryotic cells began as a symbiotic merger of prokaryotic bacteria.

Simpson, George Gaylord. *The Meaning of Evolution.* New Haven, Conn.: Yale University Press, 1949. The book that inspired young John Ostrom to study history of living things.

Stauber, John, and Sheldon Rampton. *Toxic Sludge Is Good for You!* Monroe, Maine: Common Courage Press, 1995. Authors examine chemical industry's campaigns to assuage environmental concerns.

Temin, Howard M. "Homology between RNA from Rous Sarcoma Virus and DNA from Rous Sarcoma Virus-Infected Cells." *Proceedings of the National Academy of Sciences* 52, no. 2 (August 1964): 323–329. Author proposes that the virus translates genetic code from its RNA into the cell's DNA.

Volkin, E., and L. Astrachan. "Intracellular Distribution of Labeled Ribonucleic Acid after Phage Infection of *Escherichia coli.*" *Virology* 2, no. 4 (August 1956): 433–437. Evidence of "DNA-like RNA," later called reverse transcriptase.

Wallace, George J., W. P. Nickell, and R. F. Bernard. "Bird Mortality in the Dutch Elm Disease Program in Michigan." *Cranbrook Institution Science Bulletin* 41 (1948): 144. Early evidence of unintended consequence from use of World War II–era pesticides.

8 1971–1980: You Say You Want a Revolution?

A New World

As the 1960s blended into the 1970s, the pace of biological discovery seemed keyed to the quickening pace of Western society. In a decade remembered for the Watergate scandal, the resignation of a U.S. president, the end of an unpopular war in Southeast Asia, and disco music, biological studies also roiled with the unexpected, the unprecedented, the long-awaited, and the persistently rhythmic (in the case of punctuated equilibrium, a new theory of evolution).

The field of molecular genetics changed radically as scientists achieved new means for probing, measuring, synthesizing, and ultimately manipulating DNA. Microbiologists, virologists, biochemists, and others joined in transformative investigations into the means by which viruses—especially retroviruses—interact with, infiltrate, and alter the chromosomes of host cells. They learned how to locate with precision certain viral genes by using the same catalytic enzymes that bacteria employ to protect themselves against invasion by foreign DNA. Thus, they invented methods for detecting the order in which DNA's four bases—adenine, guanine, cytosine, and thymine—are arranged.

Researchers' use of *restriction enzymes* to identify and sequence individual genes at the molecular level led to the ability to snip out specific gene sequences and then to reinsert them—eventually into unrelated chromosomes. Northern California scientists genetically altered a bacterium to behave like a frog (although only at the molecular-biochemical level).

Once a bacterium could be genetically reengineered to produce a protein normally made by the cell of an amphibian, it followed that one-celled life-forms also could be modified so that they would produce more useful proteins, such as enzymes and hormones with medical and industrial applications. Pharmaceutical companies, agribusinesses, and other industries would be willing to pay good money for such substances, or so reasoned Robert A. Swanson (1947–99), an entrepreneur with a grasp of industrial chemistry and a big idea. That idea took hold in the form of the first biochemical company. Before the decade was out, many top researchers were becoming businessmen in the new biotechnology industry.

Along the way, even the scientists most responsible for developing recombinant DNA technology worried that they had not given enough thought to potential dangers of mixing unlike species. Many leaders in the field gathered at a California seaside resort to hammer out safety rules for their new and (to many) worrisome field.

Growing understanding of how viruses and enzymes interact with and manipulate eukaryotic cells directly aided medical researchers. For example, two San Francisco–based virologists were able to establish that healthy animal cells contain genes that, when triggered by a viral infection or contamination by a carcinogenic substance, can cause cancer. The discovery of these oncogenes was a major step toward understanding and treating many cancers.

The picture of gene action, as it emerged through the 1970s, was much more complex than previously had been appreciated. Biologists came to see a dynamic genome that contained unexpected sequences of noncoding, or "junk DNA," interrupting coding sequences. This reinter-

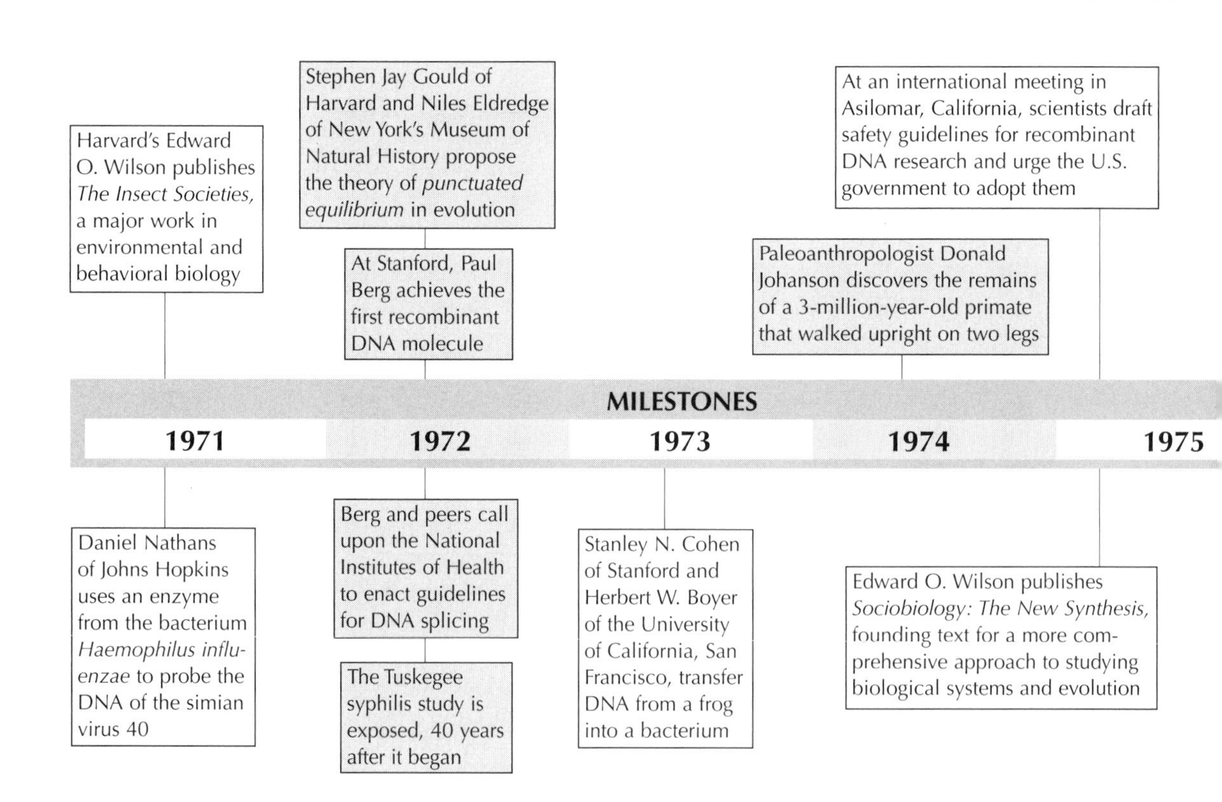

preted genome featured far more instances of genes that change position on the chromosome than previously had been known. These *transposons* became a major area of study. Gene expression came to be understood as subject to regulation by enzymatic processes. Such revelations amounted to something reminiscent of, although not identical to, the complex, highly mutable genome that maize cytologist Barbara McClintock had envisioned more than 20 years earlier. This gained the veteran researcher new respect among her peers as a visionary genius.

The tumult extended to many other fields within biology, notably evolution studies. Paleontologists and anthropologists made discoveries that overturned old assumptions about crucial, species-defining traits and the paths by which ancient species evolved into modern progeny. Theoreticians put forward new ideas about the tempo of evolution and the forces guiding the process. A broader, more holistic way of considering such forces arose, the field of sociobiology.

Although every decade of the 20th century brought great strides in biological research, the 1970s stands as a period of rapid and profound discoveries that resonated far beyond the laboratory and the classroom.

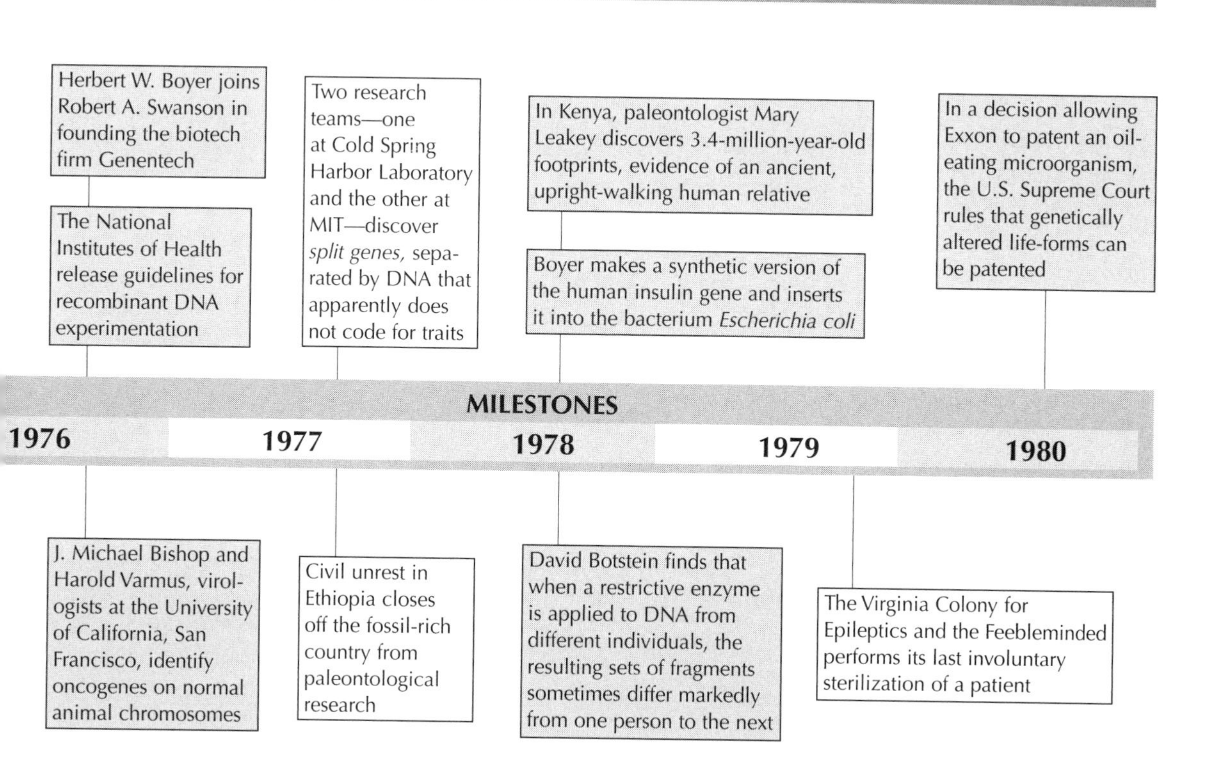

Genetic Research Crosses a Frontier

Around the same time as Howard Temin and David Baltimore's work with reverse transcriptase (covered in the previous chapter), three other microbiologists were working toward understanding a related group of enzymes that are capable of cutting bits from the DNA molecule.

Switzerland's Werner Arber (1929–), of the University of Geneva, followed up on an observation that Salvador Luria had made. He noted that when a bacteriophage attacks a bacterium, interfering with the genetic machinery of the cell, the virus also undergoes genetic changes. This work led Arber—who had studied at the University of Southern California, as well as in Zurich and Basel—to focus on enzymes produced by the bacterium. The enzymes cut to bits foreign DNA molecules. Each enzyme acts as a catalyst, dissolving the molecular bond between nucleotides in the phage DNA. Such enzymes became known as restriction enzymes for the way bacteria employ them to restrict bacteriophage growth.

Hamilton Othanel Smith (1931–), a professor of microbiology at Johns Hopkins University, built on Arber's work. The New York–born Smith, a graduate of the University of California, Berkeley, and the Johns Hopkins medical school, discovered enzymes that could snip apart foreign DNA at precise, consistent locations.

It quickly became apparent that Smith's restriction enzymes—dubbed type II—could be powerful tools for microbiology and molecular genetics. In 1971, Daniel Nathans, also of Johns Hopkins, took a type II restriction enzyme from the bacterium *Haemophilus influenzae* and used it to probe the DNA of the simian virus 40, commonly called SV40.

The son of Russian-Jewish immigrants, Nathans had grown up in modest circumstances in Wilmington, Delaware. Like many biology researchers, he had set out to become a physician. With a medical degree from Washington University in St. Louis, he had served a medical internship and residency at Columbia-Presbyterian Medical Center in New York before devoting himself to biochemical research—first at Rockefeller University, then at the National Institutes of Health in Bethesda, Maryland. At his next stop, Johns Hopkins, he was the first member of what became the Division of Genetics.

Nathans had been on a research residency in Israel when he received word from Smith about Smith's work on restriction enzymes. After returning to Baltimore, Nathans and his research team members sought an enzyme to cut apart the DNA of SV40, one of the simplest of cancer-causing viruses. They used Smith's enzyme and discovered similar restriction enzymes that cut the DNA at specific sites. This allowed them to make a "cleavage map," which is a genetic map that measures the distance between particular gene sequences as selected by the enzymes. Such mapping helped Nathans's team to pinpoint viral genes and better understand the structure and function of the virus.

Arber, Smith, and Nathans shared the 1978 Nobel Prize in physiology or medicine for this work.

Oncogenes

When virologist J. Michael Bishop (1936–) learned that Howard Temin and David Baltimore had discovered reverse transcriptase, he was both disappointed and exhilarated. The disappointment came because Bishop had just begun working with other researchers at the University of California, San Francisco, trying to solve the mystery of how retroviruses replicate their genetic information. Temin and Baltimore preempted the quest with their revelation that by means of reverse transcriptase, retroviruses use RNA to synthesize DNA. Yet Bishop also saw in the discovery exciting opportunities for virology research.

With lab partner Harold Varmus (1939–), a postdoctoral virology fellow who had joined the UCSF team late in 1970, and other graduate researchers, Bishop set to work describing the biochemical processes involved in the copying of RNA into DNA in the Rous sarcoma virus, shown to trigger cancer in chickens. They found that normal genes in healthy cells of the body can cause cancer. Called oncogenes, these genes (when functioning properly) do the routine job of controlling growth in every cell—both promoting growth and restricting it, thus achieving a balance. Infection by a virus or contamination by a carcinogenic agent (as contained in cigarette smoke) can upset this balance, leading to abnormal growth. Oncogenes thus become capable of causing cancer. Researchers had earlier thought viral genes caused cancer and had not anticipated cancer caused by a malfunction of the cell's normal genetic material.

J. Michael Bishop, chancellor of the University of California, San Francisco, and Harold Varmus, president of Memorial Sloan-Kettering Cancer Center, reunited for a photo in 2005. The former lab partners shared a Nobel Prize for their 1970s work. (Mikkel Aaland/UCSF Public Affairs)

The work of Bishop, Varmus, and their colleagues led to the identification of many specific oncogenes. Some cause cancer by activating growth at the wrong time. Others cause cancer by failing to turn off growth at the proper time.

Neither Bishop nor Varmus had set out to be research biologists. Bishop,

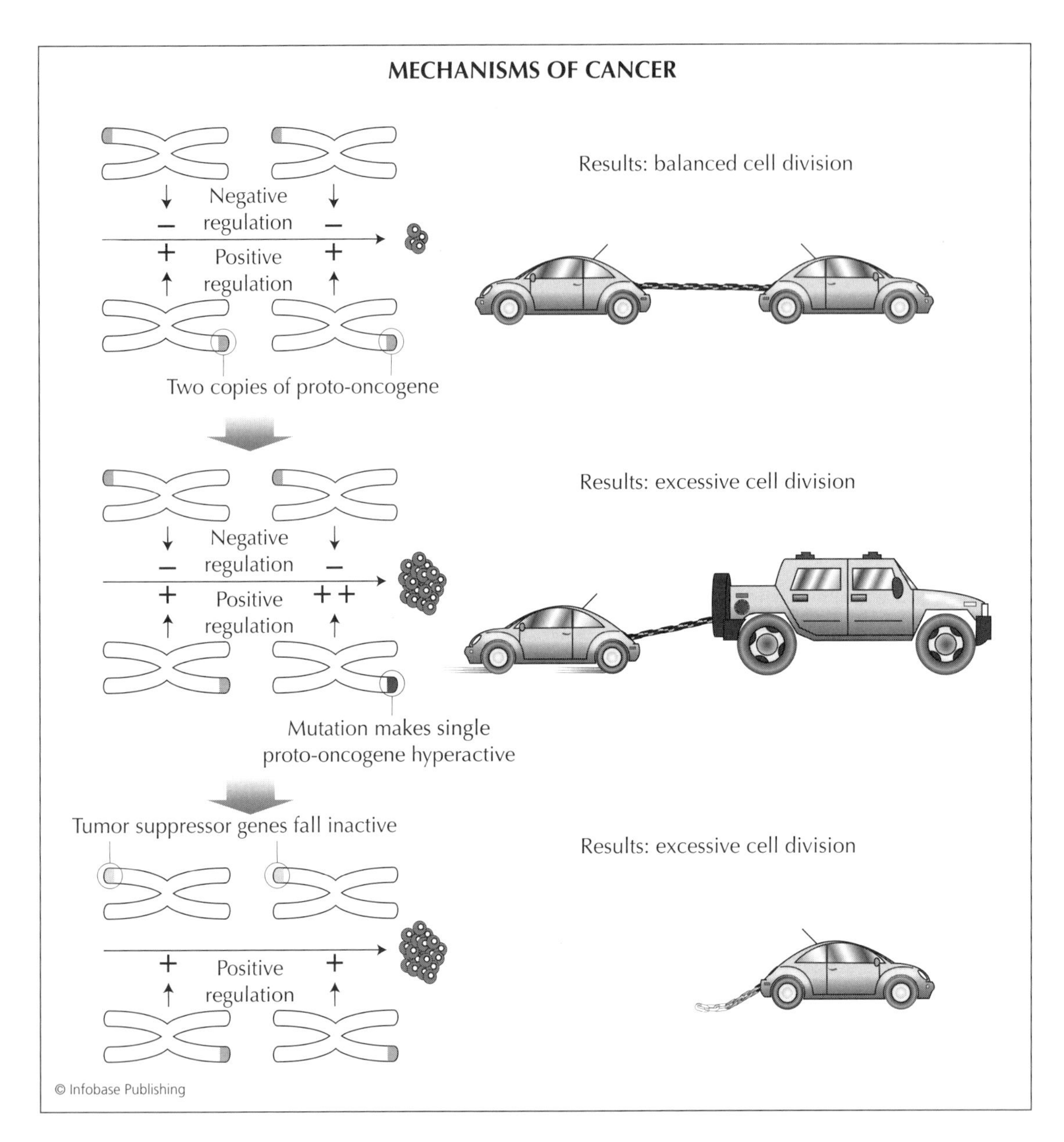

Genetic damage by mutation or exposure to a carcinogenic agent can unbalance the opposing forces between normal genes that activate growth and those that suppress abnormal growth, leading to out-of-control cell reproduction.

in particular, has written of the surprising course his life took, given his beginnings. He grew up in rural Pennsylvania, the son of a Lutheran pastor. His childhood passion was music—the piano and singing. He attended a two-room schoolhouse where he learned little science but devoured history and loved to read. Although he had decided on a career in medicine by the time he started Gettysburg College, he then found himself distracted by other disciplines—philosophy and literature among them—on the way to a degree in chemistry. It was at Harvard Medical School that Bishop decided he was better suited for a career as a researcher than as a physician. In particular, he became captivated by molecular biology. After a clinical internship in Boston, he found his way to virology research through a postgraduate training program run by the National Institutes of Health in Maryland.

Like Bishop, Varmus had started college wanting to be a medical doctor. He had grown up in Winter Park, Florida (where his army physician father had been stationed during World War II), and Nassau County, New York (on southern Long Island). Also like Bishop, Varmus was a voracious reader who found the broad intellectual smorgasbord of college delightfully distracting. In his case, English literature lured him away from science and a premed curriculum. After graduation from Amherst College in 1961, he spent an academic year at Harvard on a literary scholarship before deciding to go back to medicine. His M.D. was from the Columbia College of Physicians and Surgeons (medical school of Columbia University). Yet, again like Bishop, he served as a physician before finding his way to research through a job at the National Institutes of Health.

For their discoveries together, Bishop and Varmus shared the 1989 Nobel Prize in physiology or medicine.

Gene Sequencing

Beginning in the mid-1970s, science's growing ability to manipulate bits of DNA brought new ways for geneticists to study DNA by sorting out the order in which DNA's four bases—adenine, guanine, cytosine and thymine—occur within an isolated gene. Two simultaneous research efforts—one in England and the other in Massachusetts—resulted in slightly different methods to achieve this gene sequencing (also called sequence analysis).

In gene sequencing, scientists use a bit of DNA as a template and synthesize identical strands. They cut these fragments into different lengths. Each differs from the next by a single base. By separating the fragments and identifying the end base of each one, the researcher is able to determine the sequence in which those bases occur in the original strand.

At Cambridge University, British biochemist Frederick Sanger (1918–)—who had in 1958 won the Nobel Prize in chemistry—developed the chain termination method of DNA sequencing. Widely known as the Sanger method, it involves using restriction enzymes to cut the DNA. The base at the end of each bit is identified using *gel electrophoresis.* In gel electrophoresis, an electric charge is applied to a special gel *medium*, causing molecules to migrate so that they end up sorted by size—differentiated from one another.

Around the same time, Walter Gilbert (1932–) of Harvard University was working on the same problem. A second-generation

Harvard faculty member (his father was a Harvard economist), Gilbert (along with graduate student Allan M. Maxam) devised a method for gene sequencing that was very similar to Sanger's. The American method differs from the British largely in that it uses chemicals, rather than enzymes, to cut the DNA at specific bases. This chemical method was made possible by the growing understanding of restriction enzymes and their chemical properties.

Sanger and Gilbert each received a one-quarter share of the 1980 Nobel Prize in chemistry for their inventions. This made Sanger, the son of a Gloustershire physician, the only person to have been awarded two Nobels in chemistry.

The Cell as Factory

Paul Berg used catalytic enzymes to cut viral DNA and glue together sections of different molecules.

Almost as soon as microbiologists and molecular geneticists began to understand the properties of restriction enzymes, some researchers in

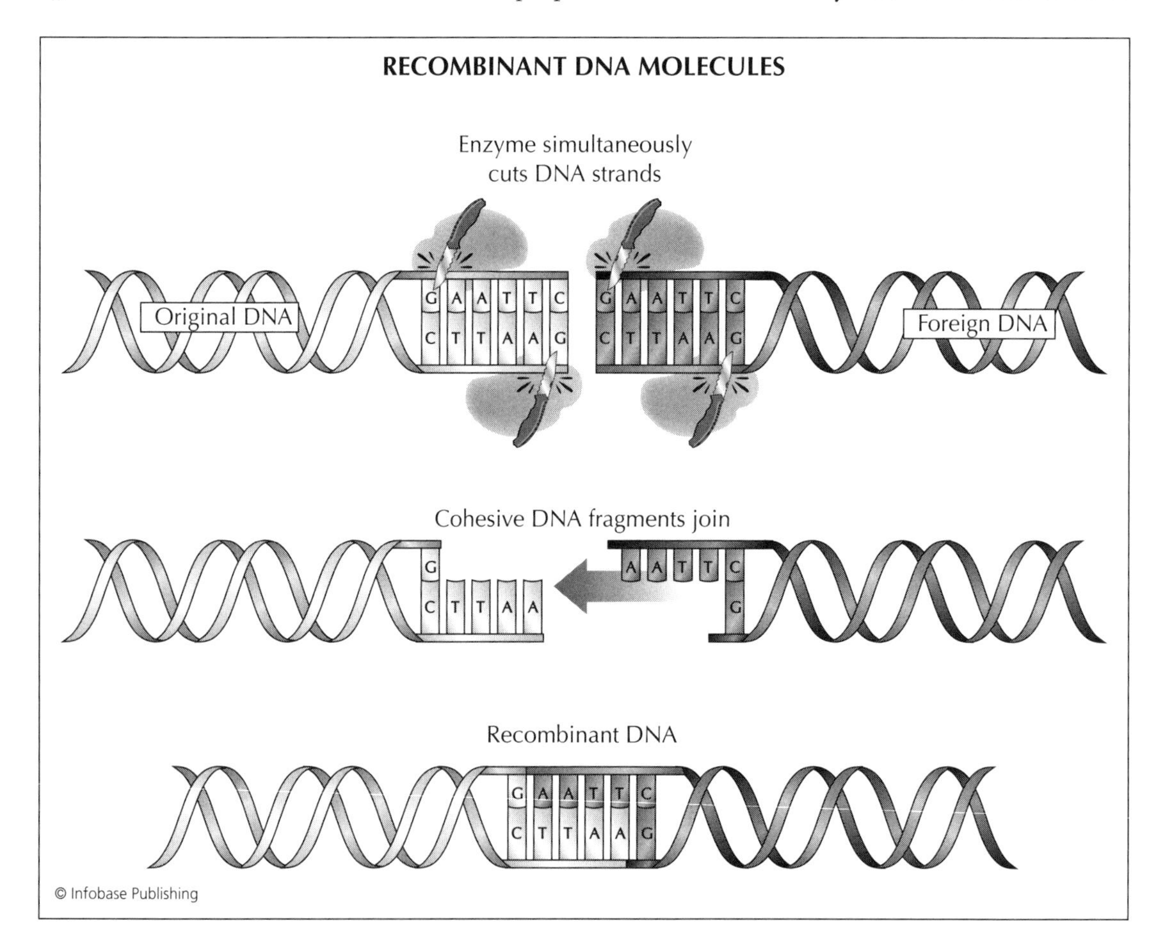

northern California began using them not only to explore the structure of DNA but also to reconfigure it.

In 1972, Paul Berg (1926–) of Stanford University used enzymes both to cut DNA and to glue sections of different DNA molecules together. Berg synthesized a ligase, which is another type of catalytic enzyme—one that helps form rather than break chemical bonds. The ligase enabled him to attach the unrelated DNA segments together. For this work, Berg shared the 1980 Nobel Prize in chemistry with Sanger and Gilbert.

In 1973, Stanley N. Cohen (1935–), also at Stanford, and Herbert W. Boyer (1936–) of the University of California, San Francisco, achieved another breakthrough that led directly to the biotechnology industry. Cohen was studying plasmids, miniscule DNA rings that float around in the cytoplasm of bacterial cells. He found a way to take a plasmid out of the cell and reinsert it in another cell. Boyer, meanwhile, had found that when certain restriction enzymes in *E. coli* cut DNA strands, they leave behind clipped ends that make it possible to paste on other pieces of DNA with remarkable precision.

At a scientific conference in Hawaii, the two California researchers got together and realized that their respective discoveries could be combined. By linking Cohen's plasmid transfer technique with Boyer's process, they soon connected a piece of DNA containing a gene from the African clawed frog *Xenopus laevis* to plasmid DNA from an *E. coli* bacterium. When the researchers put this plasmid back into an *E. coli* cell, the bacterium copied the frog DNA, and the gene directed the cell to produce a protein that was specific to the frog species.

Boyer and Cohen had found a way to turn a bacterial cell into a kind of biological factory to make specific proteins as directed by scientists. The implication was that bacteria could be genetically engineered to produce other chemicals manufactured by cells—enzymes and hormones useful to medicine and industry. In 1974, the scientists applied for a U.S. patent on this recombinant DNA technology.

Much of biochemist Paul Berg's research illuminated details of cell metabolism (Paul Berg and Stanford University Libraries)

How Not to Make a Monster

The idea of mixing vital molecular bits of dissimilar organisms sounds frightening. To the uninitiated, this new kind of genetic engineering suggested that horror fantasies about mad scientists had come true. If microbiologists could genetically cobble together a frog bacterium, what about a horrible man-insect, as in the 1958 science fiction movie *The Fly?*

Even many of the people most closely involved in the research saw a need for extraordinary caution in crossing this scientific frontier. The implications appeared great. Scientists knew that nature had long blended related species to create hybrid organisms. And human plant and animal breeders have for many centuries directed breeding to emphasize or eliminate selected genetic traits. To recombine segments of DNA from species as diverse as an amphibian and *E. coli* raised red flags, however. Bacteria cause diseases. Among other early subjects of recombinant DNA experiments was SV40—a virus shown to trigger malignant tumors in people as well as in monkeys. What if a genetically altered virus or bacterium escaped from the laboratory through an air-conditioning vent or on the cuff of somebody's trousers? How would it interact with other life-forms it would encounter? Would it find hosts or prey that the scientists who created it could not have anticipated? Could it spread disease, destroy crops, alter the landscape? Many worried that the results could be devastating.

Biologists were well aware of how introduced species can wreak huge, often destructive changes in a natural system. The 16th- through 18th-century devastation of American Indian populations by diseases that Europeans carried—diseases to which the natives had not previously been exposed and thus had developed no immunity—was a well-known example. So was the destruction of trees in the southeastern United States by the strangling Japanese vine kudzu, intentionally imported in a misguided effort to combat soil erosion.

How could microbiologists ensure that they did not accidentally introduce unfavorable or even dangerous traits into microorganisms or plants? The potential problems were enough to prompt Stanford's Paul Berg, who in 1972—almost directly after his own bioengineering breakthrough—joined 10 other researchers in writing an open letter to the National Institutes of Health. Published in the journal *Science,* the letter called for U.S. federal regulation of recombinant DNA technology.

Responding to these concerns, the National Academy of Sciences asked Berg to chair a committee that in 1974 asked researchers to stop performing certain types of recombinant DNA experiments until potential hazards were better understood. The next year, Berg and David Baltimore were among organizers of a meeting sponsored by the National Institutes of Health, a major source of funds for the research in question. The meeting brought together 100 top scientists who were either already engaged in gene splicing or likely to try it soon. A contingent of lawyers also attended, and the meeting was open to the press. Held at the Asilomar Conference Grounds, a state park on California's Monterey Peninsula, this gathering was a crucial event in the history of modern science. Some call it the Woodstock of biotechnology. The reference is to the Woodstock Music Festival, held near Woodstock, New York, in 1969. That massive rock concert defined its era in popular culture. Known by the single word *Asilomar,* the conference on recombinant DNA defined an era in molecular biology.

In their private conversations during the meeting, the participants—Nobel Prize winners and future winners among them—had opportunities to compare notes on their work and also to talk about the ethical questions raised by the new biotechnology. In the formal sessions, the scientists consciously avoided sticky philosophical issues. They concentrated on practical matters, hammering out a set of guidelines for safely working

A lodge at the Asilomar Conference Center in California, site of a 1970s conference at which molecular biologists worked out safety guidelines for their unprecedented experiments with recombinant DNA (NC Parks & Resorts at Asilomar)

with genetically altered microorganisms. They agreed, for example, to use in their gene-splicing experiments disabled bacteria that could not survive outside the lab. The National Institutes of Health subsequently adopted the rules worked out at Asilomar as "Guidelines for Research Involving Recombinant DNA Molecules." Thus, informed researchers themselves—rather than lobbyists or congressional staffers—drafted the federal regulations affecting this new field of scientific work. Further, the researchers arrived at their rules not in closed sessions but in open meetings with reporters present. The frank format lent credibility to the process.

Genetic recombination remained controversial after Asilomar and into the 21st century. Yet scientists who attended the conference, as well as their successors, point out that there never has been an instance in which dire fears about recombinant DNA have been borne out by a crisis such as epidemic disease. This is in part because of careful research, but there have undoubtedly been breeches of safety guidelines over the succeeding decades. Research has shown, however, that the cutting and recombining of DNA sequences—much of it by viral infection—is relatively common in nature, far more so than was understood in the early 1970s.

In other words, recombinant DNA is everywhere. The stuff reconfigured by human scientists comprises only a small percentage.

The Biotech Industry

In 1975, microbiologist Herbert Boyer received a phone call from Robert A. Swanson, who worked for a venture capital firm in the San Francisco Bay area. Swanson wanted to talk with Boyer about what he saw as the exciting business potential in gene splicing.

The scientist agreed to meet with the 29-year-old Swanson but expected little to come of it. What Boyer thought would be a brief meeting grew into a three-hour session during which Swanson—who had majored in chemistry as an undergraduate at MIT—convinced the UCSF researcher that there was money to be made in privately developing the process of using cells as factories to make useful hormones and proteins, the products that would become known as *biopharmaceuticals*. Swanson succeeded in persuading Boyer to become his partner in the first such commercial venture. The result, founded in 1976, was the biotechnology company Genentech.

The firm soon developed a method to mass-produce human proteins by harnessing genetically altered bacteria. Early products included human growth hormone, intended for use in children unable to produce

Herbert W. Boyer, cofounder of Genentech, invented a profitable process for synthesizing human insulin. (UCSF Public Affairs)

enough on their own, and human insulin for treatment of diabetes. A blood-clotting factor followed, as did interferon molecules for treating leukemia and immune deficiencies, and a hepatitis B vaccine. Within a few decades, hundreds of thousands of biotech companies worldwide would follow the path that Genentech was blazing—many of them started by partnerships that included top academic researchers. For example, Harvard's Gilbert joined a group of businessmen and other scientists, including MIT's Philip A. Sharp (1944–), to form Biogen, a commercial genetic-engineering research corporation based in Switzerland. Sharp would in 1993 share the Nobel Prize in physiology or medicine with Richard J. Roberts (1943–) of Cold Spring Harbor Laboratory—for their 1970s discovery of "split genes." (See "A Dynamic Genome" below.) Roberts also would join a biotech firm, New England Biolabs.

Boyer, vice president of Genentech from 1976 to 1999, had grown up in southwestern Pennsylvania with dreams of becoming a physician. While attending the local St. Vincent's College, he shifted his goal to research. After earning a Ph.D. in biochemistry from the University of Pittsburgh and doing postgraduate work in enzymology at Yale, he had joined the faculty of the University of California, San Francisco, in 1966.

Brooklyn-born and Florida-reared, Swanson had studied chemistry at MIT, but his master's degree was in business management. He had started in the venture capital business with Citicorp in New York. The firm entrusted him with opening its San Francisco office in 1973, when he was only 26. Two years later, he moved to a company specializing in the emerging field of high-tech electronics in the San Francisco Bay Area.

Much of Genentech's success—eventual billions in earnings—has been attributed to Swanson's skills. After convincing Boyer to join him in the venture, he went on to recruit other gifted researchers.

The rise of biotech companies profoundly changed the landscape of employment opportunities for scientists in molecular genetics, microbiology, biochemistry, and related fields, while also changing the pharmaceutical, agribusiness, and chemistry industries.

A Dynamic Genome

The ability to cut, splice, and isolate individual genes led many molecular biologists in the 1970s to begin reassessing the complex tangle of processes going on in genetic replication and expression. A number of bacteriologists, for example, found that certain rapidly occurring mutations corresponded with bits of DNA that—enabled by selective enzymes—cut away from one position on a DNA strand and relocated to another. This was reminiscent of what plant geneticist Barbara McClintock had described decades earlier when she wrote about transposable elements on the chromosomes of maize—so-called *jumping genes.*

McClintock had called her discovery "mutable loci" and then "controlling elements." She had in the early 1950s put forward a hypothesis

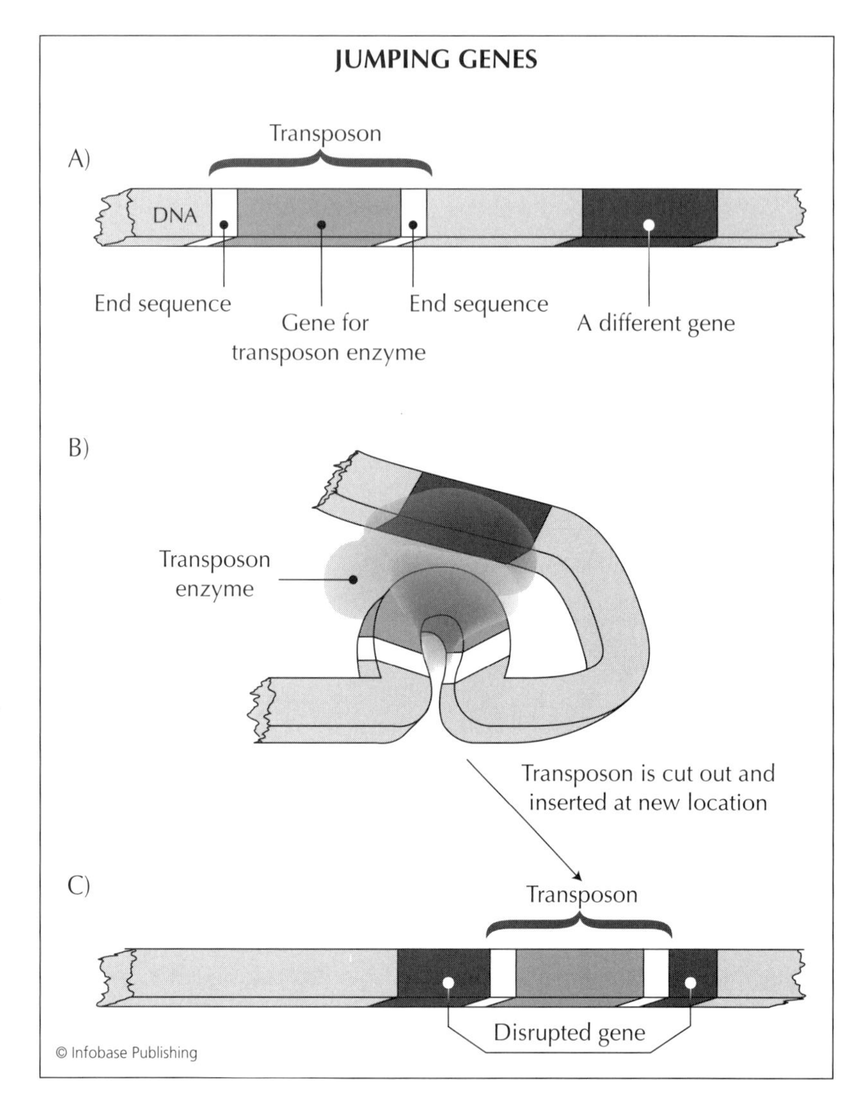

Mobile genetic elements, or class II transposons, can and do move directly from one position to another upon a chromosome. A sequence of DNA is bounded on each end by noncoding end sequences. Transposase, an enzyme that binds to DNA, cuts the transposon from one position on the DNA strand and inserts it into another, disrupting another nucleotide sequence. After Barbara McClintock first reported on the phenomenon, these sections were often called jumping genes.

that these movable bits of genetic material determined how other genes, especially those responsible for pigmentation in corn kernels, were expressed. Although other scientists had confirmed her observation of transposable elements in maize, her idea of controlled gene expression had not caught on.

McClintock's controlling elements were part of her vision of an energetic, mutable genome. She saw mechanisms regulating when and how the hereditary information contained in genes is expressed. Her approach had struck some other geneticists and cell biologists as unnecessarily complex. She seemed to be contradicting the well-established one-gene–one-enzyme theory of Beadle and Tatum. Yet a younger generation of

Veteran researcher Barbara McClintock's long-held views about the genome gained new respect in the 1970s. (Marjorie Bhavani/Cold Spring Harbor Laboratory Archives)

scientists later confirmed the idea of gene regulation—not quite by the controlling elements mechanism that she had put forward, but regulation nonetheless. Through the 1970s, transposable elements, which had come to be called transposons, became such a pervasive part of molecular genetics that a subfield of the science focused on them.

Genes are both less stable and less constant than most of McClintock's peers had previously realized. Some of them can and do move on a fairly routine basis. Many—if not most—can be turned on and off. In fact, it is essential for normal development and survival of living things that select genes be turned on and off. Genetic traits—for growth or certain metabolic functions—must be expressed at the proper time in an organism's existence and in the proper circumstance.

Jacques Monod and Francois Jacob, the French researchers responsible for naming messenger RNA, had found, for example, that *E. coli* bacteria, when in the presence of lactose, have the ability to turn on a series of genes that enable a bacterium to metabolize the sugar available in the lactose. These genes, absent lactose, remain dormant.

In 1977, two research teams—one at Cold Spring Harbor Laboratory and the other at MIT—discovered what is called "split genes." That is, they found that individual genes—the ones that encode the essential proteins of life—are often interrupted by long sections of DNA that do not code for protein structure or do anything else that scientists have yet figured out.

Richard J. Roberts, from England, led the team at Cold Spring Harbor. Kentucky-born Philip A. Sharp led the MIT group. Both worked with the adenovirus, which is among the viruses that cause the common cold. Previous studies of bacterial DNA had led to the belief among biologists that genes are made of unbroken stretches of DNA and that all the polynucleotide sequences code for protein structure. Instead, this new research showed discontinuous sequences. RNA copies, when transferring genetic information from these genes, go through a stage in which enzymatic action cuts out the noncoding sections, which came to be called *introns*. The name for a coding segments is *exon*.

Continuing research demonstrated that this discontinuous gene structure is not just present but prevalent in the cells of higher organisms, including human beings. In humans, the introns contain about 90 percent of the DNA sequence in a gene—most of which are interrupted about 10 times. So much noncoding DNA helps explain why genetic phenomena such as transposons cause fewer mutations than might otherwise be assumed. Noncoding nucleotide sequences are often referred to as *junk DNA*. The term arose because scientists did not know its purpose. Some thought it had no purpose, that it was perhaps a junk heap of discarded genes. (In the 21st century, there are researchers who focus on noncoding DNA—especially on transposons—and they have put forward a number of hypotheses about its function.)

Roberts and Sharp—corecipients of a 1993 Nobel Prize in this work—came from dissimilar backgrounds. Roberts, an only child, had grown up devising his own chemistry experiments in the old English city of Bath. Although he had not paid much attention to formal studies as a boy, he managed to win a place at Sheffield University, where he trained in organic chemistry.

Sharp, from the hill country of northern Kentucky, had grown up on a family farm surrounded by siblings, cousins, aunts, and uncles. He had earned his tuition to Kentucky's small Union College by raising livestock and growing his own tobacco crops.

Among the things the two researchers have in common is that both benefited from the guidance of brilliant mentors. In Roberts's case it was James Watson, who hired him to sequence SV40 at Harvard in the early 1970s. For Sharp, it was Salvador Luria, who brought him to MIT's Center for Cancer Research in 1974. There, he shared laboratory space with David Baltimore.

Evolving Ideas about Evolution

For many theorists, a dynamic genome suggested more possibilities for mutations that under the right circumstances could bring hereditary changes and give rise to new species. Mobile genetic elements and split genes seemed likely mechanisms for chance mutation—the engine of evolution.

Although the concept of biological evolution—an understanding that species give rise to new species—underlay virtually every aspect of biological study throughout the century, details of how and under which circumstances new species originate have been the subjects of debate among evolutionary biologists since Darwin. While some theorists have maintained that genetic adaptation occurs at a steady, gradual rate over great spans of time and many generations, others have disagreed, citing specific environmental conditions as spurs to evolution. The evolutionary biologist Ernst Mayr (1904–2005) sought to explain speciation as a phenomenon spurred by physical—that is, geological—isolation of small populations of organisms.

In 1972, two Columbia University–trained paleontologists, Niles Eldredge (1943–) and Stephen Jay Gould (1941–2002), built upon Mayr's ideas in their theory of *punctuated equilibrium.* In their 1972 essay "Punctuated Equilibria: An Alternative to Phyletic Gradualism" (published in a collection of writings titled *Models in Paleobiology*), they said that evolution, and especially the rise of new species, happens much more quickly than had traditionally been thought, in spurts that can be said to "punctuate" much longer periods of little if any change among a given population of organisms. Such a pattern, they said, is in keeping with the evidence of the fossil record, which often shows long, continuous species survival and what appear to be gaps in the record between eras. Eldredge, of the American Museum of Natural History, and Gould, of Harvard, proposed that in large, stable populations genetic changes had little chance to alter the gene pool because such changes arising in individuals would, when not fatal, inevitably blend into the whole of the species. In a small group, isolated from the general population on the fringe of its environment—perhaps an ecologically difficult fringe—selective pressures would be more likely to favor genetic change, which would gain momentum over a relatively short number of generations.

In addition to his more esoteric scientific work, the gifted writer Gould became known during the 1970s and beyond for his graceful essays on natural history. Beginning in 1974, these were published regularly in the magazine *Natural History* and collected in a series of popular books. His ideas about evolution often clashed with those of other theorists, especially Oxford University's Richard Dawkins (1946–), who argued that gene selection, not species selection, was the overwhelming force in evolution.

Born in Kenya and educated in England, Dawkins is an ethologist, or animal behaviorist. His field of biology was taking on greater prominence in the 1970s, especially as Karl von Frisch (1886–1982), Nikolaas Tinbergen (1906–88), and Konrad Lorenz (1903–89) shared the 1973 Nobel Prize in physiology or medicine—all of them for discoveries in animal behavior patterns that they had made decades earlier.

Edward O. Wilson has warned that the rapid loss of species diversity threatens the health of Earth's biosphere. (Jim Harrison/Department of Communication Services, North Carolina State University)

In 1976, Dawkins published his first book, *The Selfish Gene*, in which he stated that Darwinian natural selection is a process whereby genes use the living things that carry them to further their own survival. (This has been compared to the statement that a chicken is an egg's way of making more eggs.)

Dawkins did not mean that genes consciously act in a selfish manner but that they behave—that is, affect evolution—as if they were concerned solely with their own propagation. Thus, a gene generally programs an organism in a way that serves the organism's self-interest, but not always. For example, the male praying mantis (*Mantis religiosa*), whose genetically programmed mating behavior may include allowing itself to be devoured by the female it has just inseminated, is acting for the preservation of its genes, but not for the preservation of itself.

Tuskegee Experiment Exposed

Arguments such as those put forward by Richard Dawkins, Edward O. Wilson, and others—placing heavy influence on the role of genes in human behavior—tend to raise red flags for ethicists and social critics who detect (rightly or wrongly) the taint of genetic determinism. *Genetic determinism* is a general term for the idea that human beings are essentially the sum of their genes. This was the notion that had opened the door to eugenics-based governmental policies in the early decades of the century. (Eugenics is covered in chapter 4.)

Although the German Nazi programs to sterilize or kill so-called genetic defectives had been overwhelmingly condemned after World War II, many American laws based on eugenics were still on the books decades later, and some states were still sterilizing the developmentally disabled in the 1970s. At the Virginia asylum where Carrie Buck had been sterilized a half-century earlier (as discussed in chapter 3), the practice continued until 1979.

Americans received a harsh reminder that past attitudes had not been erased when on July 25, 1972, a story in the *Washington Star* newspaper exposed the U.S. Public Health Service's 40-year study of the effects of long-term syphilis on African-American men. Of the 600 original subjects, all poor sharecroppers living in Macon County, Alabama, 399 had been selected for observation because they were infected with syphilis. (The rest of the men, healthy, were used as *controls*.) Doctors based at the Tuskegee Institute in Alabama had recruited the men in 1932 by telling them that they had qualified for free medical care. The infected subjects were not told that they had syphilis or that the disease was spread by sexual intercourse.

Originally planned as a six-month study of the effects of syphilis on untreated men, the experiment had within its first year been extended and reconceived as a plan to follow these patients until their deaths and then autopsy them. Public Health Service researchers, with the cooperation of medical staff at the Tuskegee Institute (later Tuskegee University) actively denied effective treatment to the subjects—even after penicillin, the first proven cure for syphilis, became available in 1947. The newspaper story reported that during World War II, the researchers took steps to see that study subjects who were drafted or joined the military were exempted from mandatory treatment for venereal disease.

The study was exposed after a Public Health Service employee—having called his superiors' attention to the ethical issues involved and having failed to change their minds—alerted the press. Once the story broke—front-page coverage in newspapers across the country followed the *Star*'s report—the U.S. government finally ended the study in the fall of 1972. By then, only 74 of the infected Tuskegee Syphilis Study subjects were still alive. Forty of their wives had contracted syphilis and 19 of their children had been born with the congenital form of the disease.

Researchers and staff attempted to defend the study on the basis of its potential benefits to the understanding of syphilis. They said that information gained from the experiment would help other African Americans infected with the venereal disease. Apologists pointed out that the study had been conducted with the cooperation of Tuskegee University, an African-American institution. They had no answer, however, for the observation that such a study would never have been attempted if the intended subjects had been white, literate, and middle-class. By virtue of their race, economic status, lack of education, or all of those, the men studied had been determined appropriate experimental subjects, much as Jews had been used for cruel experiments by Nazi scientists. It can only be presumed that the 399 infected men had been used for this purpose because, like the Jews in 1930s Germany, they were judged to be a lesser strain of humanity—based on an idea that had been widely seen as not only correct but as supported by biological science in 1932, when the study began. Apparently, in at least one corner of American public health research, the idea still claimed adherents four decades later.

Gould and those who agreed with him preferred the view that survival competition takes place not only on the genetic level but also between individual organisms, species, and so on—in other words, that neither morphology nor behavior (especially not behavior) can be explained entirely in terms of gene selection.

Dawkins's views intermeshed somewhat with those of U.S. entomologist-turned-sociobiologist Edward O. Wilson, who in 1971 published *The Insect Societies.* Based on his research with ants and other social species, this comprehensive book chronicled analyses of changes in numbers, condition, and survival rates among populations of insects. It treated interactions within and between societies and between the species and their environments. Wilson followed with the immensely influential book *Sociobiology: The New Synthesis* in 1975. Seen as the founding text for a fresh and more comprehensive approach to studying biological systems and evolution, the book treats social behavior among animals as the result of genetic selection. In one chapter, Wilson proposed that human social behavior, like that of the other species he examined, flowed from biological principles. Sociobiology brings much of what are considered the social sciences under the broad heading of biology.

Wilson's Pulitzer Prize–winning 1978 book, *On Human Nature*, outlined what he sees as genetic underpinnings for interpersonal behaviors regarding ethics, sexuality, and aggression. Notably, he has applied a genetic explanation to altruism—behavior in which an individual might sacrifice personal well-being or even survival in favor of feeding or guarding another society member—especially a close family member. Although such behavior might hurt the individual's chance of breeding and passing on its genes, he explained, the behavior could increase the chance of passing along genes that the beneficiary shares with the altruistic benefactor.

As was Gould—with whom they often vociferously disagreed—Dawkins and Wilson are biologists who have written persuasively for a general audience. In the 1970s and through the end of the 20th century, the books of these and other evolutionary theorists reenergized the long-running debate over how natural selection works and helped popularize evolutionary biology and natural history.

Birds and Beasts

As evolutionary theorists debated broad principles of natural selection in the 1970s, other biologists—among them paleontologists—worked on understanding the paths whereby specific ancient lineages gave rise to modern progeny.

Peabody Museum curator John H. Ostrom's ideas about dinosaurs—that at least some of them were warm-blooded and many were more like birds than like lizards—motivated him to gain access to rare fossils from the species *Archaeopteryx lithographica*, owned by a handful of European

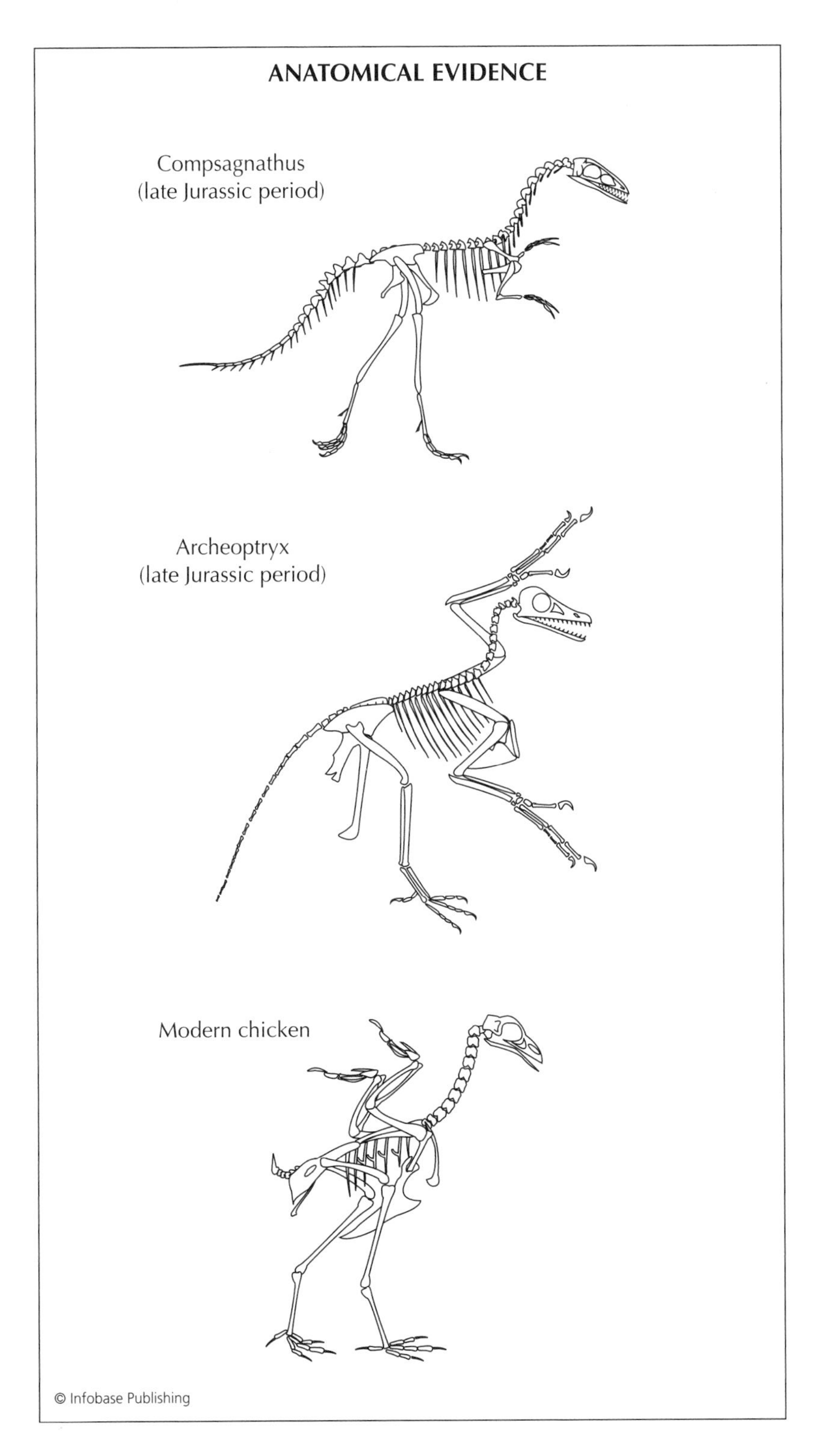

Ostrom and Bakker cited similarities in the skeletal structures of birds and certain dinosaurs.

museums. These specimens—all of them found in limestone quarries in central Bavaria—are so rare at least in part because the animals that left them were small and light-bodied, not unlike modern birds. In fact, the skeletons appear—even to the uneducated eye—to be a transitional evolutionary stage between small dinosaur and bird, with wings that end in grasping claws, beaks that held teeth, and wishbones. The most startling aspect of these skeletons, dated to about 150 million years ago, is that the rock in which they were preserved also contains the clear imprint of the creature's feathers.

In 1861, when the most complete of these fossils was identified, the announcement had sparked controversy over Charles Darwin's newly published theory of evolution. T. H. Huxley, Darwin's staunchest and most vocal supporter, hailed *Archaeopteryx* as proof of his friend's hypothesis that one line of animals adapts over time to give rise to another. Traditionalists argued that the animal instead had been an anomaly, a kind of dinosaur unrelated to modern birds.

The 19th-century debate—though never settled—was largely forgotten until Ostrom revived it in the 1970s. After his careful examination of known *Archaeopteryx* fossils, he discovered yet another skeleton of the ancient winged creature—not in a quarry, but in a drawer at a museum in the Netherlands. For more than a century, it had been misidentified as a *Pterodactyl.*

Having thus increased the number of *Archaeopteryx* remains in the world to a total of five (since increased to seven), Ostrom went on to describe this ancient animal, definitively linking its skeletal structure to those of a group of carnivorous dinosaurs called *Coelurosaurs* and also to modern birds.

Ostrom's reexamination of *Archaeopteryx* and his 1970s writings on the topic helped lead to a scientific reconsideration of the evolutionary paths of both birds and dinosaurs. He and his successors have shown that birdlike features such as feathers and air sacs within bones developed in certain dinosaurs before the evolution of birds and well before animals in this evolutionary line could fly. (Discoveries of feathered dinosaur remains in China in the 1990s supported this hypothesis.)

Ostrom's student Robert T. Bakker was particularly effective at expanding upon the teacher's ideas and popularizing a fresh view of dinosaurs. In his 1975 article "Dinosaur Renaissance" in *Scientific American,* Bakker—then working on his Ph.D. at Harvard—publicly challenged long-held ideas about dinosaurs as cold-blooded and lizard-like. That same year, a book titled *Hot-Blooded Dinosaurs: A Revolution in Paleontology,* by British science writer Adrian J. Desmond (1947–), featured illustrations by Bakker, also an artist. He depicted swift carnivores built to overtake galloping dinosaur prey—a far cry from the clumsy, tail-dragging stereotype shown in earlier illustrators' imaginings.

Like Gould, Dawkins, and Wilson, Bakker is a biologist who writes for a general, nontechnical audience. Often he has taken his case to the public when his paleontologist peers have criticized his views as extreme or unnecessarily iconoclastic. He was quicker than virtually anyone else in his field to embrace the notion that many if not all dinosaur species were endothermic, or warm-blooded. He also advanced the argument that not only are birds descended from dinosaurs but that birds *are* dinosaurs and should be reclassified as such. Today many taxonomists place birds among *Coelurosauria*, a subgroup of *Therapod* dinosaurs.

Beginning in the 1970s, when he served on the faculty of Johns Hopkins University, he has contributed to many popular books and educational videos, appeared on talk shows, and has served as consultant to makers of animatronic dinosaur models, popular films, and even dinosaur-themed video games. In so doing, Bakker has played a mighty role in drawing attention to his field. Along with his provocative ideas, Bakker draws attention to himself with his manner of dress and grooming. Whether doing field research in Como Bluff, Wyoming, or speaking in a lecture hall, he sports a battered cowboy hat shading a shaggy ponytail and an untrimmed beard that has been compared to a tumbleweed.

Upright Apes

As Ostrom and successors such as Bakker made progress in puzzling out the lineage of certain dinosaurs and modern birds, so *paleoanthropologists* in the 1970s made startling finds about the lineage of humankind.

Key fossil discoveries showed that upright-walking apes—possibly direct ancestors of *H. sapiens*—split off from other primates earlier than archaeologists and physical anthropologists had thought. Many who studied human ancestry had theorized that large brains (that is, significantly larger than those of apes) had preceded upright walking among primates. That idea proved to be wrong.

On a 1973 field expedition to the Afar region of Ethiopia, paleoanthropologist Donald Johanson (1943–) of Case Western Reserve University discovered a small, very old knee among other bones—including most of both legs—of an ancient hominid. The skeleton was eventually estimated at 3.4 million years old. The structure of the knee and legs suggested upright walking very much like that of modern humans. The next year, Johanson returned to the same area in the Horn of Africa, where he and fellow researchers found the partial skeleton, including the pelvis, of a female australopithecine—an upright walker about 3.2 million years old but with a skull very much like that of a modern chimpanzee. Overjoyed by the find, the celebrating scientists played a Beatles recording over and over at their camp that night, and Johanson found a nickname for the fossil in the song "Lucy in the Sky with Diamonds." He called her Lucy.

On the next year's expedition to Afar, Johanson and his team found the remains of approximately 13 individuals—again upright walkers with apelike skulls. The 1975 and 1976 expeditions found still more fossils.

Scientist of the Decade: Barbara McClintock (1902–1992)

Plant cytogeneticist Barbara McClintock belongs among the most accomplished biologists of several decades. Her work in the late 1920s and early 1930s (covered in chapter 4), in which she discovered ring chromosomes and confirmed the phenomenon of chromosomal crossing-over in maize, established her as leader in her field. In the 1940s and 1950s, she discovered mobile genetic elements and developed her theory of gene regulation to explain how a cell, and by extension a complex organism, activates and deactivates genetic expression. In the 1960s, she began tracing the genetic lineage of modern corn through its Central and South American ancestors.

The huge significance of one particular part of her work—the discovery of mobile genetic elements, or transposons—really gained widespread significance only in her later decades, especially the 1970s (as discussed earlier in this chapter). Through that decade and into the next, she became a scientific celebrity on the basis of that belated appreciation, reaping many awards and honors, culminating with the 1983 Nobel Prize in physiology or medicine. McClintock, who was intellectually and professionally active into her eighties, participated vigorously in belated discussions of her earlier breakthroughs.

Born in Hartford, Connecticut, in 1902, she was the third daughter of Thomas McClintock, the physician son of British immigrants, and Sara Handy, a descendant of Mayflower Puritans. Her parents named her Eleanor, although they called her Barbara instead. She later said that they had decided the latter name was less delicate-sounding and a better fit for a tough, independent-minded little girl.

The growing family—especially mother Sara—seems to have been under a lot of stress when Barbara was a toddler, perhaps because of the birth of fourth child and only son, Malcolm (whom the parents called Tom), only 18 months after Barbara. For whatever reason, the family sent three-year-old Barbara to live for a while with her father's sister and brother-in-law, a wholesale fish merchant, in Massachusetts.

Barbara grew up mostly in Flatbush, Brooklyn, where the family moved in 1908. Wearing bloomers, she played sports with the neighborhood boys. Although she sometimes skipped school just because she would rather be outdoors, she enjoyed learning and decided in high school that she wanted to go to college. Sara McClintock found her daughter's choice puzzling, but husband Thomas encouraged the girl. Barbara began her course of study at Cornell in 1919.

As recounted in chapter 4, she began working on the chromosomal analysis of maize in graduate school and saw considerable success early in her career. Although some biographical accounts of McClintock stress the obstacles and prejudices she must have faced as a woman in science, there is little evidence that such barriers held her back. Most colleagues and advisers (virtually all male) valued her work ethic and scientific insights as well as her friendship and sense of humor. By 1944, her stature in her field had become such that she was elected a member of the prestigious National Academy of Sciences—only the third woman so selected. The following year, she became the first woman president of the Genetics Society of America; she had been vice president since 1939.

In 1941, she began working at Cold Spring Harbor Laboratory, a research environment that suited McClintock's style of research almost perfectly. Instead of being saddled with classroom teaching and administrative tasks—the bane of so many university-based researchers—she was largely free to work at her own pace, following her cytological interests where they led.

They led, in the 1940s, to a long-observed phenomenon occurring in maize and more frequently in fruit flies, among other species. Called "mutable genes," "mutable loci," "mosaicism," and "genetic variegation," among other names, it involved physical traits—and thus the genes of which those traits were an expression—appearing in a distribution that seemed to defy the conventional wisdom of genetics as built on the precepts of Mendel and Morgan.

McClintock's starting point was a distribution of pigment patterns in the corn kernels of some of the maize strains she was growing. Geneticists going back to Hugo de Vries had commented upon such curious color distribution.

Through careful analysis of chromosomes, McClintock identified a *locus* upon the maize chromosome that could physically change position and seemed to cause a corresponding change in kernel color and marking. (Other scientists have commented on McClintock's eyesight, noting that she could see things under a microscope that others could not.) After years of collecting data and confirming her results—noting translocations, deletions, and insertions along the maize chromosome—she published an unusual paper titled "The Origin and Behavior of Mutable Loci in Maize." Unlike McClintock's earlier writings, this 1950 essay contained more theoretical thinking than hard data. She hypothesized the existence of a genetic element different from the gene but which, when adjacent to a specific gene's locus—its position on the chromosome—caused that locus to become changeable. Writing a few years before Watson and Crick's breakthrough work on the molecular structure of DNA, she called this additional genetic bit a controlling element. In a controversial presentation titled "Chromosome Organization and Genic Expression," she outlined her theory to gathered peers at the 1951 Cold Spring Harbor Symposium.

The presentation is controversial, in part, because later—especially in the 1970s—those who had been present had sharply differing memories of the way the audience reacted. McClintock remembered her fellow geneticists meeting what she thought of as a theoretical breakthrough with silence, skepticism, and even scorn. She said they thought she had gone crazy. Others recall that the only unusual circumstance after the talk was that nobody asked questions.

There were serious doubts among the attendees. Her findings seemed to contradict the idea—central to most genetic research at the time—that genes held their positions along the chromosome, that they could be reliably mapped. Some of her fellow researchers may also have detected in her conclusion the suggestion that genetic heredity worked not gene by gene, but in a less ordered mixture of chromosomal properties. (This idea was associated with Richard B. Goldschmidt, a University of California, Berkeley, geneticist who had long been an ally and supporter of McClintock and who was looked at by many peers as an eccentric iconoclast.)

Barbara McClintock won the 1983 Nobel Prize in physiology or medicine. (Barbara McClintock Papers, American Philosophical Society)

One reason for the lack of follow-up questions may have been that McClintock was so thoroughly steeped in her subject matter that there were few if any other researchers who could understand

(continues)

(continued)

her. She had been studying maize since the 1920s and—with her extraordinary powers of concentration and observation—she knew the organism as nobody else did or could. Maize genetics are complicated compared to those of peas or fruit flies. To get a fair hearing, McClintock may have had to bring other leading scientists up to speed in her area of study, assuming they had the time or inclination. This was something she would surely have enjoyed. Those who knew her said that she would talk at length about her ideas to fellow scientists and laypeople alike if they took the trouble to visit her in her lab.

McClintock tried to get her theory of controlling elements across again in 1953 with an article titled "Induction of Instability at Selected Loci in Maize" in the publication *Genetics*. She also embarked on lecture tours to talk about the work. Other geneticists confirmed her observation of mutable loci, which came to be called transposable elements (and later, transposons) in maize. No one, however, anticipated how important that discovery would later prove. Controlling elements, meanwhile, won few supporters.

Ultimately, McClintock said later, she decided that she stood little chance of changing minds and that she did not care to alienate other scientists. She continued her research—including a long-term exploration of the genetic characteristics of ancestral maize species—but stopped publishing her data and conclusions about transposable elements and gene regulation through the rest of the 1950s.

Her work was the focus of McClintock's life. She never married and had no children. She told friends—most of them other researchers—that she could not conceive of how other people committed to a marriage.

McClintock returned to writing about the topic of gene regulation only after the French team of biochemist Monod and biologist Jacob wrote in the early 1960s about the role of messenger RNA in regulating cell metabolism in bacteria. It was in the 1970s, however, as the new technology of gene manipulation showed how central gene transposition was to any study of biological heredity, that the science establishment came to see McClintock as someone who had been ahead of her time. By then, she had officially retired from research, but she still maintained her laboratory as an emeritus scientist at Cold Spring Harbor and remained more than able to partake in discussions of a mutable genome. She enjoyed her role as the founder of a new subfield of molecular biology—the study of genetic transposition.

In addition to the unshared Nobel Prize, McClintock was the recipient of numerous other awards, including a so-called genius grant from the MacArthur Foundation. (She was among the first class of MacArthur awardees, in 1981.) Hailed as a scientific great through the final decade of her life, she died in 1992 at age 90.

Ethiopia descended into civil violence and warfare in 1977, to the point that outside researchers could no longer go there. Johanson, who had become a curator of the Cleveland Museum of Natural History in 1974, concentrated instead on analyzing and classifying his finds. After much research and debate among themselves, he and physical anthropologist Timothy White (1950–), a young University of Michigan Ph.D. employed by the East Rudolf Research Project in North Kenya, agreed that all the fossilized bones they had found belonged to one species. This was despite a wide range of size among the skeletal remains. In 1978, Johanson and White announced their find, naming the new-old species *Australopithecus afarensis.*

In 1978, at a research site called Laetoli in Tanzania, a group led by archaeologist Mary Leakey (1913–96) found footprints that looked very much like they were made by small human beings. The prints had been left by three individuals walking in volcanic ash 3.6 million years ago. Over the intervening millennia, the ash layer containing the footprints had hardened to stone. Although Leakey and Johanson disagreed fiercely about whether or not the prints belonged to *A. afarensis* (Johanson's position) or an early member of the genus *Homo* (Leakey's), the prints were more evidence that—just as feathers had predated flying in birds—upright walking had long predated large brains and sophisticated toolmaking among hominids.

Further Reading

Access Excellence @ The National Health Museum. "Robert Swanson (1947–1999)." Available online. URL: http://www.accessexcellence.org/RC/AB/BC/Robert_Swanson.html. Accessed February 3, 2006. Biography of biotechnology pioneer Swanson.

Bakker, Robert T. "Anatomical and Ecological Evidence of Endothermy in Dinosaurs." *Nature* 238 (July 14, 1972): 81–85. Available online. URL: http://www.nature.com/nature/journal/v238/n5359/abs/238081a0.html. Accessed February 3, 2006. Paleontologist makes a case for warm-bloodedness in dinosaurs.

———. "Dinosaur Feeding Behavior and the Origin of Flowering Plants." *Nature* 274 (August 17, 1978): 661–663. Paleoecological view of interrelationship between herbivorous dinosaurs and evolving plant species.

———. "Dinosaur Renaissance." *Scientific American* 22 (April 1975): 58–78. Available online. URL: http://www.nature.com/nature/journal/v274/n5672/abs/274661a0.html. Accessed February 3, 2006. Influential article lays out Bakker's controversial ideas about what dinosaurs were and were not.

———. "Ecology of the Brontosaurs." *Nature* 229 (January 15, 1971): 172–174. Bakker discusses *Apatosaurus*'s role in ecosystem of late Jurassic and early Cretaceous periods.

Barinaga, Marcia. "Asilomar Revisited: Lessons for Today?" *Science* 287, no. 5458 (March 3, 2000): 1,584–1,585. Available online. URL: http://www.biotech-info.net/asilomar_revisited.html. Accessed April 11, 2006. Author suggests that researchers involved in cloning and stem cell work can find ethical precedent in an historic conference.

Cole, Charles, Terry Landers, Stephen Goff, Simone Manteuil-Brutlag, and Paul Berg. "Physical and Genetic Characterization of Deletion Mutants of Simian Virus 40 Constructed in Vitro," *Journal of Virology* 24, no. 1 (October 24, 1977): 277–294. Available online. URL: http://www.pubmedcentral.nih.gov/articlerender.fcgi?artid=515929&tools=bot. Accessed February 3, 2006. Molecular geneticists discuss manipulation of artificially synthesized virus.

Comfort, Nathaniel C. "The Real Point Is Control: The Reception of Barbara McClintock's Controlling Elements" *Journal of the History of*

Biology 32, no. 1 (Spring 1999): 133–162. Available online. URL: http://www.ncbi.nlm.nih.gov/entrez/query.fcgi?cmd=Retrieve&db=PubMed&list_uids=11623812&dopt=Abstract. Accessed February 3, 2006. Conventional telling of McClintock story misses most important aspect of work, author charges.

———. *The Tangled Field: Barbara McClintock's Search for the Patterns of Genetic Control.* Cambridge, Mass.: Harvard University Press, 2001. Biography sets out to separate McClintock history from McClintock myth.

Dawkins, Richard. *The Selfish Gene.* Oxford: Oxford University Press, 1976. Controversial argument that evolution, including evolution of human behavior, is overwhelmingly gene-driven.

Desmond, Adrian J. *Hot-Blooded Dinosaurs: A Revolution in Paleontology.* London: Blond and Briggs, 1975. Illustrations by young Robert T. Bakker accompany revised view of dinosaurs.

Douglas, Ed. "Darwin's Natural Heir." *Guardian*, 17 February 2001. Available online. URL: http://education.guardian.co.uk/scienceweek/story/0,,451826,00.html. Accessed April 12, 2006. In education service, online version of U.K. newspaper features profile of sociobiology pioneer.

Eldredge, Niles. *Time Frames: The Re-Thinking of Darwinian Evolution and the Theory of Punctuated Equilibria.* Princeton, N.J.: Princeton University Press, 1985. Author tells of exhaustive research and reflection that led him and Gould to punctuated equilibrium theory.

Goff, Stephen P., and Paul Berg. "Construction of Hybrid Viruses Containing SV40 and Lambda Phage DNA Segments and Their Propagation in Cultured Monkey Cells." *Cell* 4, no. 2 (December 9, 1976): 695–705. Paper describes construction and propagation of an animal virus capable of transduction.

Gould, Stephen Jay. *Hen's Teeth and Horse's Toes: Further Reflections in Natural History.* New York: W. W. Norton, 1983. Insightful, entertaining essays on evolution and related topics.

———. *Ontogeny and Phylogeny.* Cambridge, Mass.: Belknap Press, 1977. Paleontologist and theorist treats development of individual organisms in the context of the history of evolution.

———. *The Panda's Thumb: More Reflections in Natural History.* New York: W. W. Norton, 1980. Thought-provoking, illuminating essays on evolution and related topics.

Hackett, Perry B., James A. Fuchs, and Joachim W. Messing. *An Introduction to Recombinant DNA Techniques.* Menlo Park, Calif.: Benjamin/Cummings Publishing, 1984. Text on new biotechnology from field's early years.

Heller, Jean (Associated Press). "Syphilis Victims in the U.S. Study Went Untreated for 40 Years." *New York Times*, 26 July 1972, p. 1. News account of Tuskegee syphilis experiment.

Howard, Ted, and Jeremy Rifkin. *Who Should Play God?* New York: Delacorte Press, 1977. Authors argue that recombinant DNA technology is dangerous and should be stopped.

Jackson, David A., Robert H. Symons, and Paul Berg. "A Biochemical Method for Inserting New Genetic Information into SV40 DNA: Circular SV40 DNA Molecules Containing Lambda Phage Genes and the Galactose Operon of *E. coli.*" *Proceedings of the National Academy of Sciences* 69 (October 1, 1972): 2,904. Available online. URL: http://www.pnas.org/cgi/content/abstract/69/10/2904. Accessed February 3, 2006. Berg and colleagues describe experiment employing enzymes to glue sections of different DNA molecules together.

Johanson, Donald C., and M. Taieb. "Plio-Pleistocene hominid discoveries in Hadar, Ethiopia." *Nature* 260 (March 26, 1975): 293–297. Available online. URL: http://www.nature.com/nature/journal/v260/n5549/abs/260293a0.html;jsessionid=8C346FFB1D9C1642C3A53FF33F831B68. Accessed February 3, 2006. Paleoanthropologists discuss the oldest-yet discoveries of fossils from an upright-walking primate species. This is the hominid species that Johanson and Timothy White will later name *Australopithecus afarensis.*

———, and White T. D. "On the Status of *Australopithecus afarensis.*" *Nature* 207, no. 4435 (March 7, 1980): 1,103–1,104. Johanson and White discuss fossil evidence of upright-walking apes long predating larger-brained human ancestors.

Lappé, Marc. *Broken Code: The Exploitation of DNA.* San Francisco, Calif.: Sierra Club Books, 1984. Science historian examines scientific quest to understand and manipulate genes.

Lewontin, R. C. *Biology as Ideology: The Doctrine of DNA.* New York: HarperCollins, 1991. Author discusses genetic determinism and implications in age of gene sequencing.

McClintock, Barbara. "Induction of Instability at Selected Loci in Maize." *Genetics* 38 (November 1953): 579–599. McClintock attempts to win support for her theory of genetic controlling elements.

———. "The Origin and Behavior of Mutable Loci in Maize." *Proceedings of the National Academy of Sciences* 36 (June 1950): 344–355. Available online. URL: http://www.pubmedcentral.nih.gov/articlerender.fcgi?artid=1063197. Accessed February 3, 2006. McClintock introduces concept of what later will be called transposons.

Mulligan, R. C., and Paul Berg. "Expression of a Bacterial Gene in Mammalian Cells." *Science* 209 (September 1980): 1,422–1,427. Berg and colleague describe experimental step toward producing transgenic mammals.

Ostrom, John H. "*Archaeopteryx* and the Origin of Flight." *Quarterly Review of Biology* 49, no. 1 (1974): 27–47. Paleontologist discusses phylogeny and possible behavior of hollow-boned, feathered dinosaur, theorizing about how *Archaeopteryx* pointed toward modern bird evolution.

———. "*Archaeopteryx:* Notice of a 'New' Specimen." *Science* 170 (October 1970): 537–538. Author reclassifies specimen and reassesses place of feathered dinosaur in phylogeny of birds.

Thomas, R. D. K., and E. C. Olson, eds. *A Cold Look at the Warm-Blooded Dinosaurs.* Boulder, Colo.: Westview Press, 1980. Collection of writings on endothermy among ancient beasts previously grouped with reptiles.

Thomas, Stephen B., and Sandra Crouse Quinn. "The Tuskegee Syphilis Study, 1932–1972: Implications for HIV Education and AIDS Risk Programs in the Black Community." *American Journal of Public Health* 81 (1991): 1,485–1,505. Discussion of social and public health costs resulting from poorly conceived experiment conducted on unwitting human subjects.

Watson, James D., and John Tooze. *DNA Story: A Documentary History of Gene Cloning.* San Francisco, Calif.: W. H. Freeman, 1981. DNA pioneer coauthored examination of early work in gene cloning.

Wilson, Edward O. *The Insect Societies.* Cambridge, Mass.: Belknap Press, 1971. Major work in environmental and behavioral biology.

———. *Sociobiology: The New Synthesis.* Cambridge, Mass.: Belknap Press, 1975. Wilson's founding text for a more comprehensive approach to studying biological systems and evolution.

9 1981–1990: Biotech Booms; AIDS Looms

Broader Horizons, Greater Challenges

If the biotechnology industry was a green bud in the 1970s, then it began flowering in the 1980s (and many say that it will not bear the fruit of its potential until considerably later in the 21st century). The field certainly accelerated in the 1980s, in large part because of new tools for molecular biologists.

A northern California biotech company, Cetus, unveiled a remarkable new technique invented by one of its staff scientists. Called polymerase chain reaction, it exponentially multiplied what molecular biologists could accomplish, given a tiny sample of DNA. From Britain came DNA fingerprinting—useful for criminal investigations and much more. At the California Institute of Technology, multidisciplinary teams of biologists and engineers developed automatic machines to speed up and improve the accuracy of laboratory tasks, including sequencing DNA.

The technical advances made ambitious new goals seem achievable. A university chancellor had the audacious idea to sequence every gene on every chromosome of the human species. Just a few years after his suggestion, the U.S. government organized just such a long-term effort. New biotech companies formed, developed products, and sought patents, as academic and medical researchers also exploited the new methods. Doctors in Maryland inserted a gene into a little girl's blood cells to repair her disabled immune system, the first gene therapy on a human being.

There were surprises in medical research. A west coast neurologist discovered an infectious agent so different from any previously identified that many immunologists rejected his findings, dismissing them as impossible. Yet he was right in identifying rogue proteins as the source of a deadly group of brain diseases.

Two Australian researchers similarly overturned conventional medical knowledge about peptic ulcers, a common disease of the digestive system. Again, the cause proved to be something that formerly had been called impossible. In this case, it was microbes growing amid the acidic currents of the duodenum and stomach.

Stranger still, and more frightening, a baffling new medical syndrome—eventually known as AIDS—arose, breaking down the immune systems of young homosexual men. At first seemingly inexplicable, it turned out to be a disease not limited to gays, and it became a worldwide viral epidemic. Virologists and immunologists scrambled to understand it and identify its cause. Other researchers sought ways of treating the rapidly advancing plague. By the decade's end, a significant number of people understood how to prevent spreading or contracting AIDS. There were emerging medical techniques to combat it. Yet science could offer little promise of a cure, and no end to the crisis was in sight.

Out of the spotlight, molecular biologists continued to probe the workings of organisms and their cells on the smallest scale. Researchers at Yale and the University of Colorado discovered something previously unknown about RNA—that it can act as a *biocatalyst.* This considerably enhanced the theoretical possibility that the single-strand nucleic acid predates even DNA and proteins in the evolution of life.

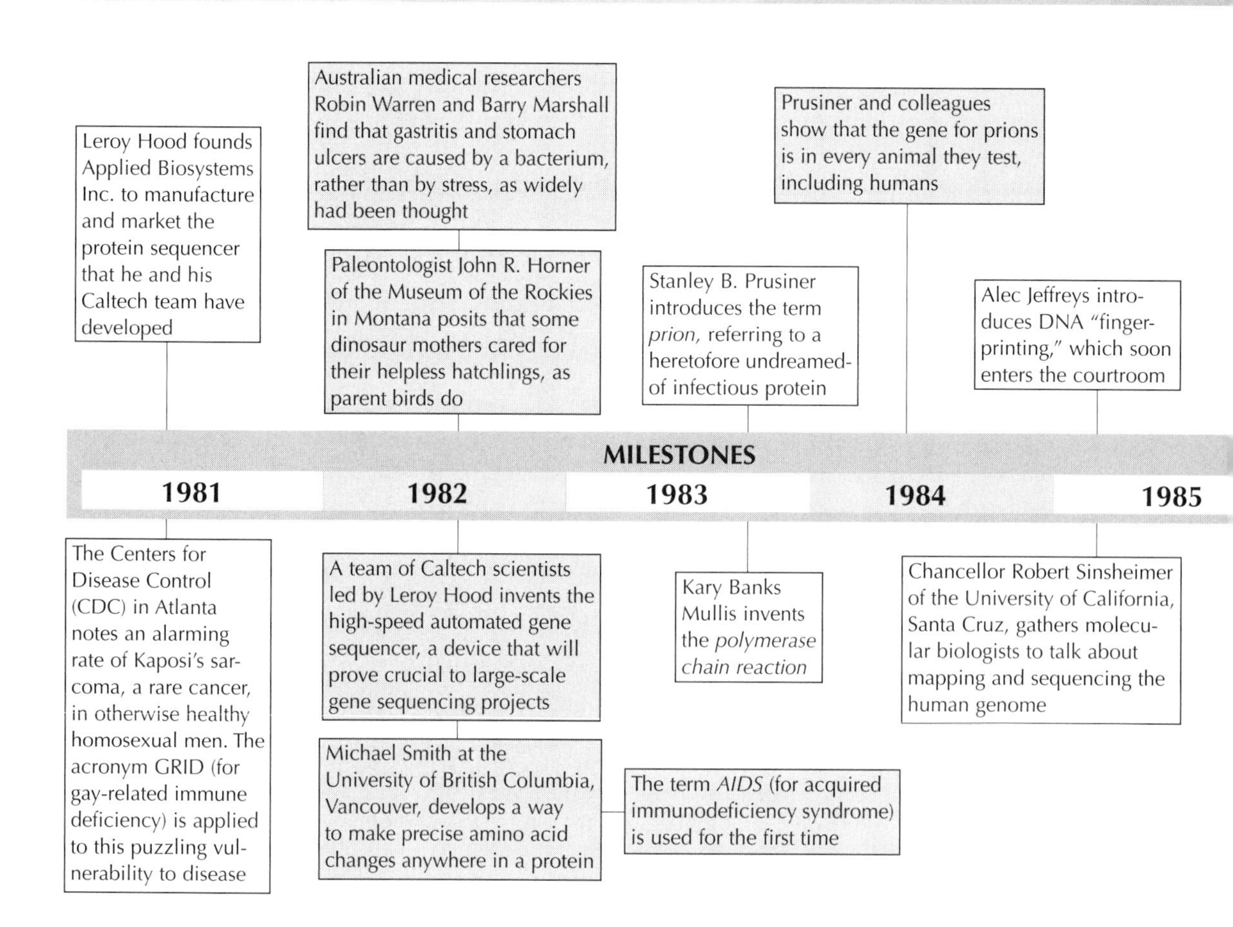

Another series of experiments, stretching from the 1960s in England to the 1980s in Massachusetts, led to the identity of genes that have evolved to play an essential but curious role: They program certain cells to die at the appropriate times so that developing organisms can achieve their proper shape and function. This cell death is part of life. Finally, biologists began to understand what controls it.

Evolutionary theories about how dinosaurs behaved and survived continued to shift in the 1980s. Paleontological finds in Montana suggested that certain among the ancient species were far more social than had previously been appreciated and far more like migratory birds in their reproductive strategies. These discoveries and other recent thinking about life in the Cretaceous and Jurassic periods were reflected at the end of the decade in a best-selling science fiction novel that also drew upon polymerase chain reaction, genetic engineering, and experimental cloning to tell the story of a theme park idea that goes horribly wrong.

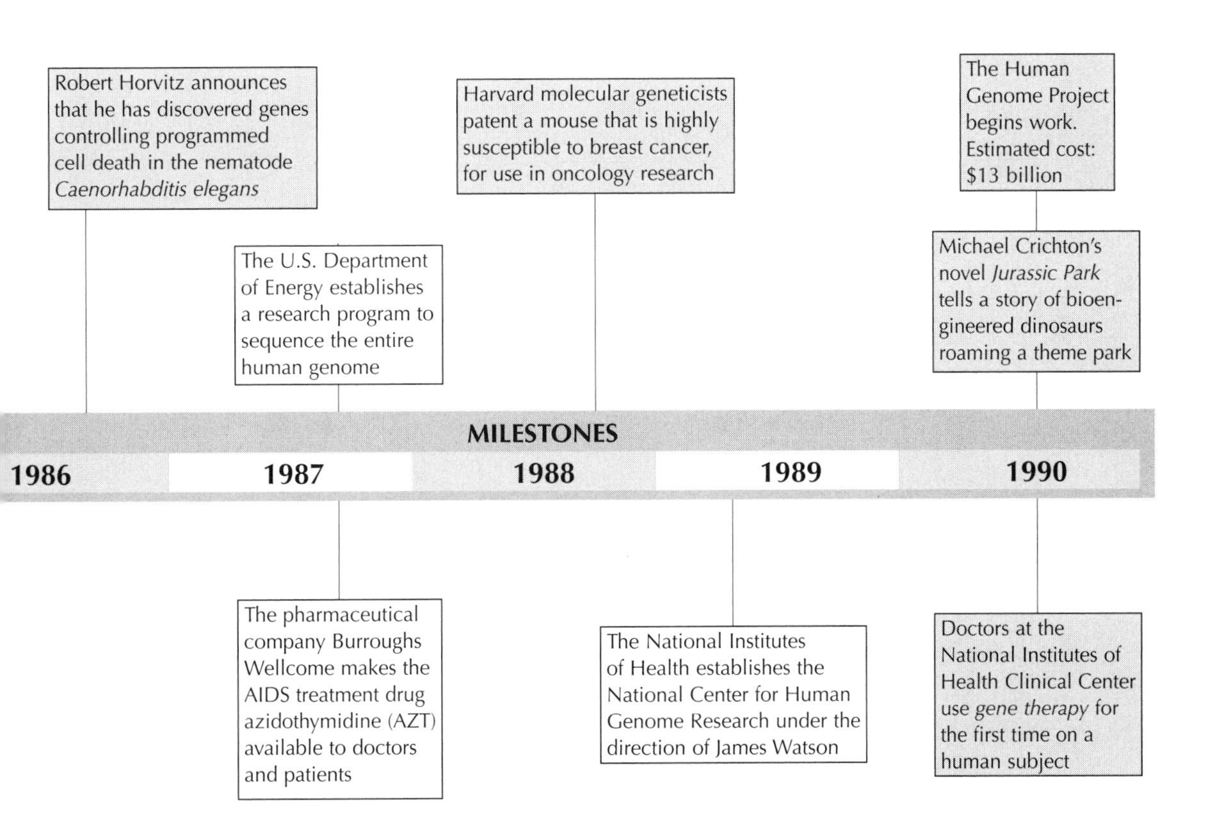

Polymerase Chain Reaction

Late on a Friday night in the spring of 1983, biochemist Kary Banks Mullis (1944–) experienced what he later described as a "eureka moment." While driving north along California State Highway 128, a world-changing technology flashed across his mind with such clarity that he distrusted the idea. It seemed too good, too easy. He wondered if something was wrong with his thought process.

Traveling from his home in Berkeley to a weekend cabin he was building in the Anderson Valley of Mendocino County, Mullis had been musing that night about his job at the biotechnology firm Cetus Corporation. He was among the biochemists there charged with synthesizing DNA. In those early days of biotech, laboratories synthesized samples of DNA large enough to work with by a gene cloning process that required growing cells in a culture of *E. coli* or yeast. It was time-consuming and expensive. Researchers wanted a better method.

Cetus had recently acquired a machine that produced *oligonucleotides*, short, single-strand nucleic acid chains that are used in DNA sequencing. The machine made oligonucleotides at a rate much faster than biochemists could handle them. This set Mullis thinking about ways to perform the entire process of duplicating DNA faster, at a pace closer to that of the oligonucleotide machine.

The idea that made him stop the car on the rural roadside so that he could grab a pen and paper—to the annoyance of his girlfriend trying to sleep in the passenger seat—was the polymerase chain reaction. Now widely known as PCR, it is a way of using an enzyme to replicate DNA—much as a living cell does so, but without using a culture of organisms as a factory.

PCR requires four ingredients. First, there is the double-stranded DNA segment to be copied. It is called the template. Next, there are the primers—two oligonucleotide lengths, each complementary to a sequence on one of the strands of the DNA template. Third, there must be nucleotides to be arranged into DNA. Finally, there is a polymerase enzyme to copy the template by linking free nucleotides to one another in the right order.

When the mixture is heated, the template DNA separates into two strands. This is called *denaturation* of the DNA. When it is subsequently cooled, the primers attach themselves to the correct sites on the separated

(Opposite page) A DNA segment provides the template. Heated, the template DNA separates into two strands. This is called denaturation. Upon cooling, the oligonucleotide primers attach themselves to the correct sites on the separated template strands. Polymerase copies template strands by attaching nucleotides to the ends until there are two identical molecules of double-stranded DNA—two where there was one. (Rapidly repeated, the process can turn out billions of copies of the original.)

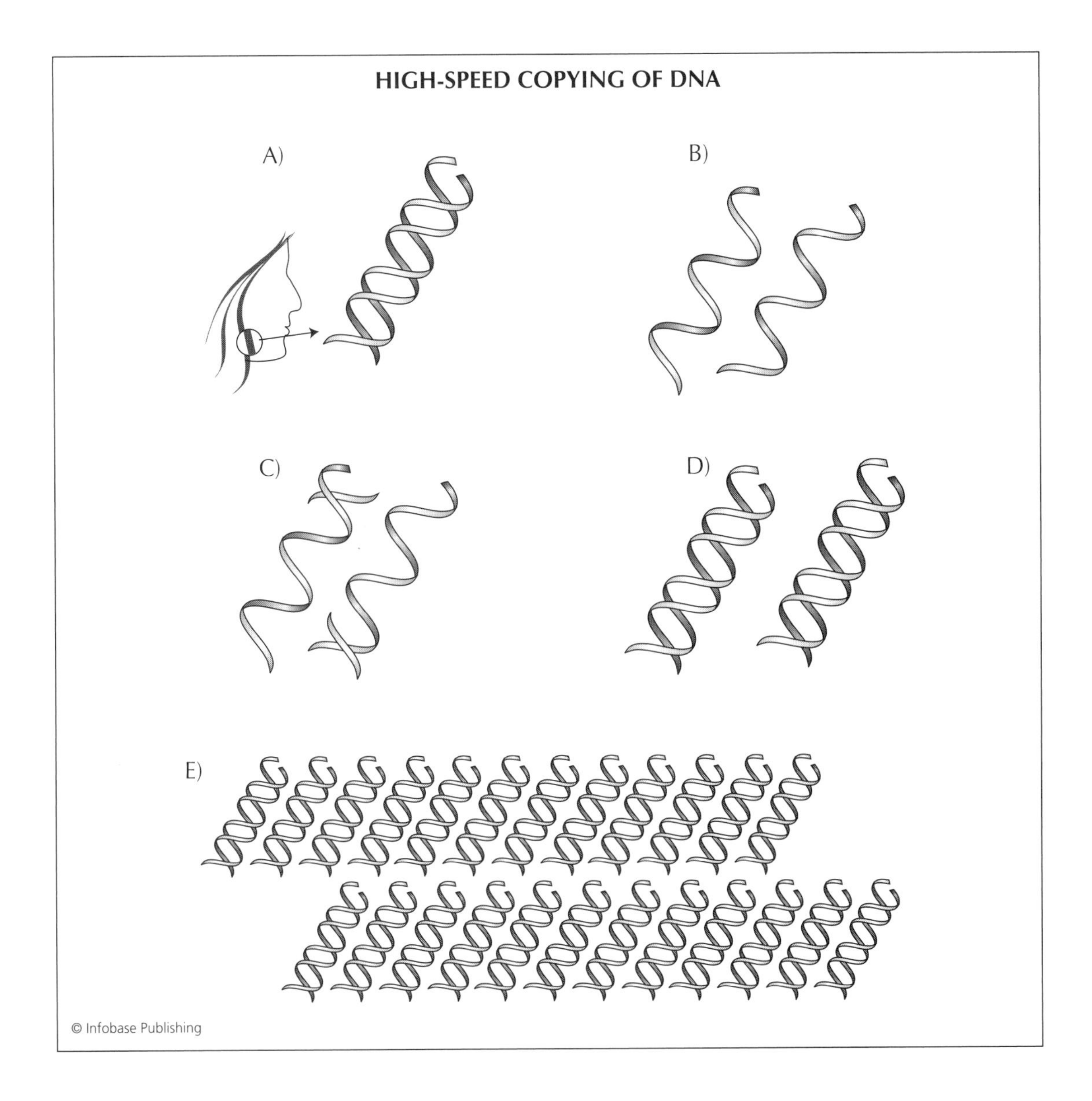

template strands. At that point, the polymerase can start copying the template strands by attaching nucleotides to the ends until there are two identical molecules of double-stranded DNA—two where there was one. Do it again, and there are four where there were two; again, and there are eight; and so on. After 30 brief cycles, a laboratory reaps more than a billion copies of the original sequence.

Mullis developed a basic working version of the process over the rest of that year. By Christmas, he had devised a process with enough promise that his colleagues at Cetus decided to invest time and effort into refining and improving this new thing called polymerase chain reaction.

By 1985, Cetus had a version of PCR reliable enough for practical applications. Yet the process remained flawed because the DNA polymerase became unstable at the high temperature required to denature the DNA. That meant lab personnel, or automated equipment, had to add more polymerase for each cycle. In 1987, Mullis thought of a way to get around this problem by using Taq polymerase. This is a DNA

Every individual's DNA contains a unique pattern of minisatellites, repeated sequences of noncoding DNA. By isolating these sequences and matching samples, a laboratory can identify the origin of genetic material.

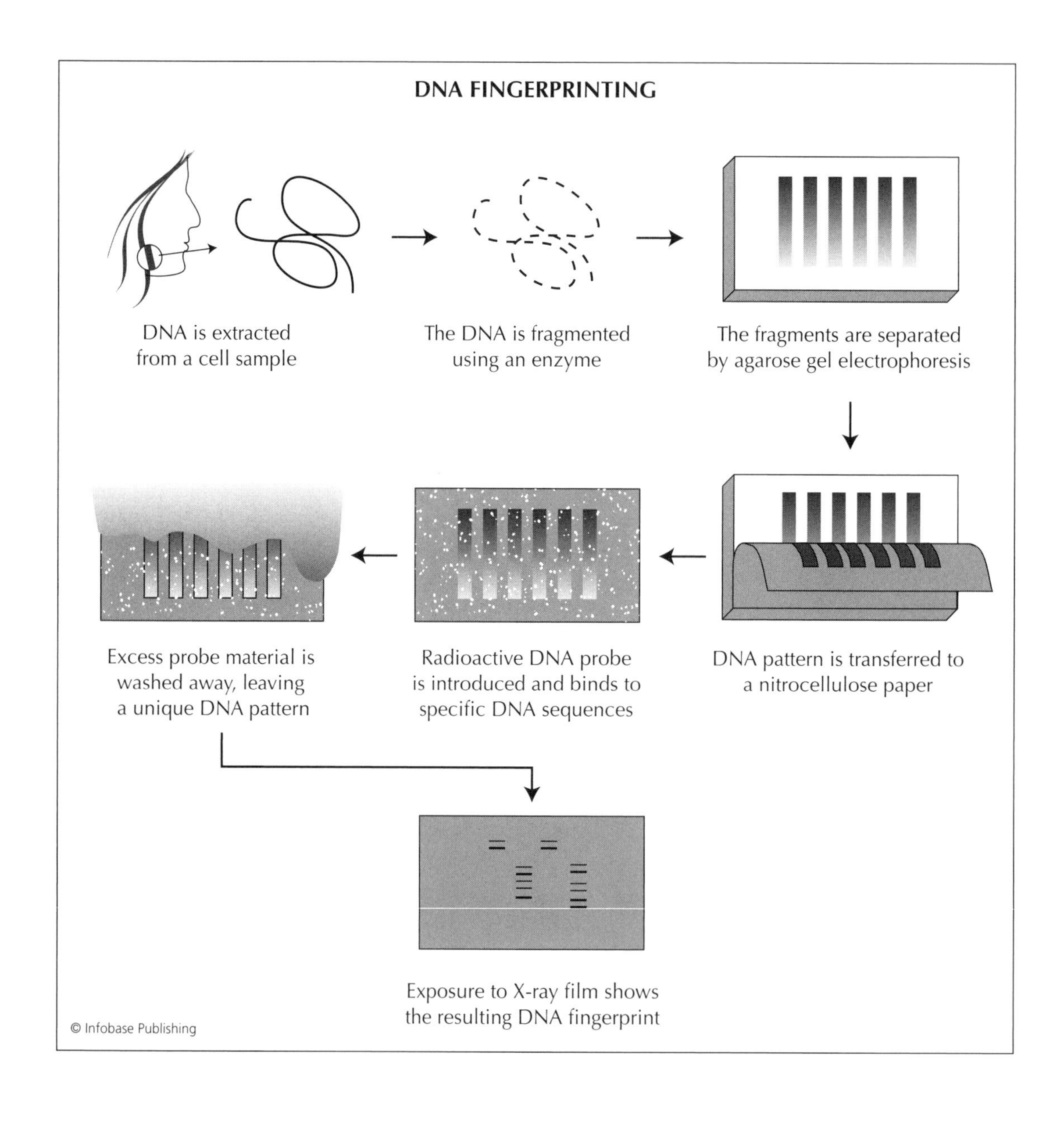

polymerase taken from the heat-tolerant bacterium *Thermus aquaticus*, which has evolved to thrive in hot springs. For that reason, the polymerase is stable at high temperatures, and Taq polymerase made PCR even faster. Biochemists coined the term *Taq* from *Thermus aquaticus*. Mullis's ultimate process is often called Taq PCR.

Once it became convenient to amplify a miniscule bit of DNA, to make from it a much larger but genetically identical sample, scientists quickly thought of many applications in biotechnology, in genetic research, in medical care, and beyond. Among the earliest examples, in the mid-1980s, PCR was used to detect sickle-cell anemia. By amplifying the gene in question, medical-genetic diagnosticians can acquire a sample large enough to sequence for a reliable reading, thus detecting the presence of sickle-cell and other hereditary diseases. It also enables doctors to diagnose bacterial and viral diseases from very small samples of infectious matter. Among many other uses, paleontologists and anthropologists use the process to amplify miniscule strands of preserved ancient DNA in fossils for the study of long-extinct species and human ancestors such as Egyptian mummies.

PCR neatly complemented genetic fingerprinting, a process introduced in 1984 by British geneticist Alec Jeffreys (1950–). At England's Leicester University, Jeffreys devised a way to use highly variant, repetitive gene sequences called *minisatellites* to identify individual strains of DNA in human beings. Law enforcement agencies quickly embraced the tool, especially in cases such as rape and sexual assault. Jeffreys's process also enabled reliable paternity testing. Investigators gained a tool enabling them to identify the remains of the victims of fires and explosions.

For inventing PCR, Mullis shared the 1993 Nobel Prize in chemistry with British-born Michael Smith (1932–2000) of the University of British Columbia. Smith was awarded his half of the prize for developing oligonucleotide-based, site-directed *mutagenesis*. This is a method for controlling genetic mutations to create precise amino acid changes anywhere in a protein, an important tool in research.

Speed Sequencing

Technological tools have been important in all areas of scientific research. In the late 20th century, the tools available for biological experimentation played an increasingly central role in accelerating the rate of discovery and even in directing the focus of research. In addition to PCR for DNA synthesis, there were new automated processes for sequencing proteins and DNA—machines invented by interdisciplinary biologist Leroy Hood (1938–) and colleagues.

Born and reared in Montana, Hood spent much of his youth outdoors—hiking, camping, horseback riding, and playing sports. He also developed an interest in biology and genetics as a boy—in part, he later

Leroy Hood and his multidisciplinary teams applied rapidly evolving technology to the needs of equally rapidly evolving molecular biology research. (North American Kyoto Prize and Leroy Hood)

said, because of the birth of a younger brother with Down syndrome, a chromosomal disorder.

On the advice of his small-town high school biology teacher, Lee Hood (as he is known) enrolled at Caltech, where his instructors included geneticist George Beadle (whose work is discussed in chapter 5) and the brilliant theoretical physicist Richard P. Feynman. Hood attended chemistry lectures by Linus Pauling. He also played in both the offensive and defensive backfield on Caltech's football team.

After graduating, Hood earned an M.D. from Johns Hopkins and returned to Caltech for a Ph.D. in molecular biology before beginning a career as a molecular immunologist. He later returned to Caltech again, as a faculty member. He said that the institution in Pasadena offered him the freedom to work across disciplines, combining his growing interest in new technologies with his background in molecular biology. In 1980, he became chair of the school's biology department.

In the late 1970s and through the 1980s, Hood and his collaborators invented faster, more efficient ways to accomplish what were becoming routine laboratory tasks. He worked with other scientists to develop machines that could carry out the processes for synthesizing proteins, sequencing proteins, and synthesizing DNA. From 1981 to 1986, he led the Caltech team of biochemists, biologists, physicists, computer specialists, and electronics engineers that developed the first high-speed automated DNA sequencer.

In chain termination sequencing, Frederick Sanger's method (discussed in the previous chapter), laboratory workers performed a number of delicate steps to bring about chemical reactions for detecting, separating, sorting, and labeling DNA fragments. The multiple steps took valuable time and provided multiple chances at a mistake being made, which would too often render the final data incorrect. The automated version of the process, as devised by Hood and his team, involved labeling the fragments with colored dyes that could be read by a computer scanner. Results were faster and, as the machine was refined, more accurate.

The Big Idea

Early in 1985, Lee Hood received an invitation from Robert L. Sinsheimer (1920–) to a workshop at the University of California, Santa Cruz (USC). Sinsheimer was a top DNA researcher who had become chancellor of UCSC. For the workshop, held in the spring of that year, he called together other leading scientists in the field. He wanted them to discuss and evaluate an audacious idea that he had been mulling over—a project to sequence the genome of the human species.

A genome is the entire genetic complement carried by the chromosomes of an organism. Sinsheimer was inspired, in part, by Frederick Sanger, who had a few years earlier sequenced the genome of a bacteriophage. There is, however, an enormous biological difference between a virus and a human being. No one knew that better than Sinsheimer, who had come to Santa Cruz from Caltech, where he had been one of the first scientists to synthesize DNA in a laboratory vessel. Yet he was taken by the idea, by its very scope. He also saw such an effort as a spur to new and better technologies.

Sinsheimer also had a background in applied technology. At MIT in the late 1930s, he had pursued chemical engineering and been sidetracked into electrical engineering. That had prepared him for a U.S. government job designing and testing airborne radar during World War II. It was only after the war that he had begun his graduate studies in biology.

As chancellor of UCSC—a relatively new part of the mighty University of California system of research institutions—and as a biologist, he had been seeking a plan for making his school a force in biological research. He envisioned an institute based among the coastal redwoods of the picturesque campus, dedicated to an incredibly ambitious long-term project.

Many at the time thought Sinsheimer had jumped the gun by quite a few years, a decade or more. To sequence the entire genome of any complex organism seemed a daunting task. Yet with technology such as Hood's DNA sequencer on the way, and with further automation improvements sure to be spurred by such a goal, others thought that sequencing the human genome, charting every DNA sequence in this remarkable primate species, was both desirable and possible.

Sinsheimer's idea did not take the form he had envisioned. For example, it was not to be centered at UCSC. The effort did, however, take form. The U.S. Department of Energy (DOE) became a sponsor of the idea in 1986, because sequencing the genome was complementary to DOE research on protecting chromosomes from the gene-mutating effects of radiation. The DOE established a research program with that aim in 1987. The following year, Congress passed a bill providing money for the DOE to join the National Institutes of Health (NIH) in a cooperative pursuit of genome research.

The NIH chose James Watson to head its part of the effort, the Office of Human Genome Research, which in 1989 became the National Center for Human Genome Research (and later the National Genome Research Institute at NIH). Actual research on the Human Genome Project began in 1990.

Bio Business, Biotech Breakthroughs

Hood's inventions brought him the 2002 Kyoto Prize in advanced technology. (North American Kyoto Prize and Leroy Hood)

The machines that Hood and colleagues were developing in Pasadena were a boon to Caltech researchers, and soon scientists at other laboratories—academic and commercial—wanted the same technology. The problem was that the Caltech machines were handbuilt, one-of-a-kind inventions. They were not mass-produced.

Hood approached the Caltech administration about forming a company to manufacture the protein sequencer, but the university had never gone into such a business venture, and its leaders had no interest in becoming entrepreneurs. So in 1981, Hood raised $2 million in venture capital to found the firm Applied Biosystems. The company eventually sold not just the protein sequencer but also Hood's protein synthesizer, DNA synthesizer, and DNA sequencer.

Hood also cofounded the biotech company Amgen, whose first product was a genetically engineered hormone (sold under the brand name Epigen) used to stimulate red blood cell formation in kidney dialysis patients, to treat and prevent anemia. It was based on a discovery achieved with the protein sequencing machine.

Epigen joined a growing field of such companies, which through the decade introduced new products,

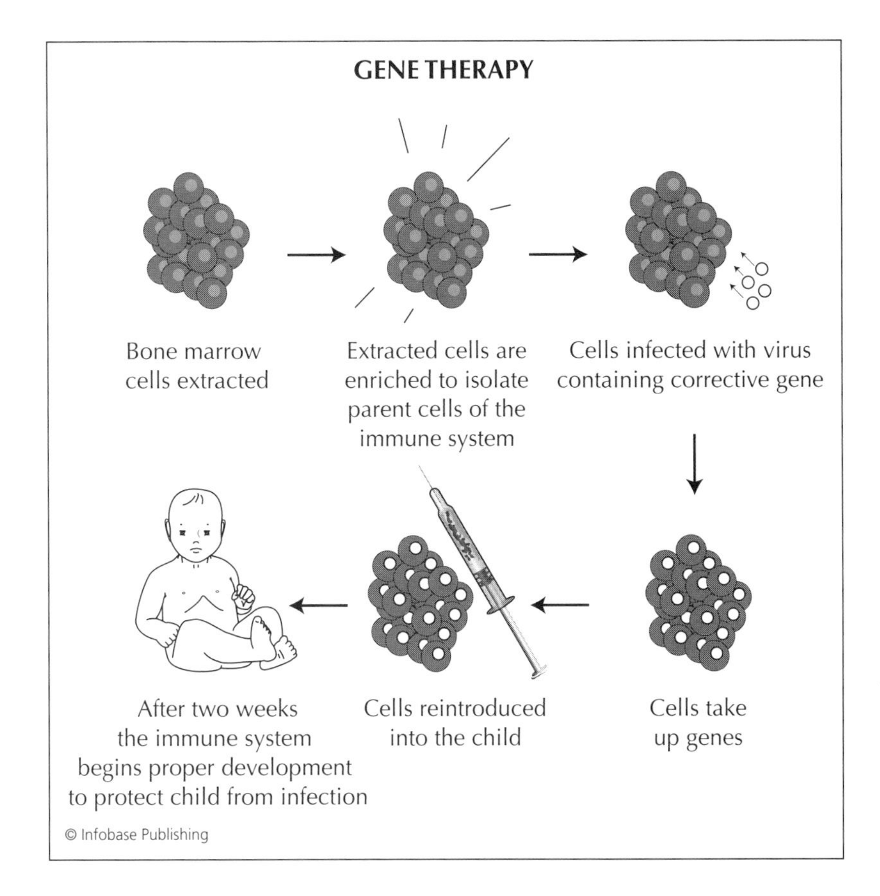

Sometimes a genetic defect, such as a gene that causes the human immune system to malfunction, can be corrected, at least temporarily, by directly introducing the healthy version of the gene into the patient.

techniques, and medical therapies achieved by manipulating genetic material. Universities joined these firms in seeking patents and government approval for their inventions.

In medicine, four-year-old Ashanti DiSilva in 1990 became the first human patient to receive gene therapy. To treat her adenosine deminase (ADA) deficiency, an immune system disorder, doctors at the NIH Clinical Center in Maryland drew a small amount of her bone marrow, isolated white blood cells called *T-lymphocytes*, and inserted a genetically altered virus carrying the ADA gene into these cells. (Often called T cells, T lymphocytes are one of two primary types of infection-fighting white cells in human blood). Then the doctors reintroduced the genetically corrected T cells into Ashanti's bloodstream.

The experiment worked, and Ashanti lived, although it took injections of more altered T cells every two months to maintain her immune system function at a level that, while functional, is much lower than in an unaffected person. This form of gene therapy subsequently worked in other ADA deficient patients. Attempts to apply gene therapy to other genetic problems have met with mixed results. Setbacks have resulted from the difficulty of modifying the human genome—much more difficult than dealing with bacteria cultures.

Among the decade's many other biotech developments:

- Genentech received approval from the U.S. Food and Drug Administration to sell genetically engineered human insulin and genetically altered tissue for use in treating heart attacks
- Harvard molecular geneticists patented a bioengineered mouse highly susceptible to breast cancer, for use in cancer research
- SyStemix Inc. patented an immune-deficient mouse with human genes, for use in immunology research
- Eli Lilly licensed its own biotech process for making insulin
- Cal Bio cloned a gene that codes for an important protein in human lungs. The gene promised treatment against respiratory complications in premature infants whose lungs were not adequately developed
- Cal Bio scientists isolated a gene for anaritide acetate, which helps to regulate blood pressure and fluid retention
- The Environmental Protection Agency gave the go-ahead for release of the first gene-altered crop, genetically engineered tobacco plants
- Advanced Genetic Sciences tested a bacterium genetically engineered to inhibit frost on a strawberry field in northern California
- The FDA approved a recombinant hepatitis B vaccine (brand name: Recombivax-HB)
- Genencor International, Inc. patented a process to make bleach-resistant protease enzymes for use in detergents
- Calgene received a patent for the tomato polygalacturonase DNA sequence, for extending the shelf life of produce
- Calgene successfully field-tested cotton plants genetically engineered to withstand herbicide application
- At the University of California, Davis, scientists developed a recombinant vaccine against rinderpest virus, deadly in cattle herds in third-world countries
- Molecular biologists at the Plant Gene Expression Center (a collaboration between the U.S. Department of Agriculture and UC Berkeley) used a high-speed gene gun to perform genetic transformation of corn plants

- Amgen developed Epoetin alfa (trade name, Epogen), a genetically engineered protein for treating patients with kidney failure
- GenPharm International, Inc. created the first transgenic dairy cow. The cow could produce human milk proteins for use in making infant formula

An Unlikely Infectious Agent

The protein sequencer developed by Hood and his partners was among the tools that came in handy as Stanley B. Prusiner (1942–), an immunology researcher at the University of California, San Francisco, sought the cause of a relatively rare but mysterious group of neurological disorders.

Born in Iowa and reared largely in Cincinnati, Prusiner is among research biologists with a background in clinical medicine. After earning an M.D. from the University of Pennsylvania, he interned and served a neurology residency at the medical center of the University of California, San Francisco. There in 1972, he first encountered an example of the diseases that would preoccupy him through the next two decades.

As a resident physician, Prusiner admitted to the hospital a woman suffering from loss of motor control and progressive dementia. The patient's condition was diagnosed as Creutzfeldt-Jakob disease, a degenerative illness of the central nervous system that is invariably fatal.

It was the first such case that Prusiner had witnessed. He became fascinated by this and related fatal illnesses in people and animals—diseases that render brain tissue spongelike, full of holes. Medical professionals presumed that the diseases were caused by a very small and slow-acting virus. That virus, however, had never been isolated or identified. In fact, it had seemed to elude earlier researchers, who had not been able to confirm that it was a virus. Prusiner set a goal for himself: to discover the molecular structure of this infectious agent.

Appointed to an assistant professorship in neurology at UCSF, Prusiner began in the mid-1970s to concentrate his research on scrapie, a disease in sheep that is similar to Creutzfeldt-Jakob in people. Others among these *transmissible spongiform encephalopathies* include Gerstmann-Sträussler-Scheinker syndrome, a fatal familial insomnia, and kuru—all three of which attack humans, although the last has been found only among the Foré tribe in Papua New Guinea. Among hoofed animals, bovine spongiform encephalopathy (known as mad cow disease) and chronic wasting disease, found in deer and elk, also belong to this category.

After years of study that involved introducing infectious cultures into laboratory mice and guinea pigs, Prusiner ran up against the problem that his preparations of what was supposed to be purified infectious matter included no nucleic acid. Without nucleic acid—RNA or DNA—there could be no virus. Everything that was known about immunology at the time said that there could be no infectious agent whatsoever without a nucleic acid. Diseases were caused by viruses, bacteria, fungi, parasites—all containing nucleic acids. All that Prusiner's preparations contained was protein.

This apparent failure resulted in the Howard Hughes Medical Institute's decision not to renew funding for Prusiner's study. At the same time, UCSF denied him tenure.

Prusiner persevered. Although he had lost one source of money, he still had a grant from the NIH. He secured other funds from private foundations and returned to work. Advocates among the UCSF faculty lobbied for him to receive tenure, and they prevailed.

Prusiner faced more hardship, however, after he announced in 1982 what he judged to be the source of the neurological diseases—an infectious protein.

He named it the *prion*, pronouncing the newly coined noun PREE-on. Much of the medical and biological establishment thought his discovery was wrong, that his findings were impossible. Proteins without nucleic acids lacked the biochemical means to replicate themselves and thus could not reproduce, could not spread. Prusiner faced not only profes-

Neuroscientist Stanley B. Prusiner defied medical orthodoxy when he announced that a rogue protein could be an infectious agent. (David Powers/UCSF Public Affairs)

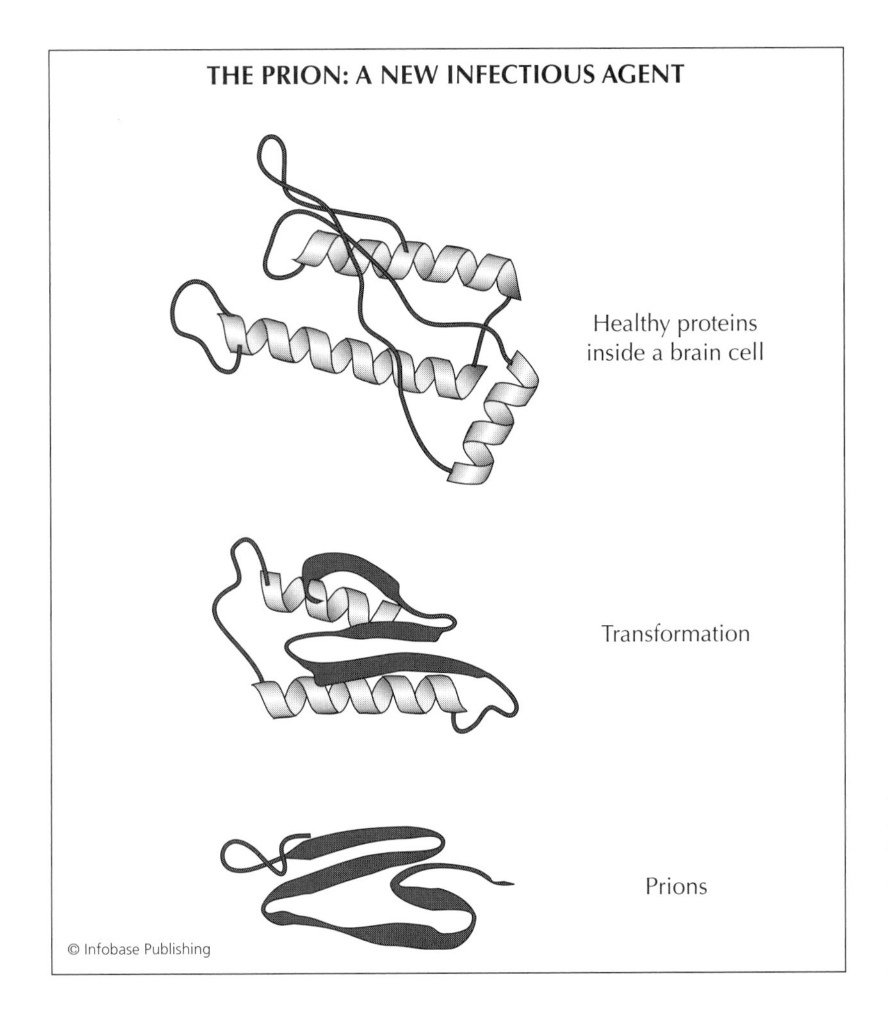

An abnormal protein can begin a chain reaction in which benign proteins lose their helical shape and unfold into flat molecular structures that build up within nerve cells and destroy them.

sional disagreement but also ridicule. Yet other researchers failed to produce results contradicting his findings.

Prusiner and colleagues announced in 1984 that prions are present in normal tissue—in every animal they had tested, including humans. In its normal molecular configuration, the protein was perfectly harmless. When folded into another, alternate configuration, a prion can initiate a molecular chain reaction that transforms neural tissue into something abnormally fibrous and deadly. In the wake of these studies, much more has been learned about transmissible spongiform encephalopathies, some of which can be acquired by eating infected neural tissue (as had happened among the formerly cannibalistic Foré people), others of which appear to be heritable or to occur randomly. This knowledge of what they are and how they spread brings science closer to understanding how to prevent and possibly even cure such unusual diseases.

Once the scientific and medical establishment acknowledged his discovery, it earned for Stanley B. Prusiner the 1997 Nobel Prize in physiology or medicine.

AIDS Rears Its Ugly Head

A much less rare, no less fatal new disease, also mysterious, suddenly challenged immunologists beginning in the 1980s. In early 1981, physicians in Los Angeles began to notice that unusual infections were showing up among young homosexual men, in such numbers as to represent a pattern. Soon thereafter, reports of similar patterns in New York and San Francisco arrived at the U.S. Centers for Disease Control (CDC).

These were diseases—a rare type of pneumonia, for example—that until then had been almost unheard of in otherwise healthy young people. A form of skin cancer called Kaposi's sarcoma had been observed almost exclusively in the elderly. Suddenly, it was striking young men. Doctors found that these men's immune systems were not functioning. They had lost their ability to fend off disease. Opportunistic infections—illnesses that a healthy person was well defended against—had moved in.

The CDC first referred to the phenomenon as GRID, for gay-related immune deficiency. That acronym, besides antagonizing advocates for gay rights, also quickly proved inadequate, as the rare infections began to appear in other segments of the population. Users of intravenous drugs proved susceptible, as did people who received blood transfusions and hemophiliacs using blood-derived clotting agents. As the disease was shown to be transmissible among the general population, concern grew sharply. The CDC gave it a more appropriate name: acquired immunodeficiency syndrome, or AIDS.

The first research breakthrough came in France. At the Pasteur Institute in Paris, immunologist Luc Montagnier (1932–) led a research team seeking a *retroviral* cause for AIDS. Retroviruses—the RNA-based viruses that use the enzyme reverse transcriptase to copy their genome into DNA—had been identified as the infectious agent behind other slow-virus diseases. In 1983, Montagnier's group discovered a retrovirus that they named "lymphadenopathy-associated virus," or LAV. A year later, Robert C. Gallo (1937–) and a team of researchers at the U.S. National Cancer Institute independently discovered a retrovirus and named it *human T lymphotropic virus type III*, or HTLV-III. Although there has since been much acrimonious discussion of who was most responsible for the discovery, it has become accepted that the Pasteur group first discovered the virus that would soon be renamed human immunodeficiency virus, or HIV. Gallo's group played an important role in establishing the virus as the cause of AIDS.

AIDS gained a higher public profile in the mid-1980s as veteran American film star Rock Hudson (1925–85) died of what was called "AIDS-related causes." Another high-profile case emerged as school

Bad Bacteria of the Belly

For most of the 20th century, medical students learned that *gastritis* and *peptic ulcers* often result from mental or physical stress that triggers the production of excess digestive acids. Diet was considered a culprit too. Treatments included bland foods, rest cures, and most often medicines to inhibit the production of stomach acid. Although medication could allow an ulcer to heal, the problem regularly recurred in many, if not most, ulcer patients.

In 1982, two Australian researchers announced that they had found out why the ulcers come back and what really causes these lesions in the mucous membrane of the stomach lining. Contrary to what had been gastroenterology dogma, the cause is not stress or lifestyle. The blame cannot be pinned upon a demanding boss. Habanero peppers play no significant role. Instead, the ulcer turns out to be an infection, a colony of microorganisms.

At the Royal Perth Hospital, pathologist J. Robin Warren (1937–) and research fellow Barry Marshall (1951–) performed biopsies on ulcer patients and used standard gastroenterology and immunology diagnostic tools to discover that the bacterium *Helicobacter pylori* causes inflammation of the stomach that can lead to ulceration.

The discovery was unexpected. According to Warren, the standard medical teaching was that no bacteria, no microorganism, could live and reproduce in stomach acid. The idea that *H. pylori* not only survived upon the lining of the stomach and duodenum but also developed long-term colonies was quite a revelation.

Frequently contracted in childhood—often passed from parent to offspring—the bacteria often remain in an individual for life. Based on subsequent research, doctors have estimated that about half of the total human population harbors the spiral-shaped *H. pylori*—a greater percentage in developing countries, lower among affluent societies—but in most instances it causes no problem or discomfort.

The work of Marshall and Warren has led to effective antibiotic treatment for the 10 to 15 percent of infected individuals in which the bacteria cause erosion of the stomach lining. By culturing the microbe, they have enabled further research, which has found connections between the bacterium and some types of stomach and lymphatic cancers.

For their discovery, Warren and Marshall shared the 2005 Nobel Prize in physiology or medicine.

officials in Kokomo, Indiana, expelled student Ryan White (1971–90) because of the HIV he had contracted from a blood product prescribed to treat his hemophilia. Public health agencies joined AIDS activist groups in getting out the word that the disease could not be spread by casual contact but only by sexual intercourse and/or contact with blood or other bodily fluids.

In the search for a treatment against HIV infection, National Cancer Institute scientists, including Robert Yarchoan (1950–) and the Japanese virologist Hiroaki Mitsuya (1950–), worked with the pharmaceutical firm Burroughs Wellcome Co. to retest azidothymidine, or AZT, which had been developed in the 1960s as a cancer treatment. It had been rejected then as ineffective and for its relatively high incidence of side effects, but Mitsuya and others thought AZT held promise against this new retrovirus.

After successful laboratory tests and then field tests in volunteer patients, Burroughs Wellcome (later GlaxoSmithKline) and the NIH had data that showed AZT could prolong the life of people with AIDS. The drug company applied for a patent and with U.S. Food and Drug Administration (FDA) approval made the medicine available to doctors and patients in 1987.

Another early treatment came in the form of cloned interferons from Genentech. The biotech firm produced alpha interferon, which is part of the human body's natural immune system. Normally, T cells in the blood produce enough of this interferon. These lymphocytes, which respond to infections or malignant cell growth, are often depleted in HIV-infected patients. In 1988, the FDA approved cloned alpha interferon as a treatment for Kaposi's sarcoma, prevalent in AIDS patients.

Treatment prolonged some lives, especially in the United States and Europe. Prevention campaigns—informing people about the dangers of unprotected sex, for example—saved lives. Yet such measures accomplished little against the global spread of AIDS in the 1980s. By decade's end, the World Health Organization estimated that there were as many as 1 million people infected with HIV—hundreds of thousands of those being heterosexuals in Africa. In less than 10 years, the disease had grown from a few reported cases to a worldwide epidemic.

Reevaluating RNA

With the public and media focused on AIDS—the urgent need for research into its causes and treatment—and on the growing realm of biotechnology, some other lines of biological research drew comparatively little attention in the 1980s. For example, outside of scientific circles, hardly anyone noted the work of Thomas R. Cech (1947–) at the University of Colorado and Sidney Altman (1939–) at Yale. Yet these two molecular biologists discovered something that altered one of their field's most basic assumptions about the workings of life. As the Royal Swedish Academy of Sciences noted in awarding them the 1989 Nobel Prize in chemistry, Cech and Altman made it necessary to rewrite biology textbooks.

What Cech and Altman discovered was that enzymes, which are proteins, are not biology's only molecular catalysts. They found that RNA can also function as a biocatalyst. This may seem a minor discovery—except that it overturned a central tenant of biological science. Until this work, biologists knew that DNA carried genetic information and that enzymes served as catalysts that could cut apart strands of DNA or bind them together. (The biotech revolution was based upon scientists' new abilities to manipulate and capitalize on restriction enzymes and other enzymatic proteins.)

RNA had been shown to be mostly a passive go-between, carrying information between DNA and proteins or—as in the case of retroviruses—serving as the carrier of genetic information itself.

This view began to shift in the late 1970s with Altman's work at Yale. Born in Montreal, Altman had come to the United States to study physics as an undergraduate at MIT. Proceeding to graduate school at Columbia University, he remained intent upon physics, but George Gamow—the great physicist who had attempted to decode DNA—redirected young Altman toward molecular biology. That path led the Canadian to work with Francis Crick and Sidney Brenner in England, and to specialize in enzyme studies.

Nobel Prize–winning biochemist Thomas R. Cech is a graduate of Grinnell College in Iowa and the University of California, Berkeley. (Paul Fetters/Howard Hughes Medical Institute News)

At Yale, Altman and colleagues focused on an enzyme from *E. coli* called RNAs P. This unusual enzyme has a molecular structure that binds a protein to an RNA molecule.

Altman separated the enzyme into its component parts. He found that the supposedly enzymatic protein, separated from the RNA, no longer performed its previous function, which was to cut strands of RNA. If he mixed the two parts of the RNAs P back together, the enzymatic function returned.

The Chicago-born Cech, meanwhile, had come to his enzyme research by way of graduate studies in biochemistry at UC Berkeley and postdoctoral studies at MIT. He had joined the University of Colorado faculty in 1978.

As Altman's team at Yale conducted further inquiries into the seeming anomaly they had run across, Cech was beginning research to understand RNA splicing in a single-celled organism called *Tetrahymena thermophila*. In carrying genetic code, RNA must often be taken apart and spliced back together to eliminate the genetic contents of noncoding junk DNA, so that the important genetic information on either side of the junk can be applied correctly to the protein-building process within a cell. Such splicing requires a biocatalyst. Conventional knowledge said the catalyst would be an enzyme.

In 1982, Cech isolated an RNA molecule in a test tube and found that, contrary to everything he had expected, the RNA began to splice itself. Soon after, Altman was able to demonstrate the same thing—that RNA can act as a catalyst. Soon other molecular biologists were finding scores of other RNA enzymes, called *ribozymes*.

Previous to this discovery, evolutionary theorists had not constructed a thoroughly satisfactory hypothesis dealing with life at its most biochemically basic, in its earliest form. DNA cannot function without catalytic enzymes, which are proteins. DNA carries the genetic information to build proteins. So if each molecule must have the other, how could either of them be the first *biomolecule*, the ancestor of all successive life?

With Cech and Altman's discovery of ribozymes, it became apparent that RNA not only possessed the ability to carry genetic information but also that it could cut and splice that information into coherent strands of functioning nucleic acid. Could the most basic building block of all life be a molecule of RNA?

Even Dinosaurs Had Mothers

Evolution is a story of nucleic acids and proteins, but the narrative would be woefully lacking without the organisms that those molecules build—especially the big, dramatic ones. Dinosaurs hold a fascination because the very thought of the largest of them having roamed this

Jack Horner, here on a fossil hunt in the Montana Badlands, has been called a paleobiologist. (Adam Hart-Davis/DHD Multimedia Gallery)

Fictive Science

Novelist Michael Crichton (1942–) saw out the decade with a fantasy novel that interwove plot elements based on some of the most provocative 1980s science. His 1990 science-fiction bestseller *Jurassic Park* employed polymerase chain reaction (PCR), genetic manipulation, gene cloning, reproductive cloning, and the mathematical-mechanical chaos theory. (The last posits that physical systems governed by seemingly predictable laws of physics and biology tend inevitably toward unpredictability.) The book also adhered to some of the latest ideas in paleontology.

In the novel, a biotech billionaire and his staff of genetic engineers have extracted bits of dinosaur DNA from blood-sucking insects that have been preserved in amber for more than 65 million years. Using PCR, the scientists have amplified the DNA. Since it is of course incomplete, they have found a way to insert crucial DNA sequences into amphibian DNA so that they can create a complete, viable dinosaur genome. Inserted into egg nuclei and incubated, this DNA brings forth living examples of long-extinct species, some of them terrifying carnivores. The biotech mogul's idea is to make these creatures the attraction at a one-of-a-kind theme park–zoo on an island near Costa Rica.

Much of this fictional cloning process is of course completely preposterous. Crichton grossly exaggerated what might be possible. Yet the author, who holds an M.D. and also trained in anthropology, knew enough about molecular biology, and about his readers, to make it all sound somewhat plausible—at least for entertainment purposes.

The dinosaurs of the book are quick-moving, warm-blooded, and social. Some of the predators display a horrifyingly adept intelligence. These are not stock, giant reptiles, but instead the dinosaurs described by such new-generation *sociopaleontologists* as Robert Bakker and Jack Horner. (Bakker as well as Horner would be employed as advisers on director Steven Spielberg's 1992 movie adaptation of the novel.) Crichton's story (in both book and film versions) probably brought some notion of genetic engineering and its potential to many thousands of people who might otherwise never have heard of it.

Pointedly, the grand experiment in Crichton's story ends in bloody disaster (far more violently and tragically in the novel than in the movie). There is the strong suggestion that humankind lacks the wisdom to exercise restraint in pushing the boundaries of the scientifically possible. There is also a moral that science utterly lacks the ability to predict outcomes.

Earth tends to stir imaginations. Fossil remains of such beasts provide a vivid visual aid for thinking about the changing Earth and the changing life upon it.

That must—at least in part—account for the lasting popularity of the many dinosaur species among children and also among adults of a certain imaginative stripe. Some of those people harness that fascination and become scientists.

The picture of what dinosaurs were—how they must have lived and looked and behaved—continued to change in the 1980s, as new paleontological finds invited fresh ideas.

Paleontologist John R. Horner (1946–)—known to virtually all as Jack Horner—in 1982 put forward the idea that certain dinosaurs displayed nesting behavior that much resembled that of migratory birds, and that part of this behavior included mother dinosaurs caring for their helpless young.

Horner, a Montana native, is unusual among scientists in that he does not hold a formal academic degree. He studied zoology and geology at the University of Montana from 1964 to 1966 and again from 1968 to 1972. In 1975, he was hired as a research assistant in the Department of Geological Sciences at Princeton University. Becoming an assistant curator of paleontology there, he led fossil-hunting expeditions. On a late-1970s dig in western Montana, Horner and his Princeton team found the first dinosaur eggs and nests to be discovered in the Western Hemisphere.

On subsequent digs, Horner found unprecedented numbers of juvenile dinosaur remains on Two Medicine Formation, an area of high ground near Choteau, Montana. Horner theorized that the area, which came to be called Egg Island by paleontologists, must have been a safe nesting ground in the late Cretaceous period.

Among their finds, a Horner-led team uncovered the remains of an adult duckbill dinosaur. It was next to a nest of hatchlings of the same kind, a species of duckbill new to the scientists. The bones of the young duckbills were not fully ossified, suggesting that they were unable to walk and would have had to stay in the nest awhile after emerging from the egg. Such a situation, Horner said, would require a degree of parental care. He named the duckbill species *Maiasaura*, which means "good mother lizard."

In a 1982 article titled "Evidence of Colonial Nesting and 'Site Fidelity' among Ornithischian Dinosaurs," Horner put forward the evidence he had gathered that certain dinosaurs were social animals that nested in colonies and that, like many migratory bird species, they returned faithfully to the same sites every year to build nests, lay eggs, and raise their young.

That same year, Horner became curator of paleontology at the Museum of the Rockies in Bozeman, Montana. In that capacity, he has made many more important fossil finds, including several skeletons of *Tyrannosaurus*. (Horner holds the controversial opinion that the giant carnivore was a scavenger rather than a predator.) In 1986, he was awarded a MacArthur Fellowship (the so-called genius grant). The announcement referred to him not as a paleontologist but as a *paleobiologist*. Among the general public, he may be best known for having served as a technical adviser on the film *Jurassic Park* and its two sequels.

Programmed Cell Death

To study biological organisms—extinct species or contemporary, dinosaurs or hominids—is to study the finite. Species come and go. Individual animals live and die. All that lives must expire. It may seem obvious that

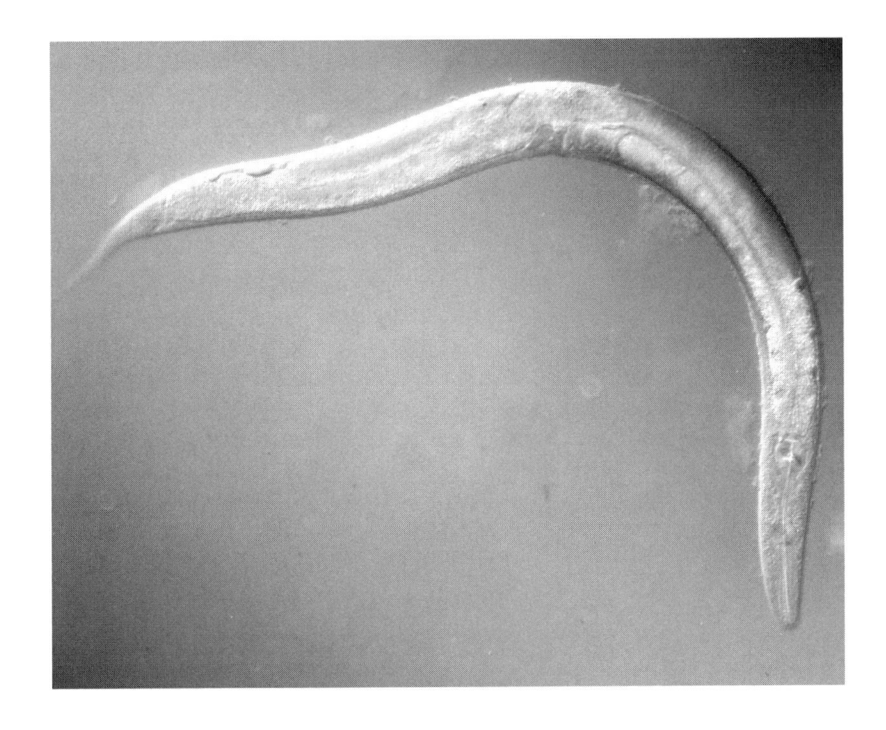

The nematode C. elegans, *valued as a research subject, feeds on microorganisms such as* E. coli. (Hulusi Cinar)

this is the natural order. It may be less obvious that selective death is part of life even within healthy developing organisms. For a plant or animal to achieve its proper form and function, select cells must die and be cast off.

Botanists had long observed programmed cell death in plants. It was also apparent as part of metamorphosis in many animals, such as frogs that develop from tadpoles. In mammal embryos, too, certain tissue is removed in the process of prenatal development. Human fetuses, for example, develop tissue between the fingers that later dies off.

After decades of studying such phenomena, biologists achieved an understanding of the process involved in the 1980s. In 1986, MIT researcher Robert Horvitz (1947–) reported that he had identified "death genes" that direct the cell-killing process in the soil nematode *Caenorhabditis elegans*, a transparent, wormlike creature about .04 inch (1 mm) in length. Horvitz also established that humans have counterpart genes.

Horvitz's discovery climaxed a series of experiments that had started at the Medical Research Council laboratories in Cambridge, England, with Sydney Brenner in the 1960s. The South African Brenner, also well known for his collaborations with Francis Crick, established *C. elegans* as a model organism. Seeking answers to fundamental questions about cell differentiation and organ development, he chose the nematode for its short generation time and also because its outer tissues are nearly clear, allowing him to observe cell division. He was able to track the actual

Scientist of the Decade: Kary Banks Mullis (1944–)

As a boy in 1950s South Carolina, Kary Mullis asked his parents to give him a chemistry set for Christmas. The reason, he later recalled, was because he wanted to figure out how to blow something up.

Although he has written of the fun he and his brothers had setting off homemade rockets fueled with sugar and potassium nitrate, Mullis grew up not to be a pyrotechnician or an ordnance expert. Instead, he graduated from the Georgia Institute of Technology in Atlanta, earned a Ph.D. in biochemistry from the University of California, Berkeley, did postdoctoral work in pediatric cardiology at the University of Kansas, and invented what is perhaps the most important and useful technique in the field of molecular biology—the polymerase chain reaction. This relatively simple method—by which a specific stretch of DNA can be multiplied into billions in a few hours—has profoundly changed the biotechnology field, along with medicine, criminal forensics, *paleobiology,* and much more. It stands with the inventions that have truly changed the world.

Yet in many ways, Mullis the Nobel laureate remains the southern boy who used to light the fuse of a rocket and then run as fast as he could to avoid getting burned in the back-blast. The scientist has set off a number of figurative explosions in the years since he won the 1993 Nobel Prize in chemistry. For one thing, Mullis—an inveterate surfer who often sports the deep tan more associated with a beachcomber than with a DNA expert—has thoroughly exploded the usual stereotypes of how a Nobel laureate should look, act, and talk.

"Eccentric" may not serve as the adjective to sum up Mullis. Many good scientists are eccentric in some way. It might be better to describe Mullis—in the patois of his adopted home, California—as "out there." In his writings, especially his popular collection of autobiographical essays, *Dancing Naked in the Mind Field,* Mullis has described experiences, thoughts, and beliefs that a more conventional scientist—one who cared about the good opinion of his peers—would be unlikely to hold, let alone admit to in public. Mullis is frank about his four marriages and other romances—describing infidelities, seductions, and betrayals. He admits to experimental and recreational use of LSD, which he learned to make while a student at UC Berkeley. He describes taking the powerful *psychotropic* drug and wandering in the woods around his cabin, allowing his altered mind to roam.

In another story involving the northern California woods, Mullis tells of a glowing raccoon who spoke to him, saying, "Good evening, doctor," after which Mullis apparently lost consciousness. His next memory was of waking up several hours later, with his clothes clean and dry—not as they would have been after a night outdoors in the humid coastal hills. The subtext here is that Mullis thinks it possible that aliens abducted him. His emphasis is on the word "possible." Because he can run no experiment to duplicate or disprove what he saw, Mullis finds it unscientific to dismiss it as untrue. It is simply unproven. He has a fondness for other unprovable phenomena. He refuses, for example, to dismiss astrology, a position that enrages astronomers. (Their discipline distanced itself from fortune-tellers many centuries ago.) Mullis also has discussed his interactions with persons occupying or traveling along what he calls the "astral plane," meaning another plane

processes whereby generalized stem cells grow into specialized cells. (The many different kinds of cells that make up an animal—bone, blood, muscle, neural tissue—all descend from a single zygote, or fertilized egg, which at first divides into undifferentiated stem cells.)

of existence, separate from what people generally perceive as reality.

Like so many scientists discussed in this book, Mullis pays little heed to boundaries between scientific disciplines. Yet his forays into other fields have been rather casual and often unwelcome. Unlike Crick—although perhaps a bit like Pauling in his later years—Mullis has often embraced controversial theories about areas of science in which he has little or no research background. Along with virologist Peter Duesberg (whose work on oncogenes is in chapter 7), Mullis believes that there is no proven link between HIV and AIDS. He has argued that the drug AZT does more harm than good and that it is the agent behind many symptoms of AIDS. He also dismisses global warming, arguing that human activity cannot affect climate.

Mullis's unusual way of looking at the world and reality did not begin with the invention of PCR, which was unveiled in 1986. Neither did it start when he was awarded the Nobel Prize in 1993. In 1968, while he was a graduate student at Berkeley, he wrote a paper titled "The Cosmological Significance of Time Reversal." Published in the journal *Nature,* the article discusses a model for the universe in which roughly half of the total mass travels backward in time. He has commented that it was much easier to get that fanciful article published than it was later to publish papers about PCR.

His radical departures from convention have enraged some peers and alienated many others. Some scientists admire Mullis for his freestyle independence. Others dismiss him as a show-off or a fool.

None of that, however, undermines the importance and the impact of PCR. Critics have charged that Mullis could not have developed his technique without the resources of Cetus Corporation, his employer at the time, and that the invention was a group achievement. There is a good deal of truth in the argument. Yet PCR was Mullis's idea. Even if someone else thought of PCR before he did (another charge by critics), Mullis acted upon his idea. He brought it to light, showed it was workable, and got it into production.

Even after his Cetus colleagues had taken up PCR, it was Mullis who stepped in and solved the problem of DNA polymerase that degraded with heat (discussed earlier in this chapter), resulting in the simple and efficient Taq PCR process.

PCR is such a powerful diagnostic tool, such a boon to researchers and investigators in so many fields, such an opener of scientific doors, that Mullis's achievement cannot be overstated.

Carrying the clout of the Nobel and the prestigious Japan Prize (also awarded to him in 1993), Mullis has become a popular speaker at universities, business meetings, and academic seminars. He may have alienated peers, but his freewheeling approach has attracted fans. Holding forth on PCR, molecular biology, and many other topics (and doing so in a thoughtful, manner that belies his loose-cannon image), he has a talent for popularizing science.

As the 21st century began, Mullis turned his attentions to immunology, inventing a method that he says can divert some of the human body's natural immune defenses against new microbial threats. He has founded a company, Altermune LLC, to develop and market this technique.

Besides holding the title of Distinguished Researcher at Children's Hospital and Research Institute of Oakland (California), Mullis serves on the board of scientific advisers of several companies. He lives in Newport Beach, California, and still spends time at his cabin in Mendocino County.

In the 1970s, Brenner used a chemical compound to bring about specific mutations in the genome of *C. elegans.* He noted which genes were linked with which mutations, tracking these genes' effects on the development of the worm's organs.

The British biologist John Sulston (1942–), a member of Brenner's research group at Cambridge, extended this work, mapping the development of cell division and cell development in the test organism. Sulston's meticulous studies showed that cell death is a normal part of the differentiation process. He discovered that certain cells in the *C. elegans* cell lineage are programmed always to die as part of the organism's development. He described this process and found connections between certain genes, the proteins they code for, and this cell death, which is called *apoptosis* (to distinguish it from necrosis, cell death through injury).

The American Horvitz had also worked with Brenner and Sulston in England. Returning to the United States in the 1970s, he continued their line of research at MIT. There, he isolated and identified two genes that control apoptosis. He was able to show how the genes work together in the cell death process and identify the corresponding process in human tissue. The combined work of these biologists showed that genetic mechanisms manage apoptosis in a delicate balance with cell division and cell differentiation.

For their combined contributions to this long-term investigation, Brenner, Sulston, and Horvitz were jointly awarded the 2002 Nobel Prize in physiology or medicine. Their work has broadened the horizons of many subfields of biology. It holds special promise for cancer research, an area where scientists seek ways to induce apoptosis in cancer cells.

Further Reading

Bahls, Christine. "First Person: Leroy Hood." *Scientist* 18, no. 7 (April 12, 2004): 16. Brief personal interview with inventor and systems biology pioneer.

Bylinski, Gene. "Heroes of Manufacturing: These Innovators Sail against the Prevailing Winds, Discovering Whole New Worlds in Biotech and Software." *Fortune* 147, no. 5 (March 17, 2003): 18–21. Available online. URL: http://money.cnn.com/magazines/fortune/fortune_archive/2003/03/17/339245/index.htm. Accessed February 9, 2006. Brisk, business-oriented account of Leroy Hood's accomplishments.

Cells Alive! "*Helicobacter pylori:* Bacteria That Cause Ulcers." Available online. URL: http://www.cellsalive.com/helico.htm. Accessed February 15, 2006. Biology site explains bacterial infections that cause gastritis and stomach ulcers.

Centers for Disease Control. "Kaposi's Sarcoma and Pneumocystis Pneumonia among Homosexual Men—New York City and California." *Morbidity and Mortality Weekly Report* 30 (July 3, 1981): 305–308. Available online. URL: http://www.cdc.gov/mmwr/preview/mmwrhtml/july_3.htm. Early report on emerging AIDS crisis.

———. "Pneumocystis Pneumonia—Los Angeles." *Morbidity and Mortality Weekly Report* 30 (June 5, 1981): 1–3. Early report of phenomenon that would prove to be the beginning of the AIDS crisis.

Cook-Deegan, Robert M. *The Gene Wars: Science, Politics and the Human Genome.* New York: W. W. Norton, 1994. History and analysis of forces that shaped the Human Genome Project.

Crichton, Michael. *Jurassic Park.* New York: Knopf, 1990. Science fiction novel weaves molecular biology, genetic engineering, and paleobiology into suspense story.

Gesteland, Raymond F., Thomas R. Cech, and John F. Atkins, eds. *The RNA World.* Cold Spring Harbor, N.Y.: Cold Spring Harbor Laboratory Press, 1999. Scholarly considerations of the likelihood of RNA's existence before the rise of life-forms.

Grainger, J. M., and D. R. Madden. "The Polymerase Chain Reaction: Turning Needles into Haystacks." *Biologist* 40, no. 5 (1993): 197–200. Article explains and analyzes PCR's function and its impact.

Hood, Leroy. "My Life and Adventures Integrating Technology and Biology: A Commemorative Lecture for the 2002 Kyoto Prize in Advanced Technologies." Available online. URL: http://www.systemsbiology.org/download/2002Kyoto.pdf. Accessed February 15, 2006. Inventor of high-speed gene sequencer recounts his life and career.

Horner, J. R. "Evidence of Colonial Nesting and 'Site Fidelity' among Ornithischian Dinosaurs." *Nature* 297 (June 24, 1982): 675–676. Paleobiologist reports novel findings from Montana fossil site.

Krupp, Guido, and Rajesh K. Gaur. *Ribozyme.* Natick, Mass.: Eaton Publishers, 2000. Scholarly work on catalytic RNA and its roles in evolution, biochemistry, and biotechnology.

Mullis, Kary B. "Cosmological Significance of Time Reversal." *Nature* 218 (May 18, 1968): 218. Paper illustrates young author's original approach to scientific topics.

———. *Dancing Naked in the Mind Field.* New York: Pantheon Books, 1998. Rollicking, quirky collection of provocative observations in autobiographical essays by the inventor of PCR.

———. "Unusual Origin of the Polymerase Chain Reaction." *Scientific American* 262 (April 1990): 56–65. The inventor looks back at the circumstances surrounding his invention.

———, F. Faloona, S. Scharf, R. Saiki, G. Horn, and H. Erlich. "Specific Enzymatic Amplification of DNA in Vitro: The Polymerase Chain Reaction." *Cold Spring Harbor Symposium in Quantitative Biology* 51, no. 1 (1986): 263–273. Mullis and colleagues announce and explain PCR.

Prusiner, S. B. *"Novel Proteinaceous Infectious Particles Cause Scrapie." Science* 9, no. 216 (April 9, 1982): 136–144. Announcement of the discovery of prions.

———, ed. *Prion Diseases of Humans and Animals.* New York: Ellis Horwood, 1992. Overview and description of spongiform encephalopathies.

Rabinow, Paul. *Making PCR: A Story of Biotechnology.* Chicago: University of Chicago Press, 1996. A critical account of Kary B. Mullis and the development of the polymerase chain reaction.

Saiki, R., S. Scharf, F. Faloona, K. Mullis, G. Horn, et al. "Enzymatic Amplification of Beta-Globin Genomic Sequences and Restriction Site Analysis for Diagnosis of Sickle Cell Anemia." *Science* 230 (December 20, 1985): 1,350–1,354. Paper treats an early medical use for PCR.

Schiele Museum of Natural History. "Hatching the Past: Jack Horner." Available online. URL: http://www.solutionscompanies.com/SchieleMuseum/HornerFeb2004.htm. Accessed February 15, 2006. Site has biography of paleobiologist, with highlights of career.

Shilts, Randy. *And the Band Played On.* New York: St. Martin's Press, 1987. San Francisco journalist's impassioned account of the early days of the AIDS crisis, attacking what author sees as government and societal indifference.

Silverstein, Alvin, and Virginia Silverstein. *AIDS: Deadly Threat.* Hillside, N.J.: Enslow Publishers, 1991. Examines origins and effects of AIDS, dispels myths, and discusses 1980s treatments and research.

Speaker, Susan L., M. Susan Lindee, and Elizabeth Hanson. *A Guide to the Human Genome Project Technologies, People, and Institutions.* Philadelphia: Chemical Heritage Foundation, 1993. Authors trace formation and early years of the Human Genome Project.

Tomei, David L., and Frederick O. Cope, eds. *Apoptosis: The Molecular Basis of Cell Death.* Cold Spring Harbor, N.Y.: Cold Spring Harbor Laboratory Press, 1991. Scholarly overview of genetically programmed cell death.

Weed, William Speed. "Nobel Dude." Salon.com. Available online. URL: http://archive.salon.com/health/feature/2000/03/29/mullis/index.htm. Accessed April 12, 2006. Interview with Kary Banks Mullis, mixed with analysis of his stature, or lack thereof, in science.

10 1991–2000: Sheep and Stem Cells

A New World

Biological science hit the front page—even the tabloids—in the final decade of the 20th century. This was the era of O. J. Simpson, a retired NFL running back accused of murder, and of Dolly, a Finn Dorset lamb unlike any before. Their stories caught the popular imagination in completely dissimilar ways. Yet both involved technicians or scientists putting to work humankind's newfound knowledge of molecular genetics.

The world watched intently in 1995 when Simpson, a Football Hall of Fame running back, went on trial in California for the murder of his ex-wife and her friend. Then everybody reacted (in either disbelief or joy, depending on point of view) as he was acquitted—despite bloodstains that were shown by DNA analysis to put him at the scene of the crime. (It turned out that the jury distrusted the handling of the evidence, not the science behind it.) DNA identification took its place as a regular part of the crime-solver's toolbox, resulting in convictions and, for the first time, the execution of a man whose DNA at crime scenes had convinced a jury of his guilt.

Dolly, born in 1997 near Edinburgh, Scotland, became famous because biologists cloned her from the nucleus of a cell taken from a mature ewe. She was the first mammal so produced. Until Dolly, scientists thought that cells from adult mammals could not be used to produce a whole animal. With her birth, researchers at the Roslin Institute proved it was possible. The implications alarmed many people. Would the future bring clones of adult humans?

The cloning of adult animals grew from the work of researchers who had created a genetically modified sheep that produced a valuable human protein—medically useful—in its milk. Once such an animal had been successfully produced, these scientists sought the ability to duplicate it. Other experiments in genetically altering mammals included introducing human genes to pigs, in an effort to make porcine organs suitable for transplants into human patients.

Genetic modification was changing agriculture, although the way was far more difficult than many in the biotechnology field had anticipated. A much-publicized attempt to grow and market the first genetically altered tomato was one company's downfall, although the effort cleared the way for other such crops by winning U.S. Food and Drug Administration approval.

Although not as sensational a story as cloning or DNA fingerprinting, a patented method to culture human embryonic stem cells also made headlines. From some quarters, it also brought public condemnation. The promise that stem cell research could lead to miraculous cures excited physicians, editorialists, and some politicians as well. Yet the technique involved destroying microscopic human embryos, a fact that seriously upset many religious leaders and right-to-life activists.

The Human Genome Project gathered momentum, challenged to a race by an entrepreneurial molecular biologist and his privately funded company. The effort to sequence the entire human genome became a sprint to the finish line at century's end. On the way, genome researchers sequenced the DNA of a strange, heat-loving, anaerobic microbe from the bottom of the ocean. In doing so, they confirmed what one U.S. researcher, Carl R. Woese (1928–), had been saying about the organ-

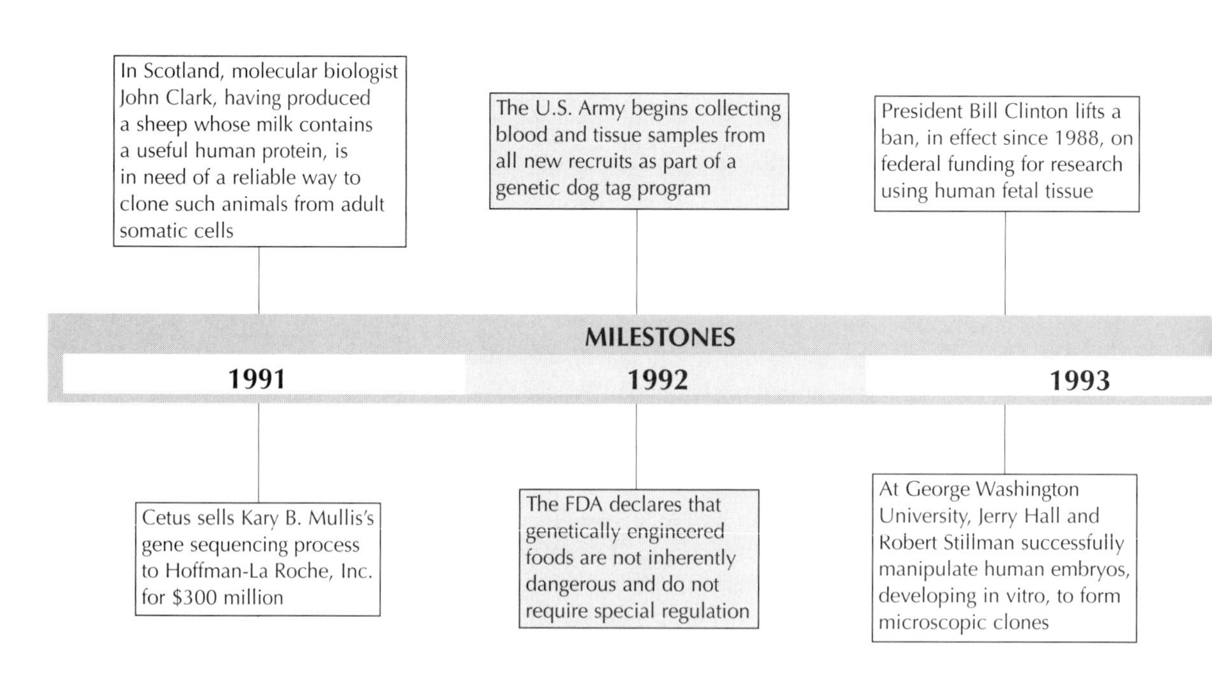

isms he had named *Archaea.* Its genes showed that Archaea belong in a separate domain of life from both bacteria and eukaryotes such as plants, fungi, and animals.

The Clone Age

Clones are as old as cells. When a single-celled organism divides asexually, without first exchanging genetic matter with another of its kind, the resulting two cells are clones—each a genetic duplicate. The English word *clone* derives from an ancient Greek term for the shoot of a plant. Gardeners know that it is often possible to cut a stem or root from one plant and use it to grow another. No mating has occurred; the second plant is a clone. It will not be identical to the first, because of differences in nutrition, hydration, soil, and so on. It is simply genetically the same—as a pair of human twins can be genetically the same yet two distinct people. So-called identical twins are clones of one another because they began as the same zygote.

In 1993, researchers at the in vitro laboratory of George Washington University's reproductive center conducted an experiment using 17 in vitro human embryos. Employing a technique called embryo splitting

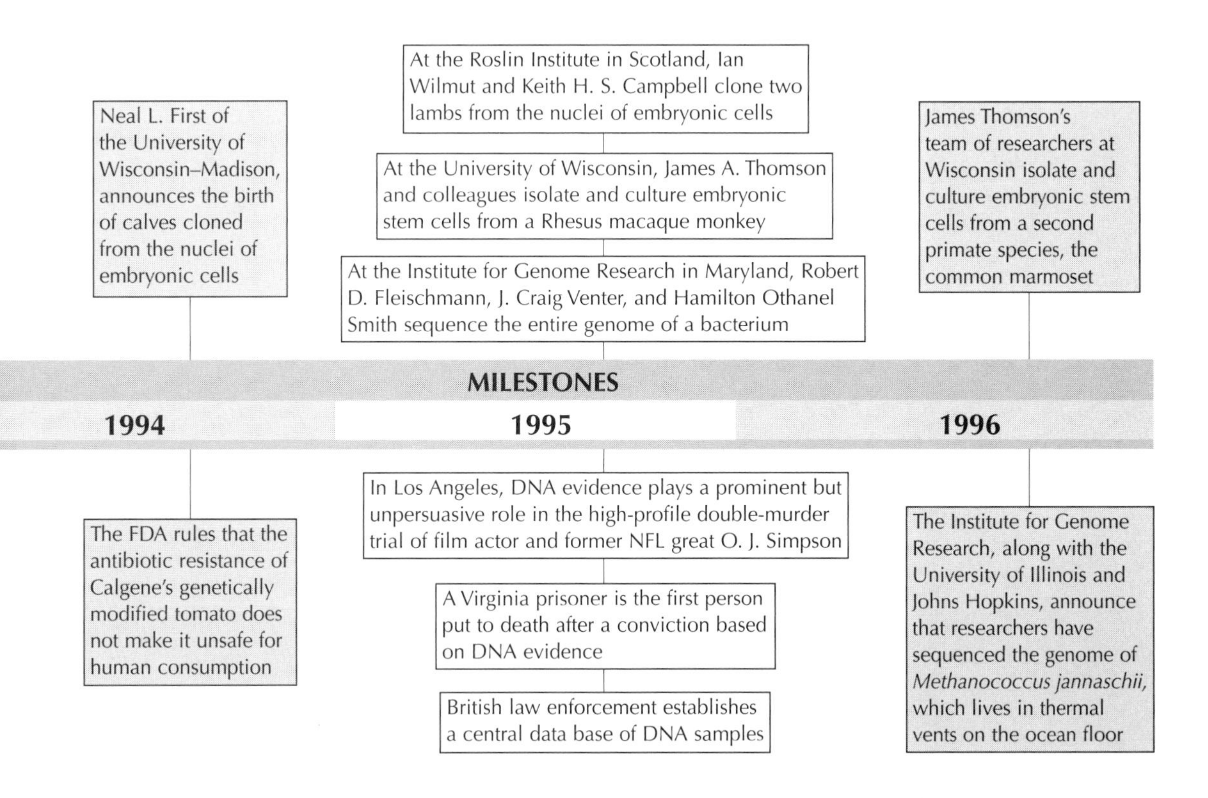

(manipulating a developing cell mass to divide into two masses), they increased the number of embryos to 48. This was a form of cloning. All of the embryos were terminated at a yet-microscopic stage. None were implanted in a woman's womb. (Implantation and birth had never been part of the researchers' intent.) When news media reported this experiment, critics—ranging from religious leaders to political figures to other biologists—roundly condemned what the scientists had done as a misuse of human entities.

In the 20th century, embryologists developed the technique of *nuclear transfer* to create clones. Nuclear transfer means removing the nucleus of an unfertilized egg cell, called an *oocyte*, and replacing it with the nucleus of a cell from another individual. The technique developed somewhat haltingly, with many failures, over several decades.

In the late 1930s, Nobel Prize–winning embryologist Hans Spemann (1869–1941) of Germany's Max Planck Institute wondered if every cell in a complex organism retained the entire complement of genetic material that had formed the whole. If so, he wanted to know if the potential that was in a fertilized egg remained in all those cells. When a zygote begins dividing to form an embryo, the first few cells formed are identical to one

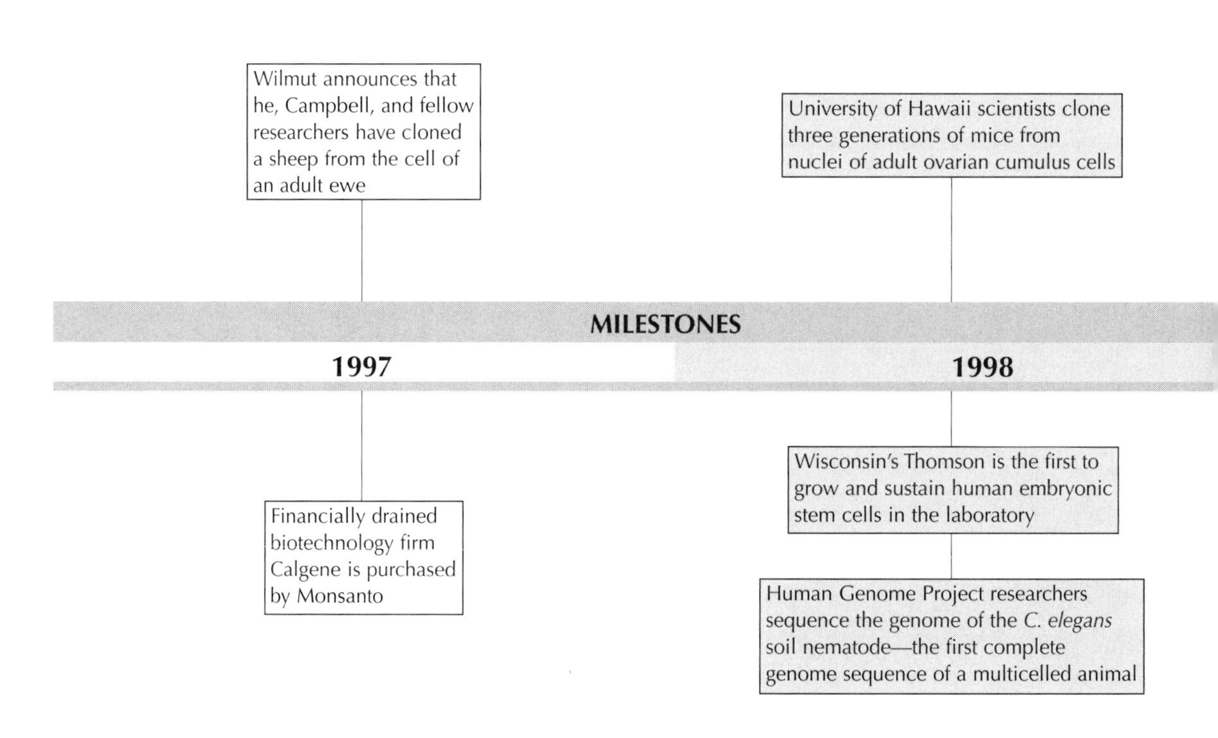

another. Until it reaches the point at which its cells begin to differentiate into those that make up bone, blood, skin, mucous membranes, and so on, each carries the potential to become any of the cell types that will make up the complete organism. These cells are *pluripotent*, able to grow into many kinds of differentiated cell types. Biologists also sometimes use the word *totipotent*, meaning able to give rise to *every* type of differentiated cell determined by the organism's genome. Only reproductive cells (sperm and egg united into a zygote) are considered totipotent. They give rise not only to all the types of cells in the adult organism but also to cells peculiar to the development of an embryo, such as those that attach to the uterine wall, form the placenta, and organize an embryo. That is why researchers cannot simply take an embryonic stem cell and implant it in the womb with the expectation of forming an embryo. Nothing would happen.

Researchers had long observed that differentiation in complex animals such as birds and mammals seems irreversible. Once a cell has differentiated, it appears unable to bring forth cells of different types from itself. Many relatively simple animal species—flatworms and some starfish among them—can be cut into pieces, each of which grows into another

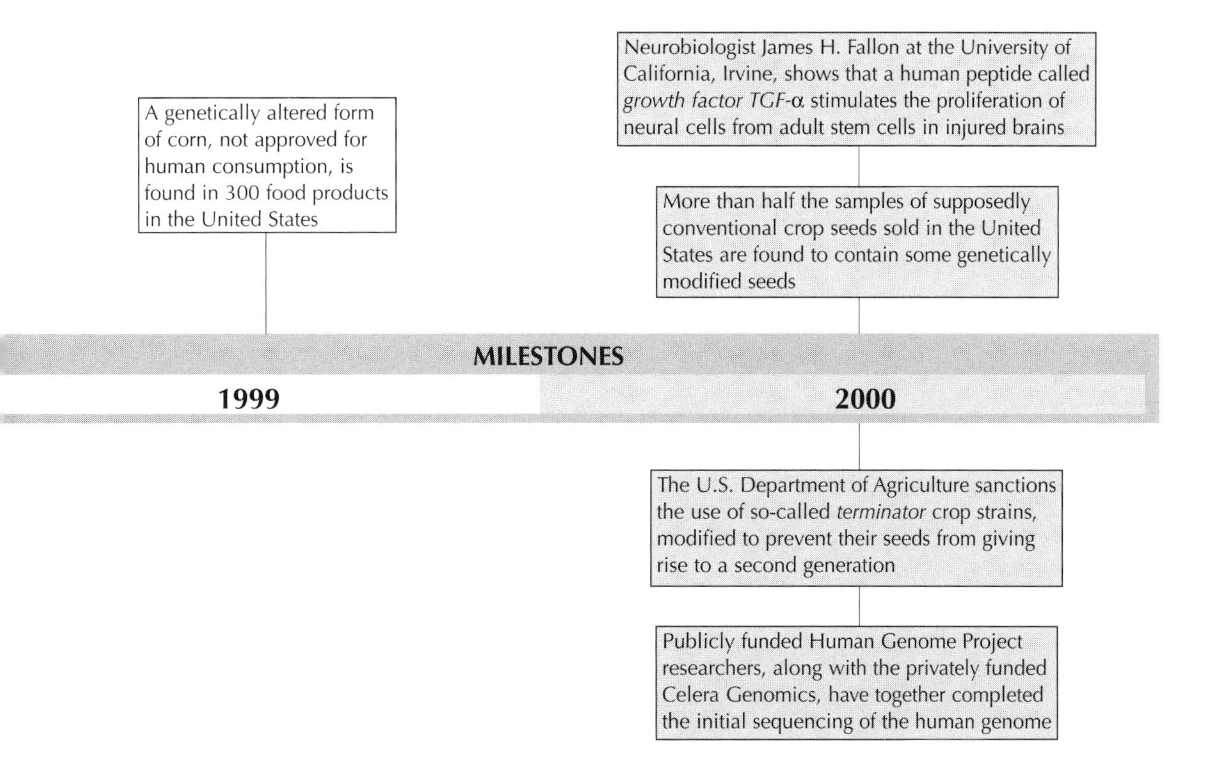

complete organism—each a clone. A large enough piece cut from the middle of a planarian may grow back a new tail and new head, but this never happens in hummingbirds, opossums, or human beings. A soldier who loses a leg to a land mine cannot regenerate the limb.

Spemann had lacked a sophisticated technique for nuclear transfer. He used a hair to tie off the nucleus of an embryonic salamander cell, halting that cell's development while the rest of the embryo progressed. At a slightly later stage of embryonic development, he untied the hair and coaxed a nucleus back into the cell whose reproduction had been arrested. That nucleus, from a stage of development a bit further along, and thus more differentiated than the formerly tied-off cell, activated the restored cell's ability to divide. Development proceeded normally.

In the early 1950s, American cytologist Robert Briggs (1911–83) and his research partner, embryologist Thomas King (1921–2000), had developed a technique in which they used a tiny glass needle to remove the nucleus from an egg of a North American leopard frog (*Rama pipiens*). *R. pipiens* has very large egg cells, making this egg easier to *enucleate* (withdraw its nucleus) than are those of many other species. When the researchers, at Philadelphia's Institute for Cancer Research, replaced the egg cell's nucleus with one taken from a newly developing embryo of the same species, the egg developed normally. Subsequent experiments using slightly older embryonic cells had not been as successful—the older the cell from which the nucleus was derived, the less likely that nucleus would function in the egg cell into which it was implanted. Later in the 1950s, John Gurden (1933–) of Oxford University had successfully taken the nucleus from an intestinal cell of an adult African clawed frog (*Xenopus laevis*) and implanted it in an enucleated oocyte. The egg then developed into a tadpole. Gurden's success would have been greater if tadpoles thus cloned had developed normally into frogs. They did not, and researchers did not know why.

Nuclear transfer cloning experiments improved over the following decades, progressing from frogs in the 1950s to mice and sheep in the 1980s. Neal L. First (1930–) of the University of Wisconsin–Madison announced the birth of calves cloned from the nuclei of early embryonic cells in 1994.

It was quite a feat to clone mammals from undifferentiated embryonic cells, but it still did not answer two questions that Spemann had asked when he started this chain of events:

1) Do differentiated cells retain their pluripotency, their ability to give rise to any of the hundreds of types of cells in a complex organism?
2) If embryonic cells lose this pluripotency, at what stage in the development of the organism do they lose it?

The answer to the first question appeared to be *no*—at least in mammals, although to some extent *yes* in frogs. As for the second question, the answer seemed somewhat uncertain. In mammals, pluripotency appeared exclusive to extremely early embryonic cells, but at how early a stage must they be harvested? Experiments with cattle in the 1980s had shown that nuclei from somewhat older embryos—those that had progressed to a cluster of 64 or even 128 cells—could be used to successfully clone calves.

At the Roslin Institute in Midlothian, Scotland, embryologist Ian Wilmut (1944–) was following this track with sheep in the early 1990s. In 1995, he and research partner Keith H. S. Campbell (1954–) took cells from a nine-day-old embryo, cultured those cells in a laboratory vessel, and implanted nuclei from the cultured cells into enucleated egg cells. Two of the eggs were then successfully brought to term in a surrogate mother. Born that summer, the resulting lambs, cloned from an established cell line of differentiated embryonic cells, were called Megan and Morag.

Wilmut and Campbell next brought forth a lamb cloned from a 26-day-old embryo. Their work drew little attention, until they announced in 1997 that they had cloned a Finn Dorset sheep from a fully differentiated cell taken from a six-year-old ewe. The original donor cell had been a mammary gland cell, and again, Wilmut and Campbell had grown a culture of such cells before taking a nucleus for implantation. The resultant lamb, a female (it could be nothing but, given that it was the clone of a female) had been born the previous summer. Workers at the institute gave her the name Dolly, after country music singer Dolly Parton.

DNA testing showed that Dolly was genetically identical to the ewe from which the original donor nucleus had been taken. She thus carried no nuclear DNA from the enucleated egg into which the nucleus had been transplanted. Neither did she carry DNA from her surrogate mother. Both the egg donor and the surrogate mother were of another breed from Dolly. Rather than Finn Dorsets, they were Scottish Blackface sheep.

How did Wilmut and Campbell's team succeed where other researchers had failed? For one thing, they refused to give up. With Dolly, the researchers achieved success on their 277th attempt. Also important was an insight that Campbell, a young cytologist who had joined the effort in 1991, brought to the cloning experiments. Earlier attempts had begun with the nucleus from a fast-dividing cell. Cells go through cycles of reproduction. Some divide rapidly and often. Others divide more slowly. Some, such as the cells in neural tissue, rarely divide once an organism has matured. They become quiescent. Most cells go through periods of growth and periods of quiescence.

In a laboratory culture, even fast-dividing cells can be made quiescent by withholding nutrients. The cells go into a resting state but will become active again when the nutrients are available for growth. In the process leading to Dolly, Campbell induced the culture of cells taken from the six-year-old ewe to become quiescent before implanting the nucleus in an enucleated egg. This proved to be a key step.

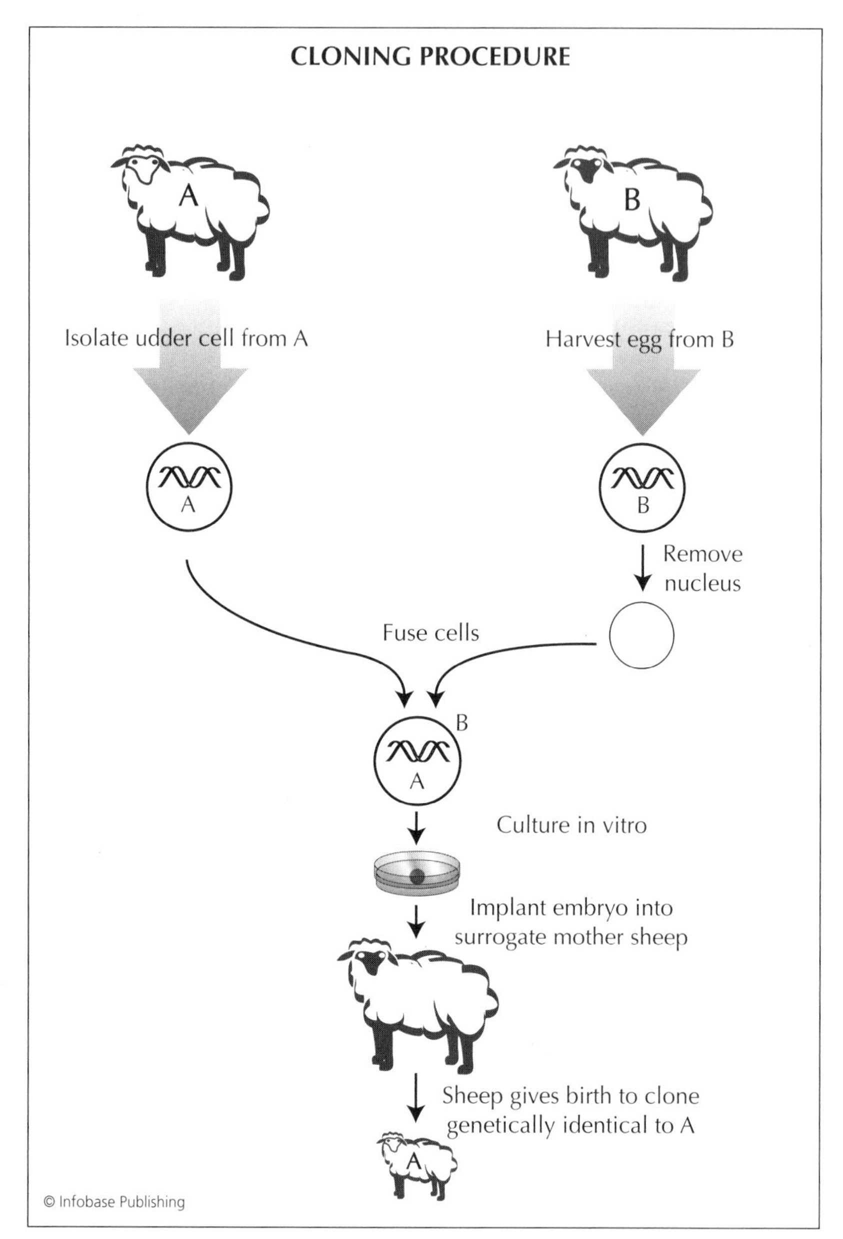

In the first successful cloning of an adult mammal, DNA was taken from a mammary gland cell of an adult Finn Dorset ewe. The DNA was fused into an egg cell taken from a Scottish Blackface ewe and inserted into the uterus of another Scottish Blackface for gestation.

Born near Warwick, England, Wilmut had grown up as a math teacher's son with a love of the outdoors. Seeking a career that would not trap him in an office or classroom, he studied agriculture at the University of Nottingham. Realizing that he did not actually want to run a farm, he switched to agricultural science. After earning a Ph.D. at Cambridge, he worked on a project there that resulted in the first calf from a frozen embryo, in 1973. That was the same year that he moved to what was then the Animal Breeding Research Organisation. It would later be renamed the Roslin Institute.

Campbell had been a medical lab technician and had worked his way to a research position. After studying microbiology at Queen Elizabeth College, London, he held laboratory jobs in Yemen and France. He assisted botanists fighting Dutch elm disease in the Alfriston Valley of England. His work at the Marie Curie Institute in Paris brought him a scholarship to study cell biology and embryology at the University of Sussex. There, Campbell explored the cell cycle in developing embryos, important preparation for his cloning research in Scotland.

Wilmut and Campbell's success with Dolly led to the cloning of other mammals from differentiated cells. Researchers tried variations on the basic cloning technology. In one such method, an electrical pulse is used to fuse the entire donor cell, not just its nucleus, with the enucleated egg. The biotech firm ABS Global in DeForest, Wisconsin, later in 1997 announced that it had a cloning technique that would work equally well with embryonic or fully differentiated cells. In 1998, an international group of scientists headquartered at the University of Hawaii announced that they had derived cloned mice from the nuclei of adult ovarian cumulus cells taken from mice that had themselves been cloned. In 1998, scientists at Japan's Kinki University cloned eight identical calves using cells taken from one adult cow. In Oregon, researchers cloned two Rhesus macaque monkeys (*Macaca mulatta*).

Somatic cell cloning had answered Spemann's questions, although it raised new ones. For example, how developmentally normal was such a clone? Dolly appeared normal and behaved as did any other lamb. She matured at the same rate as other Finn Dorsets and was able to conceive and bear lambs. There was some question, however, about whether her biological age matched her chronological age.

The cells from which she was cloned came from a six-year-old ewe. Every time a eukaryotic cell divides, the DNA replication process stops just a little short of the end of the chromosome. The DNA at the end, however, is not known to carry important genetic information. Highly repetitive, this bit provides a buffer zone called a *telomere*. A small part of the telomere is lost with each chromosomal replication. Thus the telomeres shorten as an animal matures and ages. When she was only a year old, analysis showed the telomeres of Dolly's chromosomes were shorter than those in a conventionally conceived sheep of the same age.

Later, there was evidence that Dolly may have been aging faster than a normal ewe. In 2002, Wilmut announced that she had developed osteoarthritis, more common in older sheep (and older people). Early the next year, she was diagnosed with a lung disease that required she be euthanized. She lived less than seven years, well short of the optimum Finn Dorset life span of 11 or 12.

Aside from providing esoteric scientific knowledge, the value in experiments that led to the cloning of adult animals lay in the possibility of duplicating organisms with the best genetic qualities—in wool production, milk production, meat production, and so on. Beginning the process by taking a nucleus from an adult sheep means that the breeder can choose the actual animal to be cloned, rather than a potential genetic mix.

Despite the potential benefits, this kind of cloning remained problematic through the end of the 20th century and too expensive to become standard practice. The cloning process required delicate manipulation of tiny bits of matter by hand. It put great stresses on the egg and the implanted nucleus. Frequently, it failed. There were questions about the wisdom, the safety, and the ethics of such cloning.

Genetic diversity plays an important role in nature. A great advantage of sexual reproduction, surely a primary reason why it became such a dominant method for complex organisms to make more of their kind, is in the way it mixes genes. Sexual reproduction provides for resilient populations. Diversity within the genome of a species often enables that species to survive hardship. Among a genetically varied population, there are more likely to be individuals with resistance to a particular disease-causing agent. The species is better able to survive an epidemic.

Critics asked if milk from cloned cows and goats was safe. What about meat from such animals? Proponents of somatic cell cloning argued that there was nothing nutritionally or chemically different about food products derived from clones, but objections remained at the decade's end.

Many people, scientists among them, believed that routine cloning of other mammals inevitably would lead to the cloning of human beings. Most found the prospect alarming. Cloning researchers in the 1990s took great pains to assure the public and wary governmental bodies that even if it were possible to make such clones (and the technology had not yet arrived), there were no plans to create genetic duplicates of people.

Pharmaceuticals from the Farm

In developing a technique for producing genetic replicas of grown animals, Wilmut and colleagues answered long-standing questions about the potential of differentiated somatic cells, but the research leading to Dolly actually grew from another line of inquiry—one seeking a better way to produce not just sheep but genetically altered sheep.

Scientists had been making transgenic organisms—those carrying a gene from another species—since 1970s research by Cohen and Boyer achieved *E. coli* that could produce a frog protein. That bacterium had been followed by other bioengineered microbes, most developed to produce valuable enzymes and other proteins for use in the pharmaceutical and chemical industries.

Genetic engineering had also brought about transgenic rodents—largely for the purpose of research. Geneticist Philip Leder of Harvard

(1934–) led an effort that succeeded in engineering a mouse with an oncogene inserted into its DNA, making it especially useful in studies of cancer.

John Clark (1951–2004), a molecular biologist in Scotland, followed news of such experiments closely. Something he read about a mouse modified by insertion of a gene for human growth hormone particularly impressed him. The blood of the rat-size mouse, Clark noted, contained an elevated level of the growth hormone. This gave him an idea. With colleagues at the Animal Breeding Research Organisation, Clark set out to engineer a sheep that could produce a significant amount of pharmaceutically valuable protein not in its bloodstream but in its milk.

The first step was to pair a milk production gene in sheep with a human gene for the production of alpha-I-antitrypsin, used in treating cystic fibrosis. Once they had succeeded in that task, the researchers worked on inserting the gene combination into a sheep zygote. In 1990, Clark announced the creation of Tracy, the first transgenic animal that produced a large amount of a human protein in her milk. Potentially, a flock of sheep with Tracy's engineered genome could become a reliable (and profitable) source of this valuable substance—the medicine available at every milking.

To create Tracy, however, Clark and his colleagues used a procedure that required introducing a few hundred copies of the engineered transgene (linking the human protein production with the sheep's milk production) into a freshly fertilized egg. They injected many hundreds of zygotes with the necessary genetic material. Yet only a small number of the lambs born of those zygotes expressed the crucial gene, and not all could pass on the gene to progeny. The researchers needed a way to produce multiple copies of one of these transgenic sheep, one that had matured to the point that it was proven to express the desired transgenic property.

Clark realized that an answer could be to take a cell from such an animal, grow it in a laboratory culture, and use the culture as an established source for clones of the transgenic sheep. This had never been done before, and many thought it impossible. Clark handed off the problem to Wilmut and thus began the series of Roslin experiments that produced Megan, Morag, and Dolly.

Clark and colleagues continued their transgenic experiments in the 1990s. His team produced the first mammal genetically engineered, not with the addition of a gene, but with a gene removed. It was a gene that triggered the formation of prions in sheep neural tissue.

Born in Blackpool, England, Clark had grown up in Lincolnshire. After majoring in zoology at Cambridge, he had earned a master's degree in Canada, at the University of Western Ontario. His Ph.D. work in molecular biology involved human DNA. In the 1990s, he participated in forming two biotechnology companies. By all accounts, he was a brilliant biologist and a well-rounded individual who took pleasure in music, dancing, and travel. After finishing his studies in Canada, he had taken

Tomato Soup

Genetic engineering bore fruit, literally, in the early 1990s with the Flavr Savr tomato, developed by Calgene, a small biotech firm in Davis, California. The product failed—at least in its initial outing—and the company floundered because of the failure, but Flavr Savr paved the way for hundreds of genetically engineered food crops that followed.

If in no other respect, the tomato—genetically modified to stay firm as it ripened—was important for the U.S. Food and Drug Administration (FDA) approval it won for genetically altered foods.

The idea behind the Flavr Savr was simply that commercially grown tomatoes—the ones sold in the grocery store—taste like Styrofoam, especially when the tomatoes are purchased in midwinter anywhere with a less than tropical climate. The reason behind that is that ripe tomatoes are too soft to ship without turning to mush. So, growers pick them when they are green and still hard and ship them that way. The colder the destination, the further they must be shipped and the greener they must be picked. At journey's end, the green fruit are sprayed with the hydrocarbon ethylene, which chemically triggers their skins to turn red. The spray does not trigger the tomato flesh to become tasty. The tomato looks nice and tastes awful.

To remedy this, Calgene researcher Bill Hiatt began in 1988 to focus on a particular gene in the tomato, one that codes for the enzyme polygalacturonase. Called PG for short, this is the enzyme that causes the fruit to soften as it ripens. Hiatt used reverse transcriptase to copy the DNA of the gene. He then reintroduced the gene (using a viral *vector*) in what is called the antisense direction. Essentially, that means upside down and backward. This method achieved the effect of turning off production of PG. The resulting fruit could be left on the vine longer, thus getting riper and tastier, without softening as much as standard tomatoes.

The business theory was that Calgene would be able to charge top price for these better-tasting supermarket tomatoes, especially in the upper midwest and northeastern United States. To head off consumer fears about the product, the company in late 1991 asked the U.S. Food and Drug administration about its policy on genetically altered foods. In spring of 1992, the FDA ruled that these crops would not be regulated any differently than conventional foods.

As it put together its production and marketing plan for the 1992 crop, the company also anticipated opposition to one other aspect of the tomato—it carried a genetic resistance to an antibiotic. Calgene asked the FDA for another safety ruling. The FDA ruled favorably again, but not until 1994. That meant a year's delay. It also meant no initial return on Calgene's investment. The company had to lay off workers and drastically cut its research and development budget.

Calgene made its gravest mistake by planting the genetically modified crop in a climate and soil for which the plant had not been bred. Calgene's scientists had started with a strain of tomato suited to California's Sacramento Valley, the company's

a break from science long enough that he and his wife could tour the United States. Clark became director of the Roslin Institute in 2003. Yet for all his brilliance, interests, and successes, he was not able to overcome severe depression. Clark died, apparently by suicide, in the summer of the following year.

Also in the 1990s, scientists worked toward using gene-altered animals as possible sources for organ transplants. A number of research organizations—academic and commercial—tried altering the genome of pigs

home (and a major tomato-growing region). Yet the firm contracted with Florida growers to raise its 1994 commercial crop. The resulting tomatoes, marketed under the brand name MacGregor's (after the zealous gardener in the classic Peter Rabbit stories), were not good enough to bring the prices that Calgene executives had anticipated. For what Calgene was asking, Chicago consumers could get hothouse-ripened tomatoes. The cost of producing Flavr Savr had far outstripped the return.

The Flavr Savr, though firmer than a regular ripe tomato, was not as firm as the hard, unripe tomatoes that growers, farm workers, and shippers were used to handling. The company had to sell ruined tomatoes at a steep discount to canneries and makers of soups and packaged sauces. Calgene lost more money. In 1997, the giant chemical manufacturing firm Monsanto purchased the financially drained Calgene.

If there is a lesson in Calgene's experience, it may be that genetic engineering is not magic. It will not produce an agricultural product that is automatically better or more profitable than the results of traditional farming. Other companies developed genetically altered tomatoes through the 1990s. Some were engineered to taste better and ship better, others to resist pests or stand up to chemical pesticides. Through century's end, none saw great success.

As genetically engineered crops proliferated, so did fears about consuming these products, some containing proteins that had never previously been a part of the human diet. In 1999, a gene-modified corn variety, sold under the brand name StarLink was found in more than 300 types of food products sold in the United States for human consumption. The pest-resistant corn had not won FDA approval and was supposed to be used exclusively for animal feed.

One Texas firm, a manufacturer of corn chips, tortillas, and similar products, lost millions of dollars in the resultant product recall. No report of illness was ever definitively linked to eating the goods containing modified corn.

In 2000, the firm Genetic ID of Fairfield, Iowa, conducted random tests of conventional seeds handled by U.S. agricultural distributors. More than 50 percent of the samples contained some genetically altered seeds. Besides the difficulty of isolating genetically altered crop products from the general food supply, critics of the new technology have argued that it is virtually impossible to keep genetically engineered plants from cross-pollinating with conventional crops and also with wild plants.

Also in 2000, the USDA sanctioned the use of so-called terminator crop strains. These were plants modified to prevent their seeds from giving rise to a second generation. This curb to unintentional cross-pollination raised new objections from farmers, especially those in third-world countries. If their crops yield sterile seeds, farmers cannot keep some of their harvest to begin the next year's crop; they must buy commercially grown seeds each planting season.

At decade's end and into the 21st century, the debate over the safety of genetically modified crops was not settled. Organized opposition to genetically engineered foods was stronger in many European countries than in the United States.

so that the animals produced human enzymes to block immune system complements. These complements are groups of proteins that work with other parts of the immune system to attack invaders. In Princeton, New Jersey, the biotech firm Nextran Corp. placed into pig germ cells three human genes that produce proteins which protect the lining of blood vessels from attack by the body's own immune system.

Duke University Medical Center won FDA approval and used livers from such pigs as temporary life supports for patients waiting for human liver transplants. This line of research offered much promise, but it also sparked controversy. Many people find the use of human genes to alter other animals, even for research purposes, to be highly questionable. This issue has continued to be controversial into the 21st century.

Stem Cells

In the first several hours after a mammalian egg cell is fertilized, it divides into two cells, then four, then eight, and so on. After a few days, there may be 40 to 150 cells. An outer layer of glycoprotein (molecules of protein linked to a sugar) that surrounds the zygote dissolves and what remains comprises an outer layer of cells that will become the placenta and an inner mass of cells that will grow into the embryo.

For a female to become pregnant, this *blastocyst* must implant itself into the wall of the uterus where that inner mass, the *embryoblast*, can begin growing into all the different kinds of cells that will make up the human body. The cells of the embryoblast are all the same, undifferentiated. Because of the pluripotency of these embryonic stem cells, researchers thought they had great healing potential if someone could harness them against degenerative illnesses and injury.

Animal clones such as Dolly the Finn Dorset showed that the nucleus of a differentiated somatic cell, when properly joined to an enucleated egg cell, still contains the genome for an entire organism. Yet those differentiated cells in the mammal's body never take it upon themselves to grow a new pancreas after disease ravages the old one or to mend a severed spine. Scientists saw potential for just such miracles if embryonic stem cells could be isolated, cultured, and triggered to grow into the specific tissues needed.

If stem cells could be made to grow into heart muscle cells—forming tissue to replace that destroyed in a heart attack—a damaged heart might be made whole again. If stem cells could mend the neural tissue broken in a spinal injury, perhaps a quadriplegic could regain control of his or her limbs. If the lost neurons in the brain of a Parkinson's disease patient could be regenerated, perhaps his or her motor function would come back. Patients that had been doomed to a long, slow deterioration and death might be healed.

The above are very big ifs—filled with assumptions that may never be borne out fully. Yet the potential in embryonic stem cells—if not for transplantations, then as medical research subjects—beckoned to James A. Thomson (1958–), a developmental biologist who in the early 1990s came to the University of Wisconsin from the Oregon Regional Primate Center. Using the *M. mulatta*, a monkey native to Asia, Thomson in 1995 isolated the macaque's embryonic stem cells and kept them alive in a laboratory culture. This was a first for a primate species.

He wanted to do the same with human embryonic stem cells. This was a matter fraught with difficulties—not all of them scientific. The use of

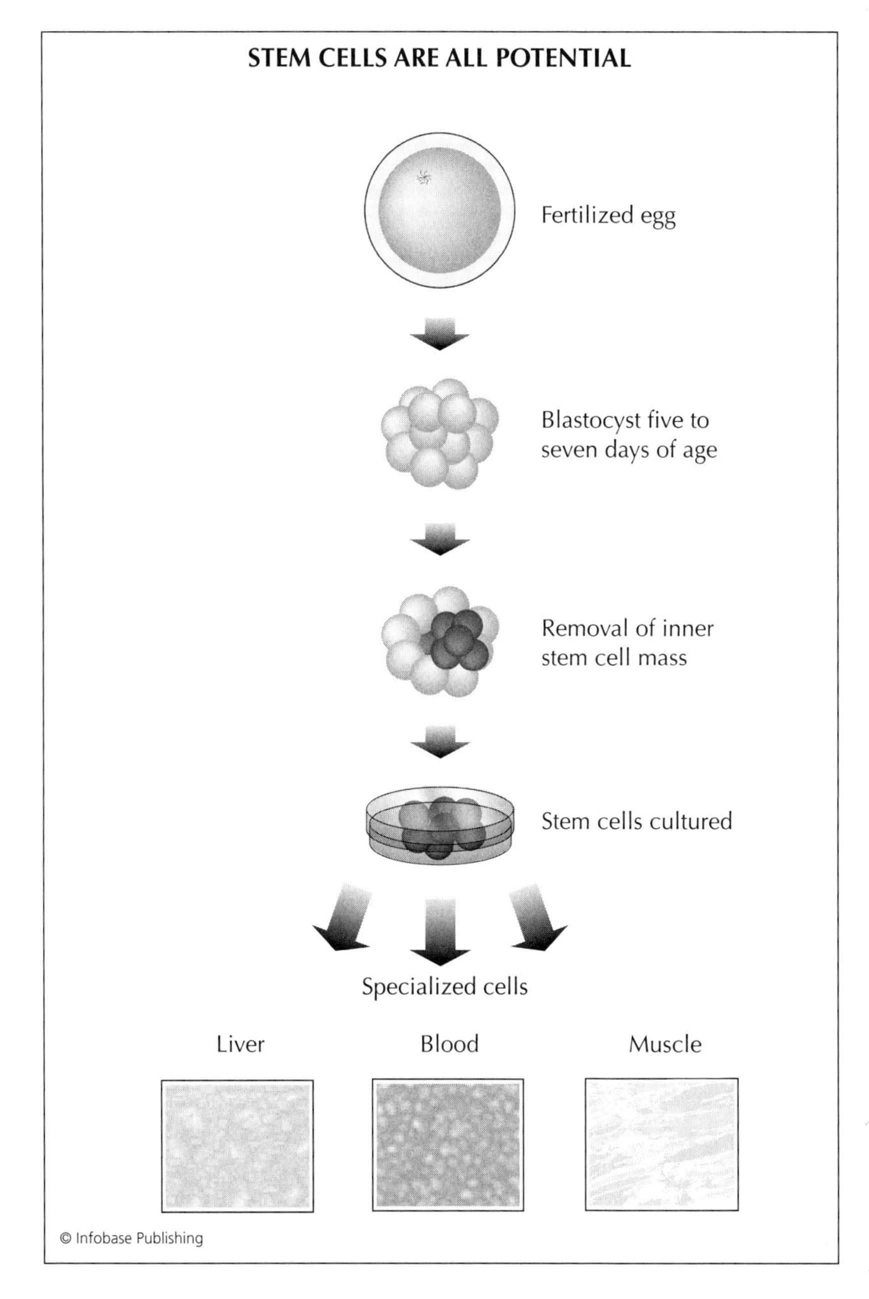

In a developing organism, stem cells divide into all the many types of differentiated tissue cells. This potential is what makes their use in medicine so promising.

human fetal tissue for medical research or therapy was—and remains—an extremely troubling subject for many who believe that it is wrong to use human tissue that has the potential to grow into a person for any research or therapeutic purpose.

James Thomson at the microscope in his Primate Research Center Laboratory at the University of Wisconsin. (Jeff Miller/University of Wisconsin Board of Regents)

In 1988, the administration of U.S. president Ronald Reagan (1911–2004) had ordered a moratorium on federal support for research into fetal tissue transplantation. The administration of Reagan's successor, George H. W. Bush (1924–) extended the moratorium, despite a recommendation from the National Institutes of Health that the ban be ended. Congress passed legislation to lift the moratorium in 1990, but President Bush vetoed the bill.

As President Bill Clinton (1946–) lifted the ban in 1993, his administration set up rules for how researchers could obtain fetal tissue for research. They were rules intended to ensure that no potential parent would choose an abortion based on a benefit that donated fetal tissue might bring to medical science. Financial incentives were also outlawed. That is, no woman could be paid for the use of an embryo formed from her egg cell.

Before beginning his quest to isolate human embryonic stem cells, Thomson consulted with medical ethicists on the moral and legal ramifications of the research. He mulled the issue privately. Thompson said that he ultimately thought about what was best for the blastocysts he intended to use, which would come from a fertility clinic. To help a woman conceive a child, such clinics routinely fertilize many of her eggs with the father's sperm *in vitro,* not within her body, but in a laboratory vessel. A zygote is then placed in a growth medium to divide for a few days. Blastocysts that a fertility expert judges most likely to grow into a healthy fetus are chosen for implantation in the womb. There are always many spares that the clinic freezes for possible future use. Most must later be discarded. Thomson decided that it was better to use such cell clusters for beneficial research than to throw them away.

To insulate the university from possible government funding prohibitions resulting from his work, he established a second, off-campus laboratory much like his lab at the Primate Research Center. This new lab was not a university facility but under the auspices of the nonprofit University of Wisconsin Alumni Research Fund (WARF). At the off-campus site (where he did many lab assistant chores himself, lacking funds for a full-time helper), Thomson succeeded in isolating human embryonic stem cells and keeping them alive, undifferentiated, in a culture for six months. He announced his success late in 1998.

Within days of Thomson's news, John D. Gearhart (1944–) announced a related breakthrough. At the Johns Hopkins School of Medicine, Gearhart had led an effort to isolate and culture embryonic germ cells. These are the egg and sperm cells within human embryos. Although harvested from six-week-old fetuses, these cells are like stem cells in that they are pluripotent—or theoretically totipotent.

The Johns Hopkins team used aborted fetuses in their research, making the work especially controversial. Any benefit derived from an aborted fetus draws extremely bitter condemnation from abortion foes.

Gearhart had taken a somewhat unusual course to his career in developmental cell biology. After spending his first six years on a farm in western Pennsylvania, he was placed in a Philadelphia orphanage. His widowed mother had felt herself unable to raise three sons alone. Keeping her youngest, she placed John and another brother in the all-boy charitable institution. John emerged at age 17, headed for the University of Pennsylvania. This in spite of an orphanage counselor who had told him college would be a waste of time.

As an undergraduate, John Gearhart remembered the farm of his first memories. He chose to study agronomy, hoping to become a plant breeder. Finding himself then fascinated by genetics, he followed the subject through graduate studies at the University of New Hampshire and Cornell University. His research topics progressed from botany to the genome of *D. melanogaster* and then mice—often focusing on the way genes regulate the formation of cells and embryos. By the early 1990s, Gearhart had isolated mouse stem cells and grown them in a tissue culture. Like Thomson in Wisconsin, the Johns Hopkins researcher saw the tremendous potential that lay in pluripotent human cells.

As the decade and the century came to an end, a few other researchers around the world were able to isolate and culture stem cells, maintaining what are called stem cell lines for research. Thomson sold stem cells to other scientists. Some of his stem cell lines were for the use of Geron Corporation, which had helped fund Thomson's research.

The next objective for stem cell therapy researchers was to discover and learn to control the biochemical signals that direct stem cells when and how to grow into specific types of cells.

Critics of embryonic stem cell research pointed out that, as with any transplantation of foreign tissue, there would be the possibility of stem cells being rejected. This could be avoided, as Gearhart has suggested, by using somatic cell nuclear transfer to begin a blastocyst that is a biological clone of the patient and then deriving the embryonic stem cell culture from this clone. The idea of creating a human clone for any purpose is highly controversial and fiercely opposed by many on religious and ethical grounds. Creating an embryonic clone so that doctors can harvest its stem cells is akin, these critics point out, to creating a full human clone simply to use its organs as spare parts.

Critics also pointed out that research might be better directed toward therapies using adult stem cells. These are the cells within the body's tissues that are responsible for healing. Adult stem cells in the skin, for example, grow into new skin, allowing a cut or abrasion to heal. Adult stem cells knit broken bones and adult stem cells in the bone marrow produce new blood cells, which is why a bone marrow transplant is essentially a form of adult stem cell therapy. Yet in mammals, adult stem cells have been found to be either unipotent—able to grow into a single kind of somatic cell—or multipotent—able to grow into a few kinds of closely related cells but not naturally pluripotent.

At the end of the century, medical researchers were trying to learn more about adult stem cells and how they might be used to treat diseases and injuries. In many cases, physicians did not even know where particular kinds of adult cells reside within the body. No one had yet succeeded in isolating adult human stem cells and growing them in a laboratory culture.

In 2000, neurobiologist James H. Fallon (1946–) and colleagues at the University of California, Irvine, showed that a human peptide called growth factor TGF-a stimulates the proliferation of neural cells from adult stem cells in injured brains. The finding may be a key to stem cell treatments. Growth factor peptides also appear to play a role in triggering the unregulated cell growth of some cancers, suggesting a possible danger in employing these proteins for therapy.

Shotgun Sequencing

Researchers who had been working on the Human Genome Project announced in June of 2000 that they had completed the initial sequencing—a rough draft of all the genes that make up human beings. Scientists from publicly funded institutions in many countries—Japan, France, Italy, and Britain among them—had participated in the massive, decade long effort, but they had to share the spotlight with commercial newcomer Celera Genomics, formed in 1998, and its president, J. Craig Venter (1946–).

Venter was a former National Institutes of Health (NIH) researcher who had grown impatient with traditional sequencing methods and had jumped to the private sector. Born in Utah, he had grown up in the San Francisco Bay Area and had served as a U.S. Navy medical corpsman in the Vietnam War before starting college.

He began his higher education at a community college and proceeded to earn a Ph.D. in physiology and pharmacology from the University of California, San Diego, in 1975. The following year, Venter became an assistant professor at the State University of New York at Buffalo. He joined the NIH in 1984.

Studying genes that control the way human nerve cells signal one another, Venter thought there had to be a quicker way to sequence genes. The preferred method, called clone-by-clone sequencing, had been speeded up by automation in the 1980s, but it still involved numerous steps as the genome is copied on the way to analysis. (The cloning referenced in the name of this method is not cell cloning, discussed elsewhere in this chapter, but gene cloning—making copies of long gene sequences using a catalytic enzyme.)

Venter decided to use a faster method often called shotgun sequencing, or more formally referred to as whole-gene sequencing. Whole-gene sequencing requires that the genome be broken into millions of pieces. The researcher puts the bits in order again by matching genetic markers, called expressed sequence tags, to their corresponding places on the chromosome.

In the 1990s, the deliberately paced clone-by-clone method was standard practice for the NIH and human genome researchers. Molecular geneticists often used shotgun sequencing for the DNA of prokaryotes, which have smaller genomes. They strongly preferred the slower method for the larger genomes of eukaryotes, considering gene-by-gene cloning more accurate. Both methods later came to be accepted, considered complementary to one another.

Venter disagreed with those who preferred the careful, slower technique. He used shotgun sequencing to rapidly identify human brain genes.

Seeing commercial possibilities in this faster method of sequencing large genomes, Venter in 1992 left the NIH to establish The Institute for Genomic Research (TIGR), financed by the biotech firm Human Genome Sciences. At TIGR, Venter and Hamilton O. Smith (Nobel Prize–winning codiscoverer of type II restriction enzymes) participated in an effort led by Robert D. Fleischmann (1952–) to sequence the genome of an entire organism, the *H. influenzae* bacterium. Their success in 1995 marked the first time the entire genome of an organism had been sequenced.

Molecular Biology in the Courtroom

In April of 1995, Timothy W. Spencer died in the Virginia electric chair, executed for a string of brutal rape-murders he had committed in the late 1980s. The evidence that led to both his arrest and multiple convictions consisted of a match between Spencer's DNA and that of semen found at crime scenes in Richmond and Arlington.

Spencer became the first person executed on the strength of evidence gathered through DNA fingerprinting. This new forensic tool had first helped police in Britain in 1986. A man had come forward to confess to two rape-murders in the English Midlands, but police suspected he was lying. At Leicester University, Alec Jeffries, inventor of the technique, used DNA fingerprinting to show that the police were right. The DNA did not match; the man could not have committed the crimes. The next year, also in Britain, prosecutors used DNA evidence to convict a rapist—the first such conviction in the world.

The technique—a probe of short, highly repetitive regions of noncoding DNA, each unique to the individual that carries it—quickly became a standard part of crime-solving, especially as courts upheld its admissibility. The Virginia Supreme Court in 1989 upheld Spencer's conviction and death sentence.

In 1995, Britain began a central database of DNA samples. Police from anywhere in England, Scotland, Wales, or Northern Ireland could submit DNA evidence for comparison to samples taken from known criminals.

Also that year in the United States, the double-murder case against former NFL running back O. J. Simpson (1947–) rested largely on DNA analysis of blood found at the crime scene, in Simpson's car, in his house, and on a glove found in his garden. In the widely reported trial, prosecutors said that much of the bloody trail, as it was characterized, was shown to match Simpson's DNA, and that there were blood traces in the car, on Simpson's sock, and on the glove that matched the DNA of victims Nicole Simpson (1959–94) and Ronald Goldman (1968–94).

The Los Angeles jury acquitted Simpson, but apparently it was not because members seriously doubted the science behind DNA fingerprinting or its reliability. After the trial, legal analysts said that Simpson's defense attorneys had successfully established reasonable doubt by convincing jurors that the police had mishandled evidence and possibly even planted it. Despite such a high-profile setback, DNA evidence continued to be seen as a remarkable and accurate new tool for crime detection.

In 1998, the U.S. Federal Bureau of Investigation established its own DNA databank, the National DNA Index System. Also in the 1990s, the U.S. Army began collecting DNA samples from new recruits. The genetic dog tag program promised aid in identifying soldiers killed in battle. (The Tomb of the Unknowns at Arlington National Cemetery stands as a memorial to U.S. service personnel whose remains could not be identified for proper burial.)

Improvements in DNA technology at century's end increased accuracy and allowed forensic scientists to make accurate matches from extremely small DNA samples. A bit of saliva on a cigarette filter or on the rim of a water glass became enough to get a match.

The full genomes of other organisms followed, both at TIGR and at labs that were part of the publicly funded Human Genome Project. The organisms included the yeast *Saccharomyces cerevisiae*, the bacterium *Mycoplasma genitalium*, and *E. coli.* In 1996, researchers from TIGR, the University of Illinois, and Johns Hopkins University announced that they had sequenced the single-celled *Methanococcus jannaschii*, which lives in thermal vents on the floor of the Pacific Ocean. What they found confirmed just how different that organism and other *Archaeons* like it are from all other types of life on Earth. There is more on this work later in this chapter.

In 1997, researchers announced the first complete genome sequence of a multicelled animal, the soil nematode *C. elegans*. Then came the fruit fly *D. melanogaster* and a plant called mouse-ear cress (*Arabidopsis thaliana*).

It may seem that the human genome researchers had wandered from their mission, but they had not. Nature is extremely conservative about preserving what works in a genome. Bacteria, worms, plants, and human beings share genes that perform similar functions in these extremely different species. Thus, learning the genome of *A. thaliana* helped geneticists as they worked on the human counterpart.

The multinational PerkinElmer Corporation founded Celera Genomics in 1998, hiring Venter as its president. The goal was to generate genomic information with commercial applications. Building on work already done by the many Human Genome Project researchers over the previous several years, Celera applied Venter's speeded-up methodology to the task of sequencing what had not yet been sequenced among the 3 billion nucleotide base pairs in the genome of *H. sapiens*. Essentially, Venter challenged the Human Genome Project to a race. Which of them could finish the complete genome first? Publicly funded researchers had little choice but to step up their pace, resulting in a tie.

After the 2000 announcement, both Celera and the Human Genome Project would publish initial results early the next year. Their reports would show that the genome contains only about 30,000 to 40,000 genes. This was much fewer than had been thought, and it meant that a far larger portion of the genome than the researchers had expected consists of noncoding DNA.

Archaea, Living Fossils

As the Human Genome Project confirmed repeatedly in the 1990s (see the Shotgun Sequencing section of this chapter, page 252), most organisms have many genes in common, and common genes perform similar functions in widely disparate species.

With the sequencing in 1996 of *M. jannaschii*, a single-celled, deep-sea *thermophile*, Genome Project researchers found something significantly unusual. J. Craig Venter of The Institute for Genome Research (TIGR) commented that almost two-thirds of the microorganism's genes were unlike anything the scientists had seen before—and he was referring to scientists such as TIGR research team leader Carol J. Bult (1962–), people who had studied and sequenced a great many genomes.

Further, the genomic blueprint showed that although *M. jannaschii* was indeed very different from better-known types of living things, prokaryotes and eukaryotes, it was more like the latter than the former. In other words, *M. jannaschii*, a microbe whose cells contain no nucleus, had a greater amount of genetic material in common with plants, fish, human beings, and other eukaryotes than with its nucleus-lacking brethren, bacteria.

Microbiologist Carl R. Woese, leader of the University of Illinois team that had participated in the sequencing, said that the genetic blueprint showed Archaea (the group of organisms including *M. jannaschii*) to be "the living fossils of our prokaryotic ancestors."

Microbes such as *M. jannaschii* used to be considered bacteria. Under a microscope they look like bacteria. But their classification had changed—or was in the process of changing—because of the work of Woese and colleagues in Urbana, Illinois. In the 1970s, the microbiologist had been studying the ribosomes in various microbes in an effort to better understand the genetic relationships among these life-forms. Ribosomes, which are about 60 percent RNA, do not change much over the course of evolution—probably because of their crucial role in protein synthesis. Nature tends to preserve that which is essential, and cells cannot function without their ribosomes. So ribosome RNA can tell a molecular biologist much about the family tree of an organism.

In 1977, Woese had announced that the RNA sequences in the ribosomes of *M. jannaschii* and microbes like it showed so little similarity to those of bacteria at large that the organisms had obviously followed separate evolutionary paths. He proposed reclassifying what had previously been called bacteria into two separate kingdoms—eubacteria (meaning true bacteria) and archaebacteria (ancient bacteria).

Those of the second type had so far been discovered in extreme environments such as *M. jannaschii*'s thermal vents at the bottom of ocean trenches, where the temperature can be as hot as 490 degrees Fahrenheit (almost 200°C). Microbiologists had previously thought of these hardy microbes as descendants of more conventional bacteria that had evolved into extreme niches. Many of them, *M. jannaschii* included, are *anaerobic*. Certain species live in deep marsh-bottom mud and even underground petroleum deposits where there is no trace of oxygen. In addition to thermal vents and hot springs, they have been found in extremely alkaline waters. Others thrive in environments so acid that no other life-form could survive. These microbes have even been found alive inside of a 200-million-year-old salt crystal.

To Woese, such extreme environments suggested the young Earth billions of years ago, before the rise of other life-forms. That led him to choose the prefix "archae-," meaning ancient. He developed a theory that archaebacteria are the oldest life-forms on the planet and a source of important data about the evolution of cells. By the mid-1990s, many scientists seeking life's cradle came to view chemosynthesis at such geothermal vents in ocean-floor trenches as a likely biochemical starting point. This line of thought complemented and reinforced Woese's ideas.

In the 1970s, most biologists had recognized a phylogenetic tree of living things that included five kingdoms: plants, animals, fungi, bacteria, and *protists* (such as protozoans, algae, and slime molds). Four of those kingdoms consisted of organisms whose cells contain nuclei. Those made up the eukaryotic *domain*. The other kingdom, bacteria, whose cells contain no nuclei, was the sole biological realm within the prokaryotic domain.

As he studied them, Woese decided that archaebacteria were so distinct from either prokaryotes or eukaryotes that they belonged in a third domain. Dropping *bacteria* from their name, he began calling them Archaea. He redrew the phylogenetic tree to reflect the change, with the three domains called Bacteria, Archaea, and Eukaria. (Prokaryote no longer qualified as a domain, as the prokaryotes now were split between two domains.) His taxonomy linked organisms not by morphological similarities, as had all such systems since Linnaeus, but by evolutionary relationship. This was as determined, where possible, through ribosome RNA analysis.

The two ideas that 1) Archaea were not bacteria and that 2) they belonged in a separate domain took years to catch on. At the end of the 20th century, some textbooks still used the term *archaebacteria*. Noted authorities, including Nobel Prize winner Salvador Luria and evolutionary biologist Ernst Mayr, disagreed with details of Woese's classification system, although not with his basic message. Continued study confirmed that Archaea were quite distinct from the rest of life on Earth, yet with similarities to both bacteria and eukaryotes.

Biologists used to think that Archaea lived exclusively in extreme habitats. Over the last two decades of the century, and especially in the 1990s, they were found in a wide range of environments, including the digestive tracts of many types of animals, from termites to cows. The fact that some of these microbes live in such extreme places, however, often without oxygen—that in fact oxygen is poison to them—has prompted speculation that they could probably survive interplanetary travel on or in a chunk of rock. In addition to being mentioned as a candidate for a very early, if not the earliest, life-form, they have also been cast in hypotheses that life may have arisen somewhere other than Earth and arrived by meteorite.

Born in Syracuse, New York, Woese graduated from Amherst College and the University of Rochester. His Ph.D. in biophysics was from Yale University. In the 1950s and 1960s, he served as a researcher at Yale, the General Electric Research Laboratory, and the Pasteur Institute in Paris. In 1996, after 30 years on the faculty of the University of Illinois, he was appointed to that institution's Stanley O. Ikenberry Endowed Chair. At the end of the 1990s, Woese continued to publish papers on the nature of the earliest life, envisioning a biochemically simple *progenote* quite unlike later cells. He wrote of a precellular community of freely exchanged genetic materials that led to the three domains of cellular life.

Scientist of the Decade: James A. Thomson (1958–)

It is difficult and probably presumptuous to say with any certainty what ultimately will result from the ability to isolate and culture embryonic stem cells. The 1998 breakthrough of James Thomson has been touted as the key to unprecedented medical miracles. Press accounts have predicted that embryonic stem cells will rebuild damaged and diseased brains and hearts. These cells, once physicians can effectively harness them, will mend broken spines. They will cause the paraplegic to walk and the blind to see. People will no longer need fear the neurological diseases named for Alzheimer and Parkinson. Other biologists have hailed Thompson's 1998 breakthrough as the seminal event in a life sciences revolution that will transform the world.

All of the above, or little of it, may come to pass a result of Thomson's work. As this book is being written, in the first decade of the 21st century, stem cell therapy remains both experimental and controversial. There are clinical applications with promise, but none is accepted therapy or shown to be cost-effective. Yet this work, like stem cells themselves, appears so full of possibilities that it seems likely to become a linchpin of 21st-century medicine.

James Thomson's comments on the issue have been considerably less hyperbolic than the above predictions. Transplantation, he has said, may not be the most fruitful use of stem cells. Transplantation refers to therapies in which undifferentiated cells are—or will be—inserted into a patient with the intention of causing those cells to grow into tissues necessary to repair the damage done by disease or injury. Thomson has said that such uses may not be as important—especially not at first—as these cells' role in experimentation.

Through the culturing of stem cells, through learning to direct their differentiation, researchers will gain unprecedented access to living human cells. New heart medicines could be tested on actual human heart cells before going into a clinical trial. Medical researchers stand to learn about cellular metabolic processes that have thus far remained elusive. The biggest benefits may be in the knowledge afforded from cultured stem cells, from information they hold about how human tissues develop and fail to develop. There will undoubtedly be benefits applicable to obstetrics and gynecology, to the prevention of birth defects, and to many branches of cancer research.

If that is so, then the University of Wisconsin researcher's place in the history of biology is secure, even without stem cell transplantation.

Thomson caught the science bug early. Growing up in his native Oak Park, Illinois, he was struck by the pleasure his fourth-grade teacher took in talking about the work of visionary inventor Buckminster Fuller. An uncle who worked for NASA reveled in the fact that he was paid for doing what he loved. Such enthusiasm made the boy think of science as fun and rewarding. At his

Thomson consulted with medical ethicists before beginning experiments with human stem cells. (Jeff Miller/University of Wisconsin Board of Regents)

Oak Park high school, Thomson's enthusiasm and intelligence translated into academic achievement. He was both a National Merit Scholar and winner of the Illinois General Assembly Award for gifted teens.

Thomson studied biology at the University of Illinois, where he qualified for a program in which a handful of outstanding undergraduates got their own private laboratories. He worked with plant geneticist Fred Meins (1942–) and became hooked on the study of how a single cell gives rise to a complex organism. After graduating Phi Beta Kappa with a bachelor's degree in biophysics, Thomson left Urbana for a veterinary medical science training program at the University of Pennsylvania. The program sent him for some hands-on vet experience at the San Diego Zoo. In southern California, he also learned hang gliding, still a favorite hobby.

Thomson received a doctorate in veterinary medicine in 1985, followed by a second doctorate in molecular biology in 1988. For his Ph.D. thesis, he probed genetic imprinting in early mammalian development.

Most other biologists working to isolate and culture stem cells, people such as John Gearhart at Johns Hopkins, were using mice as a research subject. Wanting an animal model that more closely mirrored the biology of human beings, Thomson at the University of Wisconsin worked with the embryonic cells of *M. mulatta*. His 1995 success with the monkey embryonic stem cells climaxed four years of research. In 1996, his team isolated and cultured embryonic stem cells from another species of monkey, the common marmoset (*Callithrix jacchus*) of South America. The breakthrough with human cells came two years later.

The Wisconsin Alumni Research Foundation holds six separate patents with Thomson listed as inventor—all related to stem cell research. (A patent on stem cells covers both the method for isolating a stem cell line and the cell lines so derived.) The patent for primate stem cells is licensed to the U.S. government, which funded that research through the National Science Foundation. Geron, the company that partially funded the human embryonic stem cell research holds a license to some of the cell lines.

In the early years of the 21st century, Thomson was supervising researchers working to make cultured human stem cells differentiate into four different types of adult cells—neurons, heart cells, pancreas cells, and blood cells.

Logic might say that a scientist who would engage in a controversial field of research—experiments that begin with frozen human embryos—would be the kind of person who thrives on confrontation, who plunges joyfully into battle. Logic would be incorrect in the case of Thomson. He does not seek attention or trumpet his views. When he set himself up in an off-campus laboratory at the beginning of his work involving human cells, seeking to spare the University of Wisconsin from any funding repercussions, he did it quietly, virtually in secret.

Tall and fit, balding and looking a bit rumpled, whether on his way to the lab or testifying before a U.S. Senate committee, Thomson rarely seeks attention. In 2001, on the morning after President George W. Bush (1946–) announced a new federal policy on the funding of embryonic stem cell research, Thomson knew he would be swamped with media calls for comment. Instead of showing up on campus—he is both a university professor of anatomy and chief pathologist at the Wisconsin Regional Center for Primate Research—he made himself scarce. Thomson took off for a few hours of hang gliding amid gentle hills outside of Madison. (He also enjoys hiking, canoeing, and cross-country skiing.)

Thomson was not indifferent to the president's announcement. He had taken the trouble to watch Bush's speech on television, which required going over to his neighbor's house. Thomson, who lives in Madison with his wife and two young children,

(continues)

(continued)

does not own a television set. He has explained that he and his wife, also a scientist, are not interested in watching (although they do watch movie DVDs on the computer), and they would rather their children do other things.

Bush announced a policy limiting federal funding to research using established lines of embryonic stem cells. Research using cell lines newly cultured from human embryos was not eligible for funds.

One problem with this policy, Thomson has said, is that cells grown in culture develop mutations. The greater number of generations removed from the blastocyst where they originated, the more likely they are to have mutated in ways that could make them, not just unsuitable, but perhaps dangerous, for transplantation into human patients. Since isolating earlier stem cell lines—the existing lines to which the president referred—Thomson and colleagues have made improvements in stem cell culturing, improvements that will make the new cell lines more suitable for research and safer for transplantation.

Thomson's original patented method for growing embryonic stem cells in vitro used a feeder layer of mouse cells that helped the human cells get the nutrients they needed. The use of animal cells raises the danger of introducing a virus into the embryonic stem cells. Such viruses, crossing a species barrier, might be especially dangerous to a patient.

Although Thomson has been extraordinarily careful in working around the moral, ethical, and political controversy that accompanies using cells from human embryos—even unwanted human embryos—he cannot avoid the objections of antiabortion activists and conservative religious leaders. To many, a human embryo is a human being—even when it is a frozen mass of 50 cells destined never to be implanted in a womb but instead to be discarded. They reason that it must not be violated. Many of those who decry Thomson's line of research also object to the work of fertility clinics and to in vitro fertilization in general.

In 2003, the Royal Swedish Academy of Sciences awarded Woese the Crafoord Prize in his discovery of a third domain of life. Established in 1980, there is only one Crafoord Prize per year. It goes to a scientist chosen from among the fields of mathematics, astronomy, geosciences, and biosciences—areas not directly honored by the Nobel Prizes. (The Royal Swedish Academy also selects Nobel winners in the fields of physics and chemistry.)

Further Reading

Academy of Achievement. "Interview with John D. Gearhart, Ph.D." Available online. URL: http://www.achievement.org/autodoc/page/gea0int1. Accessed March 11, 2006. Scientist discusses his career and path to stem cell breakthrough.

BBC News. "Dolly the Sheep Clone Dies Young." February 14, 2003. Available online. URL: http://news.bbc.co.uk/1/hi/sci/tech/2764069.stm. Accessed March 11, 2006. News account of passing of first mammal cloned from adult somatic cell.

Such objections, Thomson has said, may become irrelevant as this branch of research progresses. Most researchers and writers who predict revolutionary medical benefits from stem cell research have concentrated on embryonic stem cells because of their celebrated pluripotency. Yet the work of Ian Wilmut and Keith Campbell, Thomson has pointed out, show that supposedly unipotent or multipotent cells contain all the information needed to make a new organism. If the Roslin researchers could produce a lamb from the nucleus of a mammary gland cell, then it is reasonable to assume that the DNA in any human cell can serve as template for human heart tissue, neural tissue, or a new human being.

It also may prove practical to harvest useful embryonic stem cells without harming an embryo. This possibility arose in 2005 when a team of researchers in Massachusetts announced that they had begun a stem cell line using a single cell taken from the early embryo of a mouse. In August of the following year, the team—at Advanced Cell Technology (ACT) in Worcester—announced that they had accomplished the same with a human embryo. Working with leftover embryos from a fertility clinic, the researchers used a technique normally employed for early diagnosis of genetic disorders to remove a cell. When used to diagnose potential problems, the technique has been found safe for the developing embryo. The ACT team was able to culture a viable stem cell line from a *blastomere* taken this way. Team leader Bob Lanza expressed hope that the experimental technique, if it is shown to be practical and safe, may be accepted by many critics who object to conventional embryonic stem cell research. Yet progress in other areas of stem cell research may someday yield techniques that will supersede even this nondestructive method of harvesting embryonic cells.

Thomson considers it possible that the isolation and culturing of adult stem cells, or even of fully differentiated somatic cells, may someday hold all the promise that optimists at the turn of the 21st century attributed to embryonic stem cells. Whatever the future course of such research and the therapies they reap, James Thomson will have paved the way.

Boyle, Alan. "Stem Cell Pioneer Does a Reality Check." MSNBC.com, June 25, 2005. Available online. URL: http://www.msnbc.msn.com/id/8303756. Accessed March 11, 2006. Interview with James A. Thomson.

Briggs, R., and T. J. King. "Transplantation of Living Nuclei from Blastula Cells into Enucleated Frogs' Eggs." *Proceedings of the National Academy of Science* 38, no. 5 (May 1952): 455–463. Available online. URL: http://www.pnas.org/misc/BriggsKing.pdf. Accessed February 25, 2006. Paper describes early breakthrough in experimental cloning.

Elmer-Dewitt, Philip, David Bjerklie, Ann Blackman, Jeanne McDowell, and J. Madeleine Nash. "Cloning: Where Do We Draw the Line?" *Time*, 8 November 1993, pp. 65–70. Available online. URL: http://www.well.com/~ped/clips/Cloning_Cover_11.8.93.txt. Accessed March 11, 2006. Discussion of issues—ethical, scientific, and moral—surrounding human cloning.

Golden, Frederick. "America's Best: Stem Winder." *Time*, August 20, 2001, pp. 35–41. Available online. URL: http://www.cnn.com/SPECIALS/2001/americasbest/science.medicine/pro.jthomson.html.

Accessed March 11, 2006. Article about James A. Thomson and his embryonic stem cell research.

Graham, David E., Ross Overbeek, Gary J. Olsen, and Carl R. Woese. "An Archaeal Genomic Signature." *Proceedings of the National Academy of Sciences* 97, no. 7 (March 14, 2000): 3,304–3,308. Available online. URL: http://www.pnas.org/cgi/content/full/97/7/3304. Accessed March 11, 2006. Woese and colleagues discuss protein-encoding genes common to diverse members of biological domain.

Hazen, Robert. *Genesis: The Scientific Quest for Life's Origin.* Washington, D.C.: Joseph Henry Press, 2005. Author discusses research seeking pre-cellular precursor to living things.

Houdebine, Louis-Marie. *Animal Transgenesis and Cloning.* Hoboken, N.J.: John Wiley, 2003. Author discusses work of Roslin researchers and peers producing genetically modified animals.

Liu, Shi V., Jizhang Zhou, Chuanlun Zhang, David R. Cole, M. Gajdarziska-Josifovska, and Tommy J. Phelps. "Thermophilic Fe(III)-Reducing Bacteria from the Deep Subsurface: The Evolutionary Implications." *Science* 277 (August 22, 1997): 1,106–1,109. Paper discussing types of Archaea and where domain fits in phylogeny.

Love, Jamie L. "The Cloning of Dolly." Available online. URL: http://www.synapses.co.uk/science/clone.html. Accessed March 11, 2006. Accessible online resource explaining mammal cloning breakthrough.

Martineau, Belinda. *First Fruit: The Creation of the Flavr Savr Tomato and the Birth of Biotech Foods.* New York: McGraw-Hill, 2001. Author traces story of company's effort to grow and market good-tasting yet firm-fleshed tomato.

Morell, Virginia. "Life's Last Domain." *Science* 273, no. 5278 (August 23, 1996): 1,043–1,045. Science writer Morell's news commentary upon the occasion of researchers sequencing genome of *M. jannaschii.*

Nuclear Transfer: A Brief History. The Roslin Institute. Available online. URL: http://www.roslin.ac.uk/public/01-03-98-nt.html. Accessed March 11, 2006. Roslin Institute offers online information about history of cloning procedure.

Pennisi, Elizabeth. "Evolution: Genome Data Shake Tree of Life." *Science* 280, no. 5364 (May 1, 1998): 672. Article looks at surprise links between morphologically unlike species, as revealed by Human Genome Project data.

Ridley, Matt. *Genome:The Autobiography of a Species in 23 Chapters.* New York: HarperCollins, 1999. Lively look at growing body of information about the human genome and what it means, focusing on attitudes, social implications, and specific genes linked to traits, talents, and susceptibility to disease.

Shamblott, Michael J., Joyce Axelman, Shunping Wang, Elizabeth M. Bugg, John W. Littlefield, et al. "Derivation of Pluripotent Stem Cells from Cultured Human Primordial Germ Cells." *Proceedings of the National Academy of Sciences* 23 (November 10, 1998): 13,726–

13,731. Available online. URL: http://www.pnas.org/cgi/content/abstract/95/23/13726. Accessed March 11, 2006. Gearhart's team at Johns Hopkins announces isolation and culture of stem cells from embryonic germ cells.

Shreeve, James. *The Genome War: How Craig Venter Tried to Capture the Code of Life and Save the World.* New York: Knopf, 2004. Popular science writer Shreeve finds drama in story of race to finish sequencing the human genome.

Thomson, James A., Joseph Itskovitz-Eldor, Sander S. Shapiro, Michelle A. Waknitz, Jennifer J. Swiergiel, et al. "Embryonic Stem Cell Lines Derived from Human Blastocysts." *Science* 282, no. 5391 (November 6, 1998): 1,145–1,147. Available online. URL: http://www.sciencemag.org/cgi/content/full/282/5391/1145?ijkey=V5hrpPBq8DXdw. Accessed March 11, 2006. Announcement of first isolation and culture of human embryonic stem cells.

Travis, John. "Third Branch of Life Bares Its Genes." *Science News.* August 24, 1996. Available online. URL: http://www.sciencenews.org/pages/sn_arch/8_24_96/fob1.htm. Accessed March 9, 2006. News story on sequencing of *M. jannaschii* genome.

Walgate, Robert. "John Clark Dies." *Scientist* 5, no. 1 (August 26, 2004): 3. Available online. URL: http://www.the-scientist.com/news/20040826/03. Accessed March 11, 2006. Obituary and news analysis on passing of scientist who produced first transgenic sheep.

Whitaker, Leslie. "James Thompson and the Holy Grail." *Pennsylvania Gazette.* Available online. URL: http://www.upenn.edu/gazette/0102/whitaker.html. Accessed October 12, 2006. Online feature about human stem cell pioneer.

Wilmut, Ian. "Cloning for Medicine." Islamic Medical Center. Available online. URL: http://www.islamset.com/healnews/cloning/wilmut.html. Accessed March 11, 2006. Scientist who produced Dolly the cloned sheep discusses implications for medicine.

———. *The Second Creation: Dolly and the Age of Biological Control.* New York: Farrar, Straus & Giroux, 2000. Wilmut's book about the making of the first mammal clone derived from an adult somatic cell.

Woese, Carl R. "Interpreting the Universal Phylogenetic Tree." *Proceedings of the National Academy of Sciences* 97, no. 15 (July 18, 2000): 8,392–8,396. Available online. URL: http://www.pnas.org/cgi/content/full/97/15/8392. Accessed March 11, 2006. Authority on Archaea discusses horizontal gene sharing among primitive life and implications in terms of evolution.

———. "The Universal Ancestor." *Proceedings of the National Academy of Sciences* 95, no. 12 (June 9, 1998): 6,854–6,859. Available online. URL: http://www.pnas.org/cgi/content/full/95/12/6854. Accessed March 9, 2006. Woese lays out his ideas about genetic function and mutation rate in the earliest living beings.

11 *2001–2100:* What Is to Be Done?

The astonishing course of biological research in the 20th century offers many great promises for the future and just as many cautions. Prominent among the latter should be the simple admonition that life (in more than one sense of the word) is always more complex than it appears and that biological processes often prove to be even more intricate than what dedicated scientists formerly believed, sometimes what they believed even after long years of observation and experimentation.

The science of genetics once involved tracing neat rules that pea plants seemed to follow as they passed on physical traits—height, seed color and texture—to their progeny. An understanding of those rules proved hugely useful but ultimately too simplistic. Researchers had to dig deeper, to gain a view of the more complicated cellular and molecular functions that both lay at the root of Gregor Mendel's carefully recorded patterns and sometimes defied them. Genes used to be thought of as strung along a chromosome like pearls on a necklace—in fixed order. Again, a helpful and illuminating concept proved less than complete. It was assumed that every dominant gene expressed itself uniformly in an organism's phenotype. Not so, it turned out; there was more to it.

Animals and plants, organisms and their environments, bacteria and viruses, nuclei and organelles, nucleic acids and proteins—all have come into far-sharper focus through the work of biological researchers, and all have proved more surprising and less predictable than those who studied them used to think.

Recombinant DNA technology, it was expected in 1970s, would rapidly remake the world. Humankind had come within reach of medical cures previously undreamed of, agricultural miracles without precedent. Researchers had found a biotechnological arsenal with which Huntington's chorea, a genetic disorder, and famine, an economic-agricultural disaster, along with myriad other diseases and tragedies, could be resoundingly defeated. Science had learned the secret of reshaping organisms—microbes, food crops, livestock, and people—at the molecular level. Only the details, not to mention the ethics, remained to be worked out.

In the early 21st century, Huntington's disease and famine still kill their victims slowly and painfully. African children still go blind from vitamin deficiency. Heart disease and diabetes plague the overfed. Cancers, though far better understood and more successfully treated than they were decades ago, continue to disable and kill. The Earth's species are becoming extinct at an alarming rate. AIDS ravages the third world.

What happened to recombinant DNA technology? A great deal happened to it—decades of further research, applications, progress, and setbacks. After successes and failures, this work has by no means reached its conclusion. Yes, the research has encountered complications. Given the history of biological study, these ought to be expected. It has also met fierce and determined opposition on religious and philosophical grounds. To adherents, recombinant DNA research and invention remains incredibly promising. To its critics, it remains dangerous or, as some would have it, an abomination against the natural order.

More recently, stem cell research has been touted as the miracle cure of the future. Yet no less an authority than James Thomson, the pioneer of embryonic stem cells, has advised against jumping to hyperbole. Medicine may gain miraculous cures based on this line of scientific inquiry. Such cures may come very soon, but neither Thomson nor anyone else can guarantee a time of arrival. There are many hurdles yet to overcome—scientific, procedural, political, economic, and ethical.

The life sciences came so far in the 20th century that the imagination is challenged at the thought of equivalent progress by the end of the 21st century. In 1901, biologists were learning about the behavior of hereditary factors—the units later called genes—but had no idea what these units were or how they actually functioned. The very idea that hereditary factors resided within or upon chromosomes gained credence only slowly. By mid-century, biologists had learned to use analytical tools and methods borrowed from chemistry and physics. Thus equipped, they identified the molecular carrier of life's code and learned its structure. In subsequent decades, scientists cracked the code and even became able to write bits of it. What once had been viewed as a divine force, beyond the ken of science, was dissected, disassembled, reassembled, and rearranged.

A century ago, no one could envision DNA-based technology. No one imagined the intricacies that lay within living cells. No one could have glimpsed a future in which it was possible to produce a clone from an adult sheep, cat, or cow. Even if such a future were conceivable, the method for pulling off the biotechnological stunt lay far out of sight. How can 21st-century biology travel such an immense distance again? What mysteries remain? The answer to the first question is that even the most forward-looking of scientists do not know how, but history says that—barring a new Dark Ages—great leaps of knowledge and technology lie ahead. As for the second question, it would seem that every discovery within the biosciences opens up new realms of inquiry. Perhaps that always will be so.

Medicine and Public Health in a Global Village

The topics of medical research and its benefits have been touched upon only lightly in this volume—as with the discovery and development of the first antibiotics in chapters 3 and 4. Yet most of the advances in the biological sciences through the past century have had some application to the practice of medicine. The tremendous gains in knowledge and technology over the course of the last century and into this one have improved vastly the ability of physicians to prevent, diagnose, treat, and even cure an array of ailments far more numerous than had even been cataloged by their professional forbears.

Examples of the medical future coming to be can be found in the rapid development of long-awaited anticancer drugs. In June 2006, the U.S. Food and Drug Administration approved Gardasil, a vaccine against the human papilloma virus, strains of which have been shown to cause most cases of deadly cervical cancer. Meanwhile, other researchers are testing cancer vaccines aimed at getting the body to attack cancer cells themselves. Such treatments—rooted in science's greatly improved understanding of autoimmune response and the biochemical processes within cells—may soon dramatically lower incidences of many types of cancer and cure patients without subjecting them to the rigors of chemotherapy or radiation therapy.

News media announce a medical breakthrough every few weeks—a pace that likely will increase over the decades to come. Yet even with miraculous drugs and therapies, the practice of medicine will always involve the vagaries of human behavior and individual choices. Although physicians delve directly into human biology, certain aspects of their work have always been as much art as science. The science part has made incredible gains. Science will continue to master the mysteries of health and illness, but it is improbable that science will ever completely eliminate the need for canny, even somewhat intuitive, practitioners.

The realm of public health—preventing and tracking the spread of disease through large populations—has also gained significant new tools over the century past and is likely to grow vastly in sophistication in the future. Yet again, it is a field involving human variables. Human motivations, interactions, impulses, and so on are subject to much systematic study by scientists that include biological researchers—those that delve into the mechanisms of the brain and behavior, for example—but that also include anthropologists, sociologists, and economists. The biosciences make up the most obvious and most important part of public health work, but they do not comprise the entire field. Public health administration is a pursuit far more akin to politics than to laboratory research. That fact also will not change over the century ahead.

Late in 2002, a virulent and unidentified influenza-like illness broke out among rural residents of Guangdong Province, China. It quickly infected more than 300 people there, causing pneumonia in many and

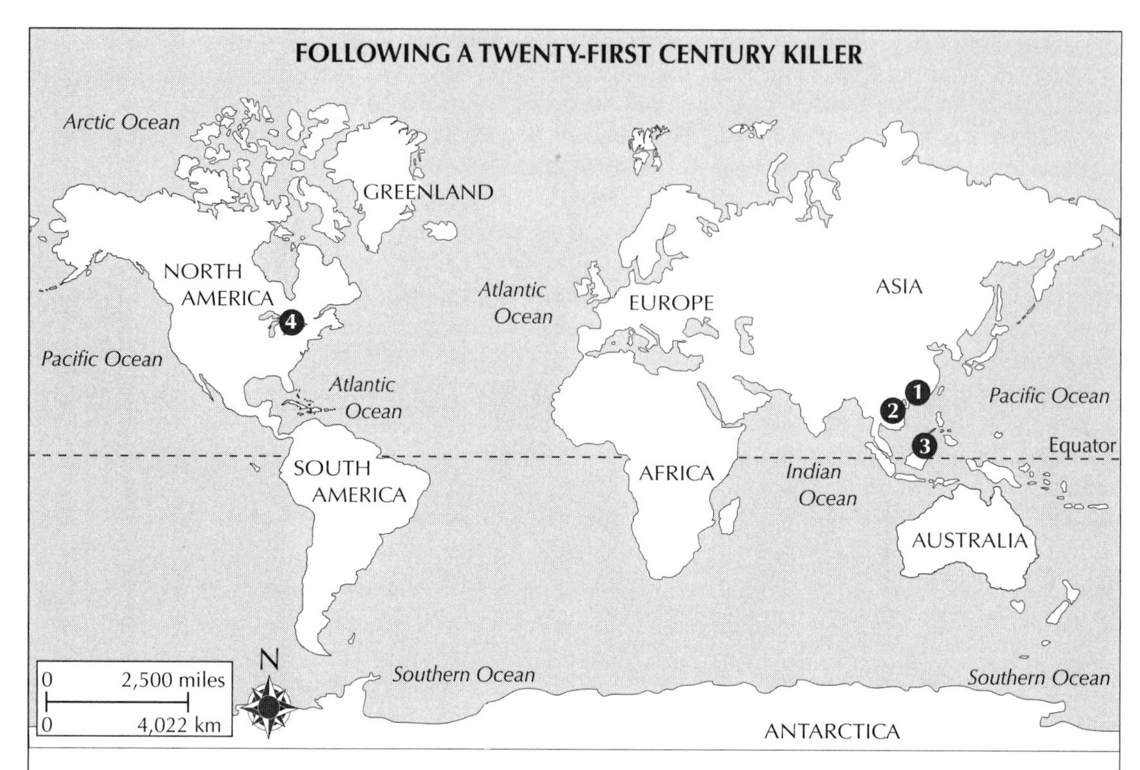

1. A doctor treats a SARS patient in Guangdong Province, China, then travels to Hong Kong, China, and stays on the 9th floor of a hotel.
2. SARS is passed to a 9th floor guest, a businessman who then flies to Vietnam.
3. SARS is passed to a 9th floor guest, a flight attendant who then flies to Singapore.
4. SARS is passed to a 9th floor guest, a tourist who then flies home to Toronto, Canada.

The rapid spread of SARS illustrated how quickly a disease can be widely disseminated in the 21st century. It put public health responses in several countries to the test.

killing five. Then the same infection appeared in the heavily populated island city of Hong Kong. With startling rapidity, it spread to Vietnam, Singapore, and Canada, as well as through mainland China.

Although it behaved like a virus, the *pathogen* was no virus previously identified. Existing antiviral drugs proved ineffective against it. Yet no bacterial source of infection could be found and antibiotic treatments also failed.

The World Health Organization took the unprecedented step of issuing a worldwide alert. Named severe acute respiratory syndrome (SARS), the illness soon had been identified in more than 20 countries on six continents. Unheard of in October 2002, SARS was a pandemic by the spring of 2003. Yet it was brought under control by midsummer of that year, after having struck more than 8,000 people and having killed nearly 10 percent of them.

The SARS crisis illustrates how quickly an infectious disease can spread in an age of frequent, easy, international jet travel. It also illustrates how quickly physicians, epidemiology researchers, and public health agencies can respond. SARS, some alarmists declared, had the potential to become a pandemic on the scale of the deadly 1918 influenza disaster, which killed at least 20 million. SARS killed fewer than 800 worldwide.

Separated by eight decades, they were entirely different diseases; to compare them is to compare an apple to a kumquat. Yet they were both worldwide viral pandemics. Research tools in the 21st century—far beyond anything available during World War I—helped greatly in understanding SARS and its spread and in tracing its origins. Researchers quickly isolated the SARS virus, finding it to be a *coronavirus* related to those that cause other respiratory and gastrointestinal diseases but different from any previously cataloged. Some of the same scientists who had been working on the Human Genome Project were able to sequence this coronavirus's single-strand RNA genome quickly—not over a span of years, but weeks. Epidemiologists traced its likely source to the meat of two mammal species—the raccoon dog (*Nyctereutes procyonoides*) and the masked palm civet (*Paguma larvata*)—sold at food markets in Guangzhou, China, capital of the province. In other words, SARS is most likely a virus of other mammals that crossed a species barrier after being consumed by human beings. The pandemic began as the coronavirus mutated and became transmissible from human to human through coughing and sneezing.

A doctor who had treated some of the original victims in Guangdong contracted the disease and unwittingly spread it to Hong Kong. There, he interacted with other travelers who flew to Singapore, Hanoi, and Toronto, taking SARS with them.

Yet, for all this knowledge, science failed to produce a vaccine against SARS. A coronavirus is difficult to culture in a laboratory. Like the *rhinoviruses* that cause most common colds, it mutates rapidly, making it especially difficult for immunologists to defend against. Public health officials' best weapons against the further spread of SARS were low-tech, time-honored tactics such as closing buildings, travel prohibitions, targeted quarantines, and public awareness. The SARS crisis illustrates the fact that virology and immunology still has some distance to travel.

In 2006, the World Health Authority and public health officials and researchers—many of them the same people who rose to the challenge of SARS—were tracking the progress of H5N1, a subtype of the avian influenza virus that is capable of infecting many species, including human beings. The fear was that the disease—widespread among birds but rare in humans—could mutate into a form transmissible from person to person.

As new viral threats arose, old ones remained formidable—some of them diseases for which there were already effective vaccines, but less than effective means for distributing and administering them to poor populations. Measles, nearly eliminated in the Western Hemisphere, still sickened millions yearly and killed hundreds of thousands of children in Africa. Polio, once nearly extinguished worldwide, saw an early 21st-century return in parts of Asia and Africa.

Clearly the obstacles to ridding humankind of deadly disease in the 21st century will be as much economic and political as immunological. Ignorance—always poverty's companion—also stands in the way. That fact is most painfully obvious in sub-Saharan Africa, where AIDS in the early 21st century had infected as many as one-third of the population of broad areas, including the countries of Zimbabwe, Swaziland, and Botswana. Many of those infected were not well informed enough to understand how to avoid contracting the HIV virus. Some—especially impoverished prostitutes—saw no economic alternative to the practices that spread AIDS, even when they knew about the risk.

Like SARS, AIDS originated as an infection spread to humans from wild animals. Researchers have linked HIV-1, the most common form of human immunodeficiency virus, to a simian immunodeficiency virus in apes. It may have crossed the species barrier through the African practice of hunting and butchering chimpanzees (*Pan troglodytes*) for food. Then, presumably, the virus mutated into a form transmissible between humans. A related human immunodeficiency virus, HIV-2, less common and found mostly in western Africa, may have followed a similar path by way of the blood of butchered African vervet monkeys (*Chlorocebus pygerythrus*).

Spread among humans largely by sexual contact, these fast-mutating viral infections were increasingly treatable early in this century, but the drugs required were extremely expensive, and AIDS was far from curable. The best tool against its further spread remained effective public information campaigns convincing people to avoid risky behavior and instructing them how to do so.

Genetic Modification and Cloning

In late 2005, a litter of five genetically modified and genetically identical piglets were born to a surrogate mother sow at a University of Missouri research facility in Columbia. What was modified about them was a kind of fat that their bodies produced and stored, a good kind often associated with salmon and tuna as well as flax seeds and other vegetable sources but rarely with the meat of four-legged beasts.

Swine are like human beings and mammals in general in that they cannot synthesize omega-3 fatty acids, which are essential nutrients and beneficial to health. To get them, genetically normal mammals need a nutritional source. The genetically modified piglets could make their own.

Employing techniques based on those that Wilmut and Campbell had used in bringing about the birth of Dolly, a large team of biologists, led by Jing X. Kang of Harvard Medical School, cloned the Missouri piglets from a cell nucleus taken from a sow that had been genetically altered to synthesize omega-3 fatty acids. To do this, they inserted a gene from the worm *C. elegans* into the genome of the sow. This gene is also found in algae and microorganisms. These beneficial fatty acids enter the aquatic food chain through algae and plankton, ending up in abundance in fatty fish. Before the work on pigs, Kang and his colleagues had successfully inserted the gene into mice.

The most obvious eventual use for pigs so modified would be as a source of pork and pork products containing these beneficial fatty acids. Yet as of early 2006, when Kang and collaborators announced their achievement, it was unlikely that anyone would soon be enjoying heart-healthy pork chops boasting all the omega-3 benefits now found in walnuts and lingonberries. These fatty acids, when people consume them in those sources or in fish, have been linked to a lower incidence of heart disease. Would the same be true if they were consumed in pork or bacon? The answer will come only after more research.

Besides the genetically modified pigs, Kang and colleagues were working on cows that could produce omega-3 fatty acids in their milk and chickens that could produce them in eggs. When will any of these products reach the supermarket? Not for quite some time, unless there are significant changes in the way genetically modified animals are viewed by consumers, watchdog groups, and public officials. As of March 2006, no genetically modified animal food product had yet been approved for human consumption by the U.S. Food and Drug Administration, and there appeared little chance that one would soon be approved. Some activists argue that even animals fed on genetically modified grains should not be used as food for people, saying they carry potential health risks that have not been adequately researched.

The piglets and others like them would certainly be used not as people food—not for many swine generations, anyway—but as research subjects. Scientists are interested in whether genetically altered meat, milk, and eggs can deliver the health benefits of fish and flax but they are also interested in whether the modified animals themselves benefit from the fatty acids their bodies can synthesize. If they do, is it possible that sometime within this century, doctors will be inserting such genes into humans to reduce the risk of cardiovascular disease?

Beyond the issue of genetic modification—widely seen as unproven—there is the issue of cloning. Cloning may well become a common way of replicating commercially desirable qualities in livestock—perhaps before the century is very old—but its methodology will have to overcome many reservations by ethicists, religious leaders, and the public at large before it will be accepted.

A central concern remains the prospect of human reproductive cloning—which many scientists and observers consider inevitable, despite widespread legislative bans against it. The ethical and moral issues surrounding this prospect involve deep-seated beliefs and provoke powerful emotions. The controversy will not be settled in a matter of years or even decades.

The Biosphere

Whether life on Earth is viewed from the molecular level up or from the planetary level down, 20th-century biological research established incontrovertibly that (to paraphrase John Donne) no organism is an island. Widely different living beings—from Archaea to elephants—are made of basically the same stuff. All life-forms share genetic mechanisms, nucleic acids, and many of the same genes. Further, all living things yet discovered share the same globe—its oceans, soil, minerals, and atmosphere. They feed upon each other and are fed upon. They support each other and are supported. They nurture one another and are nurtured—sometimes literally, as with various honey ant species (such as *Prenolepsis imparis*) that keep aphids as livestock or leafcutter ants (such as *Atta texana*) that cultivate fungus colonies for food. The fungus that those latter ants grow and feed (and feed upon) are unique to the insects' underground farms. They contribute nutrients not just to the ants but in turn to the surrounding soil—soil upon which microbes, worms, other insects, and burrowing mammals depend for shelter and sustenance.

Organisms live among, upon, and within one another. Any species—especially one at the bottom of a food chain—can prove indispensable to the health of an entire ecosystem. Every species within an ecosystem is not just a resident but an intrinsic part of that environment. "When one tugs at a single thing in nature," wrote John Muir, "he finds it attached to the rest of the world." The biological sciences have proved that notion profoundly correct many times over since the pioneering naturalist's death in 1914.

In the later part of the 20th century, new scientific disciplines arose to study the innumerable ways that living things and their environments affect one another within specific environments and in the biosphere at large. These studies have made it clear that the human species does not stand apart from all these interdependencies but is inextricably a part of them. Oxygen in the Earth's atmosphere is a by-product of photosynthesis—as in plants. Phytoplankton also gets energy by photosynthesis, thus charging the oceans with the life-giving gas.

By the first years of the present century, a great majority of scientists studying climate and atmosphere agreed that human activities—the discharge of gases such as carbon dioxide (a waste emission of energy-generating machines ranging from automobiles to coal-fired generators to fireplaces)—has been for many decades altering the balance of gases that sheathe the planet and that the process has in recent years accelerated. Agricultural practices that involve cutting down and burning great tracts of forest land, as in Brazil, result in both large emissions of hydrocarbon gases into the air and a large-scale reduction in plant life. Forests—especially the lush rain forests of the Tropics—with their abundant plant life, not to mention the cornucopia of animal life that the vegetation supports—have been shown to be like healthy oceans in that they play an important role in maintaining the planet's atmosphere.

These researchers also believe—and have shown strong evidence—that changes in the atmosphere are causing rapid changes in climate, bringing about an overall warming that can be seen melting glaciers many thousands of years old and reducing the ice cover of the Arctic Ocean.

How will these great changes, assuming they continue, affect living organisms? In countless ways, both obvious and subtle. If ocean levels rise significantly from glacier runoff, existing tidal pools and estuaries will be under deep saltwater, and their resident species will be dead or, where possible, relocated. Already, polar bears suffer and some are starving because the ice season—now drastically shortened in most winters—is their time to hunt and grow fat. A change of just a few degrees in temperature has been shown to be killing off coral in the Pacific Ocean and the Caribbean Sea, wreaking havoc among the diversity of marine life that lives on and around coral reefs. Many species will adapt and are adapting. Some migratory birds, for example, have been shown to be adjusting their seasonal habits and routes. Other species will go extinct; bringing about changes that biologists will note where they can but may not begin to understand for decades or even centuries.

Can the human species stop or reduce climate change and its impact? Should people try? Many environmentalists, as well as political leaders from virtually all the world's developed countries, believe that urgent attempts must be made to mitigate, if not reverse, damage to the environment. Some governmental programs of this type—restrictions on hydrocarbon emissions, financial incentives to industries that adopt cleaner sources of energy—have already been enacted under international agreements. Yet there are developed nations—notably the United States—that have been slow to acknowledge a problem and loathe to join with the world community in efforts to combat it.

As with other areas in which biological processes and biological knowledge affect human activities or are affected by them, science can do only so much. Again, the vagaries of human behavior—in this case politics, business competition, greed, stubbornness, pride, and complacency—figure into how, when, and whether the serious challenges of global climate change will be addressed.

In Search of Consensus

Ultimately, the biggest challenges that biologists will face in the future are sure to be cultural, political, ethical, and moral, rather than purely scientific. Barring a civilization-stunting disaster such as world war or environmental cataclysm, biological research is on track to make major advances in the decades ahead. Yet it is far from certain whether or how human society will choose to make use of much of the knowledge and many of the abilities gained. The bulk of what science reaps is sure to be accepted and celebrated, but other parts will be rejected, even outlawed.

In the mid-19th-century, Gregor Mendel—a monk in a garden—made discoveries that would decades later, well after his death, change the course of scientific history. He made these discoveries and even published his results while remaining essentially unknown, overlooked, unrecognized. Such a thing is not impossible in the 21st century, but it is extremely unlikely.

The biological sciences have long been competitive, as have other intellectual fields, but the level of competition is much more intense today, its pace much faster. Darwin published *On the Origin of Species* in 1859, 20 years after he first drafted his theory of evolution by natural selection. He might have waited even longer if it had not been for naturalist Alfred Russel Wallace (1823–1913), who had formulated a similar theory and begun writing about it in the 1850s. For all his hesitation about publishing such controversial ideas, it was important to Darwin to be first.

In the 21st century, no biologist is likely to spend two decades tweaking a theory before publishing it. Bioscience researchers are under pressure to produce, to generate grants and awards for their institutions of higher learning and—far more often since the biotech revolution—to beat other scientists to a commercial application. This heightened competition accelerates discovery and invention, but it also sometimes leads to mistakes and even to outright fraud. In March of 2006, Seoul National University fired stem cell scientist Hwang Woo Suk (1953–). Korean officials had a few weeks earlier revoked Hwang's research license after an investigative panel found that he had falsified data.

Hwang, of the university's veterinary college, reported in 2004 and 2005 that he had generated embryonic stem cells from human cells by a cloning process. His claims, hailed by stem cell research advocates as a step toward great medical cures and treatments, had been reported by news media worldwide. They had also drawn outraged condemnation from opponents of human cloning. As it turned out, the doctor and his colleagues had lied; they had cloned nothing and generated no stem cells at all. (Other researchers, meanwhile, continue to work on stem cells and their potential.)

Now, as never before, the findings of researchers are part of a wider human discourse. The Internet, the clashing ideologies facing off in real time on 24-hour news channels, the commercials for new pharmaceutical products, and the urgent environmental concerns—all of these 21st-century phenomena and more contribute to a world in which science and society are wrapped up in each other. Today technology—including biotechnology—shapes the economic course of communities and nations. Even more persistently than in past centuries, science constantly chal-

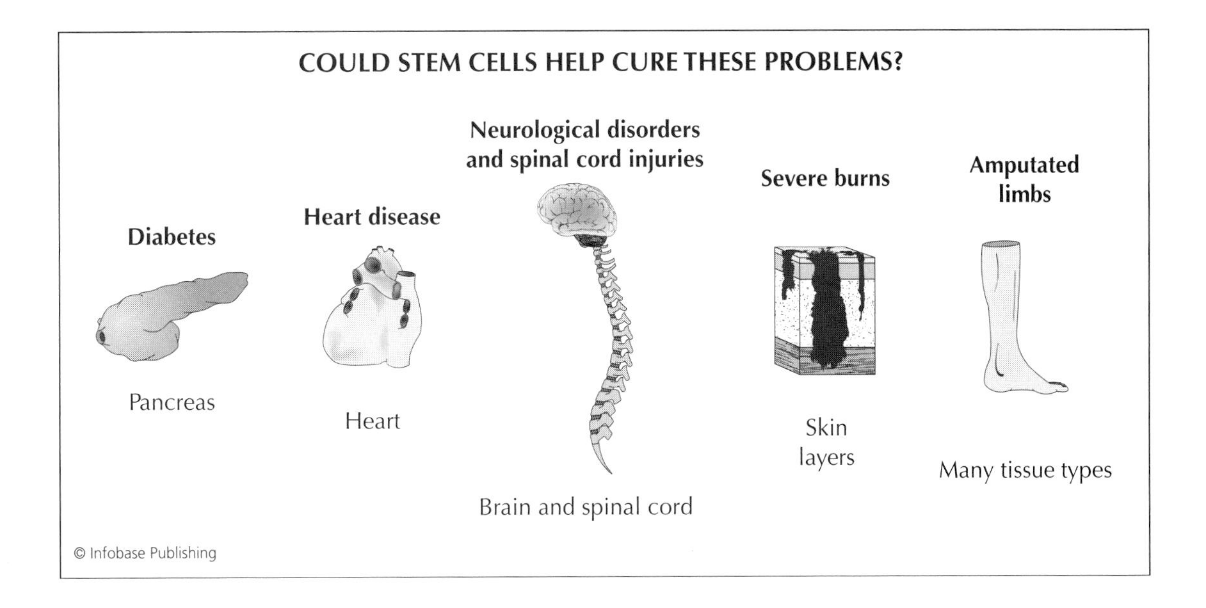

From stem cell research, medicine may achieve miraculous-seeming regeneration of tissues to treat or cure a wide range of injuries and diseases. James Thomson, a pioneering researcher in the field, has stressed that there are many problems yet to overcome.

lenges and reshapes core beliefs about the nature of reality, the nature of life, the very concept of human consciousness.

Scientific findings tend to upset the ideological status quo. People disagree. Belief systems collide. What people learn as fact and what they perceive often fail to align. Everybody knows that a full moon near the horizon looks much bigger than a full moon high overhead. Yet if one takes the scientific approach—simply holding a ruler at arm's length and measuring the moon as it appears in both positions—it proves to be the same size. Does the discovery yield disappointment or pleasure?

Once, much of humankind could be comfortable with the idea that the Earth stood immobile at the center of God's universe. Then, in the 16th century, the Polish astronomer Nicolaus Copernicus (1473–1543) showed that interplanetary reality was quite a different thing. Darwin's theory similarly knocked up against fiercely held beliefs. In Darwin's case, they were beliefs about how life had come to be on the planet, about what living things were and how they functioned, and, ultimately, about what it meant to be human. Darwinism—though a basic underpinning of virtually all biological inquiries since his time—continues to be challenged in the 21st century as unproven or as incomplete in that it does not acknowledge or require a divine creator.

Such challenges, based in faith, are not easily swept aside, nor should they be. Scientists can discover, publish, demonstrate, and influence, but they cannot order anyone to think one thing over another. Yet in the centuries since Copernicus, the notion that the Sun and other planets orbit the Earth has become quite rare. By far the majority of devoutly religious people in the 21st century see no contradiction between their faith and the scientifically established idea that the Earth orbits the Sun. It is also true that numerous people who are religiously faithful—many biological researchers among them—accept and embrace DNA science, with the incredible biochemical intricacies that have been discovered in and among the molecules of life. They value this knowledge, which illuminates the theory of evolution, of mutable, evolving life. Some even see these wonders as supportive of, rather than a challenge to their faith.

Still, the biological sciences at the end of the last century and into this one have marched up to, jostled, and even broken some societal, philosophical, and religious taboos. They will no doubt continue to stretch what society considers right, just, and normal. Even when they do not directly challenge or contradict traditional beliefs, there can be forces opposed to a line of research or its results for ancillary reasons.

For example, some U.S. religious leaders oppose any law requiring inoculation against cervical cancer. These leaders do not approve of the disease, which kills 4,000 American women every year. Yet neither do they believe it to be appropriate that 12-year-old girls be vaccinated to prevent contracting a sexually transmitted illness. Gardasil, the vaccine discussed earlier in this chapter, needs to be administered before a young woman begins having sexual intercourse. Public health advocates see pragmatic sense in requiring that the vaccine is administered around the onset of puberty, as a routine childhood inoculation. Certain conservative social critics object, noting that any such requirement would appear to sanction immoral behavior by underage girls. Some have even expressed the worry that in preventing one of the many health risks associated with promiscuity, medicine will remove a deterrent against such behavior. It may be very difficult for the two sides to find common ground.

One of the most disorienting aspects of 21st-century biology is the ability of neuroscientists to track the function of the mammalian brain—including that of human beings—so thoroughly that specific biochemical and biomechanical details can be linked to specific impulses, emotions, even thoughts. Physicians prescribe an astonishing and ever-growing array of pharmaceutical products that have been developed to correct neurochemical abnormalities. Pills bring equanimity to the stressed, cheer to the chronically depressed, and focus to children with attention deficit disorder. Yet among all the revelations of brain function and the ability to regulate it, some ask where, exactly, is the human self? Is each person, each personality, merely the sum of chemical and electrical interchanges in neural tissue? If so, what is consciousness? Is it a mere illusion? And what is an illusion but a neurological effect? By applying their mighty brain power to the subject of brain power, neurologists may be able to answer any and all such questions. Their answers, however, may always remain less than satisfactory. Human beings may never become comfortable with the idea that they are nothing but their corporeal bodies, as perceived by their corporeal minds. Perhaps they need not ever accept it. Maybe the idea will someday prove woefully incomplete, only part of a more complex bio-spiritual truth.

The sanctity of the human self, of human life, is so important to society at large that biologists must tread lightly when taking any action that presents a perceived threat to that sanctity. For some, any research or technology that harvests or manipulates a human embryo—no matter that it may be a tiny cluster of undifferentiated cells at the point harvested—will never be morally defensible. Thus, embryonic stem cell research will have opponents well into the future. In vitro fertilization, though a relatively common solution for couples who have trouble conceiving a child the traditional way, remains controversial in many quarters. The issue of cloning is of deep concern to many and not necessarily only on religious grounds. Even secular humanists have spoken out in fierce opposition to the prospect of cloned human beings.

As soon as it was technically viable to clone a kitten from a grown cat, commercial laboratories in the United States began offering—for a large fee—to duplicate a beloved pet. Presumably, a cat lover, guarding against the inevitability of Fluffy's demise, would want to make another Fluffy out of the nucleus of one of her cells. Critics point out that the cloned kitten will not necessarily be identical to its genetic source; there are variables such as gene expression and environment that will inevitably cause the two felines, though their DNA is identical, to be distinct individuals. Further, animal shelters are overflowing with unwanted cats. There is no shortage, no lack of selection. Still, as this book goes to press cats, have been and are being cloned for particular, and wealthy, owners.

If it is desirable to make a copy of a beloved pet, would it also be a good idea to clone a child? Once the technology has arrived, is it possible that some parents will bank away a few cell samples from their little boy or girl just in case something happens to him or her? Moralists, medical ethicists, religious leaders, and social critics today recoil at the idea. In the 21st century, a prevailing philosophy holds that each human individual is just that, an individual, special out of all the species. And for those that hold to a concept of a human soul—a spiritual element independent from physical reality—the cloned child could never be considered a true duplicate of the first; or could it?

If expediency were to win out over moral reservations in such cases, if it became viable and even somewhat acceptable to bank cellular insurance against the loss of a child, what else might be considered? Given enough egotism and enough money, might some human beings choose to clone themselves, to raise copies? Perhaps a woman possessed of high self-esteem might consider another like her a gift to the world. Perhaps a man might want to give his second self all the advantages that he was denied in his first childhood.

Those may be extreme possibilities, yet they are within the scope of what science will be capable of achieving. In addition to making human beings, genetic modification will present more and more opportunities to pre-shape human beings. If parents-to-be have the option of inserting a gene to make their baby resistant to a disease, less likely to develop addictions, taller, better-looking, blonde-haired, blue-eyed, will some of them opt for an engineered baby? No? What if the people down the block are doing it? What if the parents fear that theirs will be the only child in their socioeconomic class to need corrective lenses because they passed on the preemptive gene package offered by the obstetrician?

Again, there are many issues to work out. Will genetic modification of a human being be considered all right if it prevents a child from developing diabetes but not all right if its only purpose is to give her longer, thicker eyelashes? In athletics, how will the record books distinguish home runs hit by a genetically un-tampered-with batter from those hit by a man genetically engineered at conception to become a slugger? Who will draw such distinctions? Will they be legislated? If so, what will be the legal precedent? How will the laws be enforced?

The future of biology also presents ethical and philosophical problems apart from the direct application of biotechnology to the human genome. Given an intact DNA sample from an extinct animal, and a reasonably closely related species still living, it appears possible to bring back animals that died out long ago. The prospect of living dinosaurs, as in *Jurassic Park*, remains remote, because it is extremely unlikely that a viable DNA sample could have survived the 65 million years since such beasts walked. But there are more recent possibilities—the dodo bird, the passenger pigeon, perhaps even the mammoth and the mastodon. Yet even if scientists are able to do such things, should they? What are the ethical and moral issues? People wiped out the passenger pigeon; should people therefore bring it back?

In the case of huge mammals such as the mammoth (a reconstituted embryo of which could theoretically be implanted in an elephant mother), where would such a beast reside? Its Ice Age environment is long gone. Would it be created merely to live in a zoo or wild animal park? Is it ethical to revive a species simply to make it a curiosity or a research subject? What if it were possible to clone the extinct Neanderthal or *Homo habilis?*

On a broader level, how should the biological sciences respond to the state of the planet? Botanists, entomologists, and other naturalists urgently prowl endangered rain forests, seeking species yet unidentified. There may be plants with valuable medicinal properties that will be wiped out by deforestation before any scientist can discover the plant or its therapeutic value. Researchers rush to discover, catalog, perhaps even preserve valuable species. They work to measure rapid and alarming changes in habitat and the species-to-species domino effects that such changes tend to trigger over wide geographical regions.

Since trees and aquatic microbes—among many other organisms—help shape Earth's atmosphere, how far should genetic modification efforts be directed toward altering life-forms to help repair and regulate that atmosphere? Could such efforts backfire?

Again, the issues go far beyond what science is able to do and what science will soon be able to do. It is more important that people correctly decide what uses society ought to make of such incredible knowledge, what uses to make of the miraculous new abilities that biological research has wrought. Can the human brain—a mere organ within a mere organism—achieve the wisdom to make the right choices? Such considerations are certain to remain at the center of the dialogue between science and society for many decades to come.

Further Reading

Cocks, Tim. "U.S. Fears Measles Outbreak in Drought-Hit E. Africa." Reuters News Service. March 13, 2006. Available online. URL: http://www.nlm.nih.gov/medlineplus/news/fullstory_30915.html. Accessed March 30, 2006. Online news report on spread in Africa of illness no longer common in developed countries.

Eaton, Margaret L. *Ethics and the Business of Bioscience.* Stanford, Calif.: Stanford University Press, 2004. Author lays out issues of balancing safety and moral values against profit.

Fidler, David P. *SARS: Governance and the Globalization of Disease.* New York: Palgrave MacMillan, 2004. Examination of SARS crisis international implications for public health.

Finegold, David L., Cecile M. Bensimon, Abdallah S. Daar, Margaret L. Eaton, Beatrice Godard, et al. *Bioindustry Ethics.* Burlington, Mass.: Elsevier Academic Press, 2005. Serious forays into the 21st century's most pressing area of business ethics.

Fischman, Josh. "Sticking It to Cancer." *U.S. News and World Report,* 3 April 2006, pp. 56–63. News report on new anticancer vaccines.

Hockenberry, John, moderator. "Our Genes/Our Choices." Fred Friendly Seminars (video). American Museum of Natural History, 2004. Transcripts available online. URL: http://www.pbs.org/inthebalance/archives/ourgenes/transcripts.html. Accessed March 30, 2006. Panel discussion of issues medical, ethical, public, and personal surrounding new DNA technologies and therapies.

Kolata, Gina. "Cloning May Lead to Healthy Pork." *New York Times,* 27 March 2006, p. 1. Report on transgenic pigs able to synthesize omega-3 fatty acids, with reaction from scientists and nutritionists.

Liangxue, Lai, Jing X. Kang, Rongfeng Lil, Jingdong Wang, William T. Witt, et al. "Generation of Cloned Transgenic Pigs Rich in Omega-3 Fatty Acids." *Nature Biotechnology* 24, no. 4 (March 26, 2006): 435–436. Available online. URL: http://www.nature.com/nbt/journal/vaop/ncurrent/abs/nbt1198.html. Accessed March 27, 2006. Announcement of success in producing pigs able to synthesize essential fatty acid.

Omishu, Noramitsu. "In a Country That Craved Respect, Stem Cell Scientist Rode a Wave of Korean Pride." *New York Times*, 22 January 2006, p. 1. News analysis traces motive, national impact of researcher whose stem cell results proved to be fraudulent.

Smithsonian Institution. "Whatever Happened to Polio?" Available online. URL: http://americanhistory.si.edu/polio/poliotoday/expanded.htm. Accessed March 30, 2006. History of worldwide public health campaigns against infantile paralysis.

Specter, Michael. "Political Science: The Bush Administration's War on the Laboratory." *New Yorker*, 13 March 2006, pp. 58–69. In-depth news analysis about interests opposed to scientific research and their influence on the White House.

Wade, Nicholas, Cornelia Dean, and James Brooke. "Korean Scientist Said to Admit Fabrication in a Cloning Study." *New York Times*, 16 December 2005, p. 1. News report about falsified data in high-profile stem cell experiments.

Watson, James, David Baltimore, Francis Collins, Nancy Wexler, Matt Ridley, et al. "DNA Revolution—Future Visions." *Time*, 17 February 2003, pp. 60–61. Prominent thinkers in science make predictions about the course of 21st-century advances.

World Health Organization. Severe Acute Respiratory Syndrome (SARS). Available online. URL: http://www.who.int/csr/sars/en. Accessed March 30, 2006. United Nations agency traces history of worldwide public health emergency.

Nobel Prize Winners

There is no Nobel Prize category called "biology." All Nobel laureates who have won in the field of physiology or medicine have worked in areas of biology. Many scientists featured in this book won Nobel Prizes in another category. Breakthroughs in biological fields, especially molecular biology, have involved the work of organic chemists and even physicists whose contributions were directly applicable to the life sciences.

The Nobel Foundation Web site (http://nobelprize.org) provides full information, including biographies and Nobel Prize lectures for all laureates. The brief descriptions of the specific awards are quoted from pages on this site. This material is also available in book form, detailed at the end of this list.

In the Life Sciences: 1901–2000

Laureates have received the prize in physiology or medicine, except where another category is indicated.

1901

Emil Adolf von Behring (1854–1917), Germany. "For his work on serum therapy, especially its application against diphtheria, by which he has opened a new road in the domain of medical science and thereby placed in the hands of the physician a victorious weapon against illness and deaths."

1902

Ronald Ross (1857–1932), United Kingdom. "For his work on malaria, by which he has shown how it enters the organism and thereby has laid the foundation for successful research on this disease and methods of combating it."

Chemistry
Hermann Emil Fischer (1852–1919), Germany. "In recognition of the extraordinary services he has rendered by his work on sugar and purine syntheses."

1903

Niels Ryberg Finsen (1860–1904), Denmark. "In recognition of his contribution to the treatment of diseases, especially lupus vulgaris, with concentrated light radiation, whereby he has opened a new avenue for medical science."

1904

Ivan Petrovich Pavlov (1849–1936), Russia. "In recognition of his work on the physiology of digestion, through which knowledge on vital aspects of the subject has been transformed and enlarged."

1905

Robert Koch (1843–1910), Germany. "For his investigations and discoveries in relation to tuberculosis."

1906

Camillo Golgi (1843–1926), Italy, and Santiago Ramón y Cajal (1852–1934), Spain. "In recognition of their work on the structure of the nervous system."

1907

Charles Louis Alphonse Laveran (1845–1922), France. "In recognition of his work on the role played by protozoa in causing diseases."

Chemistry
Edouard Buchner (1860–1917), Germany. "For his biochemical researches and his discovery of cell-free fermentation."

1908

Ilya Ilyich Mechnikov (1845–1916), Russia, and Paul Ehrlich (1854–1915), Germany. "In recognition of their work on immunity."

1909

Emil Theodor Kocher (1841–1917), Switzerland. "For his work on the physiology, pathology and surgery of the thyroid gland."

1910

Albrecht Kossel (1853–1927), Germany. "In recognition of the contributions to our knowledge of cell chemistry made through his work on proteins, including the nucleic substances."

1911

Allvar Gullstrand (1862–1930), Sweden. "For his work on the dioptics of the eye."

1912

Alex Carrel (1873–1944), France. "In recognition of his work on vascular suture and the transplantation of blood vessels and organs."

1913

Charles Robert Richet (1850–1935), France. "In recognition of his work on anaphylaxis."

1914

Robert Bárány (1876–1936), Austria. "For his work on the physiology and pathology of the vestibular apparatus."

Physics
Max von Laue (1879–1960), Germany. "For his discovery of the diffraction of X-rays by crystal."

1915

The prize money for physiology or medicine was allocated to the Nobel Foundation special fund of this prize section.

Chemistry
Richard Willstätter (1872–1942), Germany. "For his researches on plant pigments, especially chlorophyll."

Physics
William Henry Bragg (1862–1942), United Kingdom, and William Lawrence Bragg (1890–1971), United Kingdom. "For their services in the analysis of crystal structure by means of X-rays."

1916

The prize money for physiology or medicine was allocated to the special fund of this prize section.

1917

The prize money for physiology or medicine was allocated to the special fund of this prize section.

1918

The prize money for physiology or medicine was allocated to the special fund of this prize section.

1919

Jules Bordet (1870–1961), Belgium. "For his discoveries relating to immunity."

1920

August Steenberg Krogh (1874–1949), Denmark. "For his discovery of the capillary motor regulating mechanism."

1921

The prize money for physiology or medicine was allocated to the special fund of this prize section.

1922

Archibald Vivian Hill (1886–1977), United Kingdom. "For his discovery relating to the production of heat in the muscle."

Otto Fritz Meyerhof (1884–1951), Germany. "For his discovery of the fixed relationship between the consumption of oxygen and the metabolism of lactic acid in the muscle."

1923

Frederick Grant Banting (1899–1941), Canada, and John James Richard Macleod (1876–1935), Canada. "For the discovery of insulin."

1924

Willem Einthoven (1860–1927), Netherlands. "For his discovery of the mechanism of the electrocardiogram."

1925

The prize money for physiology or medicine was allocated to the special fund of this prize section.

1926

Johannes Andreas Grib Fibiger (1867–1928), Denmark. "For his discovery of the Spiroptera carcinoma."

1927

Julius Wagner-Jauregg (1857–1940), Austria. "For his discovery of the therapeutic value of malaria inoculation in the treatment of dementia paralytica."

1928

Charles-Jules-Henri Nicolle (1866–1936), France. "For his work on typhus."

Chemistry
Adolph Otto Reinhold Windaus (1876–1959), Germany. "For his services rendered through his research into the constitution of the sterols and their connection with the vitamins."

1929

Christiaan Eijkman (1858–1930), Netherlands. "For his discovery of the antineuritic vitamin."

Frederick Gowland Hopkins (1861–1947), United Kingdom. "For his discovery of the growth-stimulating vitamins.

Chemistry
Arthur Harden (1865–1940), United Kingdom, and Hans Karl August Simon von Euler-Chelpin (1873–1964), Sweden. "For their investigations on the fermentation of sugar and fermentative enzymes."

1930

Karl Landsteiner (1868–1943), Austria. "For his discovery of the blood groups."

Chemistry
Hans Fischer (1881–1945), Germany. "For his researches into the constitution of haemin and chlorophyll and especially for the synthesis of haemin."

1931

Otto Heinrich Warburg (1883–1970), Germany. "For his discovery of the nature and mode of action of the respiratory enzyme."

1932

Charles Scott Sherrington (1857–1952), United Kingdom, and Edgar Douglas Adrian (1889–1977), United Kingdom. "For their discoveries regarding the functions of neurons."

1933

Thomas Hunt Morgan (1866–1935), United States. "For his discoveries concerning the role played by the chromosome in heredity."

1934

George Hoyt Whipple (1878–1976), United States, George Richards Minot (1885–1950), United States, and William Parry Murphy (1892–1987), United States. "For their discoveries concerning liver therapy in cases of anaemia."

1935

Hans Spemann (1869–1941), Germany. "For his discovery of the organizer effect in embryonic development."

1936

Henry Hallett Dale (1878–1968), United Kingdom, and Otto Loewi (1873–1961), Germany. "For their discoveries relating to chemical transmission of nerve impulses."

1937

Albert von Szent-Györgyi Nagyrapolt (1893–1986), Hungary. "For his discoveries in connection with the biological combustion processes, with special reference to vitamin C and the catalysis of fumaric acid."

Chemistry

Walter Norman Haworth (1883–1950), United Kingdom. "For his investigations on carbohydrates and vitamin C."

Paul Karrer (1889–1971), Switzerland. "For his investigations on carotenoids, flavins, and vitamins A and B2."

1938

Corneille Jean François Heymans (1892–1968), Belgium. "For the discovery of the role played by the sinus and aortic mechanisms in the regulation of respiration."

Chemistry

Richard Kuhn (1900–67), Germany. "For his work on carotenoids and vitamins."

1939

Gerhard Domagk (1895–1964), Germany. "For the discovery of the antibacterial effects of prontosil."

Chemistry
Adolf Friedrich Johann Butenandt (1903–95), Germany. "For his work on sex hormones."

Leopold Ruzicka (1887–1976), Switzerland. "For his work on polymethylenes and higher terpenes."

1940

One-third of the prize money for physiology or medicine was allocated to the Nobel Foundation main fund. The remaining two-thirds was allocated to the special fund of this prize section.

1941

One-third of the prize money for physiology or medicine was allocated to the main fund. The remaining two-thirds was allocated to the special fund of this prize section.

1942

One-third of the prize money for physiology or medicine was allocated to the main fund. The remaining two-thirds was allocated to the special fund of this prize section.

1943

Henrik Carl Peter Dam (1895–1976), Denmark. "For his discovery of vitamin K."

Edward Adelbert Doisy (1893–1986), United States. "For his discovery of the chemical nature of vitamin K."

1944

Joseph Erlanger (1874–1965), United States, and Herbert Spencer Gasser (1888–1963), United States. "For their discoveries relating to the highly differentiated functions of single nerve fibres."

1945

Alexander Fleming (1881–1955), United Kingdom, Ernst Boris Chain (1906–79), United Kingdom, and Howard Walter Florey (1898–1968), Australia. "For the discovery of penicillin and its curative effect in various infectious diseases."

Chemistry
Artturi Ilmari Virtanen (1895–1973), Finland. "For his research and inventions in agricultural and nutrition chemistry, especially for his fodder preservation method."

1946

Hermann Joseph Muller (1890–1967), United States. "For the discovery of the production of mutations by means of X-ray irradiation."

Chemistry
James Batcheller Sumner (1887–1955), United States. "For his discovery that enzymes can be crystallized."

John Howard Northrop (1891–1987), United States, and Wendell Meredith Stanley (1904–71), United States. "For their preparation of enzymes and virus proteins in pure form."

1947

Carl Ferdinand Cori (1896–1984), United States, and Gerty Theresa Cori, née Radnitz (1896–1957), United States. "For their discovery of the course of the catalytic conversion of glycogen."

Bernardo Alberto Houssay (1887–1971), Argentina. "For his discovery of the part played by the hormone of the anterior pituitary lobe in the metabolism of sugar."

Chemistry
Robert Robinson (1886–1975), United Kingdom. "For his investigations on plant products of biological importance, especially the alkaloids."

1948

Paul Hermann Müller (1899–1965), Switzerland. "For his discovery of the high efficiency of DDT as a contact poison against several arthropods."

1949

Walter Rudolf Hess (1895–1982), Switzerland. "For his discovery of the functional organization of the interbrain as a coordinator of the activities of the internal organs."

António Caetano de Abreu Freire Egas Moniz (1874–1955), Portugal. "For his discovery of the therapeutic value of leucotomy in certain psychoses."

1950

Edward Calvin Kendall (1886–1972), United States, Tadeus Reichstein (1897–1996), Switzerland, and Philip Showalter Hench (1896–1965), United States. "For their discoveries relating to the hormones of the adrenal cortex, their structure and biological effects."

1951

Max Theiler (1899–1972), South Africa. "For his discoveries concerning yellow fever and how to combat it."

1952

Selman Abraham Waksman (1888–1973), United States. "For his discovery of streptomycin, the first antibiotic effective against tuberculosis."

1953

Hans Adolf Krebs (1900–81), United Kingdom. "For his discovery of the citric acid cycle."

Fritz Albert Lipmann (1899–1986), United States. "For his discovery of co-enzyme A and its importance for intermediary metabolism."

1954

John Franklin Enders (1897–1985), United States, Thomas Huckle Weller (1915–), United States, and Frederick Chapman Robbins (1916–2003), United States. "For their discovery of the ability of poliomyelitis viruses to grow in cultures of various types of tissue."

Chemistry
Linus Carl Pauling (1901–94), United States. "For his research into the nature of the chemical bond and its application to the elucidation of the structure of complex substances."

1955

Axel Hugo Theodor Theorell (1903–82), Sweden. "For his discoveries concerning the nature and mode of action of oxidation enzymes."

Chemistry
Vincent du Vigneaud (1901–78), United States. "For his work on biochemically important sulfur compounds, especially for the first synthesis of a polypeptide hormone."

1956

André Frédéric Cournand (1895–1988), United States, Werner Forssmann (1904–79), Federal Republic of Germany, and Dickenson W. Richards (1895–1973), United States. "For their discoveries concerning heart catheterization and pathological changes in the circulatory system."

1957

Daniel Bovet (1907–92), Italy. "For his discoveries relating to synthetic compounds that inhibit the action of certain body substances, and especially their action on the vascular system and the skeletal muscles."

Chemistry
Alexander R. Todd (1907–97), United Kingdom. "For his work on nucleotides and nucleotide coenzymes."

1958

George Wells Beadle (1903–89), United States, and Edward Lawrie Tatum (1909–75), United States. "For their discovery that genes act by regulating definite chemical events."

Joshua Lederberg (1925–), United States. "For his discoveries concerning genetic recombination and the organization of the genetic material of bacteria."

Chemistry
Frederick Sanger (1918–), United Kingdom. "For his work on the structure of proteins, especially that of insulin."

1959

Severo Ochoa (1905–93), United States, and Arthur Kornberg (1918–), United States. "For their discovery of the mechanisms in the biological synthesis of ribonucleic acid and deoxyribonucleic acid."

1960

Frank Macfarlane Burnet (1889–1985), Australia, and Peter Brian Medawar (1915–87), United Kingdom. "For discovery of acquired immunological tolerance."

1961

Georg von Békésy (1899–1972), United States. "For his discoveries of the physical mechanism of stimulation within the cochlea."

Chemistry
Melvin Calvin (1911–97), United States. "For his research on the carbon dioxide assimilation in plants."

1962

Francis Harry Compton Crick (1916–2004), United Kingdom, James Dewey Watson (1928–), United States, and Maurice Hugh Frederick Wilkins (1916–2004), United Kingdom and New Zealand. "For their discoveries concerning the molecular structure of nucleic acids and its significance for information transfer in living material."

Chemistry
Max Ferdinand Perutz (1914–2002), United Kingdom, and John Cowdery Kendrew (1917–97), United Kingdom. "For their studies of the structures of globular proteins."

1963

John Carew Eccles (1903–97), Australia, Alan Lloyd Hodgkin (1914–98), United Kingdom, and Andrew Fielding Huxley (1917–), United Kingdom. "For their discoveries concerning the ionic mechanisms involved in excitation and inhibition in the peripheral and central portions of the nerve cell membrane."

1964

Konrad Bloch (1912–2000), United States, and Feodor Lynen (1911–79), Federal Republic of Germany. "For their discoveries concerning the mechanism and regulation of the cholesterol and fatty acid metabolism."

Chemistry
Dorothy Crowfoot Hodgkin (1910–94), United Kingdom. "For her determinations by X-ray techniques of the structures of important biochemical substances."

1965

François Jacob (1920–), France, André Lwoff (1902–94), France, and Jacques Monod (1910–76), France. "For their discoveries concerning genetic control of enzyme and virus synthesis."

Chemistry
Robert Burns Woodward (1917–79), United States. "For his outstanding achievements in the art of organic synthesis."

1966

Peyton Rous (1879–1970), United States. "For his discovery of tumor-inducing viruses."

Charles Brenton Huggins (1902–97), United States. "For his discoveries concerning hormonal treatment of prostatic cancer."

1967

Ragnar Granit (1900–91), Sweden, Haldan Keffer Hartline (1903–83), United States, and George Wald (1906–97), United Kingdom. "For their discoveries concerning the primary physiological and chemical visual processes in the eye."

1968

Robert W. Holley (1922–93), United States, Har Gobind Khorana (1922–), United States, and Marshall W. Nirenberg (1927–), United States. "For their interpretation of the genetic code and its function in protein synthesis."

1969

Max Delbrück (1906–81), United States, Alfred Hershey (1908–97), United States, and Salvador E. Luria (1912–91), United States. "For their discoveries concerning the replication mechanism and the genetic structure of viruses."

1970

Bernard Katz (1911–2003), United Kingdom, Ulf von Euler (1905–83), Sweden, and Julius Axelrod (1912–2004), United States. "For their discoveries concerning the humoral transmittors in the nerve terminals and the mechanism for their storage, release and inactivation."

Chemistry
Luis Leloir (1906–87), Argentina. "For his discovery of sugar nucleotides and their role in the biosynthesis of carbohydrates."

1971

Earl W. Sutherland, Jr. (1915–73), United States. "For his discoveries concerning the mechanisms of the action of hormones."

1972

Gerald M. Edelman (1929–), United States, and Rodney R. Porter (1917–85) United Kingdom. "For their discoveries concerning the chemical structure of antibodies."

Chemistry
Christian B. Anfinsen (1916–95), United States. "For his work on ribonuclease, especially concerning the connection between the amino acid sequence and the biologically active conformation."

Stanford Moore (1913–82), United States, and William H. Stein (1911–80), United States. "For their contribution to the understanding of the connection between chemical structure and catalytic activity of the active center of the ribonuclease molecule."

1973

Karl von Frisch (1886–1982), Federal Republic of Germany, Konrad Lorenz (1903–89), Austria, and Nikolaas Tinbergen (1907–88), United Kingdom. "For their discoveries concerning organization and elicitation of individual and social behaviour patterns."

1974

Albert Claude (1899–1983), Belgium, Christian de Duve (1917–), Belgium, and George E. Palade (1912–), United States. "For their discoveries concerning the structural and functional organization of the cell."

1975

David Baltimore (1938–), United States, Renato Dulbecco (1914–), United States, and Howard Martin Temin (1934–94), United States. "For their discoveries concerning the interaction between tumour viruses and the genetic material of the cell."

Chemistry
John Warcup Cornforth (1917–), Australia and United Kingdom. "For his work in the stereochemistry of enzyme-catalyzed reactions."

Vladimir Prelog (1906–98), Switzerland. "For his research into the stereochemistry of organic molecules and reactions."

1976

Baruch S. Blumberg (1925–), United States, and D. Carleton Gajdusek (1923–), United States. "For their discoveries concerning new mechanisms for the origin and dissemination of infectious diseases."

1977

Roger Guillemin (1924–), United States, and Andrew V. Schally (1926–), United States. "For their discoveries concerning the peptide hormone production of the brain."

Rosalyn Yalow (1921–), United States. "For the development of radioimmunoassays of peptide hormones."

1978

Werner Arber (1929–), Switzerland, Daniel Nathans (1928–99), United States, and Hamilton O. Smith (1931–), United States. "For the discovery of restriction enzymes and their application to problems of molecular genetics."

Chemistry
Peter D. Mitchell (1920–92), United Kingdom. "For his contribution to the understanding of biological energy transfer through the formulation of the chemiosmotic theory."

1979

Allan M. Cormack (1924–98), United States, and Godfrey N. Hounsfield (1919–2004), United Kingdom. "For the development of computer assisted tomography."

Chemistry
Herbert C. Brown (1912–2004), United States, and Georg Wittig (1897–1987), Federal Republic of Germany. "For their development of the use of boron- and phosphorus-containing compounds, respectively, into important reagents in organic synthesis."

1980

Baruj Benacerraf (1920–), United States, Jean Dausset (1916–), France, and George D. Snell (1903–96), United States. "For their discoveries concerning genetically determined structures on the cell surface that regulate immunological reactions."

Chemistry
Paul Berg (1926–), United States. "For his fundamental studies of the biochemistry of nucleic acids, with particular regard to recombinant-DNA."

Walter Gilbert (1932–), United States, and Frederick Sanger (1918–), United Kingdom. "For their contributions concerning the determination of base sequences in nucleic acids."

1981

Roger W. Sperry (1913–94), United States. "For his discoveries concerning the functional specialization of the cerebral hemispheres."

David H. Hubel (1926–), United States, and Torsten N. Wiesel (1924–), Sweden. "For their discoveries concerning information processing in the visual system."

1982

Sune K. Bergström (1916–2004), Sweden, Bengt I. Samuelsson (1934–), Sweden, and John R. Vane (1927–2004), United Kingdom. "For their discoveries concerning prostaglandins and related biologically active substances."

Chemistry
Aaron Klug (1926–), United Kingdom. "For his development of crystallographic electron microscopy and his structural elucidation of biologically-important nucleic acid-protein complexes."

1983

Barbara McClintock (1902–92), United States. "For her discovery of mobile genetic elements."

1984

Niels K. Jerne (1911–94), Denmark, Georges J. F. Köhler (1946–95), Federal Republic of Germany, and César Milstein (1927–2002), Argentina and United Kingdom. "For theories concerning the specificity in development and control of the immune system and the discovery of the principle for production of monoclonal antibodies."

1985

Michael S. Brown (1941–), United States, and Joseph L. Goldstein (1940–), United States. "For their discoveries concerning the regulation of cholesterol metabolism."

Chemistry

Herbert A. Hauptman (1917–), United States, and Jerome Karle (1918–), United States. "For their outstanding achievements in the development of direct methods for the determination of crystal structures."

1986

Stanley Cohen (1922–), United States, and Rita Levi-Montalcini (1909–), Italy and United States. "For their discoveries of growth factors."

1987

Susumu Tonegawa (1939–), Japan. "For his discovery of the genetic principle for generation of antibody diversity."

1988

James W. Black (1924–), United Kingdom, Gertrude B. Elion (1918–99), United States, and George H. Hitchings (1905–98), United States. "For their discoveries of important principles for drug treatment."

Chemistry

Johann Disenhofer (1943–), Federal Republic of Germany, Robert Huber (1937–), Federal Republic of Germany, and Hartmut Michel (1948–), Federal Republic of Germany. "For the determination of the three-dimensional structure of a photosynthetic reaction center."

1989

J. Michael Bishop (1936–), United States, and Harold E. Varmus (1939–), United States. "For their discovery of the cellular origin of retroviral oncogenes."

Chemistry

Sidney Altman (1939–), Canada and United States, and Thomas R. Cech (1947–), United States. "For their discovery of catalytic properties of RNA."

1990

Joseph E. Murray (1919–), United States, and E. Donnall Thomas (1920–), United States. "For their discoveries concerning organ and cell transplantation in the treatment of human disease."

1991

Erwin Neher (1944–), Federal Republic of Germany, and Richard R. Ernst (1942–), Switzerland. "For their discoveries concerning the function of single ion channels in cells."

1992

Edmond H. Fischer (1920–), Switzerland and United States, and Edwin G. Krebs (1918–), United States. "For their discoveries concerning reversible protein phosphorylation as a biological regulatory mechanism."

1993

Richard J. Roberts (1943–), United Kingdom, and Phillip A. Sharp (1944–), United States. "For their discoveries of split genes."

Chemistry
Kary B. Mullis (1944–), United States. "For his invention of the polymerase chain reaction (PCR) method."

Michael Smith (1932–2000), Canada. "For his fundamental contributions to the establishment of oligonucleotide-based, site-directed mutagenesis and its development for protein studies."

1994

Alfred G. Gilman (1941–), United States, and Martin Rodbell (1925–98), United States. "For their discovery of G-proteins and the role of these proteins in signal transduction in cells."

1995

Edward B. Lewis (1918–2004), United States, Christiane Nüsslein-Volhard (1942–), Federal Republic of Germany, and Eric F. Wieschaus (1947–), United States. "For their discoveries concerning the genetic control of early embryonic development."

1996

Peter C. Doherty (1940–), Australia, Rolf M. Zinkernagel (1944–), Switzerland. "For their discoveries concerning the specificity of the cell mediated immune defence."

1997

Stanley B. Prusiner (1942–), United States. "For his discovery of Prions—a new biological principle of infection."

Chemistry

Paul D. Boyer (1918–), United States, and John E. Walker (1941–), United Kingdom. "For their elucidation of the enzymatic mechanism underlying the synthesis of adenosine triphosphate (ATP)."

Jens C. Skou (1918–), Denmark. "For the first discovery of an ion-transporting enzyme, Na^+,K^+-ATPase."

1998

Robert F. Furchgott (1916–), United States, Louis J. Ignarro (1941–), United States, and Ferid Murad (1936–), United States. "For their discoveries concerning nitric oxide as a signaling molecule in the cardiovascular system."

2000

Günter Blobel (1936–), United States. "For the discovery that proteins have intrinsic signals that govern their transport and localization in the cell."

Glossary

acetoacetic acid a colorless compound in normal human urine

Acrididae a family of grasshoppers with short antennae, called short-horned grasshoppers

adenine one of two PURINE bases found in NUCLEIC ACIDS

adenosine triphosphate (ATP) a NUCLEOTIDE that is the universal carrier of energy in living cells

alkapton *See* HOMOGENTISIC ACID

alkaptonuria also called black diaper disease, an inherited human disorder causing inability to metabolize certain AMINO ACIDS, resulting in lack of an ENZYME that normally breaks down HOMOGENTISIC ACID. Symptoms include dark urine and, later in life, joint degeneration

allele any of the forms of a GENE at a LOCUS on a CHROMOSOME

amino acid in organic chemistry, the basic structural unit of PROTEINS

anaerobic in the absence of oxygen, applied to ORGANISMS such as ARCHAEA living in oxygen-free environments

antibodies PROTEINS manufactured by the immune system that bind ANTIGENS or MICROORGANISMS to destroy or remove them

antigen any substance foreign to the body that evokes an immune response

apoptosis genetically programmed cell death, as in tissues shed during normal fetal development

Archaea domain of life consisting of MICROBES resembling, but genetically distinct from, bacteria, often occupying extreme habitats

archaeon any member of the domain of life ARCHAEA

ATP *See* ADENOSINE TRIPHOSPHATE

bacteriophage a virus that infects bacteria

base a chemical compound with a pH value between 8 and 14. A base reacts with acids to form salts

base pairs in DNA structure, two NUCLEOTIDES on opposite complementary strands, connected by a HYDROGEN BOND of ADENINE to THYMINE or GUANINE to CYTOSINE

big bang the scientific theory that the universe emerged with great force from an extremely dense and hot state about 13.7 billion years ago

biocatalyst an enzyme or form of RNA that acts to cut or join genetic material

bioengineering shaping or redesigning an ORGANISM with BIOTECHNOLOGY. Specifically, the application of RECOMBINANT DNA technologies

biogeochemistry study of the biological, geological, and chemical processes that make up the natural environment in the BIOSPHERE

biomolecule a chemical compound of carbon and hydrogen (along with nitrogen, oxygen, phosphorus, sulfur, and sometimes other elements) that occurs in an ORGANISM

biopharmaceutical a PROTEIN OR NUCLEIC ACID used in medical therapy, produced by BIOTECHNOLOGY

biophysicist a scientist who uses the applied laws of physics in studying biological phenomena

biosphere the outer part of Earth where life occurs and which is altered by the ORGANISMS that occupy it. Includes the air, water, soil, surface rocks, and water

biotechnology a technology using ORGANISMS or derivatives of living systems for industrial, agricultural, medical, or pharmaceutical products or applications. Often used to specify RECOMBINANT DNA technologies

blastocyst in the development of the mammalian embryo, early stage just before and at implantation into wall of uterus

blastomere any of the cells of the early animal embryo

bovine having to do with cattle such as the cow and the ox

breakage-fusion-bridge cycle phenomenon during MITOSIS involving repeated breakage and rejoining of CHROMATIDS. A source of MUTATION

carbohydrate chemical compound containing oxygen, hydrogen, and carbon, consisting of a simple sugar in a chain molecular structure

catalyst a substance that speeds or enables a chemical change. In molecular biology, an ENZYME or form of RNA that acts to cut or join genetic material at specific sites

cell wall a protective layer external to the plasma or cell membrane, found in bacteria, plant cells, fungi, and some PROTOZOANS

Cenozoic referring to the Cenozoic era in Earth's history, beginning 66.4 million years ago and continuing to the present

chemotherapy the use of chemical compounds to treat disease

chloroplast structure in the cell of a green plant in which photosynthesis occurs

chromatid during MITOSIS, one of the usually paired strands of the chromosome, attached to the other by a centromere

chromatin NUCLEIC ACID and basic PROTEINS in a EUKARYOTIC cell, forming a dispersed complex that is condensed during MITOSIS OR MEIOSIS into threadlike CHROMOSOMES

chromosome microscopic structure within a cell that carries genetic information

cline a gradient of change across a spectrum of related ORGANISMS

codon in the genetic code, a sequence of three adjacent NUCLEOTIDES that usually specifies a particular PROTEIN

Coelacanthiformes biological order including the oldest-living lineage of jawed fish

coelurosaur any of a large group of dinosaurs formally known as *Coelurosauria* and ranging from the *Tyrannosaurs* to all modern birds

congenital describing a condition or trait that was present at birth

conjugation process in which lower ORGANISMS of same SPECIES exchange genetic material

control a parallel experiment, used for comparison, in which the subject (such as a laboratory rat) is not exposed to the procedure, agent, or condition that is being tested. Also, the subject in such a parallel experiment

coronavirus any of a family of fast-mutating, single-stranded RNA viruses that includes PATHOGENS of people and animals

covalent bond the molecular bond in which two atoms share an electron pair

culture in MICROBIOLOGY, the artificial growth of MICROORGANISMS such as bacteria in a prepared dish in the laboratory

cyanobacteria also called blue-green algae—a large, varied group of PROKARYOTIC organisms, most of them employing photosynthesis. True algae are EUKARYOTES

cytogeneticist one who pursues CYTOGENETICS

cytogenetics the study of genetic processes at the cellular level

cytosine one of the PYRIMIDINE bases found in a NUCLEOTIDE

denaturation the process of causing the two strands of DNA to separate, accomplished by heating it

deoxyribonucleic acid (DNA) a double-stranded, helical MOLECULE that carries the genetic information for an ORGANISM and is capable of replicating

dialectical materialism philosophy built around the idea that all change—especially economic and societal progress—results from the struggle of opposites. As expressed in the writings of Karl Marx, the philosophy of communism

differentiation the structural and functional divergence of cells as they become specialized during development

Dinosaurus the genus comprising dinosaurs

diploid having two copies of each CHROMOSOME

discontinuity as applied to evolutionary theory, any variation on the idea that SPECIES differentiate not gradually but by series of discontinuous jumps

DNA *See* DEOXYRIBONUCLEIC ACID

dominant in genetics, the type of ALLELE that is fully expressed in the PHENOTYPE
ecology the study of the relationships between living creatures and their environments
ecosystem an ecological community and the physical environment in which they live
ectothermic cold-blooded
electroencephalography a device for reading and recording brain waves
embryoblast the inner cell mass of a BLASTOCYST, the part that grows into a fetus
embryology the study of the formation and development of ORGANISMS during the stage following the initiation of MITOSIS in the zygote
endosperm in seed plants, nutrient-rich tissue formed within the embryo sac
endosymbiotic the condition of one ORGANISM living within the body or cells of another. In many instances, neither host nor SYMBIONT can survive without the other. According to one theory, ORGANELLES within EUKARYOTIC cells originated as symbiont bacteria
endothermy warm-bloodedness
entomologist a scientist who studies insects
enucleate to remove the NUCLEUS from a cell
enzyme complex PROTEINS, produced by living cells, that catalyze specific biochemical reactions within ORGANISMS
epidemic the rapid spreading of a disease, affecting a large segment of a population at one time
ethology the individual and comparative study of animal behavior
eukaryote a cell or ORGANISM that has a distinct membrane-enclosed NUCLEUS and other membrane-bound ORGANELLES
eukaryotic having a distinct membrane-enclosed NUCLEUS and other membrane-bound ORGANELLES
evolution the change in ORGANISMS over time, bringing about new SPECIES
exon a NUCLEOTIDE sequence that codes information for making a PROTEIN
gamete a HAPLOID egg or sperm cell that unites with another gamete during reproduction to form a DIPLOID zygote
gastritis inflammation of the mucous membrane of the stomach
gel electrophoresis a method whereby electric charge flowing through gel MEDIUM results in the sorting of NUCLEIC ACID or PROTEIN molecules by size
gene a discrete unit of hereditary information
gene therapy medical treatment whereby a missing gene is added or a defective gene removed, replaced, or altered
genetics the study of heredity, the passing on of the characteristics of ORGANISMS to the offspring

genome the entire genetic complement of an ORGANISM
genotype the genes or ALLELES that an ORGANISM possesses
genus a taxonomic category just above SPECIES
germ cell GAMETES, or more generally, egg and sperm cells
growth factor a PROTEIN that must be present for the normal growth and development of certain types of cells
guanine one of two PURINE bases found in NUCLEIC ACIDS
haploid having only one copy of each CHROMOSOME, as in GAMETES
heterozygous possessing two different ALLELES for a given trait
histology the study of tissue structure at the microscopic level
homogentisic acid 2,5-dihydroxyphenylacetic acid, also called melanic acid and alkapton; turns dark when exposed to oxygen
homozygous having two identical ALLELES for a given trait
hormone made by cells, a substance circulating in blood or other body fluid that stimulates activity of other cells
hybrid a new variety of ORGANISM created by crossing two distinct varieties or SPECIES
hydrogen bond a weak chemical bond formed by the attraction of a slightly positive hydrogen atom with a partially negative atom of another MOLECULE or region of the same molecule
interferon a PROTEIN secreted by cells to signal response to viruses, other infectious agents, and cancers
intracellular within a cell
intron a sequence in a NUCLEIC ACID that does not code information for PROTEIN synthesis
invertebrate any of the many species of animals without backbones, includes arthropods
in vitro in an artificial environment, such as a test tube, rather than in a living ORGANISM
ion an atom or group of atoms that bears a positive or negative charge
ionic bond a chemical bond based on electrostatic attraction between two oppositely charged ions
leucocytes white blood cells
locus in genetics, the position of a gene on a chromosome
lymphocyte a white blood cell involved in the body's immune system
lysozyme an antimicrobial chemical produced by the body that is found in mucus, tears, saliva, and other bodily fluids
macroscopic on a large scale, considered in terms of large units
Maiasaura "good mother lizard," SPECIES of duckbill dinosaur named for having tended its helpless young
matrix mechanics a mathematical interpretation of the structure and interactions of matter, describing the behavior of subatomic particles by associating their properties with numerical values arranged in a table, or matrix
medium (plural: **media)** a nutritive substance in or on which bacteria, fungi, and other MICROORGANISMS are grown for study

meiosis the cellular process of producing HAPLOID gamete cells

messenger RNA (mRNA) RIBONUCLEIC ACID that copies genetic instructions from DNA and carries them to the sites for PROTEIN synthesis within the cell

microbe a MICROORGANISM

microbiology the study of MICROORGANISMS

micrococcus any of a group of spherical bacteria such as the one that causes milk to go bad

microorganism an ORGANISM too small to see with the naked eye

minisatellite sequence of DNA whose contribution to the function of a gene, if any, is unknown, but which is repeated many times within a gene and a DNA sample

mitochondria ORGANELLES in most EUKARYOTES that produce energy for the cell

mitosis the process by which a plant or animal cell divides to form two new cells

molecule two or more atoms held together by COVALENT BONDS

mutagenesis a method for controlling genetic MUTATIONS to create precise AMINO ACID changes anywhere in a PROTEIN

mutation a change in genetic material or the trait that results from such a change

myoglobin a muscle PROTEIN that carries oxygen

naturalist a person who studies nature

natural selection mechanism by which EVOLUTION occurs as proposed by Darwin. Those members of a SPECIES that survive to breed pass on their genes to their offspring. If the environment changes, ORGANISMS best suited to the change will survive to pass on their genes while others perish. Thus, species change

neurotransmitter a chemical that relays or regulates the signal between a nerve cell and another cell

nodule a root outgrowth in a plant. In medicine, a small clump of cells

noradrenalin a HORMONE and NEUROTRANSMITTER involved in the human brain's stress response

nuclear transfer removal of the nucleus of one cell and transplantation into another

nucleic acid a complex MOLECULE made of NUCLEOTIDE chains that convey genetic information

nucleotide structural unit of NUCLEIC ACIDS including a PURINE or PYRIMIDINE base attached to a simple CARBOHYDRATE and one or more PHOSPHATE groups

nucleus a specialized structure within a cell, separated from the rest of the cell by a membrane and regulating the growth and metabolism of the cell

oligonucleotide a short sequence of NUCLEOTIDES, used by molecular biologists to detect or synthesize DNA

oncogene a modified version of a normal gene promoting or controlling growth, the oncogene can cause cancer or increase a tumor's malignancy

oocyte an unfertilized egg cell

organelle any of several membrane-enclosed structures within a cell, each with a specialized function

organism a life-form

ornithology the study of birds

ovary in animals, the structure that produces female gametes and reproductive HORMONES. In flowers, the part of the pistil in which the egg-containing ovules develop

ovule the plant structure within the ovary containing the female gametophytes; site of fertilization and seed development

paleoanthropologist a scientist who studies ancient humankind

paleobiologist a scientist who studies ancient living things

paleobiology the study of ancient life

paleoecologist a scientist who studies the ancient BIOSPHERE or aspects of it

pantothenic acid a B vitamin that the human body needs to break down CARBOHYDRATES, PROTEINS, and fats.

paramecium a single-celled, slipper-shaped PROTOZOAN that lives in water

pathogen an agent of disease, such as an infectious bacterium or virus

pathogenic causing disease

penicillin a chemical substance produced by the mold *Penicillium* that has antibacterial properties

peptic ulcer a lesion in the lining of the stomach or the upper portion of the small intestine

petri dish a circular-shaped plate used to grow bacteria in the laboratory

phagocyte a type of white blood cell that ingests and digests MICROORGANISMS and dead cells

phagocytosis process whereby a cell ingests or engulfs another cell or a bit of foreign matter

phenotype the physical and physiological traits of an ORGANISM

pheromone chemical compound by which ORGANISMS communicate, especially important among social insects

phosphate naturally occurring form of the element phosphorus, a chemical component of NUCLEIC ACIDS

phylogenetic with reference to the evolutionary relationship between organisms

phylum in TAXONOMY, a major group of ORGANISMS, divided into classes

physiochemical with regard to physical and chemical properties

physiology the study of the functions of living ORGANISMS

pistil female reproductive structure of a flower; includes the stigma, style, and ovary

placental characterized by presence of a true placenta, applied to all mammals except marsupials (which have a less developed placenta) and egg-laying monotremes (platypuses and echidnas)

plasmid especially in bacteria, a small circle of DNA that functions independently of chromosomal DNA

pluripotent able to give rise to many kinds, as stem cells that grow into many kinds of specialized cells to make up the tissues of a body

pollen an immature male gametophyte that develops in the anthers of flower stamens

polymerize chemical reaction in which two or more MOLECULES combine to form larger molecules with repeating structural units

polypeptide a molecular chain of amino acids

prion an agent of disease, a malformed PROTEIN that will link to other proteins in a chain reaction that transforms normal neural tissue, slowly destroying it

progenote that level in the EVOLUTION of life that came before PROKARYOTIC cells. Can also refer to the last common ancestor of all extant life

prokaryote an ORGANISM that does not have membrane-enclosed organelles

prokaryotic having no membrane-enclosed organelles

protein a BIOMOLECULE constructed from 20 different AMINO ACIDS linked by peptide bonds. PROTEINS perform numerous roles inside the cell

protist any among a group of EUKARYOTIC organisms, most one-celled and microscopic, that include PROTOZOA, algae, and lower fungi

protozoan (plural: **protozoa**) a EUKARYOTIC organism that does not possess a cell wall or chlorophyll, usually able to move on its own.

protozoology the study of protozoa

psychotropic affecting the brain, especially perceptions and emotions stemming from chemical balance

punctuated equilibrium theory of EVOLUTION in which large populations of ORGANISMS remain stable. New SPECIES evolve periodically, and suddenly, as the result of dramatic geological or other large-scale change that gives a survival advantage to previously marginalized species or subspecies

purine a class of double-ringed nitrogenous BASES found in NUCLEOTIDES

pyrimidine a class of single-ringed nitrogenous BASES found in NUCLEOTIDES

race cleansing euphemism for racist policies or practices in which people of certain ethnic backgrounds are expelled, imprisoned, or killed

receptor a PROTEIN that specifically recognizes and binds another MOLECULE

recessive applied to an ALLELE that does not express itself except when the dominant allele is absent

recombinant DNA genes reordered or transplanted for purposes of GENE THERAPY or BIOENGINEERING

respiration the chemical and physical process by which oxygen is delivered to the cells and carbon dioxide taken away. Also, the energy-producing oxidation process within the cell

restriction enzymes specialized catalytic PROTEINS that cut DNA into fragments at specific sites on the MOLECULE

retroviral relating to a RETROVIRUS or retroviruses

retrovirus any of a family of single-stranded RNA viruses that use the enzyme reverse transcriptase to translate their genetic code into the DNA of an infected cell

Rh blood factor a group of ANTIGENS present in most but not all people's red blood cells

rhinovirus any of a genus of viruses associated with the common cold and other respiratory disorders

ribonucleuic acid (RNA) a NUCLEIC ACID that occurs in several types whose functions complement each other and DNA in making PROTEIN within the cell. RNA is also the sole carrier of genetic code (in place of DNA) in some viruses. Some RNA also functions as a BIOCATALYST

ribose a five-carbon sugar found in living cells as part of RNA

ribosome the site of RNA-directed PROTEIN synthesis in the cell

ribozyme a MOLECULE of RNA that functions as an ENZYME

riparian having to do with a river, as in a riparian environment

salvarsan also called arsphenamine, the first CHEMOTHERAPY drug used to destroy PATHOGENIC microorganisms

semiconservative replication the idea that entwined strands of the DNA double helix replicate themselves in a process that involves unwinding from one another, with each strand able to direct the formation of a new complementary opposite, creating two double helixes, each of which conserves one-half of the original

sex-linked genes or traits encoded by one of the sex CHROMOSOMES, usually the X chromosome

sociobiology the study of organisms within the context of their interrelations within a SPECIES and between species

sociopaleobiologist a scientist who studies ancient life in the context of the interdependent relationships within a SPECIES and between species in a shared environment

species a group of like ORGANISMS able to interbreed and produce viable, fertile offspring

spermatozoa the male GAMETE

split gene in DNA, a sequence of NUCLEOTIDES that codes for a trait but that is not positioned in a contiguous sequence, having been interrupted by a TRANSPOSON of noncoding DNA

spontaneous generation the production of living ORGANISMS from nonliving matter

stamen male reproductive structure of a flower, including an anther and a filament

staphylococcal related to STAPHYLOCOCCUS

staphylococcus (plural: **staphylococci**) a type of bacteria that is spherical in shape and grows in clusters

streptococcal related to STREPTOCOCCUS

streptococcus (plural: **streptococci**) a type of bacteria that is spherical in shape and grows in chains

subshell a region within the valence shell of an atom, the valence shell being the outermost of these areas surrounding the nucleus and occupied by the orbits of a group of electrons of approximately equal energy

sulfonamides a class of chemical agents that kill bacteria

symbiont an ORGANISM that lives on or in another living thing

syphilis a sexually transmitted disease caused by a spirochete bacterium

taxonomy the scientific study of classifying ORGANISMS

T cell *See* T LYMPHOCYTE

telomere the end of an unbroken CHROMOSOME in EUKARYOTES; it is composed of a repetitive DNA sequence and serves to stabilize the chromosome

tetrahedral four-sided—describing a solid, four-sided form

thymine one of two PYRIMIDINE bases found in DNA

T lymphocyte (T cell) a type of white blood cell essential for combating virus infections and cancers

totipotent able to grow into all forms of cells comprising an ORGANISM

transduction transfer of genetic material by a viral agent such as a BACTERIOPHAGE

transmissible spongiform encephalopathies a group of diseases in several species, including humans, caused by PRIONS and resulting in the degeneration of neural tissue, especially the brain

transposon a segment of DNA that moves, often to a new position on the same CHROMOSOME, or to another chromosome

triplet in molecular genetics, a coding combination of three NUCLEOTIDE bases. *See* CODON

tropism involuntary movement that occurs in living ORGANISMS in response to external environmental stimuli, such as light or touch

tryptophan an essential amino acid found in proteins

tubal ligation a surgical sterilization method in which a woman's fallopian tubes are tied to prevent her eggs from entering the uterus

tuberculosis an infectious disease that causes small swellings to form on mucous membranes, especially in the lungs

tularemia also called rabbit fever, an acute bacterial disease spread by small animals including rabbits and also by insects and through water

vaccine a weakened or killed bacterium or virus that is injected into a human or animal, stimulating immunity to that particular ORGANISM

vector in BIOTECHNOLOGY, an agent such as a PLASMID or virus used to transfer a bit of foreign DNA into a cell. In immunology, a disease-transmitting agent such as a mosquito

virology the study of viruses and viral diseases

virulent dangerous or deadly, such as a harmful strain of a virus

wave mechanics a system for describing the behavior of subatomic particles by visualizing that they have the physical properties of energy waves

X-ray crystallography a technique used to study the structure of crystallized MOLECULES using X-rays

zoology the study of animals

Further Resources

Books

Aaseng, Nathan. *Genetics: Unlocking the Secrets of Life*. Minneapolis, Minn.: Oliver Press, 1996. Both an accessible overview and an insightful history of genetics as a field of study.

American Men and Women in Science. 22nd ed. 8 vols. Detroit: Thomson Gale, 2004. Contains 120,000 short biographical entries in the physical, biological, and related sciences.

Bryson, Vernon, ed. *Microbiology Yesterday and Today*. New Brunswick, N.J.: Rutgers University Institute of Microbiology, 1959. History covers crucial developments through early decades of the 20th century.

Bud, Robert. *The Uses of Life: A History of Biotechnology*. Cambridge: Cambridge University Press, 1993. Author looks at modern advances from long perspective of human history.

Dennett, Daniel C. *Darwin's Dangerous Idea. Evolution and the Meanings of Life*. New York: Simon & Schuster, 1995. Author explains idea of natural selection and traces its power to transform humankind's view of itself and the world, while examining pitfalls of Darwinian theory.

The Diagram Group. *The Facts On File Biology Handbook*. Rev. ed. New York: Facts On File, 2006. Convenient resource containing a glossary of terms, short biographical profiles of celebrated biologists, a chronology of events and discoveries, and useful charts and tables.

Hager, Thomas. *Force of Nature: The Life of Linus Pauling*. New York: Simon & Schuster, 1995. Biography of Nobel Prize–winning chemist who shaped course of molecular biology.

Hine, Robert, ed. *The Facts On File Dictionary of Biology*. 3rd ed. New York: Facts On File, 1999. Over 3,000 entries covering all aspects of biology, including organisms, organs, processes, and basic terminology in accessible language.

Hughes, Thomas P. *Human-Built World: How to Think about Technology and Culture*. Chicago: University of Chicago Press, 2004. The author, a science historian and sociologist, takes a broad look at humankind's relationship to the natural world, with a thoughtful eye toward the philosophical and moral shifts that come with scientific and technological development.

Keller, Evelyn Fox. *The Century of the Gene.* Cambridge, Mass.: Harvard University Press, 2000. History of genetics in the 20th century.

Kress, John, and Gary W. Barrett, eds. *A New Century of Biology.* Washington, D.C.: Smithsonian Institution Press, 2001. A collection of essays by notable biologists concerning the problems their discipline must address in the 21st century.

Lagerkvist, Ulf. *DNA Pioneers and their Legacy.* New Haven, Conn.: Yale University Press, 1998. This concise overview of cytology and molecular genetics spans work of biologists ranging from William Bateson to James Watson to Edward O. Wilson.

Lerner, K. Lee, and Brenda Wilmoth Lerner, eds. *Gale Encyclopedia of Science.* 3rd ed. 6 vols. Detroit: Thomson Gale, 2003. Provides an overview of current scientific knowledge; consists of alphabetical entries of scientific concepts and terms; written for young adults.

Lewin, Roger. *Patterns in Evolution: The New Molecular View.* New York: Scientific American Library, 1997. Informative discussion of molecular genetics in the 20th century.

Mendelsohn, Everett, ed. *Life Sciences before the Twentieth Century: Biographical Portraits.* New York: Charles Scribner's Sons, 2001. Survey of 90 men and women who made important discoveries in a variety of life science fields before the 20th century; written for young adults.

———. *Life Sciences in the Twentieth Century: Biographical Portraits.* New York: Scribner, 2000. Survey of 90 men and women who made important discoveries in a variety of life science fields during the 20th century; written for young adults.

Morange, Michael, and Matthew Cobb. *A History of Molecular Biology.* Cambridge, Mass.: Harvard University Press, 2000. Historical perspective on field of inquiry crucial to 20th-century genetics.

Narins, Brigham, ed. *Notable Scientists: From 1900 to the Present.* 2nd ed. 5 vols. Farmington Hills, Mich.: Thomson Gale, 2000. Contains 1,600 biographical profiles of scientists in the natural, physical, and applied sciences.

Parson, Ann B. *The Proteus Effect: Stem Cells and their Promise for Medicine.* Washington, D.C.: Joseph Henry Press, 2004. Although the title speaks of promise, the book also goes into some historical depth in tracing research developments beginning in the 18th century that led to modern stem cell research.

Rittner, Don, and Timothy L. McCabe. *Encyclopedia of Biology.* New York: Facts On File, 2004. Comprehensive reference of 800 A–Z entries encompassing definitions, issues, discoveries, biographies, and experiments.

Robinson, Richard, ed. *Biology.* 4 vols. New York: Macmillan, 2001. Explains biological concepts, reviews history of biology, and explores related fields; written for young adults.

Serafini, Anthony. *The Epic History of Genetics.* New York: Perseus, 2001. Graceful overview of the field from a 21st-century perspective.

Sturtevant, A. H., and Edward B. Lewis. *A History of Genetics.* Cold Spring Harbor, N.Y.: Cold Spring Harbor Laboratory Press, 2001. Scientific history benefits from the personal insights of Sturtevant, a pioneer in the field.

Yount, Lisa. *A to Z of Biologists.* New York: Facts On File, 2003. Profiles over 150 biologists, discussing their research and contributions. Includes bibliography, glossary, cross-references, and chronology.

Internet Resources

ASU Ask a Biologist. Arizona State University. Available online. URL: http://askabiologist.asu.edu. Accessed April 17, 2006. Intended as a resource for K-12 students and teachers.

Bio: Directorate for Biological Sciences. The National Science Foundation. Available online. URL: http://www.nsf.gov/bio. Accessed April 17, 2006. Contains biology news and information about NSF programs.

Biointeractive. Howard Hughes Medical Institute, 2004. Available online. URL: http://www.hhmi.org/biointeractive/index.html. Accessed April 17, 2006. Contains animations, virtual labs, and lectures on topics including cancer, DNA, and infectious diseases.

Biology Online. Available online. URL: http://www.biology-online.org. Accessed April 17, 2006. Organized into four sections: "Forum," "Dictionary of Biology," "Biology Tutorials," and "Biology on the Web."

Cold Spring Harbor Laboratory. "DNA from the Beginning." Available online. URL: http://www.dnaftb.org/dnaftb. Accessed April 17, 2006. Animated pages cover the science of DNA, genes, and heredity, and the historic research into these subjects.

Gilbert, Joanna. BiologyMad. Available online. URL: http://www.biologymad.com. Accessed August 26, 2004. Contains topic notes, concept maps, and animations on topics including cells, genetics, human biology, biochemistry, ecosystems and the environment, and plant biology.

Herrington, Jenny. "Chromosomes, Genes, and DNA." Available online. URL: http://www.biologie.uni-hamburg.de/b-online/library/cat-removed/u4aos1p2.html. Accessed April 17, 2006. Site maintained by Australia's Latrobe University features concise overview of genetics, with glossary of terms and clear explanation of DNA structure and function.

Kimball, John W. *Kimball's Biology Pages.* Available online. URL: http://www.ultranet.com/~jkimball/BiologyPages. Accessed April 17, 2006. Includes a regularly updated, online biology text based on Wm. C. Brown's 1994 edition, written by a Harvard University faculty member. Also has links to science news.

National Institutes of Health Office of Science Education. Available online. URL: http://science.education.nih.gov. Accessed April 17, 2006. Follow links under "Education Resources" for students or for the public.

NewScientist.com. Available online. URL: http://www.newscientist.com. Accessed April 17, 2006. Science and technology news, from serious research to pop science.

Nobel Foundation. Available online. URL: http://www.nobelprize.org. Accessed April 10, 2006. Biographies of Nobel laureates from 1901, news releases announcing prizes, text of laureates' lectures, as well as historical features.

Online Mendelian Inheritance in Man, OMIM. McKusick-Nathans Institute for Genetic Medicine, Johns Hopkins University (Baltimore, MD) and National Center for Biotechnology Information, National Library of Medicine (Bethesda, MD), 2000. Available online. URL: http://www.ncbi.nlm.nih.gov/entrez/query.fcgi?db=OMIM. Accessed April 17, 2006. Contains links to copious technical information regarding genetic disorders, locations of specific genes, statistics, and genome databases.

Science and Nature: Prehistoric Life: Beasts: Evolution. British Broadcasting Corporation. Available online. URL: http://www.bbc.co.uk/beasts/evolution. Accessed April 17, 2006. Access to an online game where the player must eat enough to grow from a hatchling to an adult *Allosaurus*. Other learning games include Seamonster Adventure, Caveman Challenge, and Evolution Game. Also has links to science and nature pages.

Periodicals

BioScience

Published by the American Institute of Biological Sciences
1444 I Street NW, Suite 200
Washington, DC 20005
Telephone: (202) 628-1500

Monthly journal containing overviews of current research in biology; written for researchers, educators, and students

Discover

Published by Buena Vista Magazines
114 Fifth Avenue
New York, NY 10011
Telephone: (212) 633-4400
http://www.discover.com

A popular monthly magazine containing easy to understand articles on a variety of scientific topics

Frontiers in Bioscience

Published by Frontiers in Bioscience
P.O. Box 160
Albertson, NY 11507-0160
Telephone: (516) 484-2831
http://www.bioscience.org

An online journal and virtual library with articles covering all disciplines in biology

Isis

University of Chicago Press
Journals Division
1427 East 60th Street
Chicago, IL 60637-2954
Telephone: (773) 702-7600
http://www.journals.uchicago.edu/ISIS

Quarterly publication of the History of Science Society; contains articles, research notes, and commentary on the history of science, medicine, and technology

Journal of Biology

Published by BioMed Central Ltd.
Middlesex House
34-42 Cleveland Street
London W1T 4LB
United Kingdom
Telephone: +44 (0)20 7323 0323
http://jbiol.com/home

Publishes original research articles both in print and on the Web, freely available to all

Nature

The Macmillan Building
4 Crinan Street
London N1 9XW
United Kingdom
Telephone: +44 (0)20 7833 4000
http://www.nature.com/nature

A prestigious primary source of scientific literature

Science

Published by the American Association for the Advancement of Science
1200 New York Avenue NW
Washington, DC 20005
Telephone: (202) 326-6417
http://www.sciencemag.org

One of the most highly regarded primary sources for scientific literature

Scientific American

415 Madison Avenue
New York, NY 10017

Telephone: (212) 754-0550
http://www.sciam.com

A popular monthly magazine that publishes articles on a broad range of subjects and current issues in science and technology

Societies and Organizations

American Association for the Advancement of Science
http://www.aaas.org
1200 New York Avenue NW
Washington, DC 20005
Telephone: (202) 326-6400

American Institute of Biological Sciences
http://www.aibs.org
1444 I Street NW, Suite 200
Washington, DC 20005
Telephone: (202) 628-1500

Federation of American Societies for Experimental Biology
http://www.faseb.org
9650 Rockville Pike
Bethesda, MD 20814
Telephone: (301) 634-7000

The History of Science Society
http://www.hssonline.org
P.O. Box 117360
3310 Turlington Hall
University of Florida
Gainesville, FL 32611-7360
Telephone: (352) 392-1677

The Human Biology Association
http://www.humbio.org
c/o Ted Steegmann, President (2003–07)
Department of Anthropology, University at Buffalo
380 MFAC
Buffalo, NY 14261
Telephone: (716) 645-2240

The Linnean Society of London
http://www.linnean.org
Burlington House
Picadilly, London, W1J 0BF
United Kingdom
Telephone: +44 (020) 7434 4479

Index

Note: *Italic* page numbers refer to illustrations.